Race and Politics in North Carolina, 1872‑1901

RACE AND POLITICS IN NORTH CAROLINA 1872–1901

THE BLACK SECOND

Eric Anderson

Louisiana State University Press
Baton Rouge and London

DESIGNER: Patricia Douglas Crowder
TYPEFACE: Linotype Caledonia
TYPESETTER: Service Typesetters
PRINTER: Thomson-Shore, Inc.
BINDER: John Dekker & Sons, Inc.

LIBRARY OF CONGRESS CATALOGING IN PUBLICATION DATA

Anderson, Eric, 1949–
    Race and politics in North Carolina, 1872–1901.
    Bibliography: p.
    Includes index.
    1. Afro-Americans—North Carolina—Politics and
suffrage.   2. North Carolina—Politics and government—
1865–1950.   3. North Carolina—Race relations.
I. Title.
E185.93.N6A5   305.8'96073'0756   80–16342
ISBN 0–8071–0685–2 cloth
ISBN 0–8071–0784–0 paper

For Mayte Landis Anderson

CONTENTS

PREFACE

"IT MIGHT HAVE BEEN all different, Jack," says the mortally wounded demagogue Willie Stark in Robert Penn Warren's novel *All the King's Men*. "You got to believe that." Dying historians might gasp similar sentiments, but to living ones "it might have been all different" sounds more like metaphysics than history. Yet what might have been—and why it was not—is an unavoidable part of any historical examination of the choices that led to a rapid deterioration of southern race relations in the late nineteenth century. C. Vann Woodward provoked a spirited scholarly debate twenty-five years ago when he suggested that between "Redemption" and disfranchisement there were "forgotten alternatives" for the South. The thesis has been refined in the intervening years, with many critics arguing that Jim Crow's career was longer and more regular than Woodward recognized. Howard Rabinowitz may now have closed this debate by showing that the question "How soon did segregation begin?" is an inadequate one, that the real alternative to separation was exclusion. But for all the argument, historians have returned again and again to Woodward's basic description of the ambiguous character of the era's race relations.

There were forgotten alternatives. The years between Reconstruction and 1900 were, indeed, a transition marked by "experiment, testing, and uncertainty," whatever one concludes about the origins of segregation and the gap between law and custom. Although southern Democrats were united in opposition to federal "interference" in the region, there were important differences of opinion as to the Negro's precise role in southern life—differences particularly manifest in the seldom-studied local level of politics. In many southern counties, blacks voted and held political offices well after Reconstruction. One of the most remarkable centers of black political strength was the Second Congressional District of North Carolina, where four Negroes won election to the House between 1874 and 1898 and hundreds of other blacks held lesser positions.

The history of the second district is a valuable reminder that black leaders and voters actively pursued their own goals; they were not always passive victims or clients. Our understanding will be incomplete if we concentrate only on what whites did to Negroes, neglecting what blacks achieved for themselves and how whites perceived this progress.

In particular, the second district is an illustration of the development of black leadership and the shifting white responses to that evolution. In the Republican party, the emergence of a group of black leaders produced complex interracial tensions. Time and again black Republicans demanded a stronger voice in the local party organization, especially as the black community produced a larger educated and professional class. Many white Republicans preferred more deferential black voters and found it difficult to accept the maturation of the black community.

Democrats accused the white Republicans of being mercenary hypocrites who worked with blacks solely for personal political gain. It was an unanswerable charge, for denying it only provoked the more damaging accusation of sincere commitment to "Negro domination"! There is no question that the white Republicans were often inconsistent—nor that they were essential to the success of the party. Without them the party would not have had the financial resources essential to capturing and holding certain offices, and every political argument—fair elections, for example—would have been a potentially explosive racial conflict.

No wonder, then, that the Democrats worked to disable the Republican party and to isolate dissenting whites. The comment of an editor in heavily Negro Edgecombe County in 1900 was perfectly in character: "If there were no white traitors in Edgecombe, the county would give the [disfranchising] amendment 3000 majority." Quite simply, the Republican party, with its awkward yet viable black and white partnership, represented the strongest defender of black interests.

In the Democratic party, several eminent white leaders, including Josephus Daniels, Furnifold Simmons, and Charles B. Aycock, began their political careers in the "black second" and helped determine the ultimate direction of an era that began with uneven promise. Faced with renewed black "assertiveness" (or progress), this generation which came

of age after Reconstruction chose to restrict Negro suffrage. In their judgment an experiment in democracy had failed.

"It might have been all different"? Perhaps not. But there was a time
and place when compromise appeared possible and blacks were confident that they could participate in a nearly normal way in American
politics.

ACKNOWLEDGMENTS

THIS BOOK BEGAN nine years ago in John Hope Franklin's seminar "The South since 1880." At each stage of research and writing, as a seminar paper on two black congressmen evolved into a dissertation and a book manuscript on the "black second" congressional district, I have incurred pleasant debts. My largest obligation is to Professor Franklin, who prodded me to be thorough and precise and gave good advice that I was often slow to understand. Other creditors include Arthur Mann, for his emphasis on the craft of historical writing, and Walter C. Utt, who constantly encouraged me and offered the "intelligent but ignorant" criticism of an historian of seventeenth-century France.

I would also like to acknowledge the gracious assistance of the staffs of the North Carolina Department of Archives and History, the Southern Historical Collection, East Carolina University Library, the North Carolina Collection, Duke University Library, the National Archives, and the Library of Congress, mentioning in particular H. G. Jones, Ellen McGrew, George Stevenson, Frank Gatton, Paul Hoffman, and Don Lennon. From a private "archive," Vera Jean O'Hara Rivers shared with me her knowledge of her grandfather Congressman James O'Hara.

I owe a great deal to friends who consented to read portions of my manuscript: John Christian, Kathleen Mitchell, and Steven Price, all colleagues at Pacific Union College. Joseph and Lala Carr Steelman of East Carolina University subjected the manuscript to searching criticism based on their extensive knowledge of North Carolina history. I am debtor too to Diana Artenian and Mary Jane Di Piero for their excellent editing work. Several of my students, including Bob Jackson, Diana Wallace, and Keri Edwards, performed important chores for me.

Most of all I must acknowledge the patience of my family—my wife Loretta, who long ago ceased believing my promises of "done next quarter," and my small son, who persistently attempted to derail the project.

The map of the Second Congressional District appears with the permission of the University of North Carolina Press and is adapted from Richard E. Lonsdale, *et al., Atlas of North Carolina* (Chapel Hill: University of North Carolina Press, 1967).

PART ONE

Origins, 1872–1878

Chapter 1

THE SHAPE OF THE SECOND DISTRICT

"THE SECOND CONGRESSIONAL DISTRICT is a masterpiece," sneered the Republican Wilmington *Post*. "It takes in Craven then wanders clean to the Virginia line, and turns a sharp corner around Nash and grasps Warren." "Extraordinary, inconvenient and most grotesque," wrote Governor Tod R. Caldwell, in an effort to describe the new district's shape.[1]

The Democratic members of the North Carolina General Assembly had not planned to please Republicans as they redrew the boundaries of the state's congressional districts early in 1872. Like partisan legislators in any state, they hoped to increase the power of their own party. But in 1872 ordinary calculations and maneuvers seemed invested with unusual import. Elected in 1870 amid widespread Ku Klux Klan activity, the legislature had already seriously crippled Reconstruction in North Carolina. It had impeached and removed from office Governor William W. Holden for the actions he took to suppress the Klan (which included martial law and suspension of the writ of habeas corpus), publicized charges of Republican fraud through an investigative commission, reduced government expenses, and abolished several offices. The Democratic legislators had also attempted to curb the appointing power of the Republican governor, but the state supreme court ruled the action unconstitutional. The general assembly had been reapportioned, with the state senate gerrymandered in the Democrats' favor.[2]

Congressional redistricting was part of the effort to undo Republican power. If the district lines were drawn correctly, the Democrats (or "Conservatives" as they called themselves in deference to former Whigs)

1. Wilmington *Post*, July 7, 1878; *North Carolina House Journal*, 1872–73, p. 40.
2. J. G. de Roulhac Hamilton, *Reconstruction in North Carolina* (New York, 1914), 534–71.

3

could dominate the state's congressional delegation for the next decade. In drawing borders that were friendly to their party, the Democrats created one "extraordinary" district they could never hope to carry, but a district in which thousands of Republican votes would be neutralized.

The Second Congressional District included ten counties: Warren and Northampton, both bordering on Virginia; Halifax, divided from Northampton by the Roanoke River; Edgecombe and Wilson, in the central "neck" of the political salamander; Wayne, Lenoir, and Craven, along the Neuse River; Greene, a small county north of Lenoir; and Jones, a very thinly settled county on the Trent River, south of Craven. The census of 1870, which underestimated the black population, listed 150,936 persons in these counties.[3] All of the counties were part of North Carolina's coastal plain, except Warren, which was on the border of the piedmont section.

Politically and socially the most important feature of the second district was its large Negro population. According to the more reliable 1880 census, three of the ten counties were more than two-thirds black, and with the exception of Wayne and Wilson all had black majorities. Even the two "white" counties were more than 45 percent black. Indeed, more than one fifth of the total Negro population of North Carolina lived in the second district.[4]

The combination of black counties like Craven, Warren, Halifax, and Edgecombe into one congressional district increased Democratic chances for victory in the first district, which included Pitt, Beaufort, and the counties around the Albemarle Sound; the third district, which included Wilmington, the state's largest city; and in the fourth district, which included Raleigh, the state capital. But it had other results as well. "This action may be the result of good policy on the part of the Legislature, and may give our party better chances in the other Districts of the State," commented an Edgecombe editor, "but we much fear it will not carry much enthusiasm to the ranks of the Democracy of the Second."[5] The editor's reservations were well founded. The second district was a

3. U.S. Department of Commerce, Census Office, *Ninth Census* (1870), I, 52–53.
4. U.S. Department of Commerce, Bureau of the Census, *Negro Population, 1790–1915* (Washington, D.C., 1918), 784–85.
5. Tarboro *Southerner*, February 15, 1872.

Republican and black stronghold for the next twenty-eight years—until the state disfranchisement amendment of 1900. Seven Republicans represented the district in Congress, among them Negroes John A. Hyman, James E. O'Hara, Henry P. Cheatham, and George H. White. During the same period numerous Republicans served as sheriffs, clerks of the superior court, registers of deeds, mayors, town commissioners, postmasters, and other officials. Scores of Republicans, including more than fifty blacks, represented the counties of the second district in the general assembly. Black lawyers John H. Collins and George H. White served a total of sixteen years in the office of solicitor of the Second Judicial District, a multi-county unit largely within the Second Congressional District.

Although the "black second" was their own creation, to Democrats the district became an object lesson in the abuses of "radical rule" and "Negro domination." Whenever the party was hard pressed, Democrats could conjure up visions of Republican corruption and black assertiveness from these counties, and the district became a convenient symbol of what Republicans would do if ever they returned to power.

Democratic propaganda obscured the fact that black influence in local government was far from overwhelming or irresistible. Heavy as the black population was, it stopped far short of the proportions in some Deep South counties. For example, in 1880 Negroes exceeded 90 percent of the population in Beaufort County, South Carolina, Issaquena County, Mississippi, and in several Louisiana parishes, whereas no county in the second district had a black population as large as 75 percent. Even in Warren, the district's "blackest" county, whites composed nearly 30 percent of the population.[6] As a result, politics in the district developed in a fascinating mosaic of accommodation, with white leaders playing an important role in the "Negro party" and Democratic strategists offering a variety of responses to black voters.

All of this—black politicians, racist propaganda, interracial bargains—is part of a neglected history that reveals much about the decay of race relations in late nineteenth-century America. The story of a congressional district presents itself, naturally, in a political framework. But if reader and author alike are to avoid being intellectual carpetbaggers, exploiting

6. *Negro Population,* 782–86.

thin, marshaled abstractions, the history of the "black second," must begin with a modest survey of the realm. The residents of the district were not simply Negroes or whites, Republicans, Populists, or Democrats. They were also cotton farmers, Tarheels, Primitive Baptists. Their election day behavior is best understood as part of a broad pattern which includes work customs, social relationships, and shared symbols and allegiances.

Evoking "inescapable rhythms" and frightening shadows, the poet Wallace Stevens wrote of "Thirteen Ways of Looking at a Blackbird." There are at least as many ways of approaching the second district and its people.

If one wanted, for a random example, to describe the town of Tarboro at the time the "black district" was formed, it would not be enough to say that it was the county seat of the state's largest cotton producing county (Edgecombe), had a black majority, and usually voted Republican. It was also, for one thing, a place where old names and cherished illusions counted for much, and "insults" did not pass unnoticed. As one unhappy Republican complained, Tarboro was "one of the oldest towns in the state," with "aristocracy enough to stock Great Britain . . . the fountain source for the incurable Bourbonism" which afflicted the section. Although there is no way to count them, the town certainly had its share of touchy, honor-conscious, aggressive individuals, specimens of what John Hope Franklin has called "the militant South." The editor of the local newspaper was a fervent Democrat named William Biggs who believed that public whipping should be revived as a "cheap and effective" method of controlling crime and who floated a defiant motto under the nameplate of his journal: "I AM A SOUTHERN MAN, OF SOUTHERN PRIN-CIPLES—Jefferson Davis." Twice in four years Biggs had to be arrested to prevent him from fighting duels. He emerged from an 1872 affray with black Republicans convinced that there was a "Radical" plot to assassinate him—though he admitted he had started the whole incident by whacking an insolent Negro with his cane! "The public is acquainted with the late shooting affray between Mr. A. McCabe and the editor of this paper," commented a successor of Biggs in 1875, omitting any further details as if to avoid wearying his readers. (A judge who admitted hostile relations with the editor fined McCabe one penny and costs, while disqualifying himself from ruling on the editor's conduct.) This fighting spirit was not limited to white gentlemen. Negro magistrate Robert S. Taylor resigned his post and pleaded guilty to a charge of assault, and another black leader, teacher-legislator W. P. Mabson, was fined twice in two years for fighting with rivals.[7]

But hot-tempered, traditionalist, "aristocratic" Tarboro was also an unkempt village, a sleepy, unimpressive backwater. The wealthy planter who fancied himself an aristocrat did not dare stroll too absentmindedly as he mused on the price of cotton or the future of white civilization. Pigs ran free on main street and congregated in front of the county courthouse; in fact, one summer day in 1873 the township constable counted 256 porcine pedestrians, sharing the dust with the human kind. Another unimpressive feature of Tarboro was a disreputable section of town known as "Grab All," complete with one or more black brothels.[8]

The different ways of looking at Tarboro are not unrelated or contradictory. The pigs and the pretensions, the belligerence and the obscurity all fit together, each a manifestation of a place and time that held contingent, complex answers. No local resident could have expressed the problem with the effete eloquence of a Matthew Arnold, but Tarboro—like all of the "black district"—was between two worlds, the fading Old South and an uncertain, incompletely defined new one.

For the people of Tarboro and Edgecombe County the perplexity of the times could be seen in two customs, one showing the lingering influence of antebellum paternalism, the other illustrating an opposite development. It was traditional for a planter to provide his hands with a midsummer's barbecue, once his crops had reached the point where they no longer required incessant cultivation, and to invite his friends to join in the feast. In an atmosphere of informal gaity, employer and employee, black and white, dined on "scorched pig, &c.," as one participant jocularly put it. The white planter who sponsored such a feast could imagine, as the slaveowner once did, that he was a generous patron and the Negro a grateful dependent. At the same time, in the new climate created by emancipation and Reconstruction, blacks introduced the custom of heckling white orators. Editor Biggs complained: "Edgecombe, we are in-

7. Wilmington *Post*, May 15, 1881; Tarboro *Southerner*, March 30, 1871, June 22, 1871, January 9, 1874, July 11, 1872, September 3, 1875, September 8, 15, 1876, May 7, 1875, June 30, 1876.
8. Tarboro *Southerner*, August 22, 1872, July 3, 1873, December 21, 1871, February 22, 29, 1872, May 8, 1873.

formed, is one of the few counties in the State where Democratic speakers are interrupted, hissed and talked down by colored audiences."[9]

Tarboro is simply an illustration, a convenient starting point, and another community might do as well. But to understand the Second Congressional District it is necessary to understand its mentality. The historian must approach his subject in great prowling circles, scenting and tracking to discover what was taken for granted in the earlier time.

I

For the counties of the second district, the Civil War had not been a remote conflict, fought only on battlefields in Virginia or Tennessee. Early in the war the region suffered a Yankee invasion, with New Bern, the largest town in the area, falling to the enemy March 14, 1862. Northern forces held the town for the rest of the war, using it as a base for forays into surrounding territory, including Jones, Lenoir, and Wayne counties. Late in the war, Sherman's ragged veterans swept through the area, seizing Goldsboro, an important railroad center in Wayne County, in their relentless pursuit of Joseph E. Johnston's retreating rebels.[10]

By setting in motion a large population movement, the invaders profoundly disturbed the social pattern in what was to be the "black second." As soon as New Bern fell the changes began. "The city is being overrun with [black] fugitives from the surrounding towns and plantations," the Federal commander reported immediately after the battle. The Negroes were "wild with excitement and delight," he said. "Two have reported themselves who have been in the swamps for five years." At the same time most of the town's white population fled to the interior of the state, believing that it was "dangerous for them to return." In mid-1862 a Confederate general reported that slaves were escaping to Union lines in

9. Tarboro *Southerner*, August 4, 1871, August 31, 1882, October 17, 1872.
10. See *The War of the Rebellion: A Compilation of the Official Records of the Union and Confederate Armies* (Washington, D.C., 1883), Series I, Vols. IX, XVIII, XXVII, XXIX, XXXVI, XLVII (hereinafter cited as *Official Records*); Shelby Foote, *The Civil War: A Narrative, Red River to Appomattox* (New York, 1974), 822-24; 835-37. Unless otherwise noted, "second district" will be used in this chapter to describe the twelve counties included within the Second Congressional District for any part of the period from 1872 to 1900. Thus, Bertie County will be included in 1860 and 1880 statistics although it did not become part of the district until 1883 and Vance County (created in 1881) will be included in 1900 statements despite the fact that it was removed from the district in 1891.

large numbers, costing slaveowners a million dollars a week in losses. He thought the country east of Goldsboro was "in danger of being ruined if these things continue." By January, 1865, seventeen thousand fugitive slaves had crowded into the Union-held areas of the state, the majority of them (over ten thousand) living in the vicinity of New Bern.[11]

The end of the war brought the return of most white refugees, claiming their abandoned farms and houses, but for many former slaves it was a time of new movement. Many of the freedmen who had not already deserted their old homes now did so, seeking lost relatives, testing their freedom, or responding to the lure of higher wages elsewhere. The census statistics make clear the cumulative impact of the population shifts provoked by war and Reconstruction.

As shown by Table 1, the second district counties became "blacker" in the two decades after 1860, changing from 56 percent to 61 percent Negro. Craven County, in which New Bern was located, shifted from a county with a white majority to one that was two-thirds black, and in Wayne and Wilson, the Negro populations nearly doubled between 1860 and 1880.

After 1880 the racial balance of the second district gradually shifted in favor of whites, although Negroes remained a majority. In 1900 Negroes constituted 55 percent of the population, nearly the same percentage as in 1860. Black population growth fell far behind that of whites in the eighties and nineties. Craven's Negro population increased almost 11 percent in twenty years, for example, whereas the white growth rate was more than 44 percent. In Edgecombe, Halifax, Warren, Lenoir, and Jones counties the number of Negroes declined instead of increasing.

The major cause of the negative black population statistics was the "exodus" of 1889 to 1891, a massive emigration to Mississippi and the old Southwest which cost the second district at least ten thousand residents.[12] Black population was actually growing in most parts of the district in the 1890s, but not as fast as white population, or quickly enough to recover from the "exodus" by 1900. White increases were often associated with tobacco warehouses, cotton mills, and growing towns, a

11. *Official Records*, IX, 199, 400, 477; Bell I. Wiley, *Southern Negroes, 1861–1865* (Baton Rouge, 1965), 206.

12. See Eric D. Anderson, "Race and Politics in North Carolina, 1872–1901: The Black Second Congressional District" (Ph.D. dissertation, University of Chicago, 1978), Chapter 19.

Table 1 **Second District Population 1860–1900**[a]

County	1860		1880		1900	
Bertie						
Total	14,310		16,399		20,538	
Negro	8,504	(59.4%)	9,584	(58.4%)	11,821	(57.6%)
Craven[c]						
Total	16,268		19,729		24,160	
Negro	7,521	(46.2%)	13,064	(66.2%)	14,543	(60.2%)
Edgecombe[b]						
Total	17,376		26,181		26,588	
Negro	10,497	(60.4%)	18,213	(69.6%)	16,584	(62.4%)
Greene						
Total	7,925		10,039		12,038	
Negro	4,101	(51.7%)	5,385	(53.7%)	5,778	(47.9%)
Halifax						
Total	19,442		30,300		30,793	
Negro	12,801	(65.8%)	21,162	(69.8%)	19,733	(64.1%)
Jones						
Total	5,730		7,491		8,226	
Negro	3,526	(61.5%)	4,279	(57.1%)	3,760	(45.7%)
Lenoir						
Total	10,220		15,344		18,639	
Negro	5,318	(52.0%)	8,067	(52.6%)	8,046	(43.2%)
Northampton						
Total	13,372		20,032		21,150	
Negro	7,463	(55.8%)	12,045	(60.1%)	12,118	(57.3%)
Warren[c]						
Total	15,726		22,619		19,151	
Negro	10,803	(68.7%)	16,233	(71.8%)	13,069	(68.2%)
Wayne						
Total	14,905		24,951		31,356	
Negro	6,188	(41.5%)	12,124	(48.6%)	13,419	(42.8%)
Wilson[b]						
Total	9,720		16,064		23,596	
Negro	3,777	(38.9%)	7,409	(46.1%)	9,905	(41.9%)

[a] *Thirteenth Census* (1910), Supplement for North Carolina, 596–613; *Negro Population*, 782–85; *Eleventh Census* (1890), Vol. I, Pt. I, pp. 33–34; *Ninth Census* (1870), I, 53–54.

[b] Minor boundary changes, 1860–1900. For details see David Leroy Corbitt, *The Formation of North Carolina Counties, 1663–1943* (Raleigh, 1950).

[c] Major boundary changes, 1860–1900. See Corbitt, *Formation of North Carolina Counties.*

"New South" that frequently excluded Negroes. As the Tarboro *Southerner* observed in 1900, there was political significance for Edgecombe County in the growth of Rocky Mount and Tarboro, a growth that had "wonderfully increased the white population."[13] In three counties, Lenoir, Greene, and Jones, population changes were large enough to shift the balance from Negro majority to white majority. Jones County changed most dramatically, moving from 57 percent black to 54 percent white in twenty years. Along with the declining Negro percentage went Republican weakness. No Republican congressional candidate carried any of these formerly Republican counties after 1888.

Despite these important population changes, the district's people remained, in many ways, deeply rooted and provincial, out of step with a swiftly modernizing nation. For example, almost everyone in the district claimed native birth. Throughout the thirty years from 1870 to 1900, the American-born made up more than 99.7 percent of the area's population. At a time when much of the nation was absorbing massive waves of "new immigration," foreigners in the second district were almost as rare as the two-headed chickens or six-legged calves occasionally announced in the rural press.[14] Almost equally rare were Yankees—indeed, immigrants from any other state, southern or northern. In 1880 six of the eleven district counties had non-Tarheel populations of less than 2 percent. Jones was the most insular county. In addition to its lone Irishman, the county contained twenty people from other states, including nine from neighboring southern states. The remaining group of 7,490 had been born in North Carolina, a majority, perhaps, in Jones County.[15]

At no time between 1870 and 1900 did the second district contain a town as large as 10,000 in population. The largest town, Craven County's port city of New Bern, grew more than 50 percent in three decades, yet had a population of only 9,090 in 1900. Another Neuse River town, Goldsboro, was the second largest urban center, with a population of nearly 6,000 in 1900. There were five other major towns, Kinston (Lenoir County), Henderson (Vance), Wilson (Wilson), Rocky Mount (Edge-

---

13. Tarboro *Southerner*, November 15, 1900.
14. *Ninth Census* (1870), I, 366–67; U.S. Department of Commerce, Census Office, *Compendium of the Tenth Census* (1880), rev. ed., Pt. I, pp. 523–24; U.S. Department of Commerce, Census Office, *Compendium of the Eleventh Census* (1890), Pt. I, pp. 630–34; U.S. Department of Commerce, Census Office, *Twelfth Census* (1900), Vol. I, Pt. I, pp. 514–15.
15. *Compendium of the Tenth Census* (1880), rev. ed., Pt. I, pp. 523–24.

combe and Nash), and Tarboro, ranging from 2,500 to 4,000 residents in 1900. Some of the settlements boasting weekly newspapers—parochial, confident, full of boosterism—were no more than villages. William H. Kitchin published the Scotland Neck *Democrat* in a place with about 750 residents; the home of the Warrenton *Gazette* had a population of 836 in 1900; and the Windsor *Public Ledger* and James O'Hara's Enfield *Progress* appeared in even smaller places.[16]

Economic changes beginning in the 1890s, particularly the spread of tobacco culture and the rise of new marketing centers, caused dramatic growth in several district towns. Rocky Mount, partly in Edgecombe and partly in Nash, had just 816 residents in 1890. By 1900 the town had grown 260 percent to 2,937, and ten years later the population had risen to over 8,000. Kinston more than doubled in size in the 1890s, increasing from 1,726 to 4,106. Wilson, another important tobacco town, increased about 65 percent in the decade before 1900, while Goldsboro grew by 46 percent.

Another important part of the rootedness of the district, along with its native and rural character, was its overwhelming commitment to Protestantism. Protestant Christianity, in fact, permeated the district, touching people's lives more steadily than any other institution. Yet it is not easy to describe specifically the significance of the churches in social life. The very pervasiveness of religion obscured its boundaries with politics, society, and work. Certainly the churchgoing folk of the second district did not see religion as a distinct "factor" to be weighed and assessed on its own. To them it was something like sleeping or breathing or the cycle of the seasons—so permanent and important that it could almost be taken for granted.

A modern observer might note little variety in the area's religious life, since nine tenths of the church members were either Baptists or Methodists. Baptists and Methodists, moreover, shared with most other southern Protestants a "common ethos" transcending theological fine points. As Frederick A. Bode has observed: "The conversion experience, the individual's relationship to God, personal morality, and fellowship within the church and community were what mattered to the faithful," what-

16. Figures on town size from *Compendium of the Tenth Census* (1880), rev. ed., Pt. I, p. 396; U.S. Department of Commerce, Census Office, *Thirteenth Census* (1910), Supplement for North Carolina, 574–85.

ever their formal church affiliation.[17] Less conscious of this fundamental unity, the Gilded Age Christian of Piney Grove or Snow Hill interpreted religious life from a different perspective. He saw important distinctions between a Regular Baptist, a Freewill Baptist, and a Primitive Baptist and knew very well that belonging to the African Methodist Episcopal (A.M.E.) church was different from supporting the African Methodist Episcopal Zion (A.M.E.Z.) denomination or the tiny Zion Union Apostolic church, though all were black Wesleyan organizations. In nineteenth-century terms, the four varieties of Baptists and seven types of Methodists in the district were nearly as significant as the general allegiance to evangelical Protestant principles.

No smooth talk about "common ethos" would have impressed Democratic politician William H. "Buck" Kitchin, an exponent of the old-fashioned and dogmatic in religion as in all else. His hometown, Scotland Neck, was a Baptist stronghold which invariably had a Baptist mayor. One year, according to a story told by his son, the over-confident Baptist incumbent failed to campaign, and "the Episcopalians and Methodists brought out a candidate." On voting day, the Baptist seemed headed for defeat until "Buck" Kitchin delivered a fervent stump speech defending the incumbent, deprecating "the attempt by other denominations . . . to eliminate him and deny him the salary he needed for the support of his family," and closing with language that to his son sounded like cuss words." Kitchin's parting shot was: "You may say what you think of me. You may say I am not a Christian; but the man does not live who can truthfully say I am not a Baptist and militant one." Needless to say, the incumbent was reelected.[18]

Southern Christians (and "militant Baptists," too) were divided not only by doctrinal issues, such as predestination or baptism by immersion, but also by race. In the last quarter of the nineteenth century, Negroes and whites almost never worshipped in the same congregation and usually belonged to entirely separate denominations. The Regular Baptist (Southern) and Methodist Episcopal churches, all-white organizations, were paralleled by the Negro Regular Baptists, A.M.E. and A.M.E.Z. denominations, and various smaller black groups. By the early twentieth century Primitive Baptists and Original Freewill Baptists would

---

17. Frederick A. Bode, *Protestantism and the New South: North Carolina Baptists and Methodists in Political Crisis, 1894–1903* (Charlottesville, Va., 1975), 9.
18. Josephus Daniels, *Tar Heel Editor* (Chapel Hill, N.C., 1939), 73, 177.

also divide into Negro and white denominations. A tiny minority of blacks belonged to nominally biracial groups such as Episcopalians, Presbyterians, or, rarest of all, Catholics, but even in these churches blacks and whites met in separate local congregations.[19]

Church leaders in the second district, like most of their colleagues throughout the South, preached a gospel of individual regeneration, holding that the church ought to restrict itself to spiritual matters and leave broad social arrangements to secular authorities. In theory, most ministers endorsed Edmund Burke's dictum that "politics and the pulpit are terms that have little agreement."[20]

In practice, however, some clergymen did not carry out Burke's further comment: "Surely the church is a place where one day's truce ought to be allowed to the dissentions and animosities of mankind." White political dissenters protested that the influence of the church was on occasion enlisted against them to promote the old ways in politics. A Populist leader provoked a stir, particularly in the Democratic press, when he charged in 1895 that the "church stands today where it has always stood[,] on the side of human slavery." A Bertie man complained to Populist Senator Marion Butler in 1897 that "the ministry here of the democratic persuasion" were "disgusting" church members by their abuse of Butler and would pay no attention to Populist rebuttals of a sensational statement attributed to the senator.[21] A student of North Carolina Protestantism explains: "The churches were so closely knit into the fabric of the region's life that their very 'purity' paradoxically sanctioned cultural values. . . . To support consensual attitudes that were taken to be a part of the divinely ordered scheme of things did not appear to be meddling in politics.[22]

19. On the process of religious segregation, see H. Shelton Smith, *In His Image But . . . : Racism in Southern Religion, 1780–1910* (Durham, N.C., 1972), 226–51. U.S. Department of Commerce, Bureau of the Census, *Religious Bodies, 1916*, Pt. II, pp. 147–48, 117. For black-white relations among Episcopalians, see Gaines M. Foster, "Bishop Chesire and Black Participation in the Episcopal Church: The Limitations of Religious Paternalism," *North Carolina Historical Review*, LIV (January, 1977), 49–65.

20. Edmund Burke, *Reflections on the Revolution in France and on the Proceedings in Certain Societies in London Relative to that Event* (Harmondsworth, Middlesex, Eng., 1968), 94.

21. *Ibid.*; Bode, *Protestantism and the New South*, 40–60; H. P. Harrell to Marion Butler, December 28, 1897, in Marion Butler Papers, Southern Historical Collection, University of North Carolina, Chapel Hill.

22. Bode, *Protestantism and the New South*, 14.

Perhaps the ultimate expression of a union of political and religious orthodoxy came in the prayer of a clergyman at a "white supremacy" rally in the final days of the 1898 campaign: "Give courage to the heart that we may do our duty. . . . Let us feel this day the vibrations of our coming redemption from all wicked rule, and the supremacy of that race destined not only to rule this country but to carry the Gospel to all nations, and maintain Civil and Religious Liberty throughout the world."[23]

Many white Protestants failed, in short, to live up to their own goal of a politically neutral church committed to personal salvation. Even such "individual" sins as lying, stealing, and bribery were overlooked in times of crisis. Josephus Daniels described Baptist clergyman J. D. Hufham, for years the leading Southern Baptist in the state, as a man who was "as influential in civil as in religious affairs," the friend and advisor of every Democratic governor from Zebulon Vance to Charles Aycock. "Living long in the Black District, he saw and felt the evils of the Reconstruction government and cooperated to put suffrage on the basis of intelligence. Dr. Hufham . . . made no dissent when, by one device or another, the votes of the Negroes were not counted or the Negroes were induced not to go to the polls."[24]

II

Farming was the most important economic activity in the second district, and even the few people who did not live on farms were influenced by the cycles and rituals of agriculture. Seedtime and harvest, cold and heat, dry spell and rain set the tempo for social life, commerce, and politics. Cotton was the most important crop, as in antebellum years, and a large corps of landless Negro workers did most of the backbreaking work of cultivating it. In a pattern common to the "cotton belt," district farmers also devoted thousands of acres to corn production and raised numerous swine, though they were far from self-sufficient in feed or food. Lenoir County agriculturists were typical of the rest of the area in 1879, when they planted over fifty thousand acres of corn and cotton and only six thousand acres of wheat and oats. The census of 1880 found more than seventeen thousand swine in the county—more pigs than people.[25]

23. Goldsboro *Daily Argus*, October 28, 1898.
24. Daniels, *Tar Heel Editor*, 73–74.
25. U.S. Department of Commerce, Census Office, *Tenth Census* (1880), III, 200–201, 236–37.

Although the district's agriculture showed many surface parallels to before the war, the Civil War had, in fact, revolutionized it. Previously, more than seventy thousand slaves performed the bulk of the farm labor, usually working in labor gangs under the close supervision of white men.[26] For the vast majority there was simply no opportunity to acquire any property, to enjoy freedom of movement, or to escape ignorance and illiteracy. After the war, though blacks remained at the bottom of the economic system and subject to numerous inequities, coerced labor was no longer available. Emancipation, even at its minimum, had radical results for agriculture in all of the South.

Freedom's most significant immediate result, according to economic historians Roger Ransom and Richard Sutch, was a marked decline in the supply of labor, as former slaves reserved more time for themselves and, in many cases, removed their wives and children from the fields. "Rather than work like slaves," comment Ransom and Sutch, "the freedmen chose to offer an amount of labor comparable to the standard for free laborers of the time." Across the South, black per capita work hours fell by about one third after the exhausting discipline of the lash was removed, leaving the former masters with a labor shortage.[27]

Freedom for blacks also entailed mobility, the right to change jobs or move to a more prosperous section of the county. In fact, one scholar describes this freedom of movement as "the most precious jewel of emancipation, [the black man's] ultimate reliance in resisting oppression." Even when blacks ignored legally binding contracts or debts to move, such flight "could succeed after 1865 on a scale quite impossible under the slave regime." Second district blacks did not hesitate to use this new freedom. A Tarboro editor noted in 1871 that "hundreds" of local Negroes had recently gone to Louisiana, "enticed," oddly enough, by the promise of higher wages on the sugar plantations. Those who re-

26. In 1860, there were 73,483 slaves and 7,016 free Negroes in the district. *Ninth Census* (1870), I, 53–54.

27. Roger L. Ransom and Richard Sutch, *One Kind of Freedom: The Economic Consequences of Emancipation* (Cambridge, Eng., 1977), 5–6, 44–47. Ransom and Sutch estimate that the decline in per capita hours worked may have been as great as 37 percent or as little as 28 percent. See pages 6, 45. As late as seventeen years after emancipation, one second district editor complained that blacks ought to make their wives and children work, "instead of idling, as most of them now do." Warrenton *Gazette*, January 13, 1882.

mained behind threatened "to move to Louisiana *en masse*" unless they received a larger share of the harvest.[28]

Farmers felt the disruption of war in many other ways, including losses in livestock, lost or ruined equipment, unused and overgrown land—though it is possible to exaggerate the damage suffered by a naturally resilient agricultural region. According to the somewhat unreliable census of 1870, Edgecombe County had 65 percent fewer pigs in 1869 than ten years earlier, only half as many milk cows as before the war, and 860 fewer horses. As late as 1910, in fact, the county had not returned to prewar levels for horses, dairy cattle, and pigs. In the district as a whole, improved land shrank by 170,000 acres between 1860 and 1870.[29]

The most obvious war loss, from the standpoint of many southern farmers, was that of millions of dollars invested in slave property. Although no capital was actually destroyed—it was merely redistributed—emancipation was a major shock to the southern economy, creating a capital and credit shortage for many farmers. It seemed to them that much of their wealth had simply evaporated.[30] Before the war the South had grown cotton with a system that worked because it defined labor as property and then ran its human machines as close to full capacity as possible. Using free human beings instead of slaves forced on the old system modifications that would allow it to perform with a smaller labor input in a climate of capital scarcity.

By 1870 the South had evolved the required new arrangements. As the victorious North fastened the Fifteenth Amendment to the national Constitution, social and market forces within the South had already largely eliminated the plantation system in its old form (though land ownership remained highly concentrated in many areas). In its place, farmers substituted a system of land rental—in most cases, share renting—

28. Robert Higgs, *Competition and Coercion: Blacks in the American Economy, 1865–1914* (Cambridge, Eng., 1977), 58–59, 61; Tarboro *Southerner*, May 25, June 3, June 15, October 5, 1871.

29. U.S. Department of Commerce, Census Office, *Eighth Census* (1860), *Agriculture of the United States*, 104–11; U.S. Department of Commerce, Census Office, *Compendium of the Ninth Census* (1870), 766–69; *Thirteenth Census* (1910), VII, 239, 259. On the weakness of the 1870 census, see Ransom and Sutch, *One Kind of Freedom*, 53.

30. Robert Higgs, *The Transformation of the American Economy, 1865–1914: An Essay in Interpretation* (New York, 1971), 114; Ransom and Sutch, *One Kind of Freedom*, 52.

which was "the result of a compromise between the laborers' pursuit of independence and higher incomes and the landlords' desire to retain control and minimize risk." As Robert Higgs has noted, the new tenure system was not "a method of race control imposed on helpless blacks by all-powerful whites." Indeed, "the evidence is almost entirely inconsistent with such an interpretation." Many white landowners would have preferred a form of wage labor, but they were forced to make some accommodation to the Negroes' dislike of any labor system that used the closely watched labor gangs of antebellum days.[31]

At its creation the politically "grotesque" Second Congressional District was undergoing this major economic transformation. As its landowners surrendered to the sharecropping vogue, the number of large farms fell sharply. There were over 70 percent fewer large, owner-cultivated farms (five hundred or more acres in improved land) in 1870 than a decade earlier. In 1880, when the census began reporting tenure statistics, nearly half of the farms in the eleven counties were operated by tenants of one sort or another. The total number of farms in the district, counting everything from the lowliest three-acre rented patch to the lordly one thousand-acre plantation, increased 198 percent between 1860 and 1880.[32]

Not all of the new tenants were sharecroppers, that is, workers who provided nothing but their labor, receiving in return a portion of the crop. The tenure system as it actually functioned offered a farmer a choice of contracts, each tailored to his relative wealth and willingness to gamble. Many tenants agreed to pay their landlord a fixed money value for land rent, either in cash or in some commodity like cotton. Their obligation, unlike that of share renters, was not dependent upon the size of the crop. Thus from the tenant's standpoint a fixed rent entailed greater risk than other forms of tenancy, but also held the promise of higher profits. If there were bumper crops, or prices shot up, the fixed renter needed only to pay his per-acre rent and the rest was his; in a bad year, of course, he bore all the burden of loss. A step below the fixed renter was the share tenant, who furnished his own tools, team, and supplies, and kept a much larger part of the crop than the simple sharecropper. As the system eventually worked in the second district, a

31. Ransom and Sutch, *One Kind of Freedom,* 94, 65–70; Higgs, *Competition and Coercion,* 45.
32. *Eighth Census* (1860), *Agriculture of the United States,* 210; *Ninth Census* (1870), III, 359–60; *Tenth Census* (1880), III, 62–63, 76–78.

share tenant usually received three quarters of the crop, whereas a sharecropper never kept more than one half, more often about a third. Either sort of share renter assumed less risk than the fixed renter, and as a result paid higher rent.[33] Roughly two thirds of the tenants in the district were share tenants or sharecroppers, though the proportion varied a good deal depending on place and year. By 1890 fixed renting predominated in the Virginia border area of Halifax, Northampton, and Warren, but more than 85 percent of all tenants were share renters in Wilson and Wayne, "white counties" in the central part of the district.[34]

Although the new forms of tenure originated in response to the postwar black labor crisis, they were by no means limited to Negroes. Many second district whites rented the land they tilled, a practice virtually unheard of before the war. In fact by the turn of the century, when the district was still feeling the effects of the depression of the nineties, more than 40 percent of the white farmers were tenants.[35]

The reorganization of southern agriculture was accompanied by a restructuring of the region's financial institutions. The thousands of new tenant farmers required credit to produce cotton successfully, but they were poor risks by any standard. The South needed an economical way to distribute a large amount of credit in very small units. The result was the much-criticized pattern of furnishing merchants and credit based on growing crops—the "crop lien system."[36]

33. Robert Higgs, "Race, Tenure, and Resource Allocation in Southern Agriculture, 1910," *Journal of Economic History,* XXXIII (March, 1973), 149–69; Robert Higgs, "Patterns of Farm Rental in the Georgia Cotton Belt, 1880–1900," *Journal of Economic History,* XXXIV (June, 1974), 468–80; Ransom and Sutch, *One Kind of Freedom,* 94–97. See also Rupert B. Vance, *Human Factors in Cotton Culture* (Chapel Hill, N.C., 1929), 56–57. On crop division practices, see North Carolina, *First Annual Report of the Bureau of Labor Statistics for the State of North Carolina, for the Year 1887* (Raleigh, 1887), 82–85, 120–23.

34. *Tenth Census* (1880), III, 76–79; *Eleventh Census* (1890), V, 168–70; *Twelfth Census* (1900), V, 108–11. One scholar has noted the following pattern of "rental mix" for Georgia cotton counties in 1910: "In predominantly white areas both black and white tenants tended to obtain share-rent contracts; in the predominantly black areas both black and white tended to obtain fixed rent contracts." This formula does not fit the second district exactly. Fixed renting predominated only in black counties, but not all black counties had a majority of fixed renters. A 1914 study suggested that blacks preferred fixed renting because it involved less landlord supervision than sharecropping. Higgs, "Patterns of Farm Rental," 478–80.

35. Ransom and Sutch, *One Kind of Freedom,* 88; *Twelfth Census* (1900), V, 108–11.

36. Robert Higgs comments on the country stores: "It is difficult to conceive of how any alternative financial agency—surely not banks or factors—could have pro-

Second district credit arrangements, like those for land tenure, varied from farmer to farmer. Some planters took "advances from the commission merchants in Baltimore and New York to make their crops," whereas many small farmers depended upon crossroads merchants. Most tenants looked to their landlords for credit, if not directly then indirectly through landlord-endorsed credit at a country store.[37]

Whatever its form, credit was usually expensive and its suppliers unpopular. Second district landlords admitted charging their tenants up to 25 percent over cash prices in an 1886 survey, but they accused merchants of charging even more—as much as 75 percent in some cases. "Some tenants prefer to trade independent of the landlord," observed a Lenoir landlord, "which of course, he [sic] is at liberty to do." But such a tenant had to "pay pretty well for his independence," he added, since the merchants charged high interest, taking a chattel mortgage "on everything." A Jones County man saw matters differently. "The landlord is a rapacious fellow, and has the tenant too much at his mercy." Neither a merchant nor a landlord, he thought state law should be changed to give "the merchant an equal showing with the landlord."[38]

Most tenants were more concerned with their own unequal footing in matters of credit. "The law is in favor of the landlord," said black Congressman George H. White in 1900, "and, if need be, he can use it to the detriment of the tenant. This is the general trend of the law throughout North Carolina, without the expression of it." The statute landless farmers criticized most was the Landlord and Tenant Act, a law revised by North Carolina's post-Reconstruction "Redeemers" to give the landlord a crop lien that was virtually ironclad. A simple, unwritten agreement to furnish supplies constituted a lien on a growing crop, and a tenant made himself liable for criminal prosecution if he removed any part of the crop before the rent or supplies had been paid for.

---

vided credit in such small amounts to so many poor people on such a wide scale, for only the store keepers could cheaply monitor and regulate the loans so as to minimize the losses inherent in such high-risk lending." Higgs, *Competition and Coercion*, 55.

37. *Report and Testimony of the Select Committee of the United States Senate to Investigate the Causes of the Removal of the Negroes from the Southern States to the Northern States*, Pt. I, Senate Rpt. 693, 46th Cong., 2nd Sess., 1880, pp. 49–51 (hereinafter cited as *Exodus Report*).

38. N.C. Bureau of Labor Statistics, *First Annual Report*, 82–85, 100, 130.

Although White said "the better element of our landlords" would not invoke "technical violations" of the law to reap unfair profits from tenants, the bias in the law gave an opening to the "shyster" landlord "who wants to stop me when I am disposed to go elsewhere with a view to bettering my condition." Knowing that almost any tenant over the course of time committed technical breaches of the law, the unscrupulous landlord used that "as a lever to hold them over, under a promise of immunity from prosecution in the courts."[39]

The Landlord and Tenant Act was an attempt to get around a popular measure written into the state constitution by Reconstruction reformers— the homestead exemption. By protecting from debt liability a basic minimum of every citizen's property (one thousand dollars worth of real estate, five hundred dollars in personal property), the homestead exemption was designed to benefit the poor man. But to prevent the homestead exemption from being used to deny the landlord his rent, the legislature strengthened the criminal statutes, changing into criminal offenses many acts that previously would have been the subject of civil action. As a result, a poor man, freed from the danger of losing his cabin and tools in a debt judgment, could be punished by imprisonment under a broad definition of larceny—with no distinction made between grand and petit larceny.[40] The homestead exemption also worked to make credit less available to poor men, for by limiting their liability it made them worse credit risks. The law was a well-intentioned attempt to protect persons of limited wealth, but it did not have the desired result.

In all matters of credit, the key issue is not how many tenant farmers borrowed money, or even the price of credit, but rather how many were able to "pay out" at the end of the year, that is, discharge their debts when the crop was sold. Although no exact figures are available, it is clear that the majority of tenants did pay out each year. A significant number, however, became hopelessly entangled in debt, and in 1886 a Northampton landowner estimated that a quarter of the tenants never paid out. George White testified in 1900 that in a "great many" cases

---

39. U.S. Industrial Commission, *Report of the Industrial Commission*, X (Washington, D.C., 1901), 421, 416–19.
40. *Ibid.* On the homestead exemption, see Otto H. Olsen, *Carpetbagger's Crusade: The Life of Albion Winegar Tourgée* (Baltimore, 1965), 107–108, 135–36. The exemption was one of the most popular features of the "Radical" constitution, and Democrats did not dare change it when they returned to power.

an impoverished farmer became practically "mortgaged to the land himself," going from bad to worse, unable to keep the landlord and the merchant from taking advantage of him.[41]

The South's "threefold revolution in labor, land tenure, and credit"— C. Vann Woodward's phrase—has often been described with an emphasis upon the wishes and actions of white people, and the resulting heavy burdens, grievous to be borne, of the largely passive Negroes.[42] Such an interpretation is inadequate, not only because the system burdened many white shoulders, but also because the blacks were not always and only victims. The fact of black economic achievement is absolutely central to an understanding of the postbellum southern economy; indeed, it can be considered a fourth "revolutionary" element. In spite of the obstacles to black progress, including expensive credit, unfair laws, and low wages, an important minority of blacks rose to the status of landowner, and blacks as a group enjoyed an impressive increase in income and property.

Unfortunately the sources are incomplete on the subject of black landownership, though it is easy to find references to individual blacks who were successful farmers. Isaac Forbes of Craven, a former slave, owned 1,200 acres and collected rent from fifteen tenants, according to an 1881 newspaper report. A Negro farmer in Wayne, who owned 485 acres, included some white men among his tenants in 1880. George White reported that the father of his private secretary, a farmer living near Tarboro, bequeathed his sons an estate of nearly forty thousand dollars, all earned in agriculture.[43] But when it comes to averages and aggregates, it is more difficult to estimate Negro landholding. Not until 1900 did the census break down county-by-county land tenure statistics into racial categories, and even then the numbers do not answer several important questions. The census of 1910, nine years after the second district lost its last Republican, black representative, was the first to give detailed information on Negro farms. Before the twentieth century there is only limited information to supplement the census.

41. N.C. Bureau of Labor Statistics, *First Annual Report*, 82–85, 103; Higgs, *Competition and Coercion*, 73; *Report of the Industrial Commission*, X, 419.

42. C. Vann Woodward, *Origins of the New South, 1877–1913* (Baton Rouge, 1951), 185.

43. *Carolina Enterprise* quoted in Wilmington *Post*, September 18, 1881; *Exodus Report*, 260–63; *Report of the Industrial Commission*, X, 422.

In 1879, after a careful examination of the Halifax County tax lists for the previous year, black lawyer-politician James O'Hara announced that blacks in his county owned at least 16,601 acres, or about 5 percent of the farmland in Halifax. He excluded town lots from his calculations and overlooked some property held by men over fifty, since it was difficult to tell the race of a person who was no longer required to pay a poll tax. Considering that his count was incomplete and that it was based on a year-old tax list, O'Hara thought "it would be no exaggeration to say that in my county, which is the next largest negro county in the State . . . the colored people own there in fee-simple title 20,000 acres of land." Without any extensive study, the Negro attorney guessed that blacks in neighboring Edgecombe possessed about 6,000 acres of real estate, explaining that "the people there hold their lands more intact." He added that Negroes in Edgecombe somehow had a different attitude: "The colored people over there do not seem to want to get up and acquire real estate like they do in our county. The people over there like fine horses, and I have known some colored men to pay $300 to $500 for a horse and buggy in the fall."[44]

Negroes in Vance County, which was less than half the size of Halifax County, owned about 5,147 acres in 1885. According to a "tobacco belt" business directory, 156 blacks owned land, with about half of them holding 10 acres or less. The largest Negro-owned property was Walter Bullock's 760 acres, followed by Sally Henderson's 440-acre farm. Only 9 other black landowners possessed as much as 100 acres. The county's most important black political leaders owned at least modest amounts of land, the register of deeds holding title to 13.5 acres, the general assembly member 10 acres, a town commissioner in Henderson 25, and another politician 29.[45]

By 1900 almost 3,000 black farmers owned all or part of the land they tilled. (Under the category of "owners" the census included part owners, owners and tenants, and managers, as well as simple owners, the largest group in the category.) These owners amounted to 23 percent of the total black farm operators. The proportion of owners ranged from Craven's 51 percent to only 8 percent in Edgecombe. Edgecombe's

44. *Exodus Report*, 49–50, 112–14.
45. Charles Emerson, compiler and publisher, *North Carolina Tobacco Belt Directory* (Raleigh, 1886), 589–609.

Table 2 **Negro Farm Owners, 1900**[a]

County	Percentage of black farm operators who were nontenants
Bertie	39.2
Craven	51.2
Edgecombe	8.2
Greene	11.6
Halifax	20.0
Jones	14.7
Lenoir	10.1
Northampton	25.5
Vance	26.3
Warren	29.3
Wayne	17.5
Wilson	11.9
DISTRICT	22.6

[a] Based on *Twelfth Census* (1900), Vol. V, Pt. I, pp. 108–11. These figures include part owners, owners and tenants, and managers.

immediate neighbor, Halifax, with the same crops, the same large black majority, and the same Republican politics, had a rate of Negro ownership more than twice as high as Edgecombe's, just as James O'Hara had noted in 1880.[46]

O'Hara may have been right, of course, in claiming that Edgecombe blacks fancied horses above land, but the 1910 census statistics suggest a different explanation. In that year Halifax Negroes owned over 43,000 acres, or about 12 percent of the total farm acreage in the county. In a little over thirty years the acreage owned by blacks had more than doubled. At the same time, Negroes owned less than 4 percent of the land in Edgecombe. Yet the land held by Edgecombe blacks (excluding mortgaged land and that of part owners) averaged $20.56 an acre in value. The corresponding figure for Halifax was $11.41. One reason blacks could afford to buy more land in Halifax was because it was worth less. The same process was at work elsewhere. The per-acre value of the land Wilson blacks owned outright amounted to $27.84, yet Negroes owned only 3.1 percent of the total farm acreage. In Warren County,

46. *Twelfth Census* (1900), Vol. V, Pt. I, pp. 108–11.

the Negro-owned percentage of the farmland was five times greater, but the per-acre value was $12.73.[47] In many cases black farmers bought land on the periphery, in the less prosperous counties of the district, building themselves up where land values were lower and agriculture relatively poorer.

Another way of putting it is that blacks did better in the nonplantation counties. The plantation mode of agriculture persisted in the New South, the land in many cases remaining in large parcels owned by a powerful planter, though farmed by sharecroppers. Aware of the inadequacies of previous statistics, which had concentrated on individual tillers and single "farms," the directors of the 1910 census conducted a special survey of southern plantations. Defining a plantation as "a continuous tract of land of considerable area under the general supervision of a single individual or firm, all or part of such tract being divided into at least five smaller tracts, which are leased to tenants," the study found that plantation agriculture was "extensively developed" in 325 southern counties, including 21 in North Carolina. In the second district, the census standards marked Halifax, Edgecombe, Lenoir, Greene, Wilson, and Wayne as plantation counties. With the exception of Halifax, which is a special case, each of these had a low rate of Negro farmland ownership, less than 1 acre per capita. In Edgecombe, Wilson, and Lenoir, the figure was .5 acres or less per black resident. By contrast, Halifax's black population owned 1.8 acres per capita. But then Halifax had had the largest free Negro population of any county in North Carolina in 1860, and the 62 free Negro farmers who owned real property before the war outnumbered the free black farmers in the other ten counties combined. This unique heritage, and the county's relatively lower land values, explain why Halifax was different from the other plantation counties.[48]

47. *Negro Population*, 734–41.
48. *Thirteenth Census* (1910), V, 877–89; Jay R. Mandle, *The Roots of Black Poverty* (Durham, N.C., 1978), 39–51. John Hope Franklin, *The Free Negro in North Carolina, 1790–1860* (New York, 1971), 17, 232. In the North Carolina plantation counties the plantation system had a weaker hold according to the census study, than in states like Mississippi, South Carolina, or Georgia. Plantations comprised only 17.5 percent of the land in the tweny-one plantation counties, whereas plantations made up 44.1 percent of the land in forty-five Mississippi counties. More than a third of the land in seventy Georgia counties was in plantation farms, somewhat above the regional average of 31.5 percent.

Table 3   **Negro Ownership of Farmland, 1910[a]**

County	Negro Acres	Negro Percentage of Total Farm Acres	Per Capita Negro Ownership of Farmland
Bertie	41,503	14.7	3.1
Craven	27,145	13.4	1.9
Edgecombe	10,039	3.5	.5
Greene	5,600	4.2	.9
Halifax	43,701	12.4	1.8
Jones	9,828	5.8	2.4
Lenoir	3,709	1.7	.4
Northampton	26,742	9.7	2.0
Vance	13,049	8.3	1.3
Warren	33,212	15.6	2.5
Wayne	12,489	3.9	.8
Wilson	6,167	3.1	.5
DISTRICT	233,184	8.3	1.7
STATE	1,041,006	4.6	1.5

[a] Based on *Negro Population,* 734–41, 686–89.

The black agrarians in Warren, Bertie, Craven, Jones, Halifax, and Northampton probably did as well as any in the South at acquiring land. An 1896 study suggested that Gloucester County in tidewater Virginia was "the banner county of the ex-slave States" for Negro land ownership, with blacks owning 10 percent of the total acreage in the county. Such a level of achievement was matched in several second district counties. In fact, Craven County blacks were slightly ahead of this "banner county" in 1888, holding about 11 percent of the acreage listed for taxes, as well as 11 percent of all taxable property.[49]

During the years 1872 to 1900 there was no general conviction among whites that blacks should not own land, nor any intimidation used against

49. Pitt Dillingham, "Land Tenure Among the Negroes," *Yale Review,* V (August, 1896), 201–203; Craven County, Tax List, 1888 (microfilm), in North Carolina State Archives, Raleigh. The comparison of 1888 and 1896 is imperfect because it ignores the impact of the depression of the nineties on black landowning. Some idea of the results of hard times (and the later racial crisis) may be drawn from the fact that Craven blacks owned somewhat more land in 1888 than in 1910. The tax list for 1888 shows about 32,000 taxable acres owned by blacks whereas Table 3 reports 27,000 Negro farm acres, a roughly comparable measure in a largely rural county like Craven.

blacks who purchased land. "I can not say that I know of any prejudice against the colored man's accumulating property," declared George White, though "loopholes in the law" (and sometimes Negro "ignorance and incapacity") impeded race progress. Black political leader Henry Cheatham provoked favorable comment around the state when he addressed a Negro farmers' picnic in Halifax County, urging blacks to buy land even if they had to begin with very small amounts. "The speech was sensible and to the point and can not fail to do good," observed the local white editor. Another newspaper commented: "It seems that Cheatham thinks religion, education and ownership of real estate is of more importance to the negro than politics, and he is right."[50] Unlike some modern observers, who have assumed that "mere" civic rights such as voting, holding office, and serving on juries were meaningless without sweeping economic reform, white leaders seemed to fear black participation in politics more than black landowning and the real increase in economic power it represented. Even if politics was often a largely symbolic enterprise, the ability of Negro voters and leaders to manipulate and define symbols more severely threatened southern visions of order than the thought of black farmers striving to be masters of their own farms.

As significant as the landowning minority was, it was always a small portion of the second district's total black labor force. Black owners were outnumbered, of course, by black tenants, but there was a third, even larger category, one step below sharecropping—agricultural wage laborers. Working by the month or the day, they did not qualify as farm operators in any sense. "I think it is only those who are disposed to be thrifty who rent land, and [the] others hire out for wages," said a Goldsboro banker-planter in 1880, estimating that three quarters of the blacks in agriculture worked for wages. His guess may have been a bit high, or Wayne was atypical, for the 1880 census reported approximately half of the adult black men in Halifax County as farm laborers. In 1910 North Carolina had 65,000 black agricultural laborers (not including 93,000 family farm workers) compared to 63,000 farm operators.[51]

Although most of the plantations had been broken down into tenant

50. *Report of the Industrial Commission*, X, 424; Scotland Neck *Democrat*, September 19, 26, 1895.
51. *Exodus Report*, 214; U.S. Department of Commerce, Census Office, MS Tenth Census, population schedules, North Carolina; *Negro Population*, 515.

farms, there were still large farms requiring hired hands. Edgecombe County, for example, had twenty-three owner-cultivated farms of 1,000 acres or more in 1880, covering 35,000 acres (12 percent of the county's farmland), and needing extensive hired help, especially at harvest time.[52] Nor was the demand for labor restricted to major planters. In Halifax County's Roseneath Township, a stronghold of white yeoman farmers, there were seventy-two owner-cultivators in 1880, none with more than 1,000 acres and only six in the over-500 category. Yet these farmers reported hiring labor equivalent to over ninety full-time workers. (Almost all of this labor was done by blacks; of the more than 4,700 man-weeks of labor listed by Roseneath farmers, white laborers accounted for only 185 weeks.)[53]

A farm laborer earned six to ten dollars a month, often about half of it in cash and the rest in trade or store orders. His employer usually provided him rations, shelter, firewood, and a garden plot. Working by the day, a man could make as much as fifty or sixty cents, with female workers getting no more than forty cents. White laborers were very rare in eastern North Carolina and, by most reports, earned the same wages as Negroes. A black plantation owner suggested there was some discrimination nonetheless, in that a white was likely to be boarded in the farmer's house and fed better than his colored peer.[54]

Many black laborers can only be described as permanently under-employed. A Jones County man explained: "The farm laborers are regularly employed by the month about one-half of their time; the rest of the time they work by the day or job." A landlord from Northampton claimed the laborers liked it that way: "There are many who do not care for regular work; they prefer to work by the day here and there and have plenty of time to rest."[55] But some whites were more sympathetic. The editor of the Warrenton Gazette declared that "all sensible men know that a man and wife and half a dozen children cannot support themselves" on the "pittance" usually paid. "Giving an able bodied man

52. MS Tenth Census, agriculture schedules, North Carolina.
53. Ibid.
54. Exodus Report, 64, 219, 244, 251–60; Report of the Industrial Commission, X, 423–24, 429; N.C. Bureau of Labor Statistics, First Annual Report, 82–85, 120–23, 98, 130, 132, 136.
55. N.C. Bureau of Labor Statistics, First Annual Report, 130, 103.

$80.00 a year and pay[ing] him in old clothes and in orders at a store where he has to pay fifty per cent over cash prices has well nigh ruined our labor." Another editor maintained that farmers ought to pay their workers as much as they could afford, not as little as possible. Low pay was not in the farmer's self-interest, for it led to demoralized and sometimes larcenous workers. "It should be our pleasure as it is our policy to elevate the laborer, to give him more self respect, then we will have a more honest hand."[56]

The laborers did not rely on moral suasion alone to better their situation. Edgecombe farm workers demanded fifteen dollars per month in 1870 and struck again for a dollar a day plus board in 1874. The sheriff intervened in another strike in 1889, driving irate blacks in the Sparta area out of their planter-supplied houses. On occasion the farmers had to give in to avoid economic loss. Cotton pickers in Greene County combined forces in 1890 and posted "threatening notices" against pickers who worked for less than fifty cents per hundred pounds; the Kinston *Free Press* commented: "One of these notices was posted on Mr. J. B. Sillivants' place, which he tore down. Then another one was posted threatening to burn his house down if it was torn down. It is thought that some mean white men are at the head of this move, and a reward of $100 has been offered for their apprehension." Although they did not like "the threatening manner in which it was secured" (it was never pleasant to find the workers in a strong bargaining position), the Greene planters did pay the fifty cent rate.[57] One editor tried to reason with farmers who faced cotton picking time with too few hands. "For some weeks the farmers will not have labor enough to pick the cotton as rapidly as it opens. There is a probability of some impatient ones raising the price, which is now 25 or 30 cents a hundred. No good end will be served, as there is only a given quantity of labor."[58]

Thousands of the district's farm laborers migrated in search of better opportunities, taking jobs in the Georgia turpentine industry, or Mississippi's more prosperous cotton fields, or cities in the South or North. If

56. Warrenton *Gazette*, January 13, 1882; Tarboro *Southerner*, January 14, 1876.
57. Tarboro *Southerner*, October 5, 1871, October 10, 1889; Tarboro *Enquirer-Southerner*, June 5, 1874; Kinston *Free Press*, September 25, 1890.
58. Tarboro *Southerner*, August 30, 1900.

the nonagricultural sector of the eastern Carolina economy had been stronger, there would have been closer-to-home alternatives to old clothes and eighty dollars a year.

A second district Rip Van Winkle, falling asleep in 1860, would have found much that was totally new in the agricultural system of 1880. He might have required more than one explanation before he understood emancipation, the crop lien, sharecropping, and widespread black proprietorship. But one thing would have been no surprise—cotton was still the dominant crop. Yet behind even this familiar fact lurked remarkable changes.

If cotton was king before the war, afterward it became a positive despot, dominating the area's agriculture more thoroughly in the next quarter century than ever before. By 1880 the district was producing more than twice as much cotton as before the war, and during the same period corn production fell by about a third, as the region ceased being self-sufficient. "In 1860 we produced, with the exception of wheat and probably a little bacon, all necessary food," an Edgecombe planter recalled in 1893. "From 1870 to 1890 the cotton-raisers of this district relied almost wholly upon other sections for food and forage crops; at least they did not produce more than one-fourth of the amount necessary."[59]

Cotton's hold on the district weakened somewhat in the last dozen years of the nineteenth century. In 1889 bad weather resulted in disastrously short crops. "The winter of '89 will go down through the next generation as a time of general ruin and destruction—the equal of which was never known," wrote a leading citizen of Rocky Mount. As the nation experienced a depression, cotton prices dropped sharply in the early 1890s, skidding by 1895 to only six cents a pound on the New York market. These hard times provoked a new burst of farm division and tenant making, with the majority of district farmers becoming renters in 1900. The depression also prodded many farmers to place more emphasis on food crops and alternative cash crops to cotton. In just a

59. *Eighth Census* (1860), *Agriculture of the United States*, 104–105, 108–109; *Compendium of the Ninth Census* (1870), 767, 769; *Compendium of the Tenth Census* (1880), 800–803; *Report of the Committee on Agriculture and Forestry on Condition of Cotton Growers in the United States, the Present Prices of Cotton, and the Remedy; and on Cotton Consumption and Production*, Vol. I, Senate Rpt. 986, 53rd Cong., 3rd Sess., 1895, p. 284.

decade, the amount of land planted in cotton contracted nearly 90,000 acres, a decline of more than one quarter. At the same time corn production rose markedly, in several counties surpassing antebellum standards.[60]

The most important new crops were tobacco and peanuts. Not a single second district county devoted as much as 1,000 acres to peanuts in 1889, but ten years later there was significant peanut growth in Bertie, Edgecombe, Northampton, and Halifax, with over 14,000 acres in peanuts in Bertie alone. Tobacco culture also expanded quickly, so that by 1899 six counties had planted 4,000 or more acres in the "Soverane Herb." Wilson County's 9,465 acres led the district. In 1889 only Vance County, located in the old bright-tobacco belt, could claim as many as 4,000 acres of tobacco.[61]

Despite this diversification, cotton continued to be the region's most important crop at the turn of the century, and production remained far above prewar levels. The agricultural reformers who saw "overproduction" of cotton as the root of all the farmer's woes would have preferred a much greater shift away from cotton. The other popular remedy linked with diversification, self-sufficiency, was also a remote goal in 1900. Changing from one cash crop, cotton, to others, such as peanuts or tobacco, did nothing, of course, to lessen the farmer's dependence on other areas for his food and animal feed.[62]

60. Thomas H. Battle to Elias Carr, November 16, 1889, in Elias Carr Papers, East Carolina University, Greenville, N.C.; James L. Watkins, "Production and Price of Cotton for One Hundred Years," U.S. Department of Agriculture Bulletin no. 9, Misc. Series (Washington, D.C., 1895), 12–14. Twelfth Census (1900), Vol. V, Pt. I, pp. 108–11; VI, Pt. II, pp. 176–77, 433; Eleventh Census (1890), V, 378–79, 395–96.

61. Eleventh Census (1890), V, 444–45, 483–84; Twelfth Census (1900), Vol. VI, Pt. II, pp. 565–66. On the geographical expansion of bright-tobacco culture, see Nannie May Tilley, The Bright-Tobacco Industry, 1860–1929 (Chapel Hill, N.C., 1948), 141–50.

62. Nineteenth-century farmers did not have the benefit of recent econometric research which concludes that "in rejecting the panacea of diversification, southern farmers implicitly displayed a solid grasp of their regional economy." Stephen J. DeCanio, "Cotton 'Overproduction' in Late Nineteenth-Century Southern Agriculture," Journal of Economic History, XXXIII (September, 1973), 606–33. DeCanio maintains that southern farmers responded flexibly to commodity price changes—as flexibly as did wheat farmers outside the South in the same period. Gavin Wright and Howard Kunrenther explain the dominance of cotton in terms of business risk theory, asserting that conditions in southern agriculture ecouraged farmers to gamble. Tenants had good reason to prefer cotton since there was "no prospect of raising

Many second district editors, community promoters, and politicians shared the general southern faith that the region could become prosperous by diversifying its economy and building up industry at home. Publicists for this faith (called the "New South creed" by one historian) had created a conventional wisdom emphasizing the potential productivity of the South and the broad benefits of business investment.[63] Two of the most important activities associated with the "New South" notion were railroads and cotton mills. Indeed, to some New South advocates, progress could practically be measured in thousands of spindles or miles of tracks.

At its formation, the Second Congressional District contained three major railroads built before the Civil War. North Carolina's largest city and Halifax County were connected by the Wilmington and Weldon Railroad. The Atlantic and North Carolina Railroad, partly state owned, ran ninety-five miles from Morehead City on the coast through New Bern and Kinston and ended in Goldsboro. The terminus points for the third railroad, the Raleigh and Gaston, were the state capital and Weldon. Other rail lines, largely outside the district, ran from Weldon into Virginia and from Goldsboro to Charlotte.

Railroad building proceeded at a very rapid rate in the nation and in the South during the 1880s. In the second district, new rail lines joined Rocky Mount and Wilson with Fayetteville, North Carolina, opened traffic between Scotland Neck and Kinston, and joined Tarboro and Norfolk, Virginia. Lines connecting Henderson with Oxford and Durham were also opened in the decade, and by the late nineties, the district claimed 560 miles of track.[64]

The progress of the cotton mill in the 1890s was as dramatic as the

any sizeable amount of cash income on a small farm except through cotton." Neither DeCanio nor Wright and Kunrenther see landlord-merchant "coercion" as the main impediment to diversification. Gavin Wright and Howard Kunrenther, "Cotton, Corn and Risk in the Nineteenth Century," *Journal of Economic History*, XXXV (September, 1975), 526-51. For a different view see Ransom and Sutch, *One Kind of Freedom*, 126-70.

63. Paul M. Gaston, *The New South Creed: A Study in Southern Mythmaking* (New York, 1973), 43-80.

64. John F. Stover, *The Railroads of the South, 1865-1900* (Chapel Hill, N.C., 1955), 189-93, 259; North Carolina, *Second Annual Report of the Board of Railroad Commissioners, 1892* (Raleigh, 1893), 545-53, 62, 417, 178, 95, 195, 526, 480, 150, 325; North Carolina, *Sixth Annual Report of the Board of Railroad Commissioners, 1896* (Raleigh, 1897), Pt. II, 23-30.

growth of railroads in the eighties. Twenty cotton mills operated in the towns of New Bern, Tarboro, Roanoke Rapids, Weldon, Scotland Neck, Kinston, Henderson, Goldsboro, and Wilson in 1900, nearly all of them established in the 1890s. Wilson Cotton Mills, incorporated in 1882, Kinston's Orien Knitting Mills (1890), Scotland Neck Cotton Mills (1890), and Tarboro Cotton Mills (1888) were among the oldest establishments. A third of the district's manufacturing work force worked in cotton mills by 1900.[65]

Counting the cotton mills along with all other industries, there were 733 manufacturing establishments in the district in 1900, employing about 6,900 people. The owners of these businesses, which ranged from brick factories and harness shops to saw mills and buggy construction, had invested $6,400,066.00, an average of $8,731.33 per enterprise.[66] The type of industry that predominated is readily evident from an examination of a list of businesses in any town. In Goldsboro, for instance, there were twenty-one miscellaneous industries, including two cotton mills, three brick and tiling factories, two furniture factories, two lumber companies, a plow making firm, a rice mill, and an ice company. Nine of New Bern's twenty manufacturing concerns were lumber companies. Businesses like these served the needs of an agricultural society without fundamentally altering the economic domination of farming.[67]

"Extraordinary, inconvenient and most grotesque" the governor had called the district, but his words hardly applied to the social or economic life of the area. For surely the district was highly ordinary in its commitment to Protestantism, cotton culture, and black labor, and there was nothing bizarre about a southern section that lacked major cities and seldom saw foreigners. Only the district's political shape was "grotesque." Depending on one's perspective, its political history was to be "inconvenient" and most "extraordinary."

65. North Carolina, *Fourteenth Annual Report of the Bureau of Labor and Printing, 1900* (Raleigh, 1901), 184–92; North Carolina, *Report of the Commissioner of Agriculture, 1900* (Raleigh, 1901), 240–41. The precise number of cotton mills at a given moment is difficult to ascertain, since some lists apparently included mills about to begin operation among mills already operating.
66. *Twelfth Census* (1900), Vol. VIII, Pt. II, pp. 664–67.
67. North Carolina, *Report of the Commissioner of Agriculture, 1900*, 242–53.

Chapter 2

THE DISORGANIZING CRY OF COLOR

> Our preference, as far as we have any preference in the matter,
> is, negro first, carpetbagger next and scallawag last.
> —Tarboro *Enquirer-Southerner*, May 22, 1874

THE HISTORY OF "BLACK SECOND" POLITICS is complicated, and—thanks to incomplete, one-sided sources—sometimes obscure. On occasion the historian can only conjecture concerning the motives of an historical actor who left little record save his enemies' denunciations—reconstructing, as it were, an elaborate mastodon from a few teeth, a handful of hair, and, pehaps, a lump of petrified dung. Yet despite the difficulties, the district is worthy of study in detail, for it offers a fascinating picture of southern politics in the late nineteenth century.

Two of the most important themes in this story revolve around the ideas of responsibility and conformity, especially responsibility taken by Negroes and conformity by whites. The district's large, contrived black majority made the question of black leadership an inevitable one. Who was to represent the black community? To what extent would Negroes exercise responsibility and power? Was the community as a whole capable of responding to changes in an evolving black leadership group? Such questions were awkward, even frightening, to many whites, and they called for white solidarity in facing them. White spokesmen often employed the polemical shorthand "Negro domination" to refer to the dangers of black responsibility. The antidote—"white supremacy"—required, first of all, the isolation of dissident whites by powerful pressures for conformity. Hence the arresting statement of a Democratic editor in 1874: "Our preference, as far as we have any preference in the matter, is, negro first, carpetbagger next and scallawag last." In some situations, the most distasteful person was the nonconforming native white. Neutralize him, theorized the white supremacists, and society will reach the "right" decisions about black responsibility.

The fullest elaboration of these themes, it is true, did not come until the end of the century with the North Carolina racial crisis of 1898 to 1901, but they were present in one form or another even at the formation of the second district in the twilight years of Reconstruction.

Reconstruction political patterns persisted in the Second Congressional district until 1878. Contrary to the "tragic era" stereotypes, these years were free from desperate night riders, large-scale peculations, and Negro vengefulness. Reconstruction in the second district did not mean "bayonet rule"; it was simply ordinary politics with black participation. At each election during this period, the district voters changed their congressional representative, though each time they elected a Republican. All three congressmen were native North Carolinians, two of them with important prewar political experience. The three men symbolized well the disparate groups that made up the Republican party in the South. One was a former Whig, another a former slave, and the third a common man who entered political life as a Jacksonian.

Charles Randolph Thomas was the incumbent Republican representative in 1872. He once said that he was born a Whig and had he lived in the age of Hamilton would have been a Federalist. The son of a wealthy Carteret County shipowner and merchant, Thomas had received the best education available in antebellum North Carolina. He was a graduate of the University of North Carolina and had read law with Judge Richmond Pearson, tutor of many of the state's illustrious attorneys. Thomas had been a Unionist delegate to the state secession convention, president of the Atlantic and North Carolina Railroad, and a superior court judge from 1868 to 1871. Now at the age of forty-five he was a member of the United States House of Representatives.[1]

Elected to Congress in 1870, he found his district considerably changed by the legislature's partisan apportionment of 1872. The racial balance in the district was altered by the removal of three counties with white majorities, Carteret, Duplin, and Onslow, and the addition of heavily

1. *Newbernian*, September 2, 1876; *Biographical Directory of the American Congress, 1774–1961* (Washington, D.C., 1961), 1703; John G. McCormick, "Personnel of the Convention of 1861," *James Sprunt Historical Monographs*, No. 1 (Chapel Hill, N.C., 1900), 82–83.

black Halifax, Northampton, and Warren. If the political leaders in the new counties would support him, the change was certain to mean greatly increased margins of victory, since Halifax, Warren, and Northampton gave the Republican ticket a strong vote.

But there was sentiment among some blacks, particularly in the newly added counties, for a Negro nominee. A few weeks after the reapportionment, black state legislator Edward R. Dudley felt it necessary to defend Thomas, a fellow resident of Craven County. "Admit that we are in the majority in this district," he wrote to a New Bern Republican newspaper, "is it wisdom for us as colored voters to run a colored man just because he is colored, or a white man because he is white?"[2]

John H. Collins, a Negro Civil War veteran and college graduate living in Halifax, disagreed. Dudley was out of step with "the people of the District" who were "determined to run a colored man for Congress and elect him." The nomination of a Negro was "no more than right and due to the best Educated colored Republicans in the District." He added: "I would like to know when the time will come to send colored men to Congress if not now."[3] Delighted by signs of discord in the "Radical" camp, Democrats commented frequently on the "hypocrisy" of white Republicans, who were said to use blacks only as political menials. The Tarboro *Southerner* observed: "If the colored men of this Congressional District . . . do not send one of their own race to Congress they will have no one to blame for it but themselves."[4]

The leading black congressional aspirant was thirty-one-year-old John Adams Hyman, a two-term state senator from Warren. Born a slave in the county he now represented, Hyman as a youth had been taught to read by an aged northern-born jeweler in Warrenton. The jeweler's action had angered many local citizens, who thought him hostile to slavery, and a group of village hotheads forced him to leave the state in the early days of the Civil War. Hyman also left North Carolina as an involuntary migrant, moving to Alabama as part of a slave sale. Returning home after emancipation, he had been a delegate to the state equal rights convention in 1865, a member of the constitutional convention of 1868, and a state

2. Tarboro *Southerner*, March 21, 1872; New Bern *Daily Times*, March 13, 1872.
3. New Bern *Daily Times*, March 24, 1872. Biographical details, Wilmington *Post*, January 17, 1879.
4. Tarboro *Southerner*, April 4, 1872.

senator from 1868 onward. Some Conservatives accused him of profiting from freely dispensed corruption in the legislature of 1868–1869, but the evidence was ambiguous.[5]

The Republican district convention met May 9, 1872, in the town of Wilson—a convenient midpoint between Warren and Craven, the geographical extremes of the second district. Only four of the fifteen delegates supported Hyman, and Thomas was renominated on the first ballot. (The next uncontroverted, first-ballot Republican nomination in the district would not be until 1884.) Thomas received 9 votes and 2 votes went to favorite son candidates, but these minor candidates threw their support to Thomas before the result was announced. Hyman moved that the nomination be unanimous, though one Halifax delegate loudly objected.[6]

The Democratic press reported the convention as an outrageous injustice to Negroes, who were taken advantage of by white adventurers. "They ought to know that there is not a scalawag in the state who cares a farthing for them beyond obtaining their votes," said the Raleigh *Sentinel*, edited by the flamboyant and erratic Josiah Turner. Hyman, "a distinguished citizen of Warren," "a worthy colored man of considerable legislative experience" had possibly been defeated by corrupt methods. According to the Raleigh *Daily News*, "Hyman said he had been beaten for the nomination by money."[7] But Democrats also pictured Hyman as the beneficiary of corruption. Several weeks after the convention, the Tarboro *Southerner* reported that Thomas had paid Hyman five thousand dollars. A Republican newspaper noted this claim and similar charges involving the Republican nominee in the first district and offered one hundred dollars in cash "for any substantial proof" that either candidate "or their friends, paid one cent, as charged." There is no record that the reward was ever claimed.[8]

For Thomas the nomination was tantamount to election. Democrats

---

5. *Biographical Directory of the American Congress*, 1102; Lizzie Wilson Montgomery, *Sketches of Old Warrenton, North Carolina* (Raleigh, 1924), 88–89. See following note 25 for the details of the corruption charges.
6. Raleigh *Daily News*, May 10, 1872; New Bern *Daily Times*, May 11, 1872.
7. Raleigh *Sentinel*, May 14, 1872; Raleigh *Daily News*, May 10, 1872. The Warrenton *Gazette*, November 23, 1872, reported that Hyman "and other darkies from this county" who were at the convention attributed Thomas' victory to bribery.
8. Tarboro *Southerner*, May 30, 1872; New Bern *Daily Times*, June 12, 1872.

knew they had no chance if the Republicans were united, and some suggested that the best course was to make no nomination. Other party strategists disagreed, holding that a nomination for every position was necessary to bring out the full party vote.[9]

The Democratic district convention met in Goldsboro, June 5, with a future chief justice of the state supreme court, Walter Clark, presiding. Perhaps because it was not easy to find aspirants, a nominating committee selected the congressional candidate. The man to do battle with the Radical Goliath, the committee decided, was a thirty-five-year-old Confederate veteran from Halifax named William Hodge "Buck" Kitchin, an unpolished man capable of arousing party loyalists with blistering stump speeches. "He stirred party passion as no other man of his day," remembered Josephus Daniels.[10]

Although he had "no more chance of . . . being elected than . . . of being struck by lightning," Kitchin conducted a vigorous campaign, building Democratic morale with his fiery harangues and embarrassing his restrained, cultured opponent. In a debate at New Bern, Kitchin put Thomas on the spot by promising if elected to donate three thousand dollars from the congressional salary of five thousand dollars to the education of black teachers. Would his opponent do the same? Thomas lamely replied that he could not live on two thousand dollars in the capital.[11]

North Carolina elections were curiously divided in 1872. The election for state officers and legislators took place in August, three months before the balloting for president, vice-president, and members of Congress. The August elections augured well for Thomas and could only discourage district Democrats. The Republican state ticket, led by Governor Tod R. Caldwell, carried the state by a narrow margin, and a man from the second district, Curtis Hooks Brogden of Wayne, was the successful candidate for lieutenant governor. Republican legislative strength increased by sixteen seats, though Democrats still had a majority

9. Tarboro *Southerner*, May 23, 1872.

10. Tarboro *Southerner*, June 13, 1872; *Biographical Directory of the American Congress*, 1172; Daniels, *Tar Heel Editor*, 177. Compare H. Larry Ingle, "A Southern Democrat at Large: William Hodge Kitchin and the Populist Party," *North Carolina Historical Review*, XLV (April, 1968), 178–94.

11. Wilmington *Evening Post*, July 27, 1872; Raleigh *Blasting-Powder*, June 26, 1872.

in the general assembly, thanks partly to gerrymandering. In the second district, Republican legislative candidates swept to victory in every county but Wilson. In Wayne, Republican house candidates won, but Lotte W. Humphrey, Democratic congressional nominee in 1870, carried the senatorial district. Among the winning general assembly candidates were men who would play important roles in the next few years. John Hyman was reelected to the state senate from Warren; William P. Mabson, a young black schoolteacher in Edgecombe, won a seat in the house; for the third time a Negro preacher named Henry Eppes was elected senator from Halifax; and Richard W. King, the white Republican "boss" of Lenoir, won a second term in the senate.

Three months later Thomas defeated Kitchin 20,072 votes to 11,627, carrying every county in the district save Wilson, and even there he reduced the Democratic majority to fewer than 200 votes. Two years earlier, before the gerrymandering of the district, Thomas had won by less than 3,000 votes. Now he ran with the dual advantage of overwhelming black support and the opposition's apathy toward the national Grant-Greeley contest. In Wayne County Thomas increased his margin of victory from his 1870 total of 10 to 240, and the Democratic vote in Craven fell by more than 500 from the 1870 level.[12] Although President Grant carried North Carolina by nearly 25,000 votes and the total vote given Republican congressional candidates exceeded that received by the Democrats, five members of the state's eight-man congressional delegation were Democrats.[13]

When he returned to Washington for the third session of the Forty-second Congress early in 1873, Thomas made a serious political blunder by voting for the bill to raise congressmen's salaries retroactively—the "back salary grab." Although the action was later repealed, many of his constituents did not forgive him for this vote. In the next session, which marked the beginning of his second term in the House of Representatives, Thomas introduced not a single bill and made few remarks, though he was an active member of the committee on elections.[14]

12. See appendix for complete election returns.
13. See Governor Caldwell's comments, *North Carolina House Journal*, 1872–73, pp. 40–41.
14. The "back salary grab" passed the House March 3, 1873, and was repealed on January 13, 1874. *Congressional Globe*, 42nd Cong., 3rd Sess., 2105; *Congressional Record*, 43rd Cong., 1st Sess., 626.

By the beginning of 1874 Thomas had several active rivals for the congressional nomination. E. R. Dudley, who had praised Thomas two years before, now declared him unfit for the office and harbored ambitions for the post himself. Dudley had introduced a civil rights bill in the last session of the state legislature and maintained that the second district needed as its representative an open advocate of civil rights. As early as March 12, 1874, the New Bern *Times,* which supported Thomas, saw the need to appeal for the healing of "local differences" and for an end to the "disorganizing cry of color."[15] John Hyman planned to renew his challenge, and Senator King, Lieutenant Governor Brogden, and several others were mentioned as possible candidates. A supporter of Dudley called Thomas a "would-be arristocrat [*sic*] . . . who walks the streets of New Berne with head so high that he can't notice any of the people until just before the time for the campaign to begin, and then he very graciously condescends to shake hands with a few."[16]

Thomas returned home from Washington in late March to rebuild his political strength, but railroad politics soon compounded his troubles. Governor Caldwell had pursued a policy of consolidating the state's railroad holdings, but the board of directors of the Atlantic and North Carolina Railroad (of which Thomas was a member) flouted the governor's wishes by agreeing in April, 1874, to lease the ninety-five-mile road for fifty years to a group of developers incorporated as the Midland North Carolina Railroad Company. Thomas was involved in both sides of this arrangement as he was president of the Midland company, and E. R. Stanly, president of the A & NC, was a member of the Midland board. Caldwell quickly removed Thomas, Stanley, and four others and appointed a new board led by R. W. King and L. W. Humphrey. After some legal maneuvering the projected lease was prevented,[17] but the whole episode created new opposition to Thomas.

Not one to enjoy the hurly-burly of campaigning, Thomas considered party politics in the second district a "somewhat sickening if not disgusting—*science.*" Perhaps baffled by the black opposition to him, the

15. New Bern *Times,* March 18, February 18, March 12, 1874.
16. *Ibid.,* March 14, 1874.
17. New Bern *Journal of Commerce,* March 28, 1874; Cecil Kenneth Brown, *A State Movement in Railroad Development: The Story of North Carolina's First Effort to Establish an East and West Trunk Line Railroad* (Chapel Hill, N.C., 1928), 241–42.

counseled Negroes to refrain from agitating the civil rights issue and warned them not to discriminate against white Republicans. "Whenever you raise the question of color, I'll go out. I'll repudiate [the party]," he was reported as saying.[18] The opposition to Thomas was more than a simple question of color, however, as events in predominantly black Edgecombe demonstrated. There the Republican county convention, chaired by William P. Mabson, passed resolutions repudiating "all Republican participants" in the "back salary grab," denouncing "any step or measure tending to place the nomination on a basis of color *alone*" and endorsing Alexander McCabe, a white New Yorker, for Congress. Lawyer James O'Hara, a black congressional aspirant from Halifax, reportedly "made a very sensible speech," but Mabson adherents "put him down."[19] The county conventions in Halifax and Lenoir also censured those who voted for back pay and endorsed local favorites for Congress—King in Lenoir and O'Hara in Halifax.[20]

Constituent discontent and the ambition of rivals had reduced Thomas to a weak position by the time the district convention met in Goldsboro on May 14. His cause was not helped when debate turned to the issue of color. There was applause as James O'Hara "endorsed the general sentiment that the question of color be not permitted to enter into the spirit of the convention, and that colored aspirants be not set aside on account of their color." Officeholders as well as voters should be of both races, said the New York-born attorney. Tim Lee, a white leader from Raleigh, told the convention that a Negro should be elected, that the "question of color would have to be met and decided and the sooner the better."[21]

On the first ballot Thomas received 4 votes, and seven other candidates divided the remaining 11 votes. Craven and Wayne backed Thomas, Jones and Lenoir voted for King, and no other candidate received more

18. Charles R. Thomas to Daniel L. Russell, March 8, 1874, in Daniel Lindsay Russell Papers, Southern Historical Collection, University of North Carolina, Chapel Hill. *Carolina Messenger* (Goldsboro), April 20, 1874. As a lame duck, Thomas was one of few southerners to vote for the Civil Rights Act of 1875. *Congressional Record*, 43rd Cong., 2nd Session., 1011.

19. New Bern *Republic-Courier*, May 2, 1874; Tarboro *Enquirer-Southerner*, quoted in Raleigh *Sentinel*, May 4, 1874. For McCabe's background, see J. Kelly Turner and John L. Bridgers, Jr., *History of Edgecombe County, North Carolina* (Raleigh, 1920), 249.

20. Raleigh *Era*, May 14, 1874.

21. *Carolina Messenger* (Goldsboro), May 18, 1874.

than one county's support. The peak of the Thomas strength came on the fifth ballot, when the incumbent had 5 votes. Hyman's first support outside Warren came on the seventh ballot from a Wayne delegate who broke from the Thomas ranks. The voting dragged on for twenty-eight ballots, several counties persistently supporting favorite-son candidates. At last on the twenty-ninth ballot King withdrew in Hyman's favor (as new president of the A & NC, King had every reason to prefer any candidate to Thomas) which gave Hyman a bare majority of 8. The convention then made the result unanimous.[22]

The defeat of Thomas, "the ablest representative from this State in Congress," saddened the *Evening Post*, the Republican daily in Wilmington. The result was "unaccountable," an action "which eminently gratifies our political enemies." But the Democratic *Carolina Messenger* saw Hyman's nomination as "the opening of brighter skies for the Conservative banner," and the *Newbernian*, a Democratic newspaper published in Thomas' home city, confessed: "Had we ourselves pulled the wires at Goldsboro, we would not have schemed for a different result."[23]

The Democrats' optimism was not based on hopes of capturing the Second Congressional District. The district convention met July 8, also in Goldsboro, and agreed that "it would be inexpedient to name a candidate," in effect conceding the election to John Hyman.[24] The party advantage in the change of congressmen was to be found in other races, in other parts of the state.

Since the Democratic victory of 1870, North Carolina Republicans had been able to frustrate their opponents in a series of confrontations. In 1871 the state voted with the Republicans in opposition to a state constitutional convention. The next year Governor Caldwell and President Grant carried the state. Early in 1873 Republican legislators combined with dissident Democrats to elect Augustus S. Merrimon to the United States Senate instead of Zebulon B. Vance, choice of the Democratic caucus. Democrats needed a winning issue in 1874 to defeat the Republican congressmen in the first and fourth districts, gain undisputed control of the legislature, and elect a Democratic superintendent of public instruction, the only state officer elected that year.

22. *Ibid.*
23. Wilmington *Evening Post*, May 15, 1874; *Carolina Messenger* (Goldsboro), May 18, 1874; *Newbernian*, May 16, 1874. See Raleigh *Sentinel*, May 15, 1874.
24. Raleigh *Sentinel*, July 10, 1874.

For Democrats in North Carolina, as well as many other parts of the nation, Senator Charles Sumner's civil rights bill and the danger of Negro "social equality" it represented were themes that seemed certain to win votes. Hyman's nomination, from a Democratic viewpoint, was a vivid local manifestation of the larger threat of black assertiveness. Another issue Democrats raised across the nation was reform, the need to sweep "corrupt" Republicans from office. In the second district, Democrats accused Hyman of dishonesty, reminding voters of old charges that the senator from Warren had been involved in crooked dealings in the legislature of 1868–1869.[25]

The congressional nomination was not the only exemplary outrage provided second district Democrats. In Lenoir County the GOP county convention for the first time nominated a black legislative candidate, choosing Dick Whitfield over incumbent Anthony Davis. Representative John Patrick met a similar fate in Greene, where the convention nominated Negro S. A. Busbee for the general assembly. "Everywhere the negroes are struggling for supremacy, and with decided success," commented a Democratic newspaper on the Lenoir convention.[26]

Some Republicans refused to support Hyman, though his nomination was entirely regular. William Wallace Peebles, a recent white convert

25. *Ibid.*, May 29, June 19, 1874. The charges against Hyman were not conclusive. He had been a member of the legislature's committee to select and purchase a site for the penitentiary. Two corrupt Republicans persuaded the committee to buy from them a large amount of land at inflated prices and some members of the committee apparently shared in the profit. Hyman told an investigating commission that he knew nothing about bribes to committee members and that he had been "governed by the opinions of others" in the purchase of the land, much of which he had never visited.

Hyman borrowed at least $1,000 from railroad financier George W. Swepson in 1868–69 which he did not pay back. He said Swepson's associate Milton S. Littlefield gave him $250 to 300 "for campaign purposes" during the 1868 election. John T. Deweese, Republican candidate for Congress, paid him $500 in 1868 "to be used in the campaign in Warren, Granville, and Franklin." Deweese won the election but later resigned when it was revealed that he was selling military academy cadetships. By 1876 he was living in the North and a Democrat, and he issued a statement denouncing corruption among North Carolina Republicans. Eight years after the event he claimed the $500 was used to purchase Hyman's support. See North Carolina, *Report of the Commission to Investigate Charges of Fraud and Corruption, Under Act of Assembly, Session 1871–72* (Raleigh, 1872), 316, 519–22; Raleigh *Sentinel*, September 2, 1876; Hamilton, *Reconstruction*, 380, 386, 431; see also Jonathan Daniels' biography of Littlefield, *Prince of Carpetbaggers* (Philadelphia and New York, 1958).

26. Raleigh *Sentinel*, June 9, 1874; *Carolina Messenger* (Goldsboro), June 11, 1874.

to radicalism and the Northampton senatorial candidate, withheld his support, and George Washington Stanton, white Republican leader in Wilson, was also said to be opposed to Hyman. A Halifax County Negro preacher named Garland H. White mounted an independent campaign for Congress—possibly at the instigation of prominent Democrats.[27]

A Democratic candidate for Congress emerged in the last days of the canvass, in spite of the convention's decision not to field a nominee. When the Wilson County executive committee put forward the name of a prominent local lawyer, George W. Blount, most Democrats accepted the suggestion, hoping the division among Republicans would give this unofficial nominee a chance to win.[28]

On election day Hyman defeated Blount 18,176 votes to 11,144 with 1,091 going to the maverick White. Blount carried Wayne and Wilson, each by increased margins over 1872. Most of White's strength was in Warren, and the Warrenton *Gazette* complained that "some intelligent gentlemen" had found it "expedient" to vote for Hyman, thinking that Blount had no chance and preferring Hyman to White. Other Warren whites voted for Hyman simply to gain the goodwill of the inevitable victor, or under the impression that Blount had withdrawn.[29]

Blount himself did not give up so easily, suggesting to U.S. Senator Matt W. Ransom a scheme to throw out the Hyman ballots. Since state law prohibited ballots from carrying any symbol or "device," Blount wondered whether the phrase "Republican Congressional Ticket" at the top of Hyman's ballots might not be construed to be an illegal device, as the extra line helped illiterate voters discriminate. "As between intelligent voters I would not take such ground," he admitted, "but where whole hordes hustled to the poles [*sic*] & voted just as they were required to do without knowing for whom any point may justify."[30]

Throughout the state the race issue had been useful for the Democrats. They carried all other congressional districts, elected the superin-

27. Raleigh *Sentinel*, July 9, 1874; *Carolina Messenger* (Goldsboro), July 24, 1874; Garland H. White to Matt Whitaker Ransom, December 10, 1875, White to Ransom, March 10, 1876, both in Matt W. Ransom Papers, Southern Historical Collection, University of North Carolina, Chapel Hill.

28. *Carolina Messenger* (Goldsboro), July 27, 1874; Tarboro *Enquirer-Southerner*, July 31, 1874.

29. The figure for White's vote comes from the *New York Tribune Almanac* (1875), 77. Warrenton *Gazette*, August 7, 14, 1874.

30. George W. Blount to Matt W. Ransom, August 8, 1874, in Ransom Papers.

tendent of public instruction, and captured a commanding majority in the legislature. Even in the second district they made headway, defeating the Negro house nominees in Lenoir and Greene, as well as winning the house seats in Wilson and Wayne. The sweeping Democratic victory gave the party the two-thirds strength necessary to call a constitutional convention to replace the 1868 "Radical" constitution, an important step in undoing Reconstruction. In 1875 elections, however, Republicans came close to winning control of the convention. Their candidates received more votes than the Democratic, but election irregularities in Robeson County "saved the state" for the Democrats, and the convention assembled in September, 1875, with fifty-eight Republican members, fifty-eight Democrats, and three independents. The Democrats nominated one of the independents for convention president and elected him by a 2-vote margin. Their narrow majority (increased by one after a special election in Orange County) prevented them from making as many changes in the constitution as they had hoped, though they did protect the eastern counties from "Negro domination" by putting local government under legislative control. The second district was represented in the convention by fourteen Republicans—including O'Hara, King, Mabson, McCabe, former congressman Joseph Dixon, and future state chief justice William T. Faircloth—and one Democrat from Wilson.[31]

John Hyman's record in the next Congress, the Forty-fourth, was undistinguished. An entirely silent member, he introduced bills to reimburse Jones County for the Union army's destruction of the county courthouse, to establish a lighthouse at Gull Rock, Pamlico sound, and to provide relief to Cherokees of the eastern band who had moved to the western reservation. None of these measures even emerged from committee, and the private relief bill he introduced in the second session also failed to pass. He served on the Committee on Manufactures, a body with little significance for the second district.[32]

A faithful representative who answered most roll calls, Hyman was willing to take unpopular stands. Early in the first session, for example, a Democrat-backed resolution condemning third presidential terms passed

---

31. Olsen, *Carpetbagger's Crusade*, 195–206; Hamilton, *Reconstruction*, 631–43; North Carolina, *Journal of the Constitutional Convention of the State of North Carolina Held in 1875* (Raleigh, 1875), 5–8.

32. *Congressional Record*, 44th Cong., 1st Sess., 588, 3120, 3340; 2nd Sess., 1302; 1st Sess., 250.

233 to 18. Hyman was one of the 18 nays, a fact that caused one local newspaper to jeer, "Grant ought to make him minister to China in reward for his fidelity." The Republican Wilmington *Post* thought Hyman showed manly "nerve and judgment" in opposing the Democratic third-term bugbear and wished other Republicans had done likewise. Hyman was again part of a small minority when he voted in opposition to a bill forbidding government officers and employees from contributing to or soliciting election funds in federal elections. This campaign reform passed 175 to 8.[33]

Although all but a few hundred former Confederates had had their Fourteenth Amendment disabilities removed, the matter of amnesty continued to agitate Congress. Hyman opposed blanket amnesty, but voted to consider a bill that excluded only Jefferson Davis from the benefits of forgiveness. On another major issue, resumption of specie payments, Hyman's record was inconsistent, though weighted in favor of resumption.[34]

Hyman's bill in behalf of the Cherokees suggests that he had some interest in Indian problems, though North Carolina Democrats Robert B. Vance and Alfred M. Scales were much more active advocates of the Indians' rights. Hyman voted twice to suspend the rules in order to consider a bill for relief of the Choctaw tribe and he opposed transferring the Office of Indian Affairs from the Interior Department to the War Department. He also voted to increase the number of cavalry units to suppress Indian outbreaks.[35]

Discussion of the disputed 1876 presidential election consumed much of Hyman's second session. He voted against the investigation of the elections in Florida, South Carolina, and Louisiana, and against the establishment of the electoral commission.[36]

33. *Ibid.*, 1st Sess., 228; Tarboro *Southerner*, December 24, 1875; Wilmington *Post*, December 31, 1875; *Congressional Record*, 44th Cong., 1st Sess., 1898.

34. *Congressional Record*, 44th Cong., 1st Sess., 323, 420-21, 444. There were six roll call votes related to specie resumption. Although he usually opposed efforts to repeal or delay specie resumption, two of his votes are difficult to explain. He voted against a motion to suspend the rules and pass a resolution in favor of specie resumption, and on March 20, 1876, he supported an effort to suspend the rules and pass a complete repeal of the Resumption Act. Pages 444, 1074-75, 1815-16, 1984, 5230-31, 5232.

35. *Ibid.*, 2nd Sess., 812, 2218; 1st Sess., 2686, 5696.

36. *Ibid.*, 2nd Sess., 16, 1050. William J. Poole, Jr., has pointed out the curious fact that Hyman and South Carolina Congressman Joseph H. Rainey voted with the

There were early signs that Hyman might not be renominated in 1876. Curtis Brogden, a second district native, had become governor in 1874 when Governor Caldwell died suddenly. He was little more than a caretaker governor, thanks to the overwhelming Democratic strength in the legislature and his own inclination, and it seemed unlikely that he would be nominated for a full four-year term. State supreme court Justice Thomas Settle, who had exercised significant power over federal patronage since 1873, was considered a strong contender for the Republican nomination. Long an aspirant for congressional honors, Brogden might be content to step down if he could be assured the district's congressional nomination. More than a year before the election, a New Bern newspaper noted that the governor expected "in due time to receive the nomination as a candidate for Congress."[37]

Refraining from ruling out a race for the governorship, Brogden began a quiet search for congressional support in the spring of 1876. A Goldsboro newspaper reported in May that he had visited the town several times, consulting with black leaders and weakening what had previously been near-unanimous support for Hyman. Apparently one of the governor's arguments was that a Negro candidate would hurt the North Carolina party ticket in a national election year. A Hyman adherent wrote the Wilmington *Post* to counter this argument and defend the incumbent's claims for renomination, warning that voters could become demoralized if such reasoning prevailed. John H. Smyth, a New Hanover Negro later to serve as U.S. minister to Liberia, declared that Hyman had done a good job and ought to be renominated. In the distribution of patronage, Hyman had not shown partiality to his own race, said Smyth, "a self denial no white Republican has ever practiced." Hyman, or some other "distinguished" colored Republican, ought to get

---

Democrats on one of the last roll calls related to the electoral count. The two black congressmen for some reason voted against counting the vote of the last elector, D. L. Downs of Wisconsin. There is no explanation for Hyman's vote. Since he voted with his party on all other roll calls relating to the count, this vote may simply have been a mistake. See p. 2067. See Poole's seminar paper, "The Congressional Career of Joseph Hayne Rainey, First Negro Congressman" (University of Chicago, 1971), 24.

37. Charlotte *Democrat*, August 30, 1875; New Bern *Journal of Commerce*, August 21, 1875. As early as 1873 Governor Caldwell referred to Settle as the probable 1876 candidate. John E. Huggins, "The Resurgence and Decline of the Republican Party, 1871–1876" (M.A. thesis, Wake Forest University, 1966), 46–47.

the nomination, for only a black could be an "unequivocal representative in every essential of the majority of voters in that district."[38]

As Smyth's comments suggest, Hyman was not the only black aspirant for Congress. James O'Hara was growing in favor with Negro Republicans, according to a Halifax newspaper, though "white Radicals" found he had "too much sense for them." O'Hara was "intellectually greatly the superior of Hyman, and the equal of any Radical in the District." He was also reputed to be "cunning" and "unscrupulous."[39]

Hyman was challenged in his own Warren County by a Republican faction led by Joseph Williams Thorne, a radical white "carpetbagger" who had been expelled from the North Carolina General Assembly the year before for alleged disbelief in God. Born in Pennsylvania, Thorne was one of the few Republicans who lived up to Democratic caricatures of the reforming Yankee. He apparently actually practiced "social equality" with Negroes, and as a member of the constitutional convention of 1875 was one of the three delegates to oppose a measure requiring separate schools for blacks and whites. He was a vegetarian, a believer in women's rights, and unorthodox in religion.[40]

More than two months before the district convention the bitterly partisan Raleigh *Daily Sentinel* accurately predicted the outcome. "It is rumored that the radical leaders are going to bring a tremendous pressure to bear to send Governor Brogden to congress from the 'black' district," said the *Sentinel* of May 6. "This will be attempted in order to get him off the gubernatorial track that something like harmony may be preserved in their ranks." Whether Hyman or the black voters of the district would go along with this scheme remained to be seen. "O'Hara, the negro lawyer at Halifax, is said to be smitten with congressional aspirations, and may make a lively row over the matter."

38. *Carolina Messenger* (Goldsboro), May 1, 1876; Wilmington *Post*, April 7, 21, 28, 1876. See also May 12, 1876.

39. *Carolina Messenger* (Goldsboro), February 28, 1876 (noting a report in the Weldon *News*).

40. Warrenton *Gazette*, July 7, 1876, October 1, 1875; Goldsboro *Messenger*, June 3, 1878; New York *Times*, July 1, 1878. R. A. Shotwell and Natt Atkinson, *Legislative Record, Giving the Acts Passed Session March 1877, Together with Sketches of the Lives and Public Acts of the Members of Both Houses* (Raleigh, 1877), 9. On Thorne's expulsion from the legislature see Greensboro *New North State*, March 19, 1875; Raleigh *Era*, February 26, 1875. See Raleigh *Sentinel*, July 13, 1876, for a "social equality" incident.

With insincere concern for their rights the *Sentinel* told black voters in the second district: "You do the voting and you should select the candidate without being interfered with by outside political tricksters." By mid-May the *Sentinel* reported that O'Hara and W. P. Mabson had "given in their adhesion to Brogden" and noted the (inaccurate) claims of local Republicans that Brogden could now rely on Craven, Jones, Waynes, Edgecombe, and Halifax for support. According to the Roanoke *News* O'Hara had agreed not to run against Brogden on the condition that O'Hara become district solicitor in 1878. For whatever reasons, O'Hara did not seek the nomination when the district convention assembled.[41]

Brogden's campaign was doing so well by the end of June that he came "out square for Judge Settle" in the gubernatorial race, causing the *Sentinel* editor to predict that the "well drilled" Negroes would acquiesce in the ouster of Hyman. The Republican state convention met in Raleigh two weeks before the district convention and nominated Settle for governor and William A. Smith for lieutenant governor. O'Hara was secretary of the session.[42]

When second district Republicans began gathering in Goldsboro for the July 26 convention, Smith promoted Brogden's candidacy, aided by other prominent out-of-district Republicans like federal officeholders Isaac J. Young and James E. Boyd. James H. Harris, Osborne Hunter, and Tim Lee, all of Wake County, were on hand to work for Hyman.[43] Hyman's hopes were virtually destroyed when the convention's credentials committee refused to seat the pro-Hyman delegation from Warren, recognizing instead the Thorne delegates. On the first ballot Hyman received 3 votes from Craven and Jones, Wayne County's two delegates voted for Brogden, and the remaining 10 votes were divided among seven candidates, all but one white. By the seventh ballot Brogden had 5 votes from Wayne, Jones, Wilson, and one of Warren's delegates, and Hyman had fallen completely out of the contest. Brogden won the nomination on the ninth ballot with 9 votes; Edgecombe candidate Alexander McCabe was second with 4. The convention completed its

41. Raleigh *Sentinel,* May 6, 10, 18, 19, 1876.
42. *Ibid.,* June 28, July 13, 1876.
43. *Carolina Messenger* (Goldsboro), July 27, 1876; Raleigh *Sentinel,* July 28, 1876.

business by selecting James O'Hara as presidential elector, a choice lending credence to the report that O'Hara had reached an understanding with the governor.[44]

With enthusiasm Democratic editors and orators who had made political capital from the nomination of Hyman in 1874 now sought to exploit the Republican failure to nominate him in 1876. "The nomination of Brogden is a victory of the white Republicans over negroes in the division of spoils," announced the *Carolina Messenger*. The Raleigh *Sentinel* was sure that white Republicans were insincere even in their fears that a black candidate would hurt the statewide ticket; their motives were "purely pecuniary and selfish" and blacks showed "no manhood" and "little foresight" in following "white republican masters." The elector's position given to O'Hara was an "empty honor."[45]

The "overthrow of Hyman" offered practical political possibilities to Democrats. Two days after the convention, Colonel Henry G. Williams of Wilson (a man who "ate and slept and drank politics," according to Josephus Daniels) wrote to his friend Senator Ransom about a way "to make something for our side in this district" from the events at Goldsboro. Williams had heard that Hyman would be willing to run against Brogden if the Democrats made no nomination, and since it was "more important to secure votes for the State ticket, than to take remote chances to get in a Congressman," Williams thought it wise to make no Democratic congressional nomination and encourage Hyman to run.[46] The implication was that a Republican split could produce votes for the Democratic ticket, since the pressure of a factional fight would probably tempt one of the candidates—or his friends—to make a deal with the Democrats. Democrats would be willing to "trade" with a desperate Republican congressional candidate, to aid his campaign in exchange for votes for the Democratic state ticket. Whether or not Ransom gave his approval to such a covert arrangement, this letter from a leading editor and politician illustrates well political practice in the "black second." Biracial, bipartisan deals and trades—often initiated by Democrats hop-

44. *Carolina Messenger* (Goldsboro), July 27, 1876; Raleigh *Sentinel*, July 28, 1876.

45. *Carolina Messenger* (Goldsboro), July 27, 1876; Raleigh *Sentinel*, July 28, 1876.

46. Henry G. Williams to M. W. Ransom, July 28, 1876, in Ransom Papers. Daniels, *Tar Heel Editor*, 76–77.

ing to encourage Republican divisions—were to have a long, active history in the district.

Despite rumors of widespread dissatisfaction among Republicans and reports that Hyman might run against Brogden as an independent, Hyman spoke in Warrenton in support of the Goldsboro nominee and, after a visit from the governor, issued a "card" denying that he was seeking to defeat Brogden.[47]

The "empty honor" accorded O'Hara became more important as the campaign progressed. From the start Julius A. Bonitz, German-born editor of the *Carolina Messenger*, had been appalled, declaring that "there is more Civil Rights in this pill than the nomination of Hyman would have been." Bonitz, convinced that O'Hara was a "malignant blackguard," had according to a Republican source "expressed himself pretty freely in relation to the subject of 'voting for niggers'" to some of the crowd attending the Republican convention. Bonitz reportedly said "that under no circumstances would he . . . 'support a nigger.' Some Republican in the crowd remarked that this was a mistake, because he knew for a fact that Bonitz had for years been supporting a 'family of niggers.' "[48] But other Democrats as well—indeed the same ones who professed dismay over the Republican failure to nominate a Negro for Congress—soon began to make an issue of the black elector. "Every white man in North Carolina who votes for Hayes and Wheeler will be obliged to vote for the negro elector, O'Hara," noted the *Sentinel*. "You cannot vote the radical ticket without doing so."[49]

Less than two weeks after the Goldsboro convention, former judge Albion W. Tourgée urged O'Hara to withdraw because of racial prejudice in the western half of the state, estimating that the party would lose 2,000 votes west of Raleigh if a black electoral candidate remained in the campaign. "I despise prejudice as much as you can," wrote Tourgée, "but since it is a fact, is it wise to butt our heads against it unless we may thereby reduce it[?]" If O'Hara wanted an appointive place in

47. *Carolina Messenger* (Goldsboro), July 31, 1876; Raleigh *Sentinel*, August 2, September 7, 16, 1876; Raleigh *Era*, August 10, 1876.
48. *Carolina Messenger* (Goldsboro), July 27, 31, 1876; Raleigh *Era*, August 3, 1876. The miscegenation charge was one that had been plaguing Bonitz for some time. See Wilmington *Post*, July 23, 24, 1875; *Carolina Messenger* (Goldsboro), May 25, 1876. The *Era* continued to harass Bonitz on the matter. See August 10, September 28, 1876.
49. Raleigh *Sentinel*, August 2, 1876.

compensation for stepping down, Tourgée was confident that could be arranged, "and I certainly would not blame you for making your terms in advance." Not surprisingly, O'Hara was offended by this proposal and replied in "a torrent of angry abuse," as Tourgée put it. Determined not to be pressured or manipulated by party leaders, he spurned the idea of withdrawing. Tourgée responded: "This is not a question of what *ought* to be but what *is*—as you will find before the campaign is over."[50]

As Tourgée predicted, the issue continued to plague Republicans. The *Sentinel's* editor denied that the position was one "of no significance" and said it was a sign of the degradation of the times that James O'Hara filled a place once held by antebellum giants William Gaston and Nathaniel Macon. Former judge Daniel L. Russell and William A. Smith, both Republican leaders, opposed O'Hara's being on the ticket and hinted that they might not vote for him.[51]

In the closing days of the campaign, O'Hara finally withdrew and was replaced by William J. Clarke, a white man and a former judge from Craven. O'Hara insisted that his resignation was not caused by his fellow Republicans, but that he "came to the conclusion to resign from the action and advice of prominent Democratic gentlemen, who privately advised and urged me to remain upon the ticket and 'maintain my manhood,' yet, in their public speeches, used every effort in their power to stir up and keep alive ill feeling and prejudice of caste against the negroes." O'Hara became convinced that it was the purpose of these gentlemen "to use me as an instrument to accomplish their sinister political design, and aid them in arraying race against race in North Carolina." "I may have to a certain extent yielded to caste prejudice," he said, "but by whom is this prejudice fostered, kept alive and used?" The press reaction to his withdrawal backed up his point. Oblivious to any contradiction in their position, Democratic editors returned to the

50. Albion W. Tourgée to James E. O'Hara, August 4, 1876, Tourgée to O'Hara, August 12, 1876, both in Albion W. Tourgée Papers (microfilm), Southern Historical Collection, University of North Carolina, Chapel Hill. There are two letters dated August 12 addressed to O'Hara in Tourgée's letter book. The first one is more conciliatory and may have been the one actually sent, though there is no clear indication. In the second letter Tourgée said: "Your letter is the complete exponent of the worst kind of race prejudice—mere silly spite—a foolish determination to wreak revenge for unavoidable facts, upon persons not in the least responsible for such facts. It is the spirit which has made Missi[ssi]ppi and Lousiana [*sic*] what they are and is fast hurrying South Carolina to the same end."

51. Raleigh *Sentinel*, August 27, September 26, 1876.

theme of Republican hypocrisy, an editorial in the *Newbernian* calling upon "colored fellow-citizens" to resent the "insult" and "injustice" of O'Hara's removal from the ticket, whereas a report on the next page referred to O'Hara as an "imported montebank," an "ape," and an "Imp."[52]

Former congressman Thomas formally broke with the GOP during this campaign. He declared for the Democratic nominees for president and governor in an August 31 speech in New Bern, even while maintaining his Whiggish principles. He considered both "Bourbon" Democracy and "Radical" Republicanism dangerous extremes and declared "with much earnestness" that reform in southern local government must be brought about with the aid of black voters, not by intimidation or fraud against them.[53]

As they worked to elect war governor Zebulon Vance, Democrats once again found the second district a fruitful source of campaign object lessons. The fact that Negroes bid at the hiring out of white paupers became the "Jones County outrage," played up for weeks in the press. The *Sentinel* published editorials comparing Republican county government in Edgecombe with Democratic administration in neighboring Wilson, deploring "The Tax Burden of the Negro Counties" and exposing "Radical" government in Halifax County.[54]

A few days before the election, the Democratic district executive committee announced the congressional candidacy of Wharton J. Green of Warren, a twice-wounded, twice-captured Confederate veteran with little political experience. He was to represent the third district for two terms in the 1880s, but this time Brogden thoroughly defeated him, 21,060 votes to 11,874. In fact Brogden's winning margin was the largest of any second district congressional candidate from 1872 to 1898. He carried every county except Wayne and Wilson, losing Wayne by only 37 votes.[55] But Brogden's victory provided a rare note of cheer for Re-

52. Wilmington *Post*, November 1, 1876; *Newbernian*, October 25, 1876.
53. *Newbernian*, September 2, 1876; New Bern *Times and Republic-Courier*, September 2, 1876.
54. Raleigh *Sentinel*, August 30, 31, 1876; *Newbernian*, September 9, 1876; Raleigh *Sentinel*, September 29, 30, October 3, 1876.
55. For sketches of Green, see Samuel A. Ashe (ed.), *Biographical History of North Carolina from Colonial Times to the Present* (8 vols.; Greensboro, N.C., 1905–1907), II, 120–25; John H. Wheeler, *Reminiscences and Memoirs of North Carolina and Eminent North Carolinians* (Baltimore, 1966), 459–61.

publicans in a year of "redemption." "Zeb" Vance carried the state by 13,000 votes and the legislature remained overwhelmingly Democratic, with Republicans holding fewer than a third of the seats in either chamber. In the congressional races, Brogden was the only Republican victor.

However successful Democrats were in the rest of the state, Reconstruction gave no sign of fading away in the second district. Republicans regained the ground lost in 1874 by winning the house seats in Greene and Lenoir. George A. Mebane, a twenty-six-year-old former slave from Bertie, was elected to represent the Third Senatorial District, comprising Northampton and Bertie. In Warren, J. Williams Thorne defeated the candidate of the Hyman faction and returned as a senator to the general assembly from which he had been expelled so recently. Edgecombe reelected W. P. Mabson to the state senate, and Wilson's Democratic schemer, Henry G. Williams, won in the Seventh Senatorial District. Of the mere ten Republican senators elected in the entire state six came from the counties of the Second Congressional District. Republicans, moreover, continued to dominate most of the district's county governments. In Jones, Edgecombe, and Halifax, a majority of the county commissioners were blacks, two particularly important of these being James O'Hara of Halifax and Frank Dancy of Edgecombe.[56]

When Curtis Brogden took his seat in the Forty-fifth Congress at the age of sixty-one, he was at the high point of a long career in politics. A largely self-educated man, he had announced himself a candidate for the general assembly in 1838, before he was twenty-two, and from then on was holding or seeking political office almost continuously. Before the Civil War he served ten terms in the legislature as a Jacksonian Democrat, and the legislature in 1857 elected him state comptroller, a post he held for ten years, continuing in office through the crises of secession, war, and emancipation. An opponent of secession and a supporter of franchise extension, he moved into the Republican party during Reconstruction and was elected to the state senate in 1868 and

56. Other black commissioners included Frank Whitted and Clinton W. Battle of Edgecombe; J. H. Howard, Henry Clay, and Jack Harvill of Halifax; Sandy Strayhorn, Noah Hill, and Alex. Mattocks of Jones; Wiley Lowery of Lenoir; Claiborne Faison of Northampton; and Ossian Hawkins of Warren. Levi Branson (ed.), *The North Carolina Business Directory, 1877 and 1878* (Raleigh, 1878). The commissioners listed by Branson were elected in 1876; his policy on racial identification is inconsistent. See Shotwell and Atkinson, *Legislative Record*, 9.

1870. In 1873 he took office as lieutenant governor, succeeding to the governorship when Governor Caldwell died the next year.[57] On many issues, including the "money question" and army reorganization, Brogden's stand was indistinguishable from the position of his Democratic colleagues in the North Carolina delegation. Several years later the Goldsboro *Messenger* remembered that Brogden had "made a record to which no North Carolinian could object, unless it be the party that elected him."[58]

In antebellum days a firm opponent of the Whig doctrine of internal improvements, Brogden now successfully pushed federal improvements for the Neuse River, a popular issue with his constituents. Bipartisan public meetings convened in several district towns, and delegates from four counties met in Goldsboro to elect a committee to lobby in Washington. A staunchly Democratic editor observed that he had been urging Neuse River improvements on district representatives for ten years, but "Mr. Brogden is the first one who has taken hold of the project. We wish him God speed in the good work." Brogden himself felt that his work for Neuse River improvement was the most important thing he did in Congress.[59]

The other bill Brogden introduced in his first session was also popular, though it did not pass. "Three Cheers for Governor Brogden" was the headline in a Democratic newspaper when the congressman introduced a measure to repeal internal revenue taxes on tobacco grown and produced in the United States and on liquor made from apples, peaches, or grapes, while reducing the tax on other types of liquor. "If you can get your bill through, Governor, the people of this (your) District, regardless of the past, present, or future, color or politics, will

57. *Biographical Directory of the American Congress,* 601; Ashe, *Biographical History,* VI, 106–12. (This sketch by George S. Wills is inaccurate in several respects. Brogden was never speaker of the North Carolina house, as Wills says, nor was he a member of the convention of 1868.) Raleigh *Southern Illustrated Age,* August 14, 1875; Raleigh *Signal,* May 10, 1888; *Legislative Biographical Sketch Book, Session 1887* (Raleigh, 1887), 45–46.

58. See *Congressional Record,* 45th Cong., 2nd Sess., 3853–55 for his vote on army size; 1st Sess., 241 for vote on remonetization of silver and free coinage thereof; and 1st Sess., 632–33 for vote on specie resumption; Goldsboro *Messenger,* September 4, 1884.

59. Goldsboro *Messenger,* February 28, March 11, February 7, 1878, July 10, 1879. For Brogden's prewar view of internal improvements, see *Carolina Messenger* (Goldsboro), November 8, 1875.

rise in their shoes and bless you."[60] In the second session, Brogden attracted favorable notice from the opposition press for a speech in favor of pensions for Mexican War veterans and for his bill to apportion civil appointments among the states and territories according to population. He supported in the last session a constitutional amendment to change electoral college procedures.[61]

Brogden's effort to build a new coalition in district politics came close to succeeding. He failed, as we shall see, because many in his own party were irritated by his quasi-Democratic voting record and because moderates lost influence to the uncompromising partisans in the Democratic party. Instead of bridging a gap, he fell into it.

Two changes taking effect near the end of Brogden's term marked the close of Reconstruction in the second district. Most important was a constitutional change that effectively ended majority control of local finances. For people in the second district, the center of political life was not Washington, or even Raleigh, but the county seat, and perhaps more galling to a Democrat than a Negro congressman or a Republican governor was a "Radical" sheriff or a black county commissioner. Even more disturbing than the personnel of Republican county governments was the policy of many of these governments to vote what their opponents considered huge expenditures and high taxes. One of the chief reforms that Democrats, especially from the eastern part of the state, sought in the constitutional convention of 1875 was an amendment to place county funds "beyond the reach of the large negro majorities" in counties like Warren, Craven, and Edgecombe.[62]

They achieved this goal by terminating the popular election of county commissioners and justices of the peace (magistrates). Under the new plan, as authorized by the voters in 1876, detailed in the next session of the legislature, and implemented in 1878, the general assembly elected the magistrates, who in turn elected the county commissioners. The other county offices—clerk of the superior court, sheriff, register of deeds, treasurer, coroner, surveyor, etc.—remained elective, but the body

---

60. Tarboro *Southerner,* November 15, 1877.
61. Goldsboro Messenger, March 28, 1878; Tarboro *Southerner,* February 27, 1878; *Congressional Record,* 45th Cong., 3rd Sess., appendix, 176.
62. William Eaton to David Settle Reid, September 20, 1875, in David Settle Reid Papers, North Carolina Department of Archives and History.

that controlled taxes and financial policy was indirectly chosen. Only with reluctance did Democrats in western North Carolina accept this scheme, and their commitment had to be reinforced over the years with periodic appeals to white solidarity in the face of threatened "Negro domination" in the east.[63]

Centralization of local finances was a fundamental change, rendering Republicans virtually impotent in both state and county financial policy. Although Republicans continued to elect congressmen, legislators, and sheriffs after 1878, there were very few Republican county commissioners until the fusion years of the 1890s.[64]

A second constitutional change drove home the truth that Reconstruction was over. Superior court judges were no longer to be chosen by the voters of their judicial district—a method sure to produce several Republican judges or possibly turn a talented black attorney like James O'Hara into a judge. Instead, the voters of the entire state chose the superior court judges, and unless the Republicans recaptured the state, future judges would all be Democrats.

Thus the postwar adjustment envisioned by the "Redeemers" required permanent Democratic hegemony. An isolated, largely black Republican party could be tolerated, but not a party that united a black majority and enough whites to win power. What appeared to be Democratic inconsistency in this era—in encouraging blacks to claim their rights within the GOP yet blocking them from key public positions, in attacking both "hypocritical" white Republicans and ambitious black leaders—was really a consistent attempt to disable the Republican party. Most Democrats were not so short-sighted as to limit their attacks to Negroes. They recognized that white domination had to be maintained by pre-

63. The principal eastern towns had been protected from majority rule in a similar fashion. In this area the legislature needed no new grant of authority. It used its authority over town charters to gerrymander aldermanic wards and end popular election of the mayor in a number of localities. For an example of such legislative action, see W. P. Mabson's protest against the gerrymandering of Tarboro, Raleigh Era, March 18, 1875.

Frenise Logan and Helen Edmonds erroneously assert that all county officers except register of deeds and surveyor were appointive after the constitutional changes. They thus ignore a large number of Republican officeholders. See Frenise Logan, The Negro in North Carolina, 1876–1894 (Chapel Hill, N.C., 1964), 30; Helen G. Edmonds, The Negro and Fusion Politics in North Carolina, 1894–1901 (Chapel Hill, N.C., 1951), 118.

64. The first group of magistrates chosen by the legislature in 1877 included some Negroes, but the effort at equity was dropped by the next general assembly.

serving one political organization and weakening the other—in short, by denying blacks a political vehicle for their aspirations.

By 1878 the North Carolina state machinery, including local taxing bodies, was securely in Democratic hands, but many details of the new order remained ambiguous. Much depended on the evolution of black leadership, on the reactions of men like former congressman John Hyman, James O'Hara, and younger, college-educated men who were just beginning their careers as Reconstruction came to a close.

PART TWO

James O'Hara and the Bourbon Equilibrium 1878–1887

Chapter 3

THE NEGRO MUST BE BEATEN

The Democracy of Edgecombe do not stand solely on the color line. *Honesty and representative fitness for office* are the test whose sole application is all they ask.
—Tarboro *Southerner*, March 30, 1877
We accept in good faith the recent amendments to the constitution, and renew our pledges to protect the absolute equality of all men before the law as secured by the organic law of the land.
—Resolution, Democratic convention, Second Congressional District, 1878

NO SECOND DISTRICT POLITICIAN would have seen "equilibrium" as a characteristic of the years following Reconstruction. Almost every campaign brought rancorous struggle and confusing alliances, and a political leader would likely have described the time as highly unstable. But from the vantage point of 1900, there was a Bourbon equilibrium—a brief stability built on unwritten, fragile, and inconsistent understandings. Fierce as the competition was during the era of "redemption," the political game was usually played by accepted rules.

Explosive rivalries shook the Republican district organization in the period from 1878 to 1887. Although the party suffered from disunity at many times during the twenty-eight-year history of the "black second," the nine years after Reconstruction were the worst. Twice in five elections a Democrat won because two Republicans each claimed to be the true nominee and split the party vote. Only in 1884 did a united party emerge from the GOP congressional convention.

Party discipline was better among the Democrats, but they were often confused and demoralized. "Straight-outs" and moderates debated party tactics. Should the Democracy appeal directly to Negro voters, or should it draw the color line? Should Democrats compromise in order to get the most acceptable local officers? Was political warfare to be limited and relatively civil, or should Democrats be as ruthless as in the early days of Reconstruction?

In this stable yet uncertain period, black political strength grew—despite constitutional changes that largely prevented blacks from serving as magistrates and county commissioners. These legal barriers managed to change rather than eliminate black political activity, as for the first time Negroes won lucrative executive positions like register of deeds for a large county such as Edgecombe or Halifax, or gained appointment to an important federal post like postmaster at New Bern. Beginning in 1878 a Negro held the office of solicitor for the Second Judicial District, which included the counties of Warren, Bertie, Craven, Edgecombe, Halifax, and Northampton.

One man, James Edward O'Hara, dominated the political history of these years. A candidate for the Republican congressional nomination in five consecutive elections, he was twice victorious and served four years in the House. But for party splits in 1878 and 1886 his tenure would have been longer. He was a leader in the successful antiprohibition campaign of 1881 and an architect of the statewide coalition between Republicans and "liberal" Democrats in 1882 and 1884.

The illegitimate son of an Irish merchant and a West Indian woman, O'Hara was born in New York City, February 26, 1844. Little is known of his youth, much of which was spent in the Danish West Indies. It is not clear when he returned to New York, but in 1862 he visited Union-occupied eastern North Carolina in the company of New York missionaries and decided to stay permanently. O'Hara's political experience began with work as engrossing clerk to the constitutional convention of 1868 and the legislature of 1868–1869. He spent about two years in Washington, D.C., working as a clerk in the Treasury Department and studying at Howard University.[1]

1. Vera Jean O'Hara Rivers, " 'A Thespian Must Play His Role': A Biographical Sketch of Hon. James E. O'Hara; His Life, Work, and Family" (MS in James Edward O'Hara Papers, Regenstein Library, University of Chicago), 2–9; Joseph Eliot Elmore, "North Carolina Negro Congressmen, 1875–1901" (M.A. thesis, University of North Carolina, 1964), 42; Exodus Report, 56; Congressional Directory, 49th Cong., 2nd Sess., 65. A somewhat inaccurate obituary in the New Bern Journal, September 17, 1905, said: "At the age of six years he was taken by his parents to

He received his license to practice law in North Carolina in 1873. Peter M. Wilson, later a well-known journalist, was licensed at the same time and remembered O'Hara as a "colored man . . . who knew more law than I did." The next year O'Hara won election to the Halifax County board of commissioners and for four years served as chairman of the board. In 1875 he was a delegate to the state constitutional convention. As a result of his ambition for a seat in Congress, the red-haired young lawyer began to be known in surrounding counties and gained a reputation even among his opponents for "more than ordinary intelligence."[2]

At the start of the 1878 campaign other aspirants seemed more likely to win the congressional nomination. James H. Harris, black veteran of Reconstruction and a candidate for Congress in 1870, had moved from Wake County to his native Warren with an eye on the second district nomination, and other hopefuls included Hyman, Mabson, Stanton, and Thorne.[3]

Incumbent Congressman Curtis Brogden had skillfully moved to attract Democratic support with a pragmatic, independent course in Congress, and some former opponents were now complimenting him on his work for the district. Brogden's tactics involved a gamble, of course, for his voting record made him unpopular with many Republicans. Indeed, by March, 1878, he was reported to be holding his position in his own party "by a very slender thread." But his record also made him a potentially formidable independent candidate.[4]

In the two or three months preceding the district convention, Colonel Lotte W. Humphrey of Wayne emerged as Brogden's most serious rival. As governor, Brogden had supported Humphrey, then a Democrat,

---

the West Indies where he lived until he reached manhood." Scrapbooks in O'Hara Papers. See U.S. Department of the Interior, *Official Register of the United States, 1869* (Washington, D.C., 1869), 40 (hereinafter cited as *Official Register*); *Official Register, 1871*, p. 39, on O'Hara's clerkship.

2. Peter Mitchel Wilson, *Southern Exposure* (Chapel Hill, N.C., 1927), 89; *Carolina Messenger* (Goldsboro), March 2, 1874. O'Hara was chairman of the commissioners from 1874 to 1878 not 1872 to 1876, as reported in many sources. See Halifax County Minutes of the County Commissioners, 1873–83 (microfilm), in North Carolina Department of Archives and History.

3. Wilson *Advance* quoted in Goldsboro *Messenger*, April 1, June 3, 1878.

4. Tarboro *Southerner*, December 13, 1877; Wilson *Advance* quoted in Goldsboro *Messenger*, April 1, 1878.

for the presidency of the Atlantic and North Carolina Railroad, a state-controlled line that ran from Goldsboro to the coast. Humphrey became a Republican in 1876—just as Charles R. Thomas, representative of a different faction in railroad politics, was joining the Democrats. Brogden deeply resented Humphrey's subsequent actions: "As soon as I was unable to keep him in office longer . . . he commenced his perfidious work to get me out of [Congress]. He did not wait for me to serve even my first session in Congress before he commenced his operations to get me out." Thanks to Humphrey's machinations, Brogden claimed, "I had no hearing and no chance of being heard." Besides criticizing the governor's voting record, Humphrey accused him of discriminating against blacks in the distribution of free seeds and congressional documents.[5]

Most observers expected Humphrey to win, but no one could be certain. There might be a successful "combination against him," or a black candidate like O'Hara or Harris might outdistance Humphrey if there were a "determination among the colored delegates that they are entitled to a representative of their own race."[6]

The Second Judicial District convention, less than a month before the congressional convention, vividly demonstrated the growing importance of Negro leaders and voters. John Henry Collins, an inexperienced black lawyer, was nominated on the first ballot to be the candidate for solicitor of a district that included nine counties: Wake, Warren, Halifax, Northampton, Martin, Bertie, Beaufort, Edgecombe, and Craven. "An obscure colored lawyer Solicitor in the Metropolitan District!" exclaimed the Tarboro *Southerner* in horror. One white Republican lawyer privately called the nomination "disastrous," lamenting, "It does seem that every step the Republicans in this section take is from bad to worse."[7]

5. *Speech of Hon. C. H. Brogden Delivered before the Wayne County Republican Convention at the Town Hall in Goldsboro, N.C., Saturday May 29, 1880*, 10, 12, 16, in North Carolina Collection, University of North Carolina. For a letter urging Brogden not to appoint Humphrey president of the A & NC Railroad because he was a Democrat, see L. J. Moore to C. H. Brogden, May 25, 1875, in Curtis Hooks Brogden, Governor's Papers, North Carolina Department of Archives and History.
6. New York *Times*, July 1, 1878; Thomas B. Keogh to Thomas Settle, June 9, 1878, in Thomas Settle Papers, Southern Historical Collection, University of North Carolina, Chapel Hill.
7. Tarboro *Southerner*, June 20, 1878; New York *Times*, June 23, 1878. John A. Moore to William E. Clarke, June 26, 1878, in William E. Clarke Papers, East Carolina University, Greenville, N.C. Although some Democrats claimed his nomination

The Republican congressional convention which met in Goldsboro, July 10, was orderly but deeply divided. The delegates balloted again and again without giving any candidate a majority, and as the twenty-ninth ballot was ready to be announced the vote stood at 7 for Colonel Humphrey, 6 for James O'Hara, and 2 for Israel B. Abbott, a black former legislator from Craven. The Craven delegation broke the impasse by changing its vote to O'Hara, making him the victor by 1 vote. Humphrey's support had come from the central part of the district— Edgecombe, Wilson, Wayne, Lenoir, and Greene—and his opponent had been backed by the district's extreme ends—Craven and Jones in the southeast and Halifax, Northampton, and Warren near the Virginia border.[8]

The opposition reacted quickly to the nomination of O'Hara, the second Halifax Negro to be slated for a major office within a month. "The Democratic press is shrieking all over the State that the negroes are drawing the color line," said the New York *Times*, but in actual fact, they "are tickled nearly to death because, as they think, the negroes have given them a sufficient excuse to howl on the color line and appeal to the prejudice of the whites." The editor added: "It will be observed that O'Hara is not denounced as incompetent, or that for any other good reason, he ought not to have been nominated."[9]

O'Hara was never accused of incompetence, but a host of enemies within the Republican party was soon accusing him of wily villainy. Much of the anti-O'Hara sentiment seemed concentrated in Wayne, home of both Brogden and Humphrey.[10] O'Hara's opponents said that he was corrupt and ineligible to serve in Congress because of bigamy, and late in the campaign it was alleged that he was not an American citizen.

---

was an example of Negroes drawing the color line, only three of the eight black delegates at the convention voted for Collins. Warrenton *Gazette*, June 24, 1878.

The solicitorship was quite remunerative. As solicitor in the sixth district (which at the time included Warren, Wake, Halifax, Northampton, and four other counties), Harris estimated that the office could earn from three thousand to five thousand dollars a year in fees. None of the state officers made as much as five thousand dollars a year. See J. C. L. Harris to Albion W. Tourgée, February 3, 1875, in Tourgée Papers.

8. Goldsboro *Messenger*, July 11, 1878; Raleigh *News*, July 11, 1878.

9. New York *Times*, July 23, 1878.

10. Goldsboro *Messenger*, July 25, 1878: "Our Radical candidates boldly proclaim that they will not support O'Hara." Goldsboro *Messenger*, September 5, 1878.

For about two and a half months after O'Hara's nomination, Brogden appeared to be a likely independent candidate. He was reported late in August to be "cautiously feeling his strength in his own party" and seeking Democratic assurances that their party would make no nomination. The Tarboro *Southerner* noted Brogden's reputation for honesty and said: "Our entire delegation in Congress speak well of Gov. Brogden. He is sound on the money question." The *Messenger* thought that Brogden might get "considerable Democratic support," though it would be "sheer folly" to think that he would draw the full Democratic strength, "notwithstanding that his course in Congress was honest, straightforward and satisfactory."[11]

North Carolina held state elections in August, 1878, three months before the congressional elections (in future years both elections would take place in November). The Republican party was in such disarray that it held no state convention and made no nominations for the three supreme court positions to be filled that year. But local Republican organizations remained intact, nominated legislative candidates, and gave the opposition a setback on election day. Total GOP strength rose from 46 to 57 in the 170-member general assembly, and the party once again swept the second district with only Wilson sending a purely Democratic delegation to Raleigh. In Wayne, Democrats carried the Tenth Senatorial District, but split the two house members with the Republicans. For the first time in at least a decade, Northampton elected a Democratic member of the house, but the county's senator was a Republican. Edgecombe, Halifax, and Warren selected all-Negro representation.[12]

Most of the victors in the campaigns for county offices were, as usual, Republicans, though the party was badly divided in several counties. The two Republican candidates for sheriff in Halifax had a serious effect on the congressional race. The winner in the bitter fight, James T. Dawson, did not forget that O'Hara had backed his rival, and he worked to weaken the Republican congressional candidate in Halifax.[13]

11. Goldsboro *Messenger*, August 26, 1878; Tarboro *Southerner*, August 29, 1878; Goldsboro *Messenger*, September 5, 1878.
12. The three all-black delegations were Edgecombe's Senator Frank Dancy and Representatives C. W. Battle and Dred Wimberly, Halifax's Senator Henry Eppes and Representatives J. T. Reynolds and John A. White, and Warren's Senator Isaac Alston and Representatives Hawkins W. Carter and L. T. Christmas.
13. New York *Times*, October 5, 1878. There was a serious party split in Edgecombe, where a faction led by John Norfleet, aging white Republican former mayor

As the end of summer approached with no official Democratic nominee, several men announced their candidacies on their own. B. F. Long of Warren became a candidate late in August on a Greenback platform, thinking that the Democratic party would make no nomination. In a "card" dated September 4, William H. Kitchin soon followed suit. Acting at the "solicitation of my friends of both political parties," he promised to work for the retiring of national bank notes (to be replaced by greenbacks), repeal of the Specie Resumption Act, a tax on incomes over a thousand dollars, free banking service, and other economic reforms.[14]

Brogden continued his attempt to build a new coalition, hoping his Reconstruction record would hold the gratitude of Negro voters while Democrats appreciated his congressional performance and financial views. Saying he was still undecided about making the race, Brogden tested his support in a September 10 speech in Wilson in which he "dwelt on the financial condition of the country" and pointed out his votes with the rest of the North Carolina delegation for the remonetization of silver and repeal of the Specie Resumption Act. He said he would not think of being a candidate if the Republicans had nominated a good man, but O'Hara was corrupt, immoral, and currently under indictment for malfeasance. It was necessary to defeat O'Hara to prevent the district from being disgraced.[15]

The attempts of O'Hara's Republican foes to portray him as a rogue were in strong contrast to the words of a Democratic editor shortly after his nomination: "It is by no means uncommon to hear intelligent men say that they much prefer J. E. O'Hara to represent the Second District than some of the white men who were aspirants." O'Hara was intelligent as well as polite and "conservative above his color," and "if the color

---

of Tarboro, routed the Republican incumbents led by W. P. Mabson and Alex McCabe. See Tarboro *Southerner*, June 6, 27, July 11, 1878.

14. Goldsboro *Messenger*, October 3, September 5, 1878. In the absence of a Democratic candidate, Long's action was not a defection to a third party, but rather an attempt to attract dissatisfied Republican voters. When a Democratic convention for the district was called, Long as a loyal Democrat dropped his efforts. See Warrenton *Gazette*, September 13, October 4, 1878.

15. Wilson *Advance* quoted in Goldsboro *Messenger*, September 16, 1878. Brogden's comment about malfeasance apparently refers to a Halifax inferior court indictment. See Chapter 4, pp. 81–82.

line was to be drawn between white and black republicans . . . O'Hara is the best colored man in the district for Congress."[16]

By the end of September the accusation against O'Hara that had become most important was that he was a bigamist and therefore ineligible to serve in Congress. Charges of corruption had been made freely, but the claims were vague and not very damaging; it was the bigamy charge that was the most troublesome. O'Hara had married a woman named Ann Maria Harris in New Bern, March 18, 1864. Two years later he moved to Goldsboro to accept a teaching job and although his wife visited him from time to time, she continued to live in New Bern. She became pregnant during the year, but rejected O'Hara's suggestion that she move to Goldsboro. This apparently caused a break in the relationship, for O'Hara ceased to visit or support Ann. Her child was born September 17, 1866, but it is unclear whether O'Hara ever saw the child. Ann moved to Boston and lived there for several years under the assumed name of Cowan.[17] Meanwhile O'Hara met and wooed Elizabeth Eleanor Harris, member of an important free Negro family of Oberlin, Ohio, who had come south after the war to teach the freedmen. James and Elizabeth (Libby) were married July 14, 1869, in Oberlin. Two years later the first Mrs. O'Hara returned to North Carolina while O'Hara and his second wife were living in Washington, D.C., where O'Hara was working in the Treasury Department.[18]

The Republican executive committee for the second district met in Goldsboro, September 23, to consider the bigamy charge. At first O'Hara refused to appear, then reconsidered and told the committee his side of the story. He said he had been legally divorced from Ann O'Hara in the District of Columbia, though apparently without her knowledge. The executive committee, chaired by Craven Sheriff Orlando Hubbs, was not satisfied and decided to meet again in a week. O'Hara was

16. Tarboro *Southerner*, July 25, 1878.
17. "Positive Evidence of J. E. O'Hara's Ineligibility," broadside in James Henry Harris Papers, North Carolina Department of Archives and History.
18. Rivers, " 'A Thespian Must Play His Role,' " 5, 7–9; "Positive Evidence of J. E. O'Hara's Ineligibility." During the time he was living in Goldsboro O'Hara fathered an illegitimate son named James Edward O'Hara. The mother was a daughter in the family with whom he was residing. Rivers, " 'A Thespian Must Play His Role,' " 79.

in effect called upon to prove himself innocent of the charges, and at the second meeting the committee remained unconvinced.[19]

As the committee was meeting for the second time, "Buck" Kitchin wrote Senator Ransom, "I am almost constrained to believe my chances for election are very good," if he could have financial help "*at once.*" Kitchin had already spent four hundred dollars and he hoped Ransom could use his influence to raise more, for it was possible to carry the second district "if we work and use money."[20]

The Democrats of the district met in convention October 1 to decide how to take advantage of the confusion among their opponents. Two groups favored making no party nomination. Kitchin's supporters thought their man had a better chance as an unofficial, independent candidate than as the Democratic standard-bearer (provided the other independents withdrew), whereas other Democrats believed that the most promising method of getting an acceptable congressman was "to leave the field clear for Gov. Brogden."[21]

Presiding at the congressional convention, the first in the district since 1872, was Henry Groves Connor, a young resident of Wilson destined to be speaker of the state house and justice of the North Carolina Supreme Court. Despite speeches by Dossey Battle, editor of the Tarboro *Southerner*, and Kitchin's friend Spier Whitaker urging no nomination, the convention voted in favor of a nomination, 76 1/3 to 64 2/3. By a similar margin the delegates chose "Buck" Kitchin as nominee over two other candidates.[22] The Democrats' decision to field a candidate practically finished Brogden's hopes, though some uncertainty about his intentions persisted for a few weeks.

The Republican executive committee went ahead with plans to force O'Hara out of the congressional race, calling a new convention to meet in Kinston October 15, less than three weeks before election day. "If his

19. Goldsboro *Messenger*, September 26, 1878; "Positive Evidence of J. E. O'Hara's Ineligibility"; copy of executive committee circular in *Congressional Record*, 46th Cong., 1st Sess., 1016.

20. William H. Kitchin to M. W. Ransom, September 30, 1878, in Ransom Papers.

21. Tarboro *Southerner*, October 3, 1878; Goldsboro *Messenger*, September 26, 1878.

22. Goldsboro *Messenger*, October 3, 1878. Note that Democratic conventions were organized with a much larger number of delegates than Republican conventions.

character is as bad as these Republicans now say it is," asked Bonitz of the *Messenger*, "then why was he nominated? Why has he been honored again and again by the very men who now denounce him?" What was really at stake, the editor maintained, was white domination of the Republican party.[23]

At the second GOP convention, Brogden, Hyman, Abbott, and Humphrey were among the hopefuls. To the surprise of many who expected the convention to select a prominent white man as candidate, the delegates elected James H. Harris on the fifth ballot. No delegates attended from the large county of Edgecombe, perhaps indicating county leaders' disapproval of holding a second convention.[24]

There was widespread apathy in both parties about this thoroughly muddled campaign. Robert Ransom wrote his brother from New Bern: "There is very great dissatisfaction among the White Radicals," who do not care "if the two negroes kill each other off & allow Kitchen [*sic*] to be elected." As for the other side, Ransom reported: "From what I gather here the plan of the Democrats (if they have any) is to work *quietly* & get out their full vote, fearing and believing that any outward demonstrations would only be sure to unite the factions of the Republican Party."[25]

The two Republican candidates spent more time attacking each other than the enemy. A debate between Harris and O'Hara in Snow Hill, Greene County, was probably typical. Harris prefaced his speech with the statement that O'Hara was a personal friend, then proceeded to repeat the charges against his opponent's character, the principal accusation being, once again, bigamy. O'Hara was apparently the better debater—at least at this meeting—and he replied in kind. J. W. Thorne, also present at the meeting, briefly informed the voters that he too was a candidate. The *Messenger's* correspondent called him "an intelligent man; but *voila tout*"—a man "eccentric both in politics and religion," whose political fortunes were declining.[26]

Just before the election Democrats accused O'Hara of being ineligible because he was not a United States citizen. They produced a document

23. Goldsboro *Messenger*, October 10, 1878.
24. *Ibid.*, October 17, 1878. Harris received only 26 votes from Edgecombe on election day.
25. Robert Ransom to M. W. Ransom, October 22, 1878, in Ransom Papers.
26. Goldsboro *Messenger*, November 4, 1878.

from the court records of Wayne County dated November, 1867, showing that O'Hara was a native of the Virgin Islands and had taken preliminary steps to become a naturalized American, but had never completed the process. O'Hara later explained that he had applied for naturalization "under the belief that it was required," afterward finding out "that he was born in New York City and that his parents emigrated to the West Indies when he was an infant." Thus, according to O'Hara, he was an American citizen by birth.[27]

The citizenship issue had been used against O'Hara in the constitutional convention of 1875 and would be raised several times in the next eight years. None of O'Hara's enemies seemed able to offer any conclusive evidence, however, and he served in local, state, and national offices without serious challenge.[28]

Despite rumors and accusations, and in the face of opposition from leaders in his own party, O'Hara did remarkably well on election day. His Republican rival Harris did not carry a single county and outpolled O'Hara only in Wayne and Warren. The only significant support for Thorne came from Warren. Although the Republican division allowed a Democrat to carry Warren, Lenoir, and Jones for the first time in years, O'Hara had a majority in Craven, Edgecombe, Greene, Halifax, and Northampton. O'Hara, in fact, had won the election—until the county canvassing boards in Edgecombe, Halifax, and elsewhere began officially to "count" the vote. Even after rejecting hundreds of votes, the boards were able to give Kitchin only a narrow plurality, 10,704 votes to 9,682 for O'Hara and 3,948 for Harris.

O'Hara's defeat was accomplished by careful pruning of his majorities in Edgecombe, Craven, and Halifax, counties Republicans usually carried by tremendous margins. By invoking a series of technicalities the Edge-

27. *Ibid.*, November 4, 1878, November 27, 1882; *Congressional Record*, 46th Cong., 1st Sess., 1016. O'Hara is listed as a native of St. Croix in the *Official Register, 1869*, 40; *Official Register, 1871,* 39. Apparently O'Hara learned sometime after 1871 that he was actually born in New York City. In fact, if the Goldsboro *Messenger* is accurate, he did not claim to be native born even in 1878. According to the *Messenger*, O'Hara claimed to be a citizen on the basis of his *father's* American birth. "This defense appears to be a new idea and has but recently occurred to him," the newspaper asserted. Goldsboro *Messenger*, November 4, 1878. O'Hara's granddaughter, Jean O'Hara Rivers, is unable to provide further information on O'Hara's citizenship. Telephone interview, October 26, 1975.
28. For the citizenship matter in the convention, see Raleigh *Sentinel*, September 11, 1875.

combe canvassers were able to throw out the vote in six heavily Republican precincts, where the voters had cast 1,268 votes for O'Hara and only 351 for Kitchin. The Craven County canvassers rejected the fifth ward of the city of New Bern because the place of voting had been moved a short distance from the location appointed by the county commissioners, an action costing O'Hara 470 votes, Harris 54, Kitchin none. True, the canvassers also rejected a ward Kitchin had carried, but it was a small precinct and his net loss was fewer than 40 votes. In Halifax, Littleton precinct and Kitchin's own Scotland Neck precinct were rejected, and the board adjourned before the returns from Weldon arrived. O'Hara claimed that he was thus deprived of nearly 1,000 votes in his own county.[29] There were irregularities in Lenoir County as well. Election judges in Kinston (not the county board of canvassers) rejected 225 of the 268 votes cast for O'Hara because most of the O'Hara ballots included the phrase "For members of the Forty-Sixth Congress," and the judges interpreted the expression to be an illegal "device." In two other Lenoir townships the poll-holders did the same.[30]

Who engineered Kitchin's tainted victory? The New York *Times*, labeling the event pure Democratic villainy, reported that as soon as the Democratic leaders in Goldsboro realized Kitchin was within striking distance of being elected, they sent a telegram to Tarboro stating that Kitchin would win if O'Hara got no more than 1,000 majority in Edgecombe. The canvassing board proceeded to reduce O'Hara's margin of victory to 997 votes.[31]

Editor Bonitz thought the blame (or credit) should be shared. Two years after the event (in the midst of another political campaign) he charged that most white Republicans had been opposed to O'Hara. "Very naturally the democrats made the most of this, and found in Mr. Hubbs and the white leaders generally, willing and valuable allies, and the 'counting out of O'Hara,' by reason of certain irregularities, was encouraged and more the work of white republicans than of democrats,

29. *Papers in the Case of James E. O'Hara v. William H. Kitchin, Second District of North Carolina*, House Misc. Doc. 7, 46th Cong., 3rd Sess., 1881, pp. 1–3, 12–13; Craven County Record of Elections, 1878–1900, in North Carolina Department of Archives and History. Two minor candidates received 7 votes in the two wards.
30. *Papers in O'Hara v. Kitchin*, 3; New York *Times*, December 26, 1878.
31. New York *Times*, November 20, December 26, 1878.

if not directly then indirectly, for the republican fiat had gone forth that 'the negro must be beaten.' "[32]

O'Hara himself saw events in a similar light: "In my defeat, or rather my being counted out, the Republicans had more to do with it than the Democrats, and I say that the colored Republicans of the South have more to fear from the white Republicans than from the Democrats. And there is always a combination between the white Republicans against any intelligent colored Republican who seeks to aspire to office."

The cooperation among O'Hara's enemies in his own county was particularly significant. Two white Republicans there had split the local party in their campaign for sheriff, and whereas O'Hara supported the losing candidate, Kitchin stood surety on the official bond of the winner, James Dawson. Kitchin's action was somewhat unusual for a partisan Democrat and Dawson reciprocated by favoring him in the congressional race. According to O'Hara, Dawson's friends "made a combination and counted me out. That was the reason Mr. Kitchen [sic] went on his bond."[33]

Other Republicans aided Kitchin in a less direct way. Obviously, the split in the party and the resolve of many Republicans to defeat O'Hara at any cost gave the election-cheaters their opening. And if white Republicans were the prime movers in the campaign against O'Hara, they had essential support from O'Hara's black rivals. James H. Harris, the most prominent black man in the state, accepted the nomination of the Kinston convention and ended up taking more votes from O'Hara than the county canvassing boards. Other Negroes who supported Harris included John T. Reynolds, legislator from Halifax, I. B. Abbott, and Samuel L. Perry, a black citizen of Lenoir.[34]

Perry became famous for his part in the Negro exodus to Indiana in 1879–1880, and early in 1880 when a Senate investigating committee called him to testify he took the opportunity to set the committee straight on the election of 1878: "I have noticed in several Republican papers even about being cheated out of the election there in the second Congressional district, but the man was so rotten that ran for the office that we had to lay him over. The Republicans I admit—I do not

32. Goldsboro *Messenger*, September 20, 1880.
33. *Exodus Report*, 53. See New York *Times*, October 5, 1878.
34. Kinston *Journal*, October 30, 1879.

say the Democrats—done that; we never charged it on them." Perry declared that he was a Republican but he "would vote for Kitchin [sic] a thousand times before I'd vote for any man like O'Hara, because he was a man that was a bigamist, had two wives, and was accused of being in jail in Halifax. So we laid him over, and the intelligent Republicans was satisfied."[35] Another black enemy of O'Hara was former congressman John Hyman. A few months after the election a Warren Democrat wrote to Senator Ransom recommending Hyman for a patronage job, since "he rendered valuable assistance in the Election of Capt. Kitchin who ought now to make some return."[36]

O'Hara moved quickly to seek a remedy in the courts for the dishonest election. Assisted by three able Democratic lawyers, George Howard, Fred Philips, and William H. Day, he applied to the superior court for a writ of mandamus to compel the board of canvassers in Edgecombe and in Halifax to reassemble and conduct a new, full count. Judge Augustus S. Seymour, a New York-born Republican, granted this order December 9, 1878, but the boards appealed his decision to the state supreme court. By the time the supreme court was able to act, the state canvassing board had completed the count and issued the official commission to Kitchin—after waiting as long as permitted by law for the second district matter to be resolved. In view of "the delays incident to the mode of judicial procedure," wrote Chief Justice W. N. H. Smith, "the remedy by mandamus is practically useless." More appropriate redress for O'Hara at this point, suggested the court, was a quo warranto proceeding or a contest before the House of Representatives. In other words, even if the court sustained Judge Seymour's order it was too late for O'Hara to get any benefit from that order, since the state board had already adjourned. Therefore the action was dismissed, without costs.[37]

O'Hara must have known that his prospects in the Democratic House were poor, yet he went ahead with the effort to unseat Kitchin. At every step there were obstacles. Federal law required a person intending to contest the election of a member of the House to notify that member

35. Exodus Report, 293–94.
36. Nathaniel R. Jones to M. W. Ransom, March 17, 1879, in Ransom Papers.
37. O'Hara v. Powell, et al., Vol. 80 North Carolina Reports (1879), 76–81; New York Times, December 26, 1878; Goldsboro Messenger, November 18, 1878. Compare Logan, Negro in North Carolina, 65–66. Logan is incorrect in asserting that the votes rejected in Edgecombe alone would have elected O'Hara.

within thirty days after the vote had been determined. (Just when the vote was determined in the second district was debatable, considering the complex legal proceedings.) Kitchin claimed that he never received O'Hara's notice, though O'Hara said his messenger told him it had been left at Kitchin's place of business. Kitchin issued a reply to the notice of contest on April 29, 1879, after learning that the House committee on elections had received O'Hara's notice. He prefaced his reply with the claim that O'Hara was a Danish citizen and the assertion that he had received "no lawful or sufficient notice of contest." According to federal law, the parties in an election contest had ninety days in which to collect testimony, beginning from the day on which the contestee's reply was served on the contestant. O'Hara said he and Kitchin had agreed orally that there was no need to take evidence in reference to the rejection of votes in Craven and Edgecombe, but Kitchin denied having made such an agreement. When O'Hara asked for a time extension in April, 1880, on the grounds that all written material he had prepared for the case had been destroyed when his house burned down the year before, the Committee on Elections did nothing. Just before the close of the Forty-sixth Congress, more than two years after the election, the committee reported that O'Hara was not entitled to Kitchin's seat. Recognizing that there were "very grave and important questions in dispute in this election, and that the matters in dispute concerned a far greater number of votes than the plurality of the sitting member," the committee nevertheless maintained that the evidence was inadequate as well as ineligible.[38]

So "Buck" Kitchin sat in the House as the representative of a district with an overwhelming Republican, black population. The stubborn, hot-tempered Democrat did not make an outstanding record in Congress, nor did he particularly enjoy the experience of being a national politician. "I am tired of politics & out of patience with this Congress & will say this City is the Sodom of America," he wrote to a friend during his first session.[39] A stump spellbinder, Kitchin modified his style a bit for the halls of Congress, but his oratorical methods remained, as he put it,

38. *O'Hara v. Kitchin,* House Rpt. 263, 46th Cong., 3rd Sess.; *Papers in O'Hara v. Kitchin,* 3.
39. W. H. Kitchin to Walter Clark, May 16, 1879, in Aubrey Lee Brooks and Hugh Talmage Lefler (eds.), *The Papers of Walter Clark* (2 vols.; Chapel Hill, 1948), I, 204.

"rough, candid, and, I trust, honest." More often than any of his three Republican predecessors he placed his comments into the *Congressional Record*, and these remarks reveal a good deal of his political philosophy. Although he had espoused some Greenbacker proposals during his campaign, he privately considered the party "extreme" and "off at a tangent"; indeed, once in Congress he showed himself to be an intensely partisan, old-fashioned Democrat.[40]

"I am opposed to bayonet rule," declared Kitchin in his first speech, April 3, 1879, as he spoke in favor of the rider to an appropriation bill forbidding the president to use troops at the polls on election day. He took pains to mention the harshness of Reconstruction and the evil wrought by the "unprincipled men, blood-suckers, and political buzzards" who plundered the South. At the same time he deplored the bloody-shirt rhetoric of northern Republicans.[41]

In the second session Kitchin took the floor to deliver a long address on the issue of political assessments—the practice of requiring campaign contributions from patronage appointees. Since the Republicans controlled federal patronage, he could with relish bewail the "damaging and corrupting influences of money in election campaigns," though he saw little hope for a speedy legislative remedy to an evil rooted in "our fallen nature." More fundamental changes in the political system were necessary, "a return to the great principles upon which the superstructure of our political edifice was originally based." The government should realize that it is the servant of the people, Kitchin said, and he urged that official salaries be slashed by 25 to 50 percent. In his assessment, other drawbacks to genuine reform included extravagant federal spending and the alarming centralization of authority in the national government, especially in the president's "enormous concentration of power." As a believer in states' rights, Kitchin expressed deep concern: "If there should be no change in the administration, and the executive, legislative, and judicial departments should advance as rapidly on the road to centralization for the next sixteen years as they have in the last sixteen, I believe State lines, State courts, and State governments will cease to be, and the American continent, from lakes to gulf, and from ocean to ocean, will become one consolidated government, ruled by

40. *Ibid.*
41. *Congressional Record*, 46th Cong., 1st Sess., 215–16.

some Caesar, Cromwell, or Bonaparte." Most basic of all, perhaps, the present Republican administration (headed by a "so-called President") needed to be replaced. "It would be as natural to see water in the Nile or the Mississippi flow up stream as to expect or hope for reformation under the present, or any possible republican administration."[42]

Kitchin saved his most reactionary remarks for the final session of the Forty-sixth Congress, when he was a lame duck. In an undelivered speech he showed how far out of touch he was with the Bourbon leadership of southern Democrats, including Tarheels like Matt Ransom. Commenting on the river and harbor improvement bill, a popular measure the House was sure to pass, Kitchin declared, "No gentleman who votes for this bill ought ever again to raise his voice in favor of a strict construction of the Constitution, or in favor of the reserved rights of the States, or in favor of strict economy in the administration of the Government." He then further reaffirmed the old Democratic opposition to unconstitutional, Whig-inspired internal improvements: "I am aware this is an age of progress, advancements, and civilization, and that it is urged that we must keep pace with the times . . . but, sir, principles never change. . . . If this kind of legislation was wrong and unconstitutional, and undemocratic, and non-republican twenty years ago, it is equally so today." Furthermore, much of the proposed appropriation would simply be wasted on obscure "creeks and swamps," he believed, adding, "I am sure a catfish could not navigate some of these streams in the summer season without great damage to his bottom side."[43]

Kitchin introduced few bills, none of which passed. He proposed in his first session to exempt persons making less than sixty gallons of brandy from internal revenue tax, a measure no doubt favored by many farmers in the second district who distilled modest amounts of liquor from their apple or peach crops. He later tried but failed to have a similar proposal included as an amendment to a bill revising the internal revenue laws.[44]

Early in his congressional career Kitchin's pugnacious personality drew him into a feud with his North Carolina colleague Daniel L. Russell of Wilmington, a long-time Republican elected to the House as a Green-

42. *Ibid.*, 2nd Sess., 3218–21.
43. *Ibid.*, 3rd Sess., appendix, 108–109.
44. *Ibid.*, 1st Sess., 1090; 2nd Sess., 2884. For other measures introduced by Kitchin, see 1st Sess., 1054; 2nd Sess., 763, 2754.

backer. Russell inserted into the *Congressional Record* of April 26, 1879, a statement that two Democrats—one from Florida and the other from North Carolina—owed their seats to "the fraudulent mandates of returning boards, some of whom, strange to say, are in the penitentiary." On May 1 Kitchin rose to a point of personal explanation, denying that any members of the returning boards in his district were in prison. If Russell was referring to Kitchin's district, his statement was "infamously slanderous." Then, to show why he had won, Kitchin had the clerk read a copy of the affidavit concerning O'Hara's citizenship and a Republican circular issued by Orlando Hubbs urging support for James Harris.

Two weeks later Russell replied, ridiculing Kitchin for attacking him while he was absent and calling Kitchin's remarks a specimen of "plantation manners." Russell said his statement about board members behind bars referred to a county board in Florida, not the Florida state board, as a Florida congressman had said, nor North Carolina boards, as Kitchin professed to believe. He cited the speech of a Maine representative as the source of his information, adding that if the Maine man was wrong "then I will amend the statement in that particular and acknowledge that they are not in the penitentiary, but they ought to be." The thieves who steal elections are usually sent to the legislature or the custom house rather than prison, he added sarcastically.

Russell proceeded to discuss some of the dubious methods behind Kitchin's victory. He exhibited "as one of the curiosities of reconstruction" a number of O'Hara ballots like those that had been rejected. A faint indentation made by the printer's paper-cutting machine was judged a "device" by the men counting the vote and became the basis for their refusal to accept hundreds of O'Hara's votes. Vote counters rejected other tickets because the apostrophe in "O'Hara" was imperfectly printed, said Russell, drawing laughs from the Republican side. As for the claim that O'Hara was not an American citizen, Russell said he did not know if that were true, but found it "a sorry sight to see a man defending a seat when he knows he was beaten by thousands of votes upon the excuse that the other man is not eligible."

Kitchin immediately branded Russell a traitor, a maligner of his own people. He denied Russell's charge that O'Hara had really won by 2,000 votes and insisted that only one township in Lenior had been thrown out because of the "device." Without mentioning Judge Seymour's mandamus order, he noted the judge's opinion that the Edge-combe canvassers were not criminally liable. He informed the House that a majority of canvassers in his county were Republicans, though he avoided mentioning the GOP split in Halifax. Then he attempted to corner Russell. "I want to ask that gentleman if he was court-martialed and dismissed from the confederate service?"

"How long are you going to give me to answer that question?" Russell responded. "I was court-martialed and dismissed from the confederate service for whipping a conscript officer, and I was afterward restored to the confederate service by the order of Jeff Davis." The House broke into "long and continued laughter" and Kitchin was discomfited. When the Spéaker refused to allow him to continue on the subject of Russell's war record, for it was not in order as a "personal explanation," Kitchin sat down.[45]

During the years 1878 to 1881 Kitchin gave little evidence of the virulent Negrophobia he strongly evinced in the mid-1880s. Still, he showed himself to be an extremist in the methods he was willing to use and in his uncompromising adherence to the old-time Democratic gospel. There are indications that Kitchin and his ways irritated Matt Ransom, the party boss of eastern North Carolina. Kitchin's friend and campaign advisor Spier Whitaker wrote to Ransom shortly after the 1878 election attempting to mend fences. "It is evident that certain persons have been endeavoring to estrange you from me," he said, yet "I have never said, intimated, or thought, that you did not favor the success of Kitchin." In fact he had told Kitchin to cooperate with Ransom, although Kitchin had already heard that Ransom was "at least indifferent as to his success." Kitchin's performance in Congress disappointed the senator's brother, Robert Ransom, who privately complained that Kitchin was slow in "posting himself about the vital interests of the district he so poorly & without right represents but if the people will send such creatures to high places they must & ought to suffer."[46]

45. *Congressional Record*, 46th Cong., 1st Sess., 1015–16, 1295–97. See Wilmington *Post*, May 18, 1879; Wilmington *Morning Star*, May 16, 1879. For Russell's curious war record, see Jeffery J. Crow and Robert F. Durden, *Maverick Republican in the Old North State: A Political Biography of Daniel L. Russell* (Baton Rouge, 1977), 4–10.

46. Spier Whitaker to M. W. Ransom, December 12, 1878, Robert Ransom to M. W. Ransom, March 26, 1880, both in Ransom Papers.

Chapter 4

A CARPETBAGGER'S VICTORY

THANKS TO THE ACTIONS of several thousand obscure black laborers and tenants, the second district became the object of brief national attention in 1879–1880. Inspired both by discouraging prospects at home and rumors of faraway prosperity, as many as twenty-five hundred to three thousand men, women, and children left North Carolina and migrated to Indiana, provoking Democratic fears that this "exodus" had been arranged by Republicans seeking to "colonize" a crucial swing state. One of the leaders of the movement, a black schoolteacher named Samuel L. Perry, admitted distributing a warning that "the fifteenth amendment will be repealed, and all the colored people found south of the Ohio on the 1st of May will be put back into slavery." A Senate committee energetically investigated this phenomenon, as well as the larger Kansas exodus, hearing testimony from many second district residents, including James O'Hara, a leading Democratic editor, several farmers, and representative "exodusters," without finding conclusive proof of a Republican plot. Most of North Carolina's black politicians, naturally enough, opposed the migration. O'Hara surmised that the migrants were simply "the floating population" rather than industrious colored people and said he had striven to correct reports that the federal government would give these "exodusters" aid. In fact, the excitement petered out in 1880, and life in the second district continued much as before. But for a while a heedless, powerful unease which no one could control stirred among the black masses.[1]

1. *Exodus Report*, 45, 49–71, 104, 106–108, 111, 133–48, 300, *passim*; John G. Van Deusen, "Did Republicans 'Colonize' Indiana in 1879?" *Indiana Magazine of History*, XXX (December, 1934). For a different point of view, see Stanley P. Hirshson, *Farewell to the Bloody Shirt: Northern Republicans and the Southern Negro, 1877–1893* (Chicago, 1962), 73–77. See also Nell Irvin Painter, *Exodusters: Black Migration to Kansas After Reconstruction* (New York, 1977), 251–53.

The exodus was not large enough to bring about any fundamental shift in district politics. Blacks remained in the overwhelming majority and "Buck" Kitchin's only hope of reelection lay in division among Republicans. That factionalism seemed virulent enough as the election of 1880 approached. There were several aspirants for the Republican nomination, some of them with bitter memories of the last campaign. Curtis Brogden was circulating around the district in the spring of 1880, spreading the word that he wanted to run for Congress again.[2] Colonel Humphrey, who had come so close to the nomination in 1878, hoped that this time he would succeed. James O'Hara knew he had been cheated in 1878 and was determined to seek the nomination again, despite the divisions in the Halifax party and his own legal problems.

In September, 1879, the grand jury for the Halifax superior court indicted the previous year's board of county commissioners, including O'Hara, on three counts of malfeasance in office. The available sources do not give details of the accusation, but the charge was probably based on board actions appropriating money to individual commissioners for services to the county. During the campaign of 1876 the Raleigh *Sentinel* had reported that the Halifax commissioners had allowed extra compensation to several county officials, including the sheriff, register, and chairman of the commissioners. One year during O'Hara's tenure as a commissioner, for example, he was allowed four hundred dollars extra for service as county attorney. These financial actions attracted the attention of the grand jury several times, in 1874, 1875, and 1876, but no indictments resulted. The county inferior court apparently did indict the commissioners for some reason, but minutes of the inferior court have not been preserved.[3]

Charges against three of the commissioners were dropped in March, 1880, leaving only O'Hara and J. H. Howard to face prosecution. The first of the three cases ended in a hung jury, March 18, 1880. Despite Spier Whitaker's "capital" speech for the prosecution, four of the twelve jurors voted against conviction. In the fall term of the superior court, after it became clear that O'Hara was not a candidate for any position,

2. Goldsboro *Messenger*, March 22, 1880; Kinston *Journal*, April 22, 1880.
3. Halifax County Minutes of the Superior Court, 1878–79, in North Carolina Department of Archives and History; Raleigh *Sentinel*, October 3, 1876; Spier Whitaker to Walter Clark, July 25, 1878, in Walter Clark Papers, North Carolina Department of Archives and History. It is conceivable that the 1879 indictment grew out of the transaction described in Whitaker's letter.

O'Hara and his co-defendant pleaded nolo contendere in all three cases and prosecution was dropped upon payment of costs.[4] The charges against O'Hara may have been politically motivated. In defense of his record in 1878, he had explained to the Wilmington *Post* that the indictments then standing against him (presumably in the inferior court) "were all alike, and were obtained for merely political purpose, that he had been tried and acquitted in one case, and would be in all the others when they dared to come to trial."[5]

The Republican divisions became more obvious as party conventions met in the several counties. When Wayne Republicans convened May 29 to choose delegates to the congressional and state conventions, they quickly split into two sessions. The convention began in the Goldsboro town hall, with William Smith O'Brien Robinson, a twenty-nine-year-old lawyer and the son of Irish immigrants, as chairman. Robinson and George T. Wassom, the black chairman of the county executive committee, were leaders of the anti-Humphrey faction in the party. After a tumultuous dispute over selection of the credentials committee, Humphrey and his followers—a majority of the convention—walked out to form a new convention at the courthouse. The group staying behind heard Curtis Brogden angrily vent his frustration on the absent Colonel Humphrey, calling Humphrey a "political trickster" whose duplicity had denied Brogden a renomination two years before. "I believe he would betray our Savior, like Judas did, if he had the opportunity, for like consideration."[6] Brogden would soon have reason to regret these reckless words.

Wayne's two conventions produced two sets of delegates, each claiming to be regular. When much the same thing happened in Halifax County, the Wilmington *Post* refused to publish the proceedings, since "the wrangles of our friends in Halifax" were not of general interest. The newspaper had received a report from one convention that had endorsed O'Hara for Congress, but a letter from the chairman of the executive committee asserted that the O'Hara convention was a bolting

4. Halifax County Minutes of the Superior Court, 1880–81; Goldsboro *Messenger*, March 25, 1880.

5. Wilmington *Post*, December 29, 1878.

6. Goldsboro *Messenger*, May 31, 1880; *Speech of Hon. C. H. Brogden*, 10, 13, 14. For biographical details on Robinson, see *North Carolina Biography*, Vol. VI of *History of North Carolina* (Chicago, 1919), 262.

group and that J. T. Reynolds had the support of a majority of genuine delegates.[7]

Some counties had more harmonious meetings. A Democratic newspaper described the convention in Lenoir as "orderly and well conducted" and "apparently under white control, though a majority of the delegates were colored." The Lenoir men once again endorsed R. W. King for Congress, and the Craven convention, E. R. Dudley presiding, chose county Sheriff Orlando Hubbs.[8]

Delegates from around the district met in Goldsboro July 1, hoping to nominate a man who could recapture a "safe" Republican House seat. As chairman of the executive committee, Hubbs called the meeting to order and turned the session over to temporary chairman Frank D. Dancy, senator from Edgecombe. The first order of business was resolving the credentials disputes in Wayne, Halifax, and Wilson, a task that took the credentials committee all afternoon. After making the temporary officers permanent, the convention got down to the matter of nominating candidates. Delegates suggested nine names, including Hubbs, Humphrey, O'Hara, Reynolds, and King. Although some politicians raised the quadrennial argument that a Negro nominee might hurt the national and state tickets, they were careful to appeal to black voters. A Craven white Republican offered as a reason to support Hubbs the sheriff's belief in "a proper share of offices for colored men."[9]

For six ballots the voting continued, with no candidate receiving a majority. On the seventh ballot Hubbs and Humphrey tied at 7 votes each, and a delegate from Halifax, Cary Alston, refused to vote. Apparently the O'Hara delegates had been seated from Halifax, for according to one report orders from O'Hara prevented Alston from casting his vote for Humphrey.[10] Perhaps O'Hara calculated that his own candidacy would prosper if the deadlock continued. Instead of proceeding to the next ballot at this point, chairman Dancy took the unusual step of voting to break the tie, making Hubbs the nominee by a vote of 8 to 7. His action put the convention into an uproar; for an hour, according to Brogden, "the most extraordinary turbulence [sic], disorder and confusion

7. Wilmington *Post*, June 27, 1880.
8. Kinston *Journal*, June 24, 1880; Greensboro *North State*, June 3, 1880.
9. Raleigh *Signal*, July 7, 1880; Goldsboro *Messenger*, July 5, 1880.
10. Goldsboro *Messenger*, July 5, 1880. The *Messenger* is certainly wrong in asserting that O'Hara and Hubbs were working together.

prevailed," the lights went out twice, and the police and the sheriff were called in. At some point the convention adjourned to meet again at nine-thirty the same night, and with many anti-Hubbs men absent, the later session gave the position of presidential elector to W. S. O'B. Robinson and made the nomination of Hubbs unanimous. Frank Dancy was elected chairman of the district executive committee for the next two years.[11]

The only white "carpetbagger" ever nominated in the second district, Hubbs was born on a farm in Commack, New York, February 14, 1840. His family had lived on Long Island for four generations. At the age of sixteen he left school to learn the trade of carriage and wagon building, and he later worked as a ship carpenter in Brooklyn. In 1865 he moved with his wife to New Bern—according to family history at the solicitation of his brother Ethelbert, a Union veteran who had just settled in North Carolina. Hubbs won election to the first of five terms as sheriff of Craven in 1870. His political base there was strengthened, no doubt, by the activities of his brother, who was for a time editor of the New Bern *Daily Times* and held the important patronage post of New Bern postmaster from 1874 to 1882.[12] By 1880 Orlando was chairman of the second district executive committee and a member of the party's state executive committee.

Despite his northern birth and his "alien" politics, Hubbs had apparently won the respect of local Democrats. "He is a carpet-bagger, and well spoken of by the Democrats of New Bern," commented the Kinston *Journal* on his nomination. The Democratic *Newbernian* saw Hubbs's

11. Raleigh *Signal*, July 7, 1880; Goldsboro *Messenger*, July 5, 1880; "Address of Hon. C. H. Brogden, to the Voters of the Second Congressional District of North Carolina," broadside in North Carolina Collection, University of North Carolina, Chapel Hill.

12. *Biographical Directory of the American Congress*, 1089; William S. Pelletreau, *A History of Long Island from Its Earliest Settlement to the Present Time*, III (New York and Chicago, 1903), 281–82. (I am indebted to C. W. Garrison of the Smithtown, N.Y., library for this reference.) P. C. Headley, *Public Men of To-Day* (Tecumseh, Mich., 1882), 433–34; *Who's Who in New York City and State: A Biographical Dictionary of Contemporaries* (New York, 1911), 495; Patricia H. Stewart, "Orlando Hubbs and the Corruption Charges of 1908" (Academic paper, Molloy College, 1974), 4. (I am indebted to Mrs. Stewart for a copy of her paper.) For Ethelbert's postal service, see Record of Appointments of Postmasters, Vol. 49, Record Group 28, National Archives. For his editorial career, see New Bern *Daily Times*, 1873–74, *passim*.

nomination as a "credit" to the Republican party and predicted that he would make "an honest and true" representative.[13]

A good reputation was difficult to maintain in the rough-and-tumble of a second district campaign—especially when party comrades fell to squabbling. The disputed result of the district convention revived Curtis Brogden's hopes that he might return to Congress, and he would soon be villifying Hubbs as a "fraud," "trickster," and a Yankee. But first he would have to retract his abusive language about Colonel Humphrey, the man who felt most aggrieved by Hubbs's nomination and whose support would be essential to any successful Republican rebellion. In a July 19 announcement Brogden withdrew his remarks of May 29 "as completely as if never spoken or written," explaining that he had been under the false impression that the meeting he addressed was the regular convention and that Humphrey was leading a bolting faction.[14]

For his own purposes, Humphrey had already decided that Brogden ought to run. He was willing to use the still-ambitious former governor to hurt Hubbs, a man he had reason to dislike. In the view of Humphrey and his friends, Hubbs had treacherously worked against the colonel in the first 1878 convention and now had defeated him by unfair means. The Democrats were aware of Humphrey's support for Brogden and were uncertain as to their best course. As of mid-July no date had been set for a Democratic district convention.[15]

In the meantime the regular candidates had taken to the stump. Addressing a mass meeting in Tarboro July 24, Robinson reminded his audience that "Capt Kitchin owes his seat in the U S Congress to bolting" and declared that he would support Hubbs though the candidate was not his original choice. He told the crowd to ignore "an old fossil," an obvious reference to the sixty-three-year-old Brogden. Hubbs followed him to the stand and began by offering comments on national issues and candidates. Refraining from attacking Humphrey, he simply

13. Kinston *Journal*, July 8, 1880; *Newbernian*, July 3, 1880.
14. "Address of Hon. C. H. Brogden"; Goldsboro *Messenger* quoted in Raleigh *Signal*, August 5, 1880.
15. H. G. Williams to M. W. Ransom, July 19, 1880, in Ransom Papers. The Goldsboro *Messenger*, July 15, 1878, reported that Humphrey's friends were displeased with Hubbs. "It is openly charged that having been elected chairman of the Congressional Convention by the friends of Col. Humphrey, and supposed to be a Humphrey man, he yet did all in his power to defeat the Colonel."

insisted that he had used no "wrong means" in securing the nomination. He attacked the Democratic county government system and attempted to defuse the race issue within the Republican party. After speaking of black progress and advocating Negro education he said: "It is said that a colored man should go from this district. I was nominated by colored men. If a colored man had been nominated I would have supported him. As for myself, go to my county and you'll find my record." He promised to get as many positions for competent Negroes as he could.[16]

The Wayne County Republican convention reconvened July 31 to denounce the manner of Hubbs's nomination. Two Wayne leaders who supported Hubbs, Wassom and Robinson, were even threatened with expulsion from the local party. Most important, the convention endorsed Brogden for Congress if there were no Democratic nomination.[17]

Brogden's candidacy forced the Democrats to consider the cost of compromise. It was nothing new, of course, to foster factionalism in the other party, but compromise that involved an open coalition with non-Democrats went beyond the common practice of encouraging and profiting from enemy division. If Democrats dealt with the most acceptable wing of the Republican party, did they run the risk of losing the race solidarity issue and its tremendous mobilizing power? Negotiation could lend legitimacy to "scalawags" and make it difficult again to excoriate them as opportunists. On the other hand a straight-out policy threw away any opportunity legitimately to influence elections—and left black-belt Democrats dependent upon the state regime for rewards and protection of local interests.

The dilemma was not a new one. Brogden's last attempt for Congress in 1878 had raised similar issues and many local campaigns before that had involved the matter of compromise. An arrangement existed in Warren County, for example, which had kept major county offices in the hands of white Democrats since the war. At each election a large number of Negroes supported Democrats for sheriff, clerk of the superior court, and treasurer. (The only exception to Democratic control was the office of register of deeds, held from 1878 on by Mansfield Thornton, a black Republican.) In return for black support, Democrats approved limited black officeholding in local affairs, going so far as to

16. Tarboro *Southerner*, July 26, 1880.
17. Goldsboro Messenger, August 2, 1880.

elect a Negro county commissioner in 1878. Former congressman John Hyman's influence was crucial in maintaining this arrangement over the years, though it eventually weakened his position in the Republican party.[18]

One arrangement generated pressures for further accommodation, for Democrats now had a stake in their opponents' party affairs. What would happen if an unacceptable faction took control of the Warren Republican party? When the Democrats made no legislative nominations in 1874, the Warrenton *Gazette* reported: "There are some gentlemen in the county who are attempting to create sympathy, one for the [George H.] King and the other for the Hyman wing." The *Gazette*'s strongly partisan editor, H. A. Foote, called for party unity: "We can not see that the Conservative gentlemen of the county are called upon to espouse either side." But not all Democrats agreed, and Foote later complained that he had been denounced for his stand as "officious, presumptuous and dictatorial."[19]

Conservative gentlemen could even find themselves voting for a black candidate in preference to a white one. White Republican J. Williams Thorne ran for a seat in the legislature in a January, 1875, special election, and some Democrats worked for the other Republican nominee, a Negro, in spite of the fact that a white Democrat was running. When Thorne won election to the state senate in 1876 the Democratic *Centennial* expressed regret: "We were very much in hope that the ticket nominated by the Hyman party would be elected. We of course knew that they were all Republicans, but believed the men on the Hyman ticket to be the best men and of more kindly feelings." The editor added that it was "to be regretted that every white man in the county did not cast his vote for the Hyman ticket" in order to defeat the "bitter and vindictive" radicals who "had done much to disturb the harmony and good feeling between the races in the county." There was some comfort

18. North Carolina General Assembly, Legislative Papers, 1881, Petition for colored magistrates from twenty-one Warren County Democrats, in North Carolina Department of Archives and History. Nathaniel R. Jones to M. W. Ransom, March 17, 1879, petition from John R. Turnbull *et al.* to Matt W. Ransom and Z. B. Vance, March 3, 1879, both in Ransom Papers. Warrenton *Gazette*, August 9, 1878. Whites also supported Negro candidates for positions on the Warrenton board of commissioners. Warrenton *Gazette*, May 5, 1882, April 25, 1884. See Raleigh *Daily Sentinel*, August 28, 1874.

19. Warrenton *Gazette*, July 31, 1874, July 30, 1875.

in the victory of the Hyman candidates over two radical blacks in the House races.[20]

By 1880 Foote was printing a letter to the editor maintaining that the party had "all to lose and nothing to gain" by nominating a "straight out" ticket for every position. The author noted "two distinct parties" among the colored people and mentioned talk of a possible division of the legislative ticket with the "Liberal" or moderate Republicans. Nothing came of this, for the moderates did not nominate any Democrats, but the fact that it was proposed showed how far compromise could go.[21]

The issue of compromise and coalition divided Democrats in other places as well. Lacking a Warren-type arrangement, Edgecombe Democrats faced numerous defeats. After the 1878 elections, the editor of the Tarboro *Southerner* had had enough: "We believe that if a policy of concession had prevailed during the late canvass, or rather at its inception, the democrats might have been represented in the State legislature and in the county offices. We have seen, year in and year out, that the nomination of a 'straight out ticket' has resulted in always the same defeat." In view of these failures, perhaps it was time to lay aside the old policy and try "new and other methods," providing, of course, that Democrats acted as a unit. "We believe that the majority favor a liberal policy."[22]

But it was easier to follow a "liberal policy" in local contests than in a campaign covering ten counties and involving a national office. What would pass unnoticed in the Halifax town elections might anger Democrats throughout the state in a congressional race. Brogden did his best to convince district Democrats to take the unprecedented step of tacitly endorsing an independent Republican by making no nomination of their own. These tactics were clearly demonstrated in a broadside he issued (probably in September) "To the Voters of the Second Congressional District of North Carolina." This campaign document began

20. Warrenton *Gazette*, January 22, 1875; Warrenton *Centennial*, November 17, 1876.
21. Warrenton *Gazette*, July 23, 1880.
22. Tarboro *Southerner*, August 8, 1878. Apparently Edgecombe Negroes did cooperate with Democrats in the election of magistrates under the 1868 constitution. In 1875 William P. Mabson told the state senate that the majority of justices of the peace in the county had been Democrats and that Republicans voted for them. See the Raleigh *Era* (weekly), March 18, 1875.

with a disingenuous description of the disputed July 1 convention and Hubbs's record. Attempting to capitalize on the bitter divisions of 1878, Brogden attacked Hubbs as "responsible more than any other man for all the disorganization in the Republican party in the last two or three years." The second convention in 1878 had really been called because Hubbs wanted a second chance for his own nomination. (Hubbs supported Abbott in the second convention, and there is no indication that he was a candidate himself.) After advising Republicans to rally around Harris, the "traitor-like" Hubbs had refused to support Harris himself, alleged Brogden.

Brogden accused Hubbs of using a forged letter to secure the executive committee's selection of Frank Dancy as temporary chairman of the convention, but he offered no proof. (Besides, Dancy became permanent chairman by a vote of the entire convention.) And Brogden denounced Dancy's behavior when the "voting ceased" on the seventh ballot, without explaining that the chairman had broken a tie vote. The former congressman cited the opinion of James O'Hara and convention secretary Hiram L. Grant to show that Hubbs had not been legitimately nominated. Considering all this, he asked, "will good Republicans vote to reward Mr. Hubbs treachery and treason to the Republican party?"

If Brogden appealed to Republican resentments, he asked for Democratic votes on the basis of the issues. The time demanded "reform of the most radical character," he said, particularly in the present "unequal and unjust" system of taxation which oppressed "the farmer and the laboring man" while exempting "the bondholders and privileged classes from taxation." Hubbs was an outsider who would do nothing for the district. "On the all-important question of tariff taxation, he will vote in favor of the Northern manufacturers and against the best interests of the people of our own State. We had just as well have a man from Rhode Island or Vermont to represent us as Mr. Hubbs."

Not only was Hubbs a carpetbagger (though Brogden avoided using the word), he was a man with no legislative experience. In contrast, Brogden had deep local roots and had served almost twenty-five years in various legislative bodies. He reminded voters of his efforts while in Congress regarding river improvement, tax reduction, and civil service for North Carolina.

Both men had reputations for official probity, but the former congressman suggested that Hubbs showed "little respect for the binding obligations of an official oath," citing an incident from four years earlier to prove his point. Hubbs had been one of the sureties for Tim Lee, sheriff of Wake, and when Lee defaulted, the Wake superior court sent Sheriff Hubbs an execution for $15,000 against the property of Hubbs and two other signers of Lee's official bond. According to Brogden, Hubbs returned the execution with the notation: "No property to be found to satisfy the within execution." Hubbs was lying, Brogden implied, either when he swore he was worth $5,000 to sign the bond, or when he did not satisfy the execution against Lee.[23]

Dislike of Hubbs brought James O'Hara and Brogden together during this campaign, O'Hara sharing the belief that Hubbs was largely responsible for the 1878 debacle. Late in September Brogden and O'Hara planned a speaking tour in Jones, Lenoir, and Green, and O'Hara was reported to be making an "open and bitter fight upon" Hubbs in Halifax.[24] Brogden apparently "withdrew" his criticism of two years earlier, or perhaps O'Hara was less of a "disgrace" to the party when he was working with Brogden.

The Democratic district executive committee decided to submit the question of a nomination to the party rank and file and called a convention for September 28 in Goldsboro. The implications of making no nomination were much clearer in 1880 than two years before: since the Kitchin forces favored an official nomination, a vote for no nomination was probably a vote in favor of Brogden. A delegate from Wayne, where Brogden lived, offered a resolution opposing a nomination because "dissensions . . . in the Republican ranks which are widening every day would instantly cease after a Democratic nomination." Strongest support for this motion came from Wayne, Lenoir, and Greene counties, but the delegations from Craven, Edgecombe, Halifax, Northampton, and Warren were solidly opposed. By a vote of 88 to 47, the convention tabled the proposal. With the session's really important decision disposed of, the delegates nominated Kitchin by acclamation. As predicted, the nomination ended the open division in Republican ranks. "I have been

23. "Address of Hon. C. H. Brogden."
24. Kinston *Journal*, September 23, 1880; Goldsboro *Messenger*, September 30, 1880.

withdrawn as a candidate ever since the nomination of Hon. W. H. Kitchin," Brogden announced near the end of the campaign.[25]

Even if Kitchin had little chance of winning, his nomination—and his aggressive campaign oratory—might help bring out the full party vote. In the state gubernatorial contest between Republican Ralph P. Buxton and Democrat Thomas J. Jarvis every vote was important. Succeeding to the governorship when Zebulon B. Vance resigned to take a seat in the U.S. Senate, Jarvis had all the advantages and liabilities of incumbency. Buxton and other GOP candidates were denouncing the county government system, condemning Jarvis' support for the sale of the state interest in the Western North Carolina Railroad, and reminding voters of Democratic election fraud in Robeson County in the 1875 constitutional convention election. Democrats defended their party record, emphasizing their commitment to education and reminding Negro voters of the insane asylum and normal school provided for them by a Democratic legislature.[26]

Hubbs won easily on election day, but Kitchin polled 14,305 votes—more than 2,000 more than any previous Democratic congressional nominee in the "black second." Part of Kitchin's good showing was due to a dishonest election in Halifax County, his home. One of the Democrats running for the legislature "openly announced" a month before the election his intention to count the county for Democrats, saying "they had sent to South Carolina and learned how to do it." Official returns gave Kitchin 2,487 votes in Halifax—800 more than any Democrat had received before in a congressional election. Hubbs was given only 1,772 votes in a county that had given the Republican nominee over 3,000 votes in 1872, 1874, and 1876. Even in the disastrous 1878 campaign the two Republican nominees had a combined vote of over 2,000. The vote miscounters did not escape punishment, however. For the first time following such an incident a federal grand jury indicted seven Halifax election officials, two of whom were convicted and fined.[27]

25. Goldsboro *Messenger*, September 27, 1880; Kinston *Journal*, September 30, 1880; Goldsboro *Messenger*, October 28, 1880.

26. Kinston *Journal*, August 12, October 14, 1880.

27. William E. Clarke to James A. Garfield, December 2, 1880, in James A. Garfield Papers, microfilm copy in Library of Congress. Raleigh *News and Observer*, June 9, 1882; New York *Times*, June 17, 1881, June 10, 1882.

Hubbs did well in the rest of the district, failing to carry only the usually Democratic Wayne and Wilson, though even in Wilson he cut the Democratic margin to 198 votes. His district-wide majority was almost 5,000 despite the Halifax machinations. Kitchin's reputation for ruthless election tactics made him distasteful to some fastidious Democrats, such as the strong-minded Reverend William Closs, a leading Methodist clergyman from Edgecombe. Normally Closs was a staunch Democrat and had earlier gained fame for a mocking remark made as a witness in the court of Judge Samuel Watts, a native Republican. When Watts challenged him to define the word "scalawag," Closs had replied that a scalawag was a person who thought the Negro to be his equal and was right. Tarheel Democrats cherished this sally and it was repeated even outside the state. But in the 1880 election Closs made it clear that he was not a blind partisan. Replying to reports that he had voted the Republican ticket, he wrote a letter to his son which was published in the Toisnot *Sunny Home* shortly after the election. "I voted for no Republican but Mr. Hubbs," he said. "I did not vote for him because he is a Republican, but because he has the reputation of being an honest man and he never obtained a seat in Congress by fraud."[28]

In the state elections the Democrats were less effectively organized than in 1876, and Buxton came within 6,000 votes of defeating Jarvis. Many Republicans thought Buxton would have won, but for false counting of the votes.[29] At no time in the next fifteen years did the GOP come as close to capturing the governorship—at least as the votes were officially counted.

The two parties' legislative strength remained about the same. In the second district Republicans elected their house candidates in Craven, Edgecombe, Jones, Greene, Lenoir, Northampton, and Warren. One of Craven's representatives was a young black lawyer named George Henry White, soon to be a leading district politician. Republicans also did well in the state senate races. The Second Congressional District included

28. Kinston *Journal*, November 18, 1880. On the Watts incident, see Daniels, *Tar Heel Editor*, 129. It should be noted that Hubbs was a Methodist and Kitchin a militant Baptist.
29. For example, see W. E. Clarke to James Garfield, December 2, 1880, in Garfield Papers. Comments of W. A. Moore in Republican state convention, Raleigh *News and Observer*, June 15, 1882.

parts of nine senatorial districts; Republicans carried four of the five districts that were completely within the "black second." R. W. King won a third term as senator from Lenoir and Greene, the eleventh district, and the senator from the nineteenth district (Warren) was Hawkins W. Carter, a Negro who had already served three terms in the general assembly. Vote fraud cost Republicans Halifax County, where for the first time since the beginning of congressional Reconstruction returns showed that three Democrats (Senator Spier Whitaker, Representatives William H. Day and M. T. Savage) had been elected. Their Republican opponents contested the results before the general assembly, to no avail.[30]

Most local offices continued to be controlled by Republicans. In 1880 Republican sheriffs won in Craven, Jones, Lenoir, Edgecombe, and Northampton. James T. Dawson had virtually no opposition in Halifax.[31] Two black registers of deeds were elected, John C. Dancy in Edgecombe and Mansfield Thornton in Warren. Wilson voters elected an independent Democrat to a second term as sheriff, which was as close to political unorthodoxy as the county ever came. Greene was generally a Republican county, but a Democrat ousted the incumbent sheriff. Democratic sheriffs gained reelection in Wayne and Warren.

In the 1880 election, as in all others, the vast majority of Republican voters were Negroes, though probably more whites voted for GOP candidates than Democrats were usually willing to admit. In Trenton township, Jones County, for example, black and white registration was practically equal, the Negroes having an eight-voter edge in 1880. Yet Hubbs defeated Kitchin 148 to 89 and ran behind a popular Republican legislative candidate who received 166 votes. The editor of the Kinston *Journal* estimated on the basis of census returns that Lenoir had 145 more potential white voters than voting-age blacks. Hubbs carried Lenoir by nearly 300 votes, whereas Kitchin polled only 1,065 votes in in a county that had 1,546 white males eligible to vote. The *Journal* noted that "a good fair number of whites have gone republican," but added that "a respectable number of negroes have from the beginning

30. See N.C. General Assembly, Legislative Papers, 1881, reports of Jackson v. Whitaker, Davis v. Day.
31. See Halifax County Record of Elections, 1878–1896, in North Carolina Department of Archives and History, on Dawson's opposition. He defeated two candidates 2,942 votes to 131.

invariably voted the regular Democratic ticket, especially in Falling Creek township," and at least 100 white men never went to the polls at all because they were disgusted with politics. The local Republican candidates apparently had greater support from white voters than the candidates for state or national positions. The Republican candidate for sheriff led Hubbs by over 100 votes.[32]

Although Reconstruction had given way to "Redemption" and the South was supposedly solid for Democracy, Hubbs was not the only "carpet-bagger" to serve in the Forty-seventh Congress. He was joined by Horatio Bisbee of Florida, Chester B. Darrall of Louisiana, and Joseph Jorgensen of Virginia. Whatever his opponents might say about his origins, Hubbs worked to advance local interests, introducing unsuccessful bills for the erection of a marine hospital and a public building in New Bern, and the building of a lighthouse at Wilkinson's Point. He also attempted to increase the appropriation for improvement of the Trent River from five thousand to ten thousand dollars, also without success. Unlike his relatively loquacious predecessor, he said not a word on the floor of the House.[33]

With the election of Hubbs, second district politics seemed to be returning to normal after the aberration of Kitchin's term in the House. Democrats were firmly mired in the minority, unable to win except in the white counties or where they used fraud or made compromises. Republicans had recovered from the paralysis of 1878, though they continued to be divided by personal ambition and local interests. Blacks were gaining power as elected officials and in Republican party affairs.

But there was a strong feeling that blacks got less than a fair share of federal patronage. "Two colored clerks and a few route agents are all that represent the race in the postal department," complained A.M.E.Z. Bishop J. W. Hood in 1880. Apparently, he was unaware of Littleton Postmaster Winfield F. Young, a black who was appointed

32. Jones County Record of Elections, 1878–1908, in North Carolina Department of Archives and History; Kinston *Journal*, July 15, 1880; unpublished compilation of North Carolina election returns (Second Congressional District, 1880) in North Carolina Department of Archives and History; Lenoir County Record of Elections, 1880–1900, in North Carolina Department of Archives and History.

33. *Congressional Record*, 47th Cong., 1st Sess., 289, 564, 2nd Sess., 3447. Hubbs was a member of the Committee on Mines and Mining and the select Committee on Public Health. For private bills introduced by Hubbs, see 1st Sess., 216, 453, 732, 4532, 2nd Sess., 182, 738, 1197, 2104.

while John Hyman represented the second district. "Leave Newbern and Wilmington," continued Bishop Hood, "and you will have to hunt a long time to find a man in the revenue department."[34] Other blacks had jobs as laborers, watchmen, and clerks in Washington, D.C., but the major positions everywhere went to whites. Represented by a white northerner, the second district gave little indication that it would become a remarkable political stronghold for blacks.

34. *North Carolina Republican* quoted in Wilmington *Post*, April 11, 1880.

Chapter 5

A MAN NOT EASILY SUBDUED

A WELL ORGANIZED PROHIBITION MOVEMENT flooded the legislature of 1881 with petitions for an antiliquor law. Little suspecting the uproar that would follow, the legislature enacted a law prohibiting the manufacturing of all liquors except wine and hard cider and forbidding the sale of any type of liquor except by a specially licensed druggist or physician. The law would go into effect October 1, 1881, unless a majority of the voters in a special August referendum rejected it.[1]

The referendum cut across race and party lines and almost undid the political order so carefully constructed by Democratic "Redeemers." Both sides courted Negro votes and welcomed black orators to their rostrums. Men who had perhaps never before applauded a Negro speaker cheered the protemperance speeches of Joseph Charles Price, a youthful clergyman destined for national prominence in the next decade. On the opposite side, "wets" welcomed the aid of James O'Hara and other blacks.[2]

For O'Hara the prohibition election was the beginning of a political comeback. At the end of 1880 his public career had seemed in ruins, since during that year he had been prosecuted in the courts, stymied in his contested election case against Kitchin, and defeated in his bid for Congress. Still an effective speaker and a talented politician, however,

1. Daniel Jay Whitener, *Prohibition in North Carolina, 1715–1945* (Chapel Hill, N.C., 1945), 59–67. J. G. de Roulhac Hamilton, *North Carolina Since 1860*, Vol. III of *History of North Carolina* (6 vols.; Chicago, 1919), 207, is incorrect in stating that the referendum took place on October 1.
2. Daniels, *Tar Heel Editor*, 196. For a similar suspension of color-line politics, see John H. Moore, "The Negro and Prohibition in Atlanta, 1885–1887," *South Atlantic Quarterly*, LXIX (Winter, 1970), 38–57.

O'Hara's energetic part in the prohibition campaign gave him wide exposure and the opportunity to build new political strength.

O'Hara was the most active black delegate to the antiprohibition convention held in Raleigh, June 1, 1881. In a largely white group which included prominent men of both parties, O'Hara won a place on the resolutions committee and on the executive committee of the permanent organization that was formed. Making clear that he was not a whisky dealer, he spoke "at some length" in opposition to the prohibition law, charging that it would promote the ambitions of certain politicians, not temperance. The report of the committee on resolutions, which O'Hara presented, denounced the prohibition law as sumptuary legislation, unenforceable and subversive of liberty. It would create new taxes and generally do more harm than good.[3]

Against the wishes of many party members, Republican state chairman John J. Mott moved to align the party with the antiprohibition movement and to saddle the Democrats with responsibility for the law. His strategy was to use liquor as a political issue to build a coalition against incumbent Democrats, just as the state debt issue had been used by Republicans in Virginia since 1879. His actions displeased important Republican prohibitionists such as Thomas B. Keogh, former state chairman, former governor William W. Holden, future governor Daniel Russell, former treasurer David A. Jenkins, and Bishop J. W. Hood. Other Republicans opposed the bill but thought the prohibition election should be nonpartisan.[4]

The election placed a number of second district Republicans, including Congressman Hubbs, in a difficult position. A nondrinker himself, Hubbs supported curbing the liquor traffic, but he did not want to oppose an official action of the Republican state committee, which under Mott's leadership had condemned the prohibition measure. He found it convenient, therefore, to be out of the state—for health reasons—at the height of the campaign. His friend Robert E. Hancock, Jr., a white Republican of Craven, wrote to the Wilmington *Post* after the election to deny that Hubbs was hostile to the party's course on the issue.[5]

3. Raleigh *News and Observer*, June 2, 1881.
4. Whitener, *Prohibition*, 70–71; Raleigh *News and Observer*, June 10, 16, 26, 1881. See Greensboro *North State*, 1881, *passim*, for opposition to Mott.
5. Wilmington *Post*, September 11, 1881.

The election was an overwhelming defeat for prohibition, the "dry" forces carrying only three counties in the entire state.[6] If the coalition that won the election could be maintained and the momentum of the victory harnessed to other purposes, calculated Mott and his colleagues, the incumbent "Bourbon" Democrats would be defeated in 1882. As a member of the executive committee of the Anti-Prohibition Association and a leading opponent of prohibition, O'Hara was in a position to profit if this strategy were adopted.

O'Hara's prospects for 1882 were also enhanced by black Republicans' increasing dissatisfaction with their subordinate role in the party. The restiveness was statewide and was particularly focused on the unequal distribution of federal patronage. Just before the prohibition campaign began in earnest, a group of about seventy-five Negro leaders met in Raleigh to discuss their grievances. The meeting's import was well represented by O'Hara, who "thought the negro had been too long figuring with broom and spittoon" and "wanted a negro at the head of affairs—deputies were played out."[7]

The Negro protest was strongly encouraged by William P. Canaday, white editor of the Wilmington *Post*, and the delegates warmly praised him. A month before the black conclave he wrote that his advocacy of more colored appointments had been "very bitterly criticized by many of the leading white Republicans of the state." He estimated that 350 federal officials in North Carolina received $800 and up a year, but "not more than twenty of that number are colored." Negroes "have never drawn the color line," he asserted, sharing offices with white Republicans even in places where blacks had a large majority. As an example of black Republican faithfulness, he cited O'Hara's 1876 withdrawal from the slate of Republican presidential electors.[8]

6. Whitener, *Prohibition*, 73.

7. Raleigh *News and Observer*, May 18, 1881; Wilmington *Post*, May 29, 1881.

8. Wilmington *Post*, April 17, 1881. Canaday estimated that there were 120,000 Republicans in the state, "at least" 70,000 of whom were black. The Greensboro *North State*, representative of a different faction in the party, eventually endorsed the demand for more Negro officers, as did the Republican state committee. See Greensboro *North State*, June 30, 1881, July 13, 1882; New York *Times*, May 28, 1881. A second black convention, also encouraged by Canaday, met in March, 1882, to discuss the exclusion of Negroes from juries in many counties. A number of second district figures spoke, including E. R. Dudley, George White, Frank Dancy, and George Wassom, but the proceedings do not mention O'Hara. Wilmington *Post*, April 2, 1882.

Congressman Hubbs, however, was not one who refused to recognize black office seekers. For William A. Boyd, a black politician from Warren, he secured a position folding documents for the House, a job paying $720 a year. He helped get Osborne Hunter, Jr., a leader in the black North Carolina Industrial Association, a $1,200-a-year clerkship in the Department of the Interior. Another Hubbs patronage appointee was Richard C. Ward, a twenty-two-year-old Warren Negro who served as a laborer in the general office of the Post Office Department. In an editorial comment Canaday's *Post* described Hubbs as a Republican "who does not think that the color of a man's skin disqualifies him for office."[9] Still, the best places went to white Republicans. Hubbs used his influence to gain for his friend Robert Hancock, Jr., the position of superintendent of the document room, House of Representatives, with a salary of $2,000 per year. Walter P. Williamson, state senator from Edgecombe, earned yearly compensation of $1,600 as postmaster of Tarboro.[10]

O'Hara could have profited more directly from the general black dissatisfaction if Hubbs's record on Negro patronage had been worse. Yet O'Hara's campaign certainly gained strength from the widespread conviction that black Republicans ought to hold more important positions. It was only a small step from the demand for a fairer distribution of patronage to the notion that a district with a huge black majority should have a black representative.

Besides O'Hara and Hubbs, there was a third major congressional aspirant. The Goldsboro *Messenger* had "every reason to believe" that Colonel L. W. Humphrey, Wayne GOP convert, would be the "nominee of the republicans in this district," that is "unless he is again sold out by means of bribery and trickery, as was the case two years ago."[11] He had come within one vote of the nomination on each of his previous attempts, and this time—anxious to avenge the "trickery" of 1880—he did not intend to be denied.

Republican state leaders could only hope that the result in the second district would be clean and decisive. The party was moving toward

9. *Official Register, 1883,* I, 12; *Official Register, 1881,* I, 549; *Official Register, 1883,* I, 517. Ward later served three terms in the general assembly. For biographical details, see *Assembly Sketch Book, Session 1885, North Carolina* (Raleigh, 1885), 46. Wilmington *Post,* February 5, 1882.

10. *Official Register, 1883,* I, 12; II, 549.

11. Goldsboro *Messenger,* June 1, 1882.

an alliance with independent Democrats and another disputed convention would only play into the hands of the "Bourbons." It was already clear that large numbers of white men were willing to desert the Democratic banner. Seeking to inject the previous year's coalition into the 1882 campaign, the executive committee of the state Anti-Prohibition Association met in Raleigh on May 2 and passed a resolution (offered by O'Hara, the only black member) calling for a mass convention of the "liberal, independent voters of the State, without regard to former political affiliations" to meet in the state capital in one month. The purpose of the convention, according to an address issued to the people of North Carolina, was to adopt principles and candidates "opposed to the party organization which forced" prohibition upon the state. The liberal movement aimed to restore "local self-government," extend public education, purify the ballot box, and "forever" settle the issue of prohibition. William Johnston of Charlotte, a Democrat who had been the "original secessionist" candidate for governor against Vance in 1862, replaced Republican Thomas N. Cooper as chairman of the organization.[12]

When the Liberal convention met, O'Hara took such a large role that the Raleigh *News and Observer* ridiculed the session as the "Mott-O'Hara convention" and declared him "the best speaker" in the convention. "Beside him the converts, or new issue Republicans, who spoke, cut but a poor figure." As in the 1881 antiprohibition convention, O'Hara was a member of the committee on resolutions and the state executive committee. The Liberals called for the repeal of indirect county government, repeal of the inoperative prohibition act, and application of liquor taxes to education—a platform that facilitated collaboration with the Republicans. They nominated former congressman Oliver H. Dockery, a Republican, for congressman-at-large, and George N. Folk, an independent Democrat, for associate justice of the supreme court. At least four fifths of the delegates were white men.[13]

Within a week two other important conventions met. On June 12 the Republican convention for the Second Judicial District renominated district solicitor John H. Collins over two rivals, George H. White of Craven and Walter P. Williamson of Edgecombe. The convention also

12. Raleigh *News and Observer*, May 3, 1882.
13. Raleigh *News and Observer*, June 14, 8, 1882; Raleigh *State Journal* quoted in Wilmington *Post*, June 18, 1882.

ruled on an important matter that affected the congressional race. The legislature of 1881 had changed the house representation for a number of counties, including Northampton, Craven, and Warren in the second district. Craven and Warren had been reduced from two representatives each to just one apiece, whereas Northampton had been increased from one to two house members. Since the size of a county's convention delegation depended upon legislative apportionment, there was an argument over whether the new or old apportionment should be followed. The judicial convention decided to use the new representation, giving Northampton 4 votes and Craven 2.[14] (There was good reason to maintain the old representation for Warren, because part of the new county of Vance—created from Granville, Franklin, and Warren—still voted with Warren on judicial matters.) This policy hurt George White in the judicial convention and would weaken Hubbs if followed in the congressional convention.

Two days later North Carolina Republicans convened in Raleigh to write a platform and choose candidates. Although there were lingering divisions over Mott's handling of the prohibition election, most Republicans were ready to try coalition with the independents, a tactic that had been successful in neighboring Virginia. More in evidence than either of his main rivals, James O'Hara predicted victory for the coalition if the votes were honestly counted. His growing importance in the state was shown by a convention resolution thanking Mott, O'Hara, and two other leaders for their work in arranging coalition.

Craven County provoked a long debate when it claimed to be entitled to 4 votes instead of the 2 it was assigned. After many speeches on both sides—for the decision would affect other counties whose legislative representation had been changed—Mott said he believed current legislative representation should be the basis for convention votes, not new representation. The delegates then voted 134–56 against the convention chairman's ruling that Craven had only 2 votes. But making current representation the rule created other problems, for with this criterion new counties such as Vance and Durham would have no delegates, since of course they were not represented in the legislature of 1881. After "heated discussion" the two new counties were allowed 2 votes each. Perhaps

14. Tarboro *Southerner,* June 15, 1882.

with the consequences for the second district convention in mind, O'Hara denounced this inconsistent action in "an exceptionally hot speech," declaring that the convention's decision had denied Northampton its rightful number of delegates. Standing in front of Dr. Mott, a revenue collector, he excitedly assailed the "revenue wing" or "government wing" of the party.

The convention nominated Dockery and Folk and passed resolutions similar to those endorsed by the Liberals. Hubbs moved to add an endorsement of President Arthur, and delegates from each congressional district then chose a man for the executive committee and three members were elected at large. After the second district selected a white federal employee for its representative, O'Hara complained that the "revenue wing" of the fourth district (meaning, perhaps, revenue collector I. J. Young) had interfered with the second district. Only two of the eleven members of the executive committee were Negroes and almost all were federal officeholders.[15]

For all O'Hara's activity in the coalition movement, he still trailed his rivals in the quest for the congressional nomination. As the second district convention approached, Orlando Hubbs was the front runner, with endorsements from county conventions in Craven, Warren, Lenoir, and Jones. Humphrey's support came from Wayne and Greene, O'Hara was favored in Northampton and Halifax, and Wilson endorsed George W. Stanton. Edgecombe's delegates were apparently uninstructed. Depending on the number of votes allotted to Northampton and Craven, Hubbs had 10 to 12 votes, Humphrey 6, and O'Hara 6 to 8. "Neither of the three can command enough votes on the first ballot and a hot contest may be looked for," predicted the Goldsboro *Messenger* on the eve of the convention.[16]

Since 1874 each Republican district convention had been held in Goldsboro, but the 1882 meeting convened in Wilson, perhaps to deny Humphrey any advantage that might result from holding the conven-

15. Raleigh *News and Observer*, June 15, September 3, 1882; Wilmington *Post*, June 18, 1882. I. J. Young, J. S. Leary, T. N. Cooper, and J. B. Eaves were all associated with the Internal Revenue Department. W. P. Canaday was customs collector for Wilmington, Palemon John was a customs inspector, and Willis Bagley was an assistant U.S. district attorney. See *Official Register, 1881, 1883*.

16. Weldon *News* quoted in New Bern *Weekly Journal*, June 22, 1882; Raleigh *News and Observer*, June 6, 1882; Goldsboro *Messenger*, July 17, 1882.

tion in his home county. District chairman Frank Dancy called the convention to order at noon July 19 and as the first order of business appointed a strongly pro-Hubbs credentials committee, at least two members of which were indebted to Hubbs for federal patronage. On the vexing question of representation from Craven and Northampton, a majority of the committee recommended that each be allowed 4 votes. Debate on the majority report took up the rest of the day. Defenders of 4 votes for Craven read a telegram from John Mott, while opponents of the credentials report complained of rings and "revenue men." In the end the majority report was adopted by a vote of 17–15.[17]

The next day a full house gathered to watch the convention; a number of Democrats also came to town, perhaps hoping for a "radical row." (On the first day O'Hara had appealed to the delegates to behave in an orderly way, so that the press could not truthfully call the convention a "pandemonium.") By a vote of 17–15 the Hubbs faction succeeded in electing as permanent chairman Llewellen G. Estes, a Union veteran and postmaster, over Humphrey supporter Hiram L. Grant, also a postmaster and Union veteran. The convention proceeded to consider five men for the congressional candidate: Hubbs, O'Hara, Humphrey, Stanton, and I. B. Abbott. Edward R. Dudley, a deputy collector of internal revenue from Craven, pointed out that Hubbs was not present to defend his interests; instead, he was in Washington insuring that a quorum was present for the vote on South Carolina Negro Robert Smalls's election case. Another Hubbs supporter read a telegram from Smalls praising Hubbs. John H. Hannon, a black delegate from Halifax, nominated O'Hara, declaring that the candidate from the second district ought to be a Negro. A white observer reported: "The negroes were aroused to a sense of the imposition too long practiced upon them and they were now determined to have their rights." O'Hara attempted to calm the crowd, showing by "the influence which he wielded over this turbulent mass that he was the ruling spirit of the convention," according to Josephus Daniels' Wilson *Advance*.[18]

At this point, before the voting began, Colonel Humphrey judged that

17. Tarboro *Southerner*, July 27, 1882; Wilmington *Post*, July 23, 1882; Wilson *Advance*, July 21, 1882. Under a new plan of organization the total number of votes changed from 15 to 30. Obviously the delegates from Craven were allowed to vote on their own case.

18. Wilson *Advance*, July 21, 1882; Wilmington *Post*, July 23, 1882.

he could not win and decided to withdraw. Climbing up on a table, Wayne alternate George T. Wassom (O'Hara's brother-in-law) withdrew Humphrey's name and told the convention that the combination of O'Hara's 8 votes from Halifax and Northampton with Humphrey's 9 votes from Wayne, Greene, and Edgecombe produced an absolute majority of 17 for O'Hara. Wassom therefore moved the nomination of James E. O'Hara by acclamation, putting his motion to the delegates (and the audience), who roared their approval. "The audience was almost a unit for O'Hara and they joined in the vote. The noes were very faint," said the Tarboro *Southerner*. Stating that he saw evidence of a "disposition to carry out a preconcerted plan by mob force," chairman Estes boldly declared Hubbs the "nominee" and adjourned the convention. For his part, O'Hara made a speech accepting the "nomination" and vowing to stay in the race to the end.[19]

After the convention broke up in confusion, the O'Hara forces issued a statement signed by eighteen delegates declaring that they "did endorse and ratify" the nomination of O'Hara, though the signers did not claim to have actually voted for him in the convention. All the delegates from Greene, Northampton, Wayne, and Halifax, as well as three from Edgecombe and one from Wilson signed the statement; no one from Craven, Jones, Lenoir, or Warren endorsed it. The Hubbs faction produced a declaration from chairman Estes and sixteen other delegates affirming "that it was our intention to have voted for the Honorable ORLANDO HUBBS . . . and that we would have voted for him on the first ballot; and we do hereby declare the Honorable ORLANDO HUBBS the regular nominee of the Republican party."[20]

To further complicate matters, the names of three Northampton delegates, all black, appeared on both statements. Claiborne Faison, John W. Pope, and S. G. Newsom explained this discrepancy by asserting that they had signed the O'Hara statement under "intimidation of mob violence," and about a month after the convention the three issued a repudiation of their earlier support of O'Hara's claim.[21] If Faison, Pope, and Newsom intended to vote for Hubbs, they were ignoring the wishes of the convention that had elected them. The Northampton

19. New Bern *Daily Journal*, July 21, 1882; Tarboro *Southerner*, July 27, 1882; Wilmington *Post*, July 23, 1882.
20. New Bern *Weekly Journal*, July 27, August 3, 1882.
21. New Bern *Daily Journal*, August 31, 1882.

convention (of which Pope was chairman) had endorsed O'Hara with a resolution declaring that it was right that the "sun-scorched citizens of Ham" in the second district "be once represented in Congress by a Representative of their own color." A later Northampton convention, meeting shortly after the district convention to nominate a county ticket, again endorsed O'Hara.[22] When sentiment in their county was so strong for O'Hara, why did the three delegates support the white incumbent?

Rumors circulating after the convention suggest one possibility. The Tarboro *Southerner* reported: "Hubbs' friends, it is asserted, spent at least five thousand dollars. . . . The anti-Hubbs' men from this county say that Hubbs was backed by the entire Revenue Department in the State." According to a Goldsboro report, the Hubbs men were willing to pay a thousand to fifteen hundred dollars per delegate, "which completely baffled the friends of Col. Humphrey." "The Humphrey faction charged that money and the promise of Federal patronage was used against them, and that one of Col. Humphrey's strongest supporters went back on him under tempting inducements." Could "tempting inducements" also have been behind the strange behavior of the three supposed O'Hara men?[23]

It is probable that Humphrey and O'Hara had planned to cooperate on the representation issue and in the election of convention officers. Both men had an interest in cutting Craven's votes and keeping the chairmanship out of the control of the front runner. But Hubbs's friends (for Hubbs himself was absent) managed to secure help from several delegates on whom the anti-Hubbs forces had relied, including the Northampton three. District chairman Dancy also used his influence on Hubbs's behalf. When the convention awarded 4 votes to Craven and the Hubbs faction successfully organized the convention, the Humphrey-O'Hara managers realized that they had been outmaneuvered. To counteract the lubricant of lucre they saw at work in the defection of key delegates, they joined forces and invoked O'Hara's popular strength by Wassom's acclamation gambit—a sort of stentorian remedy to a rigged

22. Wilmington *Post*, June 11, 1882; Weldon *News* quoted in Raleigh *News and Observer*, August 5, 1882.
23. Tarboro *Southerner*, July 27, 1882; Goldsboro *Messenger*, July 24, 1882. For an accusation of bribery against Humphrey, see Warrenton *Gazette*, July 28, 1882.

convention. Such an explanation is plausible, at least, though the evidence is incomplete.

In the confusing aftermath of the convention, Faison, Newsom, and Pope made the mistake of signing both candidates' victory claims. Perhaps they did not care to announce their intended vote for Hubbs to the pro-O'Hara crowd, but at any rate, their error limited their usefulness to Hubbs. "We are informed that one of the Northampton delegates to the Republican Congressional convention received a draft for $600 for his vote," said the Weldon *News* a few days after the convention, "and went to headquarters to get his money, but failed to get it. It is said another delegate received a draft for $500, payment of which was afterward refused."[24] Again there is little evidence, but it would be understandable if the bribers felt relieved of their obligations by the delegates' erratic course—at least until a clarifying statement was issued.

The relationship between the second district feud and the state issues was curious and grew even more curious. John Mott's plan to parlay antiprohibition sentiment into a victory over the "Bourbons" brought resistance from a minority who had sympathized with prohibition or did not relish cooperating with old Democratic enemies. The Greensboro *North State*, a Republican newspaper critical of Mott, welcomed the nomination of O'Hara, "a man of pluck, ability and extensive experience." According to the editor: "The second district is the first ground where the Republicans have taken a stand against the would-be masters of the party—the revenue ring." The Goldsboro *Messenger* also saw the second district conflict as a battle involving "Mott's whole 'infernal revenue crew.'" Mott supported Hubbs in order to weaken the influence of Colonel Humphrey, who was opposed to the coalition movement.[25] No one seemed to notice the incongruity of Mott the antiprohibitionist favoring Hubbs the teetotaler or Humphrey the anti-Liberal supporting O'Hara the coalitionist.

O'Hara's color was one of the sources of his strength. Since the formation of the district, many Negroes had thought the "black second" deserved a black representative. Hannon's nomination speech for O'Hara appealed to this sentiment, just as Hubbs's defenders and the telegram from Smalls attempted to counteract it. No doubt many black Republi-

24. Weldon *News* quoted in Raleigh *News and Observer*, August 5, 1882.
25. Greensboro *North State*, August 3, 1882; Goldsboro *Messenger*, July 24, 1882.

cans found it frustrating that the district had not elected a Negro to Congress since 1874. But it would be misleading to describe the struggle as a simple conflict between white and black Republicans—as the New York *Times* did when it reported that "the colored men, or a few of them, have been inspired to rebel by one O'Hara."[26] Such an explanation ignores the white Republicans who worked with O'Hara, as well as the many black leaders who supported Hubbs. O'Hara's postconvention statement included the signatures of Hiram L. Grant and John T. Sharpe, both active, well-known white "radicals." And Leonidas J. Moore, a white attorney from Craven, took the stump in O'Hara's behalf. Most important of all, Humphrey threw his influence behind O'Hara after his own hopes were disappointed. There were also reports that Governor Brogden, at this point sorely displeased with state party leadership and policy, contributed eighteen hundred dollars to the anti-Hubbs campaign.[27]

But black leaders in Warren, Craven, and Lenoir strongly opposed O'Hara. A few days after the Wilson convention, a meeting of Warren Republicans endorsed Hubbs, insisting that if the O'Hara and Humphrey supporters had allowed a fair ballot the incumbent would have been nominated. Among the Negroes who spoke in favor of Hubbs were George H. King, state legislator, former congressman John Hyman, and Jacob H. Montgomery, candidate for the legislature. In Lenoir County two successful black businessmen and politicians, Wiley Lowery and Lewis H. Fisher, favored Hubbs, as the county's delegates had done in the convention. E. R. Dudley of Craven was an active campaigner for Hubbs, and James City, a black town across the river from New Bern, was said to be "solid" for the former sheriff.[28]

Yet if there was no clear racial division among Republican voters, 1882 was a turning point for black officeholding. For O'Hara personally,

26. New York *Times,* August 11, 1882.
27. Tarboro *Southerner,* July 27, 1882; New Bern *Nut Shell* quoted in Goldsboro *Messenger,* August 17, 1882; New Bern *Daily Journal,* September 15, 1882; Charlotte *Journal* quoted in New Bern *Daily Journal,* October 22, 1882; Goldsboro *Messenger,* September 4, 1884. See Goldsboro *Messenger,* July 17, 1882, for a communication from Brogden (published under the pseudonym "Justice") critical of the GOP. See also October 19, 1882, for his opposition to coalition.
28. Wilmington *Post,* August 6, 1882; New Bern *Weekly Journal,* August 10, 1882; Goldsboro *Messenger,* August 17, 1882; New Bern *Daily Journal,* October 5, 1882.

another defeat might finish his hopes of going to Congress, and this knowledge gave him determination to overcome his rival. "We are of the opinion that O'Hara is not a man easily subdued," observed the New Bern *Nut Shell*. A man of "talent and irrepressible energy," he was doubtless planning an unrelenting battle, and the *Nut Shell* predicted that the present campaign would "fix his destiny one way or another."[29] For the second district, the victory of a Negro candidate in 1882 might enable future black representatives to be elected more easily. If O'Hara lost, the district could become like other southern, black, Republican districts that almost never nominated Negroes—the second and fourth districts in Virginia, for example.

Other blacks were also pursuing important offices in the counties of the Second Congressional District. John H. Collins was seeking a second term as solicitor of the Second Judicial District, and George T. Wassom hoped to win the solicitorship in the third district. Collins, Wassom, and O'Hara represented a challenge to the cohesion of the GOP and to the plan for coalition with Liberals. E. E. Smith's Goldsboro *Enterprise*, one of the largest black newspapers in the state, warned Liberals that they must support the black triumvirate if they expected to receive Negro votes themselves. The *Enterprise* also reminded white Republicans that they owed their victories to Negroes. As for colored voters, those who valued liberty and appreciated "true manhood" would stand by the three candidates.[30]

On August 24, about a month after the controverted district convention, chairman Estes reconvened the convention in Wilson. This time everything went Hubbs's way. Only twenty-two delegates attended and Halifax and Greene were not represented at all, but the Hubbs faction claimed strengthened legitimacy in the unanimous endorsement of the session. Perhaps in an effort to appeal to as many voters as possible, Hubbs praised both the coalition movement and Senator Ransom—despite the coalition's goal of capturing the legislature and electing a new senator in 1883.[31]

The Republican split presented opportunities as well as dilemmas to the Democrats. Was it possible that the Republican disarray would enable

29. New Bern *Nut Shell* quoted in Goldsboro *Messenger*, August 17, 1882.
30. Goldsboro *Messenger*, August 7, 1882.
31. Wilson *Advance*, August 25, 1882.

a Democrat to win a seat in Congress? The editor of the New Bern *Journal* thought so and urged that a candidate be chosen, but obviously ruled out the last nominee: "No 'counting in' politician should be tolerated. The party that follows or condones that practice ought to be defeated."[32] "There is no chance of electing a congressman from this district," said the Tarboro *Southerner* in rebuttal, and the party should refrain from making a nomination. The editor of the *Southerner* insisted that his opposition was not based on a desire for "trading" with the enemy for votes, but on a belief that "nothing but good can result" from Republican factional fights. If allowed to continue, the battles within the Republican party were likely to break down black political solidarity, but if the Democrats made a nomination the strife would cease.[33]

Other Democrats advanced similar arguments. "Dont [sic] let the Democratic Ex. Com. for the 2nd Cong District bring out a candidate," wrote Fred Philips of Edgecombe to Secretary of State William L. Saunders. Philips, Democratic candidate for superior court judge, explained: "Hubbs and O'Hara have gotten things into a great mess, and it . . . looks right here as if we might have two republican tickets out in Edgecombe—At any rate wisdom dictates prudence in bringing out candidates in the negro counties when such disaffection exists." When the district executive committee called a convention though recommending that no nomination be made, the Goldsboro *Messenger* commented: "The party has much to gain by keeping up the O'Hara and Hubbs feud."[34]

What did Democrats stand to gain from the Republican fight, if there was no chance to elect a congressman? Proponents of a nomination had little doubt that dubious schemes were afoot. "We dislike very much to see Democrats 'trading' and 'hunnyfugling' with Republicans, which will certainly be done should we fail to make a nomination," said the Wilson *Siftings*. The accusation was repeated after the district convention resolved that a nomination would be "inexpedient and injudicious" and

32. New Bern *Daily Journal*, August 25, 1882. The *Journal* had a different attitude toward the legislative race in Jones County: "If the Democrats nominate a man it will solidify the Republicans and why not let them fight it out among themselves?" September 15, 1882.
33. Tarboro *Southerner*, September 21, 1882.
34. Fred Philips to William L. Saunders, August 29, 1882, in William L. Saunders Papers, North Carolina Department of Archives and History. Goldsboro *Messenger*, October 2, 1882.

requested Democratic voters not to support any unofficial "volunteer candidates." The New Bern *Journal* interpreted the action to mean that Democrats should vote for one or the other of the Republican candidates. "The 'traders' in Halifax, Northampton, Edgecombe and Wayne will carry out the plan arranged several weeks ago," charged the newspaper.[35]

Trading was in fact the main reason for Democrats to encourage the Republican feud. A week after the Democratic convention Hubbs issued a letter to the voters of the district announcing his decision to withdraw from the race. "It is obvious," he said, "that our Democratic friends intend to make the heated contest for Congress in this district a means of trading off our State and Legislative tickets." Also Hubbs had heard that the Democrats intended as well to surprise the Republicans with a last-minute congressional candidate. The Liberal-Republican combination hoped to elect a congressman-at-large, an associate justice of the supreme court, a slate of superior court judges, and a majority of the legislature, but this would be impossible, in Hubbs's opinion, if disunity prevailed in the second district. Since O'Hara clearly meant to stay in the field, Hubbs felt he had no choice but to withdraw for the good of the party— even though he was the "fairly nominated" choice of the district. Apologizing to loyal supporters for his retreat, Hubbs said that "nothing but a firm belief that a continued struggle will give the district and State to the enemy would cause my withdrawal."[36]

One Democratic newspaper reacted to Hubbs's withdrawal by predicting that the party's majority in the state would be "several thousand less than it would have been if he and O'Hara had both remained in the field"—directly implying that the trading charges were accurate. The Republican Wilmington *Post* was jubilant at the restoration of unity in the second district. By stating that victory in the state was now insured, the *Post* showed that it also assumed that trading had been planned.[37]

The tide had been running against Hubbs for a month or more. When Halifax Republicans met August 26 to select local and legislative tickets, the secretary of the state executive committee, J. C. L. Harris, was present and spoke "in high terms" of O'Hara, promising that the com-

35. Wilson *Siftings* quoted in New Bern *Daily Journal*, September 29, 1882; New Bern *Weekly Journal*, October 12, 1882.

36. Goldsboro *Messenger*, October 23, 1882.

37. Charlotte *Journal* quoted in New Bern *Daily Journal*, October 22, 1882; Wilmington *Post*, October 22, 1882.

mittee would "recognize Mr. O'Hara as the regular Republican candidate." Almost a month before the event, the Greensboro *Patriot*, a Democratic paper, was predicting that Hubbs would quit the campaign. By mid-October "it was tolerably apparent that O'Hara would beat him," according to the Raleigh *News and Observer*. About the same time, a correspondent from La Grange, Lenoir County, wrote the New Bern *Journal* that O'Hara's support was increasing among black voters who had been "solid" for Hubbs until recently. (Only a few weeks before, former state senator Henry Eppes had been shouted down in La Grange when he attempted to make an O'Hara speech.)[38]

Hubbs may have been promised a patronage post as a consolation prize. After the election he sought appointment as the United States marshal for the eastern district of North Carolina. John Mott wrote to William E. Chandler, the member of President Arthur's cabinet most interested in the affairs of southern Republicans, asking him to aid "our mutual friend Mr. Hubbs." Mott's attitude toward the second district fight apparently differed from the majority of the state committee, for he said Hubbs "was no doubt the choice and nominee of the Convention in his Congressional District," but he had stepped down to help the general ticket, a "magnanimous" sacrifice that deserved reward. According to Mott, "we said at the time Mr. Hubbs was entitled to the gratitude of the party and any favor it could bestow on him in the state." Hubbs spoke to President Arthur about the matter, but O'Hara supported the incumbent, who was retained.[39]

The battle between Hubbs and O'Hara, it should be mentioned, revived several old accusations. O'Hara, like Brogden two years before, criticized Hubbs as a supporter of a high protective tariff and author of the debacle of 1878. He also accused his opponent of not giving offices to Negroes and remaining silent during the prohibition campaign. In an era familiar with bosses and rings, real and imaginary, politicians were wont to brand their opponents the puppets of sinister managers. O'Hara

38. Wilmington *Post*, September 10, 1882; Greensboro *Patriot* quoted in Raleigh *News and Observer*, September 21, 1882; Raleigh *News and Observer*, October 12, 1882; New Bern *Weekly Journal*, October 19, 1882; New Bern *Daily Journal*, October 4, 1882.

39. John J. Mott to William E. Chandler, December 12, 1882, in William E. Chandler Papers, Library of Congress. J. B. Hill to M. W. Ransom, January 30, 1883, in Ransom Papers.

claimed Hubbs was the creation of Estes, whereas Hubbs said O'Hara was Humphrey's tool. The squabbling candidates also reminded voters of O'Hara's alleged bigamy and Hubbs's supposed dishonesty in relation to Tim Lee's official bond.[40]

Following the vicissitudes of the campaign, the election itself was anticlimactic with O'Hara unopposed and certain to win. Neither factionalism nor fraud could deny him victory this time. The denouement to the Republican feud did not displease all Democrats. "While we are opposed to O'Hara and think him unfit for the position," said the Tarboro *Southerner*, "candor compels us to say that he will make a better representative than his immediate predecessor."[41] Even with no opposition O'Hara garnered over 18,000 votes. Halifax resoundingly rejected the vote frauds of 1878 and 1880 by giving its adopted citizen 4,340 votes; the federal verdicts rendered in June in the Halifax cases of 1880 had perhaps deterred the county's election-rigging veterans. (W. H. Day, one of the dubious Democratic victors in 1880, had joined the Liberals, partly in anger over Governor Jarvis' refusal to help the indicted election officials or accept responsibility for their crimes.)[42] Craven County gave O'Hara only 1,138 votes, far less than half the number Hubbs received in 1880. A scattering of about 1,200 votes went to other candidates in the district.

In the state election the Republican-Liberal coalition lost by a narrow margin. The coalition candidate for congressman-at-large, Dockery, came within 400 votes of defeating the Democratic nominee, Risden T. Bennett. A Republican won the U.S. House seat in the first district, and Tyre York, a Liberal, was elected from the seventh district. Opposition strength in the general assembly increased to sixty-eight members. Altogether it was the strongest challenge to the Democratic party in a decade.[43]

Republicans continued to dominate county and legislative positions in

40. New Bern *Weekly Journal*, August 3, 1882; Tarboro *Southerner*, August 31, 1882; Goldsboro *Messenger*, September 25, 1882.
41. Tarboro *Southerner*, October 19, 1882.
42. Daniels, *Tar Heel Editor*, 186; Wilmington *Post*, June 18, 25, 1882. On the 1880 Halifax frauds, see Chapter 4 herein, p. 91.
43. Vincent P. De Santis is inaccurate when he asserts that North Carolina Republicans lost ground to the Independents (Liberals) in this election. He does not note that the Liberal candidate for congressman-at-large was a Republican. The statement that the Republicans failed to win a single black-belt county in North Carolina is inconsistent with O'Hara's victory and the legislative returns. Vincent

the second district. In Wayne a Republican ousted the incumbent register of deeds and an independent Democrat and a Republican defeated the regular Democratic candidates for the state house. The Goldsboro *Messenger* attributed the defeat to antiprohibition sentiment and continuing Democratic divisions over the liquor issue. Democratic voters on either side of the issue "scratched" candidates not to their liking.[44] Greene's Democratic sheriff lost his place by 4 votes. The Republican candidates for clerk, sheriff, treasurer, coroner, and surveyor ran virtually unopposed in Halifax, and John H. Hannon, the candidate for register, overwhelmed his Democratic rival, 4,330 to 1,653. Despite the usual Republican divisions in Edgecombe, John C. Dancy was reelected without opposition to the office of register of deeds. Mansfield Thornton, black register in Warren, faced a serious challenge from former sheriff Nathaniel R. Jones, but he won with a majority of nearly 500 votes. The most interesting electoral battle in Craven was between two Republican factions, one led by Sheriff Mayer Hahn, the other by Daniel Stimson, a wealthy white Republican. Hahn won, but the split in the party was not healed. The Republican ticket swept the major offices in Lenoir, although the Democrats captured the county's house seat. Craven, Edgecombe, Greene, Halifax, and Warren sent straight Republican delegations to Raleigh. When the contested election case from Northampton was resolved, it too had purely Republican representation.[45]

O'Hara's victory was the beginning of a brief period of calm in the "black second." For four years he would represent the people of his district in two Democratic Congresses, building a legislative record of vigor and skill. An outsider and a Roman Catholic, this articulate, olive-skinned lawyer was in many ways untypical of his district, yet his career was a symbol to both black and white of the future of Negro participation in politics. He had overcome repeated frustrations—resigning from the electoral ticket in 1876, losing an election by fraud in 1878, facing a malfeasance trial in 1880—before rising to prominence as a leader in the antiprohibition and Liberal movements. Wresting the nomination from a determined incumbent, he was truly a man "not easily subdued."

P. De Santis, *Republicans Face the Southern Question: The New Departure Years, 1887–1897* (Baltimore, 1959), 180–81.

44. Goldsboro *Messenger,* November 20, 1882.

45. See N.C. General Assembly, Legislative Papers, 1883, Parker v. Peebles (House).

Chapter 6

BUSINESS ALL THE TIME

IN THE SPRING OF 1883, as Orlando Hubbs retired to the cultivation of a "model farm" near New Bern, James O'Hara visited Washington in preparation for his service in the Forty-eighth Congress. A letter signed "Veritas" in the Washington *Bee*, a black newspaper in the capital, rejoiced that with the end of the Forty-seventh Congress "the last brace of colored congressmen belonging to the older class of negroes will retire." (The writer was referring to John R. Lynch of Mississippi and Robert Smalls of South Carolina.) Men of this class had "sat only as figure-heads, merely demonstrating that the negro has a right to be an M. C.," contributing little to the legislative process and failing to get good patronage appointments for their black constituents. The one colored man in the Forty-eighth Congress, O'Hara, was "an able man" who belonged to the "younger class of colored men," and "Veritas" predicted a brilliant future for him. A few months later the editor of the *Bee* noted that O'Hara was "business all the time" and suggested that he would "do more than a half dozen of the others we have had put together."[1]

The congressman-elect's visit to Washington may have been related to several accounts he had to settle in the second district. L. G. Estes—Hubbs's creator according to O'Hara's campaign charge—was replaced as Enfield postmaster in March, 1883. In Lenoir County, O'Hara rewarded white Republican William A. Coleman, a former mayor of Kinston who had supported him in the battle with Hubbs, by having him appointed postmaster of the town. O'Hara recognized the services of John T. Sharpe by securing the Wilson post office for his wife Virginia, replac-

1. Wilmington *Post*, April 1, March 18, 1883; Washington (D.C.) *Bee*, February 17, July 21, 1883. Veritas called O'Hara "Mr. O'Hand."

114

ing Mary C. Daniels. Josephus Daniels thought his mother was being punished for *his* fiercely partisan editorials. O'Hara's brother-in-law George T. Wassom received a place in the Railway Mail Service.[2] O'Hara also prevailed upon internal revenue officer Isaac J. Young to fire Edward R. Dudley, an energetic black campaigner for Hubbs. Dudley had been a deputy collector since Hyman's tenure in Congress and was furious, protesting to Young in a long, angry letter and calling O'Hara a "man of notorious record."[3]

The Democratic legislature, perhaps unwittingly, also helped O'Hara consolidate his hold on the district. In redrawing congressional district lines in 1883, the general assembly moved Wayne County into the third district and added Bertie and Vance to the second. Whatever the intention—and there was no need for politicians to discuss publicly such subjects—the effect was to increase the "blackness" of the "black second," for Wayne had a white majority, whereas Vance (recently formed from parts of Granville, Franklin, and Warren) and Bertie had strong black majorities. The removal of Wayne relieved O'Hara of a troublesome group of politicians, including Governor Brogden and the ever-ambitious Colonel Humphrey. They had supported him in the last election, it is true, but they might take a different course in the next campaign. If Humphrey had calculated on reaping favors from his aid to O'Hara, the new boundaries sharply limited any obligation. The legislators were probably moved by other considerations, such as the need to make the close first district "safer" by removing Bertie, and perhaps the desire of Wayne Democrats to be delivered from the black district.[4]

When the first session of the Forty-eighth Congress convened in December, 1883, O'Hara had little time for legislative accomplishments before the opening of the 1884 campaign. He reacted to the recent Supreme Court decision which largely nullified the Civil Rights Act of 1875 by introducing a resolution calling for a constitutional amendment

2. See Record of Appointments of Postmasters, Vol. 49, RG 28, NA; George E. Miller to M. W. Ransom, May 19, 1885, Henry G. Connor to M. W. Ransom, December 30, 1882, both in Ransom Papers. Daniels, *Tar Heel Editor*, 208; *Official Register, 1883*, II, 363.

3. Clipping from *Western Sentinel*, November 8, 1883, in Charles N. Hunter Scrapbooks, Charles N. Hunter Papers, Duke University. See also Raleigh *State Chronicle*, November 3, 1883.

4. See Wilmington *Post*, November 2, 1883, on Bertie and the first district.

on civil rights.[5] He introduced a measure to reimburse depositors in the defunct Freedman's Savings and Trust Company, presented the familiar measure to build a public building at New Bern, and, like John Hyman, proposed government aid for North Carolina Cherokees.[6] He sponsored thirteen private bills for relief, claims, or pensions, two of which passed the House during the first session.[7] Despite his campaign comments on Hubbs's predilection for a high tariff, he voted with most Republicans to kill a tariff reduction bill. When he voted with the majority (rather than with the "bitter extremists") to abolish test oaths for House members the Democratic Goldsboro *Messenger* decreed: "James E. O'Hara shall receive his meed of praise."[8]

O'Hara was at the zenith of his power in 1884. A member of the executive committee of the Republican congressional committee, one of ten vice-presidents of the National Union League, and a leader in party affairs in North Carolina, he had no serious opposition in his home district.[9] The district convention, meeting earlier than usual in 1884, was a dull affair compared to previous years. The choice of Halifax as site of the meeting was just one indication of O'Hara's complete control, and when delegates arrived on April 29 they found a banner stretched across the street by the courthouse: "For Congress, Hon. James E. O'Hara—The Peoples' Choice." About three hundred people attended the proceedings, including a number of Democratic "interested spectators." I. B. Abbott, who had been thought to be a candidate himself, was elected chairman and as he took the chair expressed the expectation that O'Hara would be nominated. No rival candidates were suggested and the delegates nominated O'Hara by acclamation. "O'Hara was loudly and persistently called for, and upon taking the stand, completely broke down and was unable to utter but one word—'thanks.'" After choosing a presidential

5. *Congressional Record*, 48th Cong., 1st Sess., 282.

6. *Ibid.*, 347, 102, 1028.

7. *Ibid.*, 102, 103, 282, 391, 1028, 1355, 1979, 2727, 1520, 1525, 4049.

8. *Ibid.*, 3908, 219; Goldsboro *Messenger*, January 28, 1884. One historian has accused O'Hara of "neglect of public business" for taking leaves of absence amounting to forty-nine days during this session. The charge is completely unfair. O'Hara was not present during most of April, but his absence is justified considering that the district convention met April 29 and the state convention was held May 1. Smith was unwilling to concede normal fence-mending privileges to the black congressman. Samuel Denny Smith, *The Negro in Congress, 1870–1901* (Chapel Hill, N.C., 1940), 118–19.

9. Goldsboro *Messenger*, March 13, 1884, notes O'Hara's position with the Union League.

elector and delegates for the national convention, the session adjourned in unwonted order.[10]

Two days later the state GOP convention met in Raleigh, with O'Hara and the second district much in evidence. The delegates chose second district veteran L. W. Humphrey as chairman, John C. Dancy secretary, and elected the Negro congressman one of four delegates-at-large to the national convention. Once again North Carolina Republicans were seeking to cooperate with the independent Liberal movement to defeat regular Democrats, and because the governor and state officers were to be chosen in 1884, this election presented a greater opportunity than the contest two years earlier. O'Hara offered a resolution establishing a fifteen-member committee to meet with a similar Liberal committee to arrange coalition and settle on mutually acceptable candidates, and when the resolution passed he was appointed a committee member.[11]

When the Liberal-Republican negotiations were complete, Congressman Tyre York, a Liberal from western North Carolina, headed the coalition ticket as the gubernatorial candidate, whereas the nominees for lieutenant governor, secretary of state, treasurer, superintendent of public instruction, auditor, and associate justice of the supreme court were all Republicans. The ticket included three men from the counties of the second district: Wilson's leading Republican George W. Stanton for secretary of state, youthful Francis D. Winston for superintendent of public instruction, and Charles A. Cook, Liberal lawyer from Warren, for attorney general.

Second district Democrats had no higher hope in this campaign than to bring out the full party vote in resistance to the anti-"Bourbon" insurgents. Clearly there was no chance of defeating O'Hara by any honest methods. The district convention held June 18 in Weldon was the first in eight years that did not debate the expediency of a nomination. Apparently no one questioned that a nomination ought to be made—or that the nominee would lose in November. Wilson lawyer Frederick A. Woodard (partner of H. G. Connor) defeated William W. Carraway of Lenoir, 172–37. "Of course there is no probability of his election," said a friendly newspaper, "but his high character . . . and his force on the

10. Unidentified clipping in O'Hara Scrapbooks, O'Hara Papers. Goldsboro *Messenger*, May 1, 1884.
11. Raleigh *News and Observer*, May 2, 1884. The Liberal convention reelected O'Hara to the state executive committee. Raleigh *Register*, May 7, 1884.

stump will bring out the full Democratic vote and prove of great value to the party."[12] So discouraged were the Democrats that some indulged in the luxury of grumbling. Bertie, Craven, Greene, and Jones had not been represented at the district convention, though delegates from Craven and Jones arrived just after adjournment. The New Bern *Journal* criticized the slighting of Craven and Jones, the inconvenient site of the meeting, and the undue influence of Wilson County. (The nominees for Congress, national delegate, and alternate were all Wilsonians.) Carraway wrote a letter raising questions about the regularity of the call for the convention.[13]

O'Hara was well enough known that Francis W. Dawson, editor of the Charleston (S.C.) *News and Courier*, wrote to Senator Ransom with an odd scheme to defeat him. "I can place at your command, if you want him, a colored canvasser who ought to be of considerable service in your colored district." Dawson admitted that his black orator was not a man "of high moral character" but said he was "aggressive" and "fluent"—just the man to "clean out O'Hara on the stump if you give him the opportunity." Dawson thought the man could be hired for a hundred dollars a month or perhaps less. (This black Democrat was named Byas. As Dawson explained: "Some years ago he had a little difficulty with one of our reporters, and as the local paper said at the time, 'was shot in that portion of his person which is described by the second syllable of his name.'") Ransom must have thought there were better ways to spend Democratic dollars, for there are no reports of an imported black exhorter ranging the district to embarrass O'Hara.[14]

O'Hara was one of the state's few victorious Republicans on election day. He received 22,309 votes, more than any other candidate in the entire history of the "black second," 1872 to 1898, and carried every county in the district except Wilson and Lenoir; in Edgecombe and Halifax his majorities exceeded 1,700 votes. But Woodard accomplished his goal, too, for 15,699 men cast their ballots for him—the best Democratic showing to date.

Aided by the less-than-enthusiastic support many Republicans gave

12. Wilson *Advance,* June 26, 1884; Woodard's name is frequently misspelled "Woodward." For example, see Logan, *Negro in North Carolina,* 35, 40.
13. New Bern *Weekly Journal,* June 26, 1884.
14. F. W. Dawson to M. W. Ransom, August 13, 1884, in Ransom Papers.

former Democrat York, Congressman Alfred M. Scales won the governorship by a margin larger than Vance's 1876 victory.[15] Democrats swept all the other congressional races and cut Republican legislative strength by more than half—to its lowest point since the formation of the state party. Add to this the national victory of Grover Cleveland and Tarheel Democrats had good reason to be elated.

Republicans slipped even in the counties of the second district, where Democratic house candidates won in Greene, Jones, Lenoir, and, of course, Wilson. A Republican split permitted a Democratic senator and two representatives to be elected in Halifax, and the GOP lost Northampton's three general assembly seats, although there was an election contest over the senate seat, which the county shared with Bertie.[16] Republicans maintained traditional strength in five counties. George H. White triumphed in the Craven senate race, Robert S. Taylor, a Jamaican-born Negro, was elected Edgecombe senator, and in Warren County Jacob H. Montgomery won the senate seat. Republican house candidates were successful in Bertie, Vance, Craven, Warren, and Edgecombe. The biggest Republican loss in local government came in Lenoir, where long-time Sheriff James K. Davis and Register Bruton L. Taylor lost to Democrats and the county went into a decade of Democratic control.[17] Incumbent officers were reelected in Halifax, Craven, Warren, and Jones, including Negroes Mansfield Thornton and John H. Hannon.

However strong O'Hara was in his district and state, as he returned to Washington for the second session of the Forty-eighth Congress he was merely one obscure member in a large legislative body, his actions in this and other sessions of Congress generally drawing little public attention. A large metropolitan daily might briefly describe a black congressman because of his rarity, a local weekly note an occasional vote or bill introduced, and the black press comment flatteringly on a speech or refute white criticism. But no one printed extensive interviews with O'Hara on pending legislation or current issues and he was seldom

15. Scales defeated York by 20,335 votes. *North Carolina Manual* (Raleigh, 1913), 1004.
16. See N.C. General Assembly, Legislative Papers, 1885, Newsum v. Mason.
17. Josephus Daniels and his brother Charles established the Kinston *Free Press* in 1882. "A fighting Democratic paper," the *Free Press* helped defeat Taylor and other Republicans. (In his memoirs Daniels mistakenly identified Taylor as clerk of the court.) Daniels, *Tar Heel Editor*, 89.

pressed about why he voted a certain way. Even friendly sources tell little about his life as a member of the House of Representatives.

For two days in mid-December, 1884, however, O'Hara's name appeared on front pages around the nation after he offered a controversial amendment to the Reagan interstate commerce bill. His amendment provided: "Any person or persons having purchased a ticket to be conveyed from one state to another, or paid the required fare, shall receive the same treatment and be afforded equal facilities and accommodations as are furnished all other persons holding tickets of the same class without discrimination." In explanation O'Hara briefly cited several legal arguments showing that Congress had the authority to legislate in this area and denied that he was proposing "class legislation" or discussing a "race question." The amendment was "plain, healthy legislation" seeking to guard "the rights of every citizen of this great Republic, however humble may be his station in our social scale." Having already passed a law to protect animals transported by rail, now in the process of regulating rail freight rates, Congress ought to "throw a shield around the citizen's rights" by passing his amendment, O'Hara argued. Although Congressman John H. Reagan of Texas, sponsor of the bill, complained that the bill should not be enlarged to include the transportation of people, the House passed O'Hara's amendment 134–97, with a number of northern Democrats among the yeas.

The next day, December 17, Congressman Charles F. Crisp, a Georgian, introduced an amendment to follow O'Hara's: "Nothing in this act contained shall be so construed as to prevent any railroad company from providing separate accommodations for white and colored persons." Crisp declared that the amendment passed the day before went "even further" than the Civil Rights Act of 1875—the "social-equality law." "Why agitate anew this question? The law is well settled. The rights of the colored man are absolutely protected. Nobody wants to interfere with his rights."

Black Congressman Robert Smalls (elected in a special election after the death of white Republican Edwin W. M. Mackey) took the floor next to challenge Crisp's comments, especially his claim that Georgia law provided blacks and whites equal accommodations in railroad travel. Speaking for Negroes, he said they had "no objection to riding in a separate car when the car is of the same character as that provided for the white people to ride in." Black travelers might buy a first-class ticket at the beginning of a trip across several states, but when they arrived in Georgia they were forced by white passengers to move to a sooty, second-class, Jim Crow car as railroad officials looked the other way. In South Carolina, however, Smalls proudly noted that no discrimination was made "among persons traveling through the State."

Alabama Congressman Hiliary A. Herbert accused O'Hara of presenting the amendment, especially the phrase "without discrimination," in order to force "certain gentlemen on this side" to vote against the whole bill. Southern Democrats, said Herbert, had no objection to equal accommodations, but the common carriers ought not be deprived of the "natural right" to provide "equal accommodations in separate cars." O'Hara replied that his amendment really had nothing to do with color, that he believed "no matter whether a man is white or black he is an American citizen, and that the aegis of this great Republic should be held over him regardless of color." His amendment protected the white man "who may not occupy so high a social station as some of his more favored brethren" as well as the Negro. He noted that blacks and whites rode together in every northern state, and even in North Carolina. To the applause of his Republican colleagues, he concluded: "Let the man be white or black, humble or great, plebian or aristocratic, if he pays his fare, if he decently behaves himself, he is entitled to the same right as his money and desire prompt him."

An Arkansas member offered a substitute for Crisp's amendment eliminating all reference to race. "But nothing in this act," said the substitute, "shall be construed to deny to railroads the rights to classify passengers as they deem best for the public comfort and safety, or to relate to transportation between points wholly within the limits of one State." "What the gentlemen admit here to be the rights under the law of travelers carried by common carriers I am willing to vote for," said Congressman Clifton R. Breckinridge, "but when you seek to prevent the assorting of passengers or the providing of equal but separate accommodations from the standpoint of public convenience or public safety, you then introduce a social question into a question of commerce."

This comment presented an opportunity to the fat, witty congressman from Maine, Thomas B. Reed, who said he was "very much pleased" to see the Breckinridge amendment. "This at once ceases to be a question of politics or color, and has now become a question of assortment," he observed sarcastically. "Now, I appeal to this House, engaged as it is in the pursuit of wicked monopolists, if it intends to confer upon them a privilege of assortment without rights of law? Why, surely we must have some Treasury regulations as to the method of assortment." There was great merriment when the rotund Republican asked, "Are we to be assorted on the ground of size? Am I to be put in one car because of my size and the gentleman from Arkansas into another because of his?" Would people be assorted on the basis of moustaches, complexion, or beards?

Reagan said Reed was "very facetious" but surely railroads had a right to assort passengers, to separate ladies from "a drunken man or rowdy," for example. As for O'Hara's amendment, he attached "no importance" to it. Unlike some of his southern colleagues, he did not think the amendment added anything new to the law or forced integrated travel. It meant only that railroads had to give first-class facilities to first-class ticket holders.

There was considerable disagreement about the effect O'Hara's amendment would have. Crisp thought it was designed to "prevent a separation of the colors" and was an attempt to strike at southern white sentiment against association with blacks. But Ethelbert Barksdale of Mississippi was sure that the amendment would "not prevent railroad companies from providing separate accommodations for persons" and said he would vote for the bill even with the offending amendment attached. Several Democrats complained that O'Hara's amendment had been used by Republicans to arouse southern opposition to the interstate commerce bill, the real purpose being to defeat the bill. Representative Thomas M. Browne of Indiana denied that equal accommodations in rail travel was a social issue. "The time has come when there ought to be an end to this caste legislation, and I hope the time is not far distant when every white American citizen can sit down beside a respectable colored man without feeling that he is disgraced by the mere association, especially when it is simply occupying perhaps a distant seat in the same railroad car."

If the matter were not already confused enough, the House proceeded to vote in a circle. By a vote of 137–127, Breckinridge's amendment was substituted for Crisp's, and the House then voted to pass the amendment as amended. After that West Virginia Republican Nathan Goff moved to add to the amendment as adopted the phrase *"Provided,* That no discrimination is made on account of race or color," reaffirming O'Hara's basic point. This the House approved 141–102 with seventy-nine members not voting. The issue came up for a third day when, amid Republican laughter, Congressman Barksdale presented yet another qualification of O'Hara's amendment, providing that "furnishing separate accommodations, with equal facilities and equal comforts, shall not be considered discrimination." The House passed this 132–124 and then by 8 votes rejected the attempt of a Michigan congressman to amend Barksdale's addition to the bill with the statement that "such separation shall not be made on the basis of race or color." The Reagan bill eventually passed the House by a larger than two-to-one margin, but O'Hara voted against it. His black associate Smalls was among the yeas.[18]

Attaching an antidiscrimination rider to the interstate commerce bill was a clever move, and some Democrats could not bring themselves to believe that the Negro congressman had been the author of the amendment. He must have been "put up" to it, perhaps by Thomas Reed, who was in turn "prompted by some sharp railway presidents or attorneys."[19] It was true that many Republicans opposed the interstate commerce measure, and no doubt they enjoyed the confusion O'Hara's amendment produced among the bill's advocates. But O'Hara's strong and continued interest in civil rights needed no prompting. He suggested on January 6, 1885, an amendment to a pension appropriation bill to insure that the "mode and manner provided by the law and regulations for the payment of white persons entitled to pensions shall apply to and govern the payment of all pensions." A Democrat commented: "I believe it is the law now, but if it is not it should be the law," and the motion was adopted without debate. Six days later O'Hara introduced a bill forbidding racial discrimination in restaurants and other public places in the

18. *Congressional Record,* 48th Cong., 2nd Sess., 296–97, 316–23, 332–33, 339–43, 554. Reagan's biographer described O'Hara's amendment as a "devious attempt to defeat" the bill. Ben H. Proctor, *Not Without Honor: The Life of John H. Reagan* (Austin, 1962), 255. For an analysis of these votes, see Lawrence Grossman, *The Democratic Party and the Negro: Northern and National Politics, 1868–92* (Urbana, Ill., 1976), 110–12.

19. Goldsboro *Messenger,* December 25, 1884; Washington (D.C.) *Bee,* December 27, 1884.

District of Columbia. When it seemed that the bill would never emerge from committee, Robert Smalls succeeded (when O'Hara was absent) in adding it as an amendment to a bill regulating the sale and manufacture of liquor in the district, but the Senate failed to take any action on this House bill.[20] During this session O'Hara also introduced a private relief bill, attempted to gain a maintenance appropriation for a river in his district, and spoke briefly in favor of a private pension measure.[21]

O'Hara was very active in the first session of the Forty-ninth Congress. He introduced bills to provide federal aid to common schools, to regulate District of Columbia restaurants, and for reappraisal of the *Planter*, the ship captured by Robert Smalls during the Civil War. As in the Forty-eighth Congress, he proposed relief for depositors in the Freedman's Savings and Trust Company and erection of a public building in New Bern. He presented a bill for improvement of the Cashie River, a district waterway, and another bill to amend the act relative to the charter of the Freedman's Savings and Trust.[22] He introduced eleven private, pension, or relief bills, five of which passed the House. Included among these private bills were measures to pension the wife of a black soldier, to allow the widow of a Republican politician to be buried in the Federal cemetery at New Bern, and to pension the mother of a Negro veteran.[23] O'Hara was assigned to the Committee on Expenditures on Public Buildings and the Committee on Invalid Pensions. He took a significant part in the latter, presenting over one hundred reports to the House on the committee's behalf.

He made no lengthy set speeches but offered brief comments on several issues. Saying that he represented a constituency composed of a "large class of unorganized labor . . . which must in the very near future be organized for its own protection," he endorsed a bill setting up arbitration machinery for settling labor disputes. He rejected, however,

20. *Congressional Record*, 48th Cong., 2nd Sess., 501, 632, 2057–59; Washington (D.C.) *Bee*, February 28, 1885. A copy of the bill that included Smalls's amendment (House Resolution 7556) is in the O'Hara Papers.
21. *Congressional Record*, 48th Cong., 2nd Sess., 57, 1857, 783.
22. *Ibid.*, 49th Cong., 1st Sess., 345, 1351, 1887.
23. *Ibid.*, 345, 1887, 2882, 4251. House Resolution 6192 was to pension Mary Norman, wife of a Negro soldier; H. R. 7364 was to allow Harriet B. Lehman to be buried in the New Bern Federal cemetery; and H. R. 8486 was to pension Rebecca Morris, mother of a Negro veteran. See *House Reports*, 49th Cong., 1st Sess., Nos. 1107, 2013, 2946.

criticism of the Blair education bill made by some friends of the arbitration bill. The seventy-seven million dollars to be spent on education would "return in bounties fifty-fold," he said.[24]

O'Hara opposed a bill to tax oleomargarine, charging that "under the guise of protecting the poor man from oleomargarine and spurious butter, it seeks to destroy one industry of the country for the purpose of building up another"—the dairy industry. He particularly objected to a section of the bill creating new officers in the Internal Revenue Department to enforce it. Reminding Democrats of their campaign calls for lower taxes and reduction in the federal bureaucracy, he said ironically: "The revenue officer, the spy, the accuser of his neighbors, the United States prosecuting attorney are no longer tyrants but guardian angels to the health and liberty of the poor man."[25]

In a debate on pensions for Civil War veterans, O'Hara took the floor to criticize the Democratic chairman of the Committee on Invalid Pensions and to defend an increase in the already large government spending for Union soldiers. The pension question, he told the House, "is not such a bugbear to the people of this country as some gentlemen here seem to suppose." North Carolinians—including Union veterans—"cheerfully" paid state taxes to support a program of pensions for Confederate veterans. "More than that, in my own county some of these pensioners on the confederate rolls are to-day occupying Federal positions; and nobody complains." Was he thinking of the new Democratic postmaster at Enfield, a wounded former Rebel?[26]

After lawless whites murdered a group of Negroes in Carrollton, Mississippi, O'Hara introduced a resolution calling for a five-man investigating committee to ascertain the facts "and to report, by bill or otherwise, such measure as will check or prevent in future the wanton and barbarous destruction of human life." Unanimous consent was required to introduce this resolution out of regular order and Reagan of Texas objected because the "resolutions proposed to deal with a subject over which we have no constitutional power." Later O'Hara was able to introduce the resolution and it was referred to the Rules Committee, where it was never heard of again. The *News and Observer* commented

24. *Congressional Record*, 49th Cong., 1st Sess., 3073.
25. *Ibid.*, 5395–96.
26. *Ibid.*, 6369; Goldsboro *Messenger*, August 10, 1885.

on O'Hara's resolution, insisting that the Carrollton affair had no relation to politics, "and O'Hara can not give it any political color."[27]

Already defeated in his battle for a third term, O'Hara offered only one bill, a measure for the relief of the pilot and crew of the *Planter*, in the second session of the Forty-ninth Congress. He spoke only twice, once in eulogy of Illinois Senator John A. Logan and later in opposition to President Cleveland's veto of a veterans' pension bill. His speech on pensions placed particular emphasis on black veterans, quoting Benjamin F. Butler's testimony on the valor of Negro troops in his command.[28]

In debate on a bill regarding the cattle disease "pleuro-pneumonia" O'Hara successfully moved to include an investigation of hog cholera in the duties of a proposed board of experts, saying this disease was very important to people in his section. He offered another amendment, this time to the District of Columbia appropriation bill, banning salary discrimination "between male and female teachers holding the same grade of certificate and performing similar duties," but the motion was ruled out of order.[29]

O'Hara voted five times to override presidential vetoes of pension bills and each time the House sustained Cleveland. Two other votes during this session illustrate his independence. The House passed the "Mormon bill," a harsh crackdown on polygamy, by the overwhelming vote of 202–40, with O'Hara as one of the few opponents. He found himself voting with such unlikely allies as John Reagan and North Carolina Democrats Risden T. Bennett and Thomas G. Skinner, and on the opposite side from Robert Smalls. Late in the session he voted for a motion offered by Tarheel Democrat William R. Cox to suspend the rules and pass a bill repealing the Tenure of Office Act. Republican stalwarts like Reed, William McKinley, and Smalls voted the other way.[30]

O'Hara had represented his district well during his four years in Congress. One can only wonder how much stronger his legislative record would have been had his party been in the majority.

27. *Congressional Record*, 49th Cong., 1st Sess., 2893, 3136; Raleigh *News and Observer*, April 8, 1886. Also in this session O'Hara offered a minor amendment to a river and harbor appropriation bill, which was accepted, p. 3894.
28. *Congressional Record*, 49th Cong., 2nd Sess., 289, 1839, 2209.
29. *Ibid.*, 1118, 1171.
30. *Ibid.*, 1300, 1921, 2077–78, 2696, 1882, 2700. O'Hara's specific objections to the "Mormon bill" are nowhere recorded.

Chapter 7

THE NECESSARY COLOR LINE

Drawing the color line is wrong in principle. The Democratic party has time and again in convention assembled declared their purpose not to interfere with the rights of the negro as guaranteed by the Constitution of the United States and of the State of North Carolina. All the legislation by the party in this State has been consistent with these declarations. The colored man is deprived no right before the law on account of his color. . . . Then why seek to array one race against the other? The negroes are citizens, and have the right of suffrage. Why not teach them to exercise this right with intelligence? To draw the color line will but put them in the hands of bad men and keep their prejudices aroused to the highest pitch.

—New Bern *Weekly Journal*, November 25, 1886

THE ELECTION OF A DEMOCRATIC PRESIDENT in 1884 caused many North Carolina Democrats to reconsider their party's relations with the state's Negro citizens. Although the party had made overtures to blacks before, particularly in 1877 and 1878, these efforts had been half-hearted and ineffective. Never completely rejecting black votes, the Democracy often appealed to Negroes in the spirit of a Wilmington newspaper comment: "If the colored people will trust us and vote with us we will act for their interests just as we do for the interests of the women and minors, who do not vote at all."[1]

Even before election day some voices were calling for the party to write off Negroes entirely. William H. Kitchin, elector-at-large in 1884, sparked considerable controversy when he publicly declined to make further appeals for the black vote. "I do not think that I ought to say it," the not-always-discreet former congressman told a Democratic audi-

---

1. Wilmington *Democrat* quoted in Wilmington *Post*, April 26, 1878.

ence, "but . . . I stand here to-night as the advocate of a government by white men, by the virtue and intelligence of this country; I stand here to-night to appeal to no colored man for his support. I feel honestly that I have no right to appeal to him." According to Kitchin, a divine decree made the Negro different from the white man. "Now I say to the colored man do the best you can. For years I have talked to you and I have persuaded you for what I thought was the best, but you have disregarded my advice. I have always told you we could do without you, and I tell you here today in the name of common sense and in the name of heaven and in the presence of angels, if there be such things, that we can and will do without you."[2]

An alternate view was that color-line politics was a burden to be rid of as soon as possible. "For a good many years it has been perfectly apparent to close observers that the division of parties according to race could not continue in this country," said the Goldsboro *Messenger* a few weeks after Cleveland's narrow triumph. The color line made sense only as a southern defense against the solid North, and the election of a Democratic president by the votes of the South joined by four northern states created a new political situation. The newspaper noted Governor Jarvis' prediction that a large minority of Negroes would soon be voting Democratic, that white solidarity would break down as a result, and future elections would be fought on issues like the tariff and not on the color line: "The Governor said that the division of parties according to color was a standing menace to the people of the State, and especially so during election campaigns, and that every man who wished for his State's and the general welfare should be glad to see the color line disappear from the politics of the Southern States."[3] Jarvis expected blacks to divide politically when they saw that their rights were secure under a national Democratic administration. But the color line in politics would not simply fade away in the glow of the 1884 victory. Democrats would have to encourage Negroes to leave the GOP, showing blacks their stake in Democratic success and sharing with them the privileges of incumbency.

If Democratic overtures were forthcoming, some blacks were prepared

2. Raleigh *Register*, July 16, 1884. See Raleigh *Register*, August 27, 1884, Raleigh *News and Observer*, August 21, 1884, on the controversy provoked by Kitchin's remarks.
3. Goldsboro *Messenger*, November 24, 1884.

to respond. Former Northampton legislator Paul F. Hayley wrote to Senator Ransom shortly before the new administration took office, asking to be continued in his job as route agent in the Railway Mail Service, though he had no claims on the Democratic party and had "not labored for its success." He hoped that "the time has come when I can affiliate with the best people of the South in political matters, as I well know my best interests are identified with that class of people." If Ransom would back him, Hayley promised: "I will not give you, your son, nor, your friends any trouble in the County or District so far as my influence extinds [sic]."[4]

Nathaniel R. Jones, former Democratic sheriff of Warren, urged Ransom to work for the retention of another Negro route agent, John R. Hawkins, a "well educated," "intelligent," "well behaved" young man. Hawkins and his father were moderate Republicans who kept out of politics except to vote and who had the respect of "the genteel white people of their acquaintance." There had been no complaints about Hawkins' performance, he wrote, and "Besides all of this the retention of John Hawkins in his place will greatly strengthen the Administration & the Democratic party with the better class of negroes and render the election of good white democrats to the County offices in the Counties having negro majorities easier and more certain."[5]

These were tentative approaches, of course, requiring time and cultivation to produce significant results. But the Democracy had been out of power twenty-five years and most Democrats were too anxious to see the federal service purged of Republicans to be concerned with any cautious courting of Negro leaders and voters. The editor of the *Messenger* was a good example of this impatience, this inability to appreciate subtle changes. Less than two years after Cleveland's victory he was quoting with approval a comment from the Fayetteville *Observer* on the futility of seeking Negro Democrats: "We do not suppose that a Democratic candidate in all of North Carolina will appeal to the colored people for votes. It would be a thankless task, if he should."[6]

The *Observer's* comment was wrong on both counts, at least in the second district. The campaign of 1886 was marked by two serious at-

4. P. F. Hayley to M. W. Ransom, February 18, 1885, in Ransom Papers.
5. N. R. Jones to M. W. Ransom, March 13, 1885, in Ransom Papers.
6. Fayetteville *Observer* quoted in Goldsboro *Messenger*, October 4, 1886.

tempts to persuade blacks to vote for Democrats, and both had a measure of success. In Craven County Democrats agreed to support the dissident "reform" wing of the Republican party for the county offices in return for their support for Democratic legislative nominees. And in the congressional race the Democratic candidate made the strongest appeal to black voters that any Democratic nominee had ever made in the history of the "black second."

The effort would have been impractical if James O'Hara had been able to maintain the control of the district which he had in 1884. But O'Hara's popularity was waning and he was under attack from several rivals of both races. Part of his problem was what one editor called North Carolina's "unwritten law that no man can serve more than two terms" in Congress. The *People's Advocate*, a black newspaper in New Bern, argued: "Mr. O'Hara has been in Congress for four years. This we take it, substantially disposes of his claim to be returned. In a district with eight thousand majority, equality of candidates being conceded, our man can't hope to be returned more than twice." There were other men eager to represent the second district in Washington. The choice of the *Advocate* was Leonidas J. Moore, a local white attorney who had previously supported O'Hara. Israel B. Abbott, black leader from Craven, declared himself a candidate against O'Hara as early as April, 1886, and by the end of July he was the *Advocate*'s second choice. In O'Hara's own county, white lawyer John A. Moore wanted "to try on the colored brother's sandals," as a Democratic newspaper put it. Vance County's treasurer Robert E. Young, a wealthy white landowner, brother to I. J. Young, was lining up support for his own congressional ambitions.[7]

O'Hara had problems in addition to the popular prejudice in favor of rotation in office. Some of his constituents complained that he was too distant, that he forgot them while he was in Washington. No doubt a few of them read with displeasure a report from the Chicago *Inter-Ocean* reprinted in the Washington *Bee*: "There is an aristocracy among the colored people of Washington as well as among the white, and quite as exclusive." What the *Inter-Ocean* described as "high-toned

7. Warrenton *Gazette*, March 14, 1890; New Bern *People's Advocate*, July 31, 1886; Washington (D.C.) *Bee*, June 26, 1886; Salisbury *Star of Zion*, April 9, 1886; Raleigh *News and Observer*, July 15, July 21, 1886.

colored society" revolved around Francis Grimké's 15th Street Presbyterian church and included former senator Blanche K. Bruce, John
Mercer Langston, Richard T. Greener, Charles B. Purvis, and others.
Although they were Catholics, the O'Haras were said to be part of this
genteel "coterie." The *Inter-Ocean* reporter described Libby O'Hara as
"one of the loveliest ladies in Washington," a highly educated woman
who spoke French, played Beethoven, and was "up in art and literature
to a degree that would make some of her white sisters blush for envy."
The revelation that she had "a white governess for her children" could
not have been politically helpful to her husband. The article went on to
describe the balls, dinner parties, receptions, and formal visitation of the
black elite.[8]

O'Hara's opponents scattered complaints shotgun style. They condemned him because "he failed to have Negroes appointed to prominent
places in the District," because he did not "recognize his constituents,"
because he was alleged to be "ashamed" of the Negro. O'Hara "won't
send his children to a colored school," said his enemies, and "when his
colored constituents call on him treats them with disrespect and indifference." "He is above his colored constituents when he meets them in
Washington. . . . He does nothing for the district, he spends his
time and money in the north." The old charges that he was a bigamist
and a foreigner were revived as well.[9]

John C. Dancy, editor of the African Methodist Episcopal Zion newspaper *Star of Zion*, had an explanation for O'Hara's troubles. Although
he was no longer a resident of the district, the twenty-nine-year-old
editor had been born in Edgecombe and maintained an interest in
district politics. "If Hon. J. E. O'Hara had only proved half so true to
his friends, who risked everything in his support, as he has to his enemies, who have spared no opportunity to stab and destroy him," wrote
Dancy a few weeks before the nominating convention, "he would not
now find them indifferent and careless" as he sought renomination. He

8. Chicago *Inter-Ocean* quoted in Washington (D.C.) *Bee,* January 30, 1886.
This article reports that Mrs. O'Hara was "nearly white," which is inaccurate. Interview with Vera Jean O'Hara Rivers, February 26, 1975.
9. Washington (D.C.) *Bee,* June 26, 1886; Goldsboro *Messenger,* September 16,
1886; Washington (D.C.) *Bee,* September 25, 1886. "Jas. E. O'Hara is an American
citizen and not a foreigner," affirmed the *Bee,* June 26, 1886.

added: "It is a maxim in political warfare to never forsake, ignore or desert your friends, if you would succeed."[10] Dancy may have disapproved of O'Hara's appointment policy, thinking that too many deserving men had been slighted in the distribution of patronage, or his comments may have been inspired by O'Hara's alleged failure to cater to constituents, but he clearly referred to opposition to O'Hara from within the Republican party.

O'Hara's handling of patronage may have been unpopular. Although he made a few changes (like the removal of Dudley and Mrs. Daniels), he had seemed content to leave most offices under his influence undisturbed. He did not, for example, change many of the postmasters in the district. When he took office only one Negro managed a post office of significance, and that was Winfield F. Young of Littleton, appointed in 1875. In July, 1884, O'Hara secured the appointment of another black postmaster, Edward A. Richardson, at New Bern, one of the most important post offices in the region. O'Hara's supporters in Edgecombe County may have wanted him to remove Hubbs's appointee Walter P. Williamson at Tarboro, but Williamson remained in office until the Cleveland administration replaced him with the widow of a Confederate general. In the Edgecombe town of Whitakers, O'Hara appointed old foe L. G. Estes to the postmastership about a year and a half after he had been removed in Enfield. Was it this sort of thing Dancy had in mind when he complained about O'Hara's being true to his enemies? (Estes wrote to Ransom after the Democrats captured the federal government and explained that he had taken the position only to prevent O'Hara from appointing a Negro. He also proposed a scheme to send one Democrat to the general assembly from Edgecombe in return for Democratic support for a Republican county slate.) In the county seats of Snow Hill, Henderson, Warrenton, and Jackson, O'Hara made no changes. His laissez-faire attitude is summed up in a letter he wrote to Senator Ransom just after the Democratic accession to power, asking that the incumbent postmaster be retained at Enfield, O'Hara's home. "I would respectfully ask that the same courtesies be extended to me at this my own office as was extended you at the Weldon office." He exaggerated only a bit when he said, "I have made no change for

10. Salisbury *Star of Zion,* August 6, 1886.

political reasons in my district" (especially if political changes are defined as Democrat-Republican shifts). O'Hara told Ransom that there were just two Republican postmasters in Halifax and none in Northampton.[11]

Perhaps the district's hungry office seekers forgot how limited O'Hara's influence was. Both Houses in which he served were controlled by Democrats, which meant that Democrats filled most of the House offices —doorkeeper, sergeant-at-arms, clerks, messengers, laborers, etc. He could not reward a friend with a job like superintendent of the documents room, as Hubbs had done. In O'Hara's second term, the federal executive was also under Democratic control, and he could do little as a party that had been out of power for a generation made wholesale removals in the internal revenue and customs service, in the postal department, and in the judicial department. Senator Ransom even ignored his request on the Enfield post office, replacing O'Hara's man with a wounded Confederate veteran.

Once again the evidence is sketchy, but O'Hara may have counted on the argument of a black man for a black district to pull him through his troubles. For as the late August convention date approached, his strongest rival appeared to be Robert E. Young, a white man. In mid-July Young's friends claimed that he had support from Bertie, Jones, and Northampton, and the Warren and Vance country conventions endorsed him in the next two weeks. There were rumors that if O'Hara lost the nomination he planned to run as an independent "mainly on the ground that he was a colored man and that that was the 'black district.' "[12]

Disorderly proceedings in several county conventions and the district judicial convention adumbrated the disaster that would hit the party. At the Northampton convention July 15, for example, one faction among the delegates favored Young, the other faction preferring "a colored man or a choice from the county" (an illustration of the complex cross currents of race and localism in district politics). Amid great confusion, the Young faction's candidate for permanent chairman was

11. Information on postmasters based on Record of Appointments of Postmasters, Vols. 49, 69, RG 28, NA; L. G. Estes to M. W. Ransom, September 28, 1885, J. E. O'Hara to M. W. Ransom, April 29, 1885, both in Ransom Papers.
12. Raleigh News and Observer, July 12, 27, August 5, July 17, August 26, 1886.

elected (or seized the chair), precipitating a bolt by the other faction, which ultimately endorsed O'Hara.[13]

For the first time, the Second Judicial District convention "broke up in a row." Would-be solicitor George White claimed to have had the support of a majority of the delegates "and would have been nominated had a vote been reached," according to the *Star of Zion*, but Collins, the incumbent, printed a circular asserting that he had been "fairly and honestly nominated" and had the support of a "large majority" of Republican voters. A third candidate for solicitor, Francis Winston, denounced mob rule and declared that no one had been legally nominated.[14]

The congressional delegates convened in Kinston on August 25 and quickly fell into chaos. Executive committee chairman William W. Watson of Edgecombe, an O'Hara supporter, called the session to order and then ordered the convention hall cleared of all delegates and spectators! His unusual action may have been intended to forestall any attempt to control the convention by mob methods, but a large number of delegates ignored him, chose a more cooperative chairman, and proceeded to nominate Israel B. Abbott on the second ballot. Nine of the eleven counties in the district were represented in some fashion in this first meeting. When it adjourned, a second session, meeting in the same hall and claiming to be composed of regular delegates, nominated O'Hara. Not surprisingly the whole affair was "noisy and disorderly."[15]

Although he had worked for several months to get the nomination and was a leading contender, R. E. Young refused to allow his name to go before the splintered convention. "It was thought up to yesterday that Young had rather the inside track on O'Hara and that he would get the nomination," said the *News and Observer* the day after the convention.[16] In the future he would work for political power in the black district by less direct methods.

13. *Blade*, July 23, 1886, and unidentified clipping (correspondence from R. J. Perry), in O'Hara Scrapbooks, O'Hara Papers. Craven's convention also broke into two meetings (New Bern *Weekly Journal*, July 15, 1886), and two sets of delegates emerged from Halifax. Washington (D.C.) *Bee*, September 25, 1886.
14. Salisbury *Star of Zion*, August 27, 1886; New Bern *Weekly Journal*, August 26, September 25, 1886; Raleigh *News and Observer*, August 26, 1886.
15. New Bern *Weekly Journal*, August 26, September 2, 1886; Washington (D.C.) *Bee*, September 25, 1886; Raleigh *News and Observer*, August 26, 1886.
16. Raleigh *News and Observer*, August 26, 1886.

Forty-three-year-old Israel Braddock Abbott had considerable political experience and had been mentioned as a congressional hopeful in several previous campaigns. Born a free Negro, he was by trade a carpenter. During the Civil War he was assigned to work on Confederate forts and served for a time as an officer's servant. "Being dissatisfied, he wrote a pass for himself and ran away, reaching New Berne, Dec. 18, 1861," and remained in hiding until the Union forces captured the town the next spring. He served in the general assembly of 1872–1873, represented the second district as a delegate to the Republican national convention in 1880 and as an alternate in 1884, and was an active member of the Good Samaritan Lodge, editing the fraternal newspaper in New Bern for several years. Abbott claimed that except for "undue influence" he would have been nominated long before. Of "unmixed African blood," he was described as short in stature and a good debator.[17]

The complexions of the two Republican candidates would become something of an issue in the next three or four months. The *News and Observer* noted criticism of O'Hara: "There are many who say that he is never seen among the darkies except at nominating and election times, and that he holds himself too much above the black man anyhow, being himself of a ginger-cake hue." I. B. Abbott, however, "prides himself on the fact that he is a genuine colored man, a pure blood negro, black enough to draw the color line on," reported a New Bern journalist. An Abbott supporter wrote to the Washington *Bee*: "During the canvass prior to the convention O'Hara made the fight that a colored man should represent the district (meaning of course himself.) But his color is much doubted down here, still they gave him a man not colored but black; a true representative of the race, and a native of the district."[18] But the matter of skin color was not the major issue in the campaign against O'Hara, as Furnifold Simmons would later claim. Long before anyone knew that Abbott would be a nominee, O'Hara was under fire for other reasons. And when election day came he received "far more of

---

17. Raleigh *Examiner* quoted in New Bern *Times,* February 25, 1874. This sketch erroneously gives his first name as "Isaac." Wilmington *Post,* March 21, 1880, January 8, 1882; New Bern *Weekly Journal,* September 2, 1886; Salisbury *Star of Zion,* September 3, 1886.

18. Raleigh *News and Observer,* September 1, 1886; New Bern *Weekly Journal,* September 2, 1886; Washington (D.C.) *Bee,* September 25, 1886. See also Washington (D.C.) *Bee,* October 9, 1886.

the unadulterated black votes than did his opponent who was of un-mixed Negro blood," as John Dancy pointed out.[19]

Even before the chaotic Republican convention produced two candi-dates, Democrats were talking of good chances for "the right kind of man" to take advantage of Republican disunity and carry the district. After the convention the News and Observer was cautiously optimistic: "In view of the radical dissensions in the second congressional district it may not be impossible to select a democrat." Even so, there were not many men who desired the nomination. When the Democrats met in Wilson on September 1 only one name was presented and the delegates unanimously selected Furnifold M. Simmons.[20]

A youthful lawyer and Trinity College graduate, Simmons would later become state party chairman and serve thirty years in the United States Senate. But in 1886 he had less political experience than either O'Hara or Abbott—both of whom were ten years his senior. He had never held elective office, failing in an effort to represent his native Jones County in the 1875 constitutional convention. He had an important family connection, however, since from 1874 to 1883 he had been L. W. Hum-phrey's son-in-law. Eliza Humphrey Simmons died in 1883 and Simmons remarried in the summer of 1886, but the colonel was still willing to help the young man.[21]

A half-century later Josephus Daniels remembered: "It was freely charged that Colonel L. W. Humphrey . . . manoeuvered a split in the unruly [Republican] Convention and paid the campaign expenses of the Negroes to keep them in the race, so that Simmons, his son-in-law, could be elected." The leading Tarheel Republican newspaper charged during the campaign of 1888 that a group of "Democratic negroes" under the leadership of Humphrey bolted the Republican convention and put out a pseudo-Republican candidate for the purpose of helping Sim-mons. An Abbott supporter suggested in September, 1886, that O'Hara had bargained to elect the Democratic candidate in order to repay his

19. J. Fred Rippy (ed.), Furnifold Simmons, Statesman of the New South: Memoirs and Addresses (Durham, N.C., 1936), 16; Salisbury Star of Zion, March 24, 1887.

20. Wilson Advance quoted in New Bern Weekly Journal, August 12, 1886; Raleigh News and Observer, August 28, 1886; Wilson Advance quoted in New Bern Weekly Journal, September 9, 1886.

21. A Biographical Congressional Directory, 1774-1903 (Washington, D.C., 1903), 798. New Bern Weekly Journal, September 9, August 5, 1886.

debts to Humphrey. But more plausible is the explanation of John Dancy: "Col. Humphrey encouraged both O'Hara and Abbott to continue their fight and thus secured the defeat of both."[22] Humphrey's role must not be exaggerated, however. O'Hara was certainly his own man, and it seems unlikely that Abbott was a Humphrey puppet, though both men may have accepted the colonel's cash. Humphrey did not single-handedly create the divisions in the second district, though he may have encouraged them.

For the first time since "Buck" Kitchin offered to donate part of his salary for the training of colored teachers in 1872, a Democratic congressional candidate made a serious appeal to Negro voters. Simmons told a Craven County crowd "that while he was an unflinching Democrat, he was not one of the kind that set no value upon the colored man's vote." According to the New Bern *Weekly Journal*, he told the Negroes that "he wanted their votes, and if elected . . . would represent them better . . . than either of his opponents." Simmons was addressing black voters in the ordinary language of politics, telling what he could accomplish for them in Washington.[23]

Simmons' call for black support coincided with an unusual effort by the Craven County Democracy to cooperate with black voters. The local Republicans were divided into two camps, one faction led by Sheriff Mayer Hahn and the other by Daniel Stimson, a wealthy white man who wanted to be sheriff.[24] Stimson had unsuccessfully challenged Hahn in two earlier elections, causing a full-scale party schism in 1882. Craven Democratic leaders moved in 1886 officially to arrange a coalition between the Stimson "reform" wing of the GOP and the Democracy in order to elect two Democrats to the general assembly. In return Democrats would support the Stimson county ticket, including Stimson for sheriff and Orlando Hubbs for register of deeds.

The editor of the New Bern *Journal*, H. S. Nunn, gave the movement his strong support. Craven County was handicapped, he told his readers, by sending minority party representation to Raleigh, because many important questions affecting the county were "virtually disposed

22. Daniels, *Tar Heel Editor*, 176; Raleigh *Sentinel*, August 3, 1888; Washington (D.C.) *Bee*, September 25, 1886; Salisbury *Star of Zion*, April 14, 1887.
23. New Bern *Weekly Journal*, October 14, 1886.
24. Stimson had one of the largest tax bills in the county. See Craven County Tax List, 1887 (microfilm), in North Carolina Department of Archives and History.

of in caucus." With Democratic representation Craven would have a more effective voice in matters like county boundaries—there had been a recent unpopular change in the line—and state railroad policy. County Democrats' dissatisfaction at being a noncontiguous part of the Second Judicial District could also have been avoided had the county sent Democrats to the general assembly. In short, representation in the legislature made "all the difference imaginable." Voting for the coalition ticket would not hurt Democrats any more than voting for Greeley had— or offend Republicans more than supporting Tyre York, quipped Nunn.[25]

The Craven coalition obviously involved a good deal of interracial cooperation. Black former legislators E. R. Dudley and Willis D. Pettipher served on the alliance's central committee, and Dudley edited a procoalition newspaper, the *Republican*. The Democratic nominee for the senate spoke to voters in the black village of James City, perhaps the first Democrat to address a "public gathering" there, surmised the *Journal*.[26]

Both Simmons and the Craven coalition were partly successful in attracting black votes in the surprising 1886 elections. Simmons won less than a majority of the vote in the district, defeating O'Hara 15,158 to 13,060. O'Hara demonstrated that he still had the support of most Republicans by outpolling Abbott in all but two counties, and these two, Edgecombe and Warren, furnished three quarters of Abbott's 5,020 votes. O'Hara carried Bertie, Greene, and Halifax—Vance, too, until the canvassers rejected nearly 500 of his ballots.[27] A Democratic source would later estimate that Simmons received "not less than twenty-five hundred colored votes," and Simmons himself considered aid from "the better class of colored men" the basis of his success.[28] But even more important were the votes Abbott took from O'Hara—more than twice Simmons' 2,098 victory margin. The Craven coalitionists fell 200 to 300 votes short in their campaign to overthrow the Hahn Republicans, but by rejecting returns in several precincts the canvassing board was able to declare Stimson and company the victors. The board justified its action

25. New Bern *Weekly Journal*, July 29, August 19, 1886.
26. *Ibid.*, July 29, October 14, 1886. The Craven factional fight was not related to the one at the district level. See September 2, 1886.
27. Raleigh *News and Observer*, November 5, 1886.
28. Raleigh *State Chronicle*, February 2, 1888; Henderson *Gold Leaf*, June 7, 1888.

with the claim that voters had been intimidated in some precincts that Hahn carried, but the state supreme court eventually ruled in favor of the Hahn ticket and the general assembly seated the two Republican candidates.[29]

Across the state the Republican party showed amazing strength. Weakened by the defeats of 1884, plagued by division that produced two rival state committees in 1886, the North Carolina GOP had seemed moribund, yet the party won seventy-three seats in the legislature and with the aid of independent Democrats controlled the house. Although the Republican judicial slate lost, for the first time since Reconstruction Republican congressional candidates won in the fourth district, where John Nichols, a long-time Republican, ran as an independent with labor support, and in the fifth district, which elected John M. Brower.

In 1884 O'Hara had triumphed even as second district local and legislative candidates faltered. Now as O'Hara was defeated, the party recovered the 1884 losses. Bertie, Edgecombe, Craven, Greene, Halifax, Jones, Vance, and Warren elected straight Republican delegations to the general assembly. Francis Winston, youthful and wellborn, was elected to represent Northampton and Bertie in the senate. After eight years out of office, Henry Eppes returned to the senate from Halifax, and Charles A. Cook, now a full-fledged Republican instead of Liberal, won the Warren senate seat. In Wayne, temporarily out of the second district, the voters sent old Curtis Brogden to the state house, where his career had begun almost fifty years earlier. Democratic house candidates won in Wilson and Lenoir. Northampton elected a Democrat, R. H. Stancill, and a Negro, Ned Rawls, to the house in another example of black-white coalition. Although a "simon-pure" Democrat, Stancill reportedly received "over five hundred colored votes."[30]

Republicans did well in local elections throughout the district. The party won Greene, ousting the Democratic sheriff, and Halifax, reelecting Negro Register John H. Hannon. There was a three-way race in Edgecombe, where Joseph Cobb, veteran of Reconstruction, became sheriff once again, and Frank M. Hines, a Negro, was elected register. Blacks in Warren challenged the long-standing arrangement with local Democrats by electing a Negro, H. H. Falkener, clerk of the superior

29. See Raleigh *Signal,* December 30, 1886, on "The Craven County Fraud."
30. Raleigh *News and Observer,* November 10, 1886.

court over William A. White, who had been in the office for more than two decades. Henry P. Cheatham, an 1882 honors graduate of Shaw University, was reelected register in Vance. Jones voters defeated their Democratic sheriff, and in Lenoir, Sheriff James Sutton barely defeated Bruton Taylor, 1,453 to 1,442 in an election complicated by the liquor issue. (Local prohibitionists, led by James Mewboorne, resolved not to support candidates opposed to local option.)[31]

What caused this near-defeat for the Democracy? Charles B. Aycock, young Goldsboro lawyer, thought it was a combination of hard times, Democratic overconfidence, and "failure to draw the color line."[32] Not everyone agreed, but it was an ominous excuse. The Bourbon equilibrium —with its acceptance of Negroes as permanent voters, its rejection of political violence, and its considerable toleration of black Republican officeholders—was coming to an end.

31. New Bern *Weekly Journal,* September 23, 1886.
32. Raleigh *State Chronicle* quoted in Goldsboro *Messenger,* November 15, 1886; New Bern *Weekly Journal,* November 25, 1886.

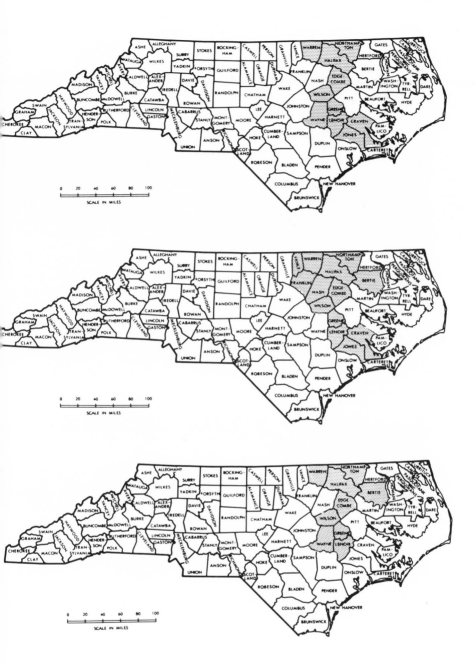

Second Congressional District boundaries in 1872, 1883, and 1891 (based on
present county boundaries).

University of North Carolina Press

Former slave John Adams Hyman, the first North Carolina Negro elected to Congress, served from 1875 to 1877.

Courtesy of Division of Archives and History, Raleigh, N.C.

An important white Republican from the "black second," Curtis Hooks Brogden
held a number of offices, ranging from governor (1874–77) and congressman
(1877–79) to member of the legislature.

Courtesy of Division of Archives and History, Raleigh, N.C.

James Edward O'Hara, congressional aspirant in five consecutive elections, posed with his family in a formal portrait probably taken during his stay in Washington, 1883 to 1887.

Courtesy of Regenstein Library, University of Chicago

"I cannot live in North Carolina and be a man," declared George Henry White, when he announced his decision not to run for a third congressional term in 1900.

The son of William Hodge "Buck" Kitchin, Claude Kitchin won election to the House from the second district in 1900, and went on to become an extremely influential congressman.

Courtesy of Division of Archives and History, Raleigh, N.C.

PART THREE

Party Realignment
1887–1895

Chapter 8

THE FIRST WHITE SUPREMACY CAMPAIGN

> Yes I did say and now say the color line sharply drawn is our
> only hope in this State. Blot it out as King Grover has done his
> best to do, and this state would go more than fifty thousand
> republican majority; if the republicans were smart and de-
> clare[d] . . . for white supremacy in the South, they would
> bury the democratic party forever.
>
> —William H. Kitchin, 1887[1]

IN FEBRUARY, 1888, former congressman John Hyman sat
down to write a leading white Democrat in Warren County, scrawling
"Personal" in the upper left hand corner of the page and underlining it
twice. "I beg leave to Explain to you inregards to the matter I mensun to
you on yesterday," he wrote Marmaduke J. Hawkins. "I have information
from all over the 2nd Dist. that if I carry Warren county the outher Co.
will give me thar strenk in the Dist. Convention." First, however, he
had to defeat white Republican Charles A. Cook in Warren County, and
he had no money for transportation and campaign expenses. But "if I
can get some help at this time to by a out fitt I think I can bet any
white Republican in this Dist." Assuming that a Democrat would be
equally interested in foiling white Republicans, Hyman requested: "Will
you please see your farther and outher friends . . . give me the lone of
. . . one Hundred and fifty Dollars[.] I am satisfied that I can come
out [a]head[.] I will Promas this much that I will sertenly Defeat Mr.
C. A. Cook in this County and any outher white man in the Republican

---

1. W. H. Kitchin to Z. B. Vance, [December, 1887] in Zebulon Baird Vance
Papers, Southern Historical Collection, University of North Carolina, Chapel Hill.

Party of this Dist. as I am satisfied the col[.] voters of this Dist. are tired of being drawn by thar white Reps. Bosses."[2]

Hyman had spent the decade since his retirement from Congress in obscurity, taking little part in district politics. At the end of his House term, President Hayes had appointed him collector of internal revenue for the second revenue district, a well-paying patronage post, but pressure from friends of the incumbent collector caused the president to revoke his order within a few days.[3] Failing in his efforts to be renominated in 1878, Hyman turned to local Democrats for assistance. Twenty-one Warren Democrats, including former congressional nominee Wharton Green and Sheriff Nathaniel Jones, signed a petition asking Senators Ransom and Vance to use their influence and "good offices" in securing for Hyman "a position that will afford him a living" since he was "penniless & poor with a large family on his hands." Sheriff Jones emphasized Hyman's worthiness in a separate letter: "As you know, he has always supported the best men, he could get from the Democratic party for County officers and has gone so far in that matter that he has seriously impaired his popularity & influence with his own party." Hyman called on the two senators in Washington during March, 1879, and they helped him get a government job. Hoping for something better, he served for a time as a postal clerk in Richmond, Virginia, then moved to the District of Columbia where he worked as a $2.25-a-day watchman in the government printing office from 1883 to 1886.[4]

In the fall of 1887 Hyman left Washington to return to Warrenton with renewed congressional ambition. W. Calvin Chase's *Bee* reported that Hyman's chances for the congressional nomination were good and praised him as a man who had worked for black patronage while in Congress. Republicans throughout the state would "show their gratitude" for Hyman's fine record, predicted the *Bee*, "by aiding this injured man."[5]

There is no record that Hyman received the loan he requested from

2. J. A. Hyman to M. J. Hawkins, February 7, 1888, in Marmaduke J. Hawkins Papers, North Carolina Department of Archives and History.
3. Goldsboro *Messenger*, June 25, July 5, 1877; Raleigh *Register*, June 26, July 3, 1877; Charlotte *Observer* quoted in Tarboro *Southerner*, July 13, 1877.
4. J. R. Turnbull and others to M. W. Ransom and Z. B. Vance, March 3, 1879, N. R. Jones to M. W. Ransom, March 17, 1879, J. A. Hyman to M. W. Ransom, August 31, 1880, all in Ransom Papers. Goldsboro *Messenger*, March 27, 1879; *Official Register*, 1883, I, 625; *Official Register*, 1885, I, 599.
5. Washington (D.C.) *Bee*, December 10, 1887.

Hawkins. Despite the *Bee's* flattery, he had little political strength and his campaign may have seemed a poor investment to a realistic politician. Yet his letter is significant for what it reveals about party politics in the district. Hyman took for granted that white Democrats and black Republicans had a common interest in weakening the influence of white Republicans. As an experienced professional, he knew without reflection that black-belt Democrats feared white Republicans as a threat to white solidarity. He also knew, from his own misfortunes, that white Republicans often refused to share fairly the privileges of party power. Hyman's letter also provides a hint of one of the major changes in party alignment in the years 1887 to 1895. During this chaotic period, as a farmers' revolt shook the Democratic party, eastern Democrats would strive to drive white men from the Republican party, the only biracial institution in their society.

History seldom repeats itself as clearly—and as quickly—as in North Carolina during the last twelve years of the nineteenth century. The 1888 state election anticipated the famous "white supremacy" campaign of ten years later. Faced with a politically conscious Farmers' Alliance, an attractive Republican gubernatorial candidate, and a large black vote, the Democracy desperately invoked the race issue to escape defeat. In the next year the general assembly tightened suffrage laws to limit Negro voting, and the Republican party in the eastern black belt was crippled. But discontented white farmers began leaving the Democratic party in 1892 to join the Populists, and two years later a Populist-Republican coalition captured the state legislature. The fusion legislators made possible a revival of black political power by revising election laws and reestablishing directly elected local government. The alliance between Populists and Republicans was always unwieldly, yet it maintained enough cohesion to elect a state administration in 1896. Democrats regained control of the legislature by repeating and intensifying the tactics of 1888 in the fiercely fought 1898 campaign, and after victory, as in 1889, they enacted new suffrage restrictions. This time the Democratic legislators were more thoroughgoing, producing a constitutional amendment to disfranchise most Negroes. In 1900 the voters ratified the amendment and elected a Democratic governor.

The first half of this cycle, from the end of the Bourbon era to about

1895, transformed the second district. After 1890 Republicans could no longer count on electing legislators from such former strongholds as Bertie, Edgecombe, Halifax, Northampton, even Warren. Democrats controlled most county governments, either by electing their own men or by refusing to accept the official bonds of many Republican victors. The boundaries of the district shifted in 1891, and a Democrat won the congressional seat in 1892 and 1894. Little more united than in previous years, Republicans suffered bouts of factionalism in 1888 and 1894, though there were no elections with two Republican congressional candidates.

Yet as the GOP disintegrated a curious florescence of black political power occurred. In a development related to the departure of important white leaders, blacks were appointed to more federal offices than ever before. The major post offices in Rocky Mount, Wilson, Windsor, Halifax, and Littleton, as well as several smaller places were administered by black postmasters. Unable to win elective offices, numerous minor politicians gained jobs in the federal bureaus in the District of Columbia.

The Democrat Furnifold M. Simmons represented the second district in Washington at the beginning of the period of party realignment and a decade later would be leading North Carolina Democrats to a sweeping, statewide victory on a platform of strident racism. In 1888, however, his tone was still conciliatory. Elected after significant appeals to the black vote, his performance in the Fiftieth Congress had been unusual.

On a number of issues he continued to court Negro support. He proposed to reimburse depositors in the Freedman's Savings and Trust Company, an action President Cleveland had endorsed in his 1886 annual message.[6] This future champion of white extremism also introduced a bill to establish a commission "to inquire into the progress of the colored race" and, like his black predecessor, presented a measure to give federal aid to common schools.[7] In his first speech, March 5, 1888, Simmons announced that the Republican party had lost control of the southern Negro vote. Disillusioned by Republican "false promises," black voters saw white southerners "burdening their property with excess

6. *Congressional Record*, 50th Cong., 1st Sess., 635; Abby L. Gilbert, "The Comptroller of the Currency and the Freedman's Savings Bank," *Journal of Negro History*, LVII (April, 1972), 139.

7. *Congressional Record*, 50th Cong., 1st Sess., 3250, 1343.

taxation to educate the black man" and understood from Cleveland's performance that there was nothing to fear in Democratic ascendancy. The future opponent of black voting promised to oppose any Republican attempts to disfranchise Negroes by reducing southern representation in Congress.[8]

If one judged a representative by the bills he introduced, it would be difficult to distinguish Simmons from earlier Republican representatives of the district. His bills for constructing public buildings in New Bern and Henderson, and for surveying four local waterways could have been presented by almost any district representative. Local pride rather than partisan politics motivated his advocacy of a revenue cutter and a federal road for New Bern. Simmons' eighteen private bills included six previously introduced by James O'Hara.[9]

The youthful congressman spoke several times on economic issues. He blamed the present tariff system on Republican "vultures of protection," who impoverished the farmer and constricted foreign trade, but he maintained that the internal revenue system ought to be substantially repealed before the tariff was reformed. On May 15, 1888, he somewhat reluctantly endorsed the party plan for tariff reduction: "I would . . . be lacking in frankness if I should say or pretend that this bill in its present shape is wholly acceptable to me, or, in my opinion, to the people of North Carolina."[10] Simmons later took the floor to defend a 100 percent duty on imported rice. "If there be any industry in this country that does need protection," he said, "and within the revenue limit and regulated by the revenue principle there are many, it is this particular industry of rice cultivation in the South." Such protection, he claimed, would largely benefit "the colored laborers of the South, in whom the Republican party professes such interest." Removing the duty would bring southern farmers into competition with cheap Chinese labor, said Simmons. These sentiments caused an opponent to accuse

8. *Ibid.*, 1749, 1750.
9. For the bills on public buildings and waterways, see *Congressional Record*, 50th Cong., 1st Sess., 7741, 357, 1529, 1922, 2678. For the New Bern bills, see 357, 635. For private bills, see 468, 3199, 2199, 7759, 5282, 724, 2724, 329, 1662, 4934. (I have assumed that Garrett C. Moye, Garrett C. Moge, and Garett G. Moze are all the same person.)
10. *Congressional Record*, 50th Cong., 1st Sess., 4181–84. The Tarboro *Southerner* objected to Simmons' position on internal revenue and tariff reform, May 24, 1888.

him of being "a protectionist of the ultra type," though the Republican member added, "He is for the protection of those articles in which he and his constituents are interested, and for which I do not blame him."[11]

A few days later Simmons again attacked the internal revenue system, which was unpopular with many Tarheels. He spoke in support of amendments repealing federal taxes on fruit brandy and certain tobacco products. At least these obnoxious levies should be abolished, he declared, even if it was impolitic to end immediately the entire system. Simmons thought the present taxes were a blight on the "poor man's orchard" and an injury to the "small cigar manufacturers in my district."[12] His predecessors Curtis Brogden and "Buck" Kitchin could have heartily applauded these sentiments.

Simmons' congressional record, in short, seemed a promising one to carry into a reelection battle. He had defended local interests, denounced internal revenue, and attempted to conciliate the Negro vote. If Republicans were divided, perhaps he could repeat his feat of 1886 without appealing to racial fears.

There was no shortage of Republican politicians who coveted Simmons' place. The woods were full of them, as the country editors liked to say, and they began making plans months before the campaign.[13] No Republican would succeed, of course, unless harmony were reestablished in the party. The two district committees produced by the bitter O'Hara-Abbott feud of 1886 would have to work together before the district could hold a unified convention. Meeting January 19, 1888, in Wilson, these committees agreed to consolidate, choosing Wilson Hicks of Vance, a member of the Abbott faction, as chairman of the unified committee.[14]

When battle for the nomination began in earnest during the spring of 1888, Vance Register Henry Cheatham and Leonidas J. Moore, a white attorney, collected more delegates than any other aspirants. Conventions in Craven, Jones, Lenoir, and Greene endorsed Moore. In the northern end of the district Cheatham won the support of Vance and Halifax

11. *Congressional Record*, 50th Cong., 1st Sess., 6082–85.
12. *Ibid.*, 6425–26.
13. Raleigh *Signal*, April 14, 21, 1887; Raleigh *State Chronicle*, March 17, 1887; Raleigh *Signal*, December 22, July 21, 1887; Salisbury *Star of Zion*, September 24, 1887; Raleigh *Signal*, February 9, 1888.
14. Wilson *Advance*, January 26, 1888.

counties. "Disorder, confusion, antics, foul language" marked the Edge-combe County convention according to the Tarboro *Southerner*, and rival factions split the session. A quiet campaign on behalf of Cheatham by the local, all-black chapter of the Knights of Labor had undermined what had been solid support for Sheriff Joseph Cobb. The Negro chair-man of the convention, William Lee Person, appointed a pro-Cobb credentials committee which preserved a Cobb majority by ruling in favor of a contesting delegation from one township. Following what had become customary in the district, the Cheathamites organized an opposition convention amid "confusion and fearful noise." As a result two Edgecombe delegations would appear at the state and district con-ventions.[15]

The district convention was held in Weldon, a site that no doubt pleased Cheatham, since Halifax County supported him. Candidates and delegates arrived in town throughout the day on May 29, gathering in small caucuses to discuss the prospects and, in some cases, to wager on the result of the next day's deliberations. Wearing badges of blue and gold, Cheatham and his followers came down from Vance in a special railroad car. The Weldon *News* noted eleven men who wanted to be nominated, including Charles Cook, George Mebane, Hyman, O'Hara, Cobb, and Cheatham.[16]

Almost as soon as executive committee chairman Wilson Hicks called the convention to order his authority was challenged. W. W. Watson of Edgecombe, chairman two years earlier, questioned whether Hicks had the right to appoint a credentials committee, but the convention voted to sustain Hicks. As the credentials committee considered disputes from Craven, Vance, and Edgecombe, hopeful politicians entertained the convention with speeches. Everyone realized that Cheatham's hopes for victory hung on the credentials committee's decision about Edge-combe. If the convention seated the four Cobb delegates—as the state Republican convention had done a few days earlier—Cheatham could count on the votes of no more than twelve of the twenty-eight delegates. If the Cheatham delegation were recognized, he could win the nomina-tion on the first ballot. When the majority report endorsed the Cheatham-

15. Kinston *Free Press*, May 10, 17, 24, 1888; Henderson *Gold Leaf*, April 19, 1888; Tarboro *Southerner*, March 29, 1888.
16. Weldon *News* quoted in Wilson *Advance*, June 7, 1888.

ites' claims in Edgecombe, the convention erupted into a "deafening" din. W. Lee Person, a Cobb delegate, charged the platform and tried to seize control of the meeting, with assistance from Watson and others. According to a pro-Cheatham report, "This created considerable confusion as the delegates and citizens who were in favor of having a peaceable convention went to the aid of the chairman." The Weldon *News* reported that "everybody was shouting and no one was listening." In the uproar Watson moved that George Mebane be nominated by acclamation, and the insurgents shouted their approval. In the same way, national delegates and a presidential elector were chosen.[17]

After ten minutes of disorder, the Mebane supporters "adjourned," and the regular convention resumed. Three of the eight members of the credentials committee presented a minority report in favor of the Cobb delegates, but the convention voted it down 11–7. The committee chairman complained later that he had been tricked into signing the majority report, which he opposed.[18] For permanent chairman of the convention, the delegates chose Claiborne Faison of Northampton, one of the three delegates who had played such an equivocal role in 1882. His signing of both rival candidates' statements may have made him temporarily unpopular, but it did not permanently discredit him.[19] In the constantly shifting, intense competition of the second district, most politicians found it practical to forget the dubious deeds of the last campaign—especially if the man were useful now. The disorderly anti-Cheathamite W. Lee Person would be thanking Cheatham in less than two years for a valuable federal appointment.

Despite the many aspirants, only two names, Cheatham and Cook, were put in nomination. Angry at the pro-Cheatham credentials report, Moore's supporters refused to participate in the nomination process, and when the roll was called Bertie, Lenoir, Jones, Greene, and Craven did not vote. Cheatham defeated Cook on the first ballot 16–2. A delegate from Jones and another from Lenoir at this point consented to vote

17. Weldon *News* quoted in Wilson *Advance*, June 7, 1888.
18. Raleigh *Signal,* August 30, 1888.
19. In a deposition of February 20, 1883, Willis Bagley, a white Republican lawyer from Northampton, said Faison had become unpopular in the county for his course in 1882. N.C. General Assembly, Legislative Papers, 1883, Parker v. Peebles.

and the result changed to 20 votes for Cheatham with no opposition, though eight delegates still abstained.[20]

The only candidate to profit from the Weldon Republican convention was Furnifold Simmons, for it now appeared that 1888 would repeat the campaign of two years earlier: two black Republican candidates and a Democratic victory. In fact, many Republicans assumed that Simmons had something to do with the Republican division. The day after the convention a black politician from Bertie, Mebane's home, wrote Senator John Sherman, noting the "disgraceful affair" in the second district and charging that Mebane "was hiard by certain parties to rase a row and claim the nomination[.] We all knew what was going to be done before the convention[.] [T]his was done to elect a democrat." But whatever his purpose in claiming the congressional nomination, George Allen Mebane was far from a political nobody. He had been elected to the state senate in 1876 and 1882 and apparently served with some distinction. He had also edited a black newspaper, the *Banner-Enterprise* of Raleigh, in association with E. E. Smith and John H. Williamson. Mebane probably considered himself a more experienced and capable politician than his youthful rival, whose only experience in politics came as Vance register of deeds.[21]

Mebane's strategy was to use his claim to force a new district convention. He wrote to Cheatham on June 2: "The interest of the Republican party and especially of our race demands that there be but one candidate in the race for Congress" and suggested that both of them "re-submit" their claims "to the Republicans of the district and let them decide whether they will have either of us or some other."[22] In reply Cheatham insisted that he was the regular nominee and had no right to refuse to do his duty. "I shall spare no pains in making a bold and aggressive fight for the success of the Republican party," he told Mebane, "especially since the Democrats are doing so much to split and confuse the Republican ranks."

20. Weldon *News* quoted in Wilson *Advance*, June 7, 1888.

21. W. H. Outlaw to John Sherman, June 1, 1888, in John Sherman Papers, Library of Congress. The Greensboro *North State* described Mebane as a leader among Senate Republicans (March 8, 1883). For one of the few extant issues of the *Banner-Enterprise*, see May 31, 1883.

22. Raleigh *Signal*, August 30, 1888. W. Lee Person also called for a new convention on a mid-June visit to Kinston. See Kinston *Free Press*, June 21, 1888.

"If you are the choice of the people," responded Mebane on June 11, "you can have no fear in resubmitting your claims to them." There was no time for further delay. "Both of us cannot be elected," he said, suggesting as a "last resort" compromise that both candidates submit the issue to the state executive committee. "Or, I am willing to submit to any proposition that may be suggested by you which affects both of us alike." Mebane added: "It is currently reported that you are hired by the Democrats to run against me for the purpose of again electing a Democrat from this district"—just what Cheatham's friends had been saying about Mebane. When it was clear that Cheatham would not accept a second convention, Mebane dispatched a letter of acceptance to the committee that had notified him of his "nomination," enclosing his correspondence with Cheatham to show his own efforts at "amicably adjusting the matter."[23]

Throughout the summer the two men vied for support, each blaming the other for the continued Republican division. Again and again Cheatham's supporters accused Mebane of being a hired tool of the Democrats, of "working in the interest of the Democratic party," and Mebane's men responded in kind. James O'Hara tried to keep the congressional dispute out of a Republican rally in Enfield, but Cheathamites erected their own stage and insisted on hearing a "two hour's outburst of eloquence" from their champion. According to a partisan report, O'Hara "orated to the gnarled oaks of a secluded grove," unable to draw a large crowd, even with the aid of a brass band.[24] W. Lee Person, chairman of the Mebane district executive committee, issued a set of anti-Cheatham resolutions adopted at a July 22 meeting of the committee, only to have one of the alleged members of the committee, Claiborne Faison, publish an angry letter declaring that the use of his name was unauthorized and branding Mebane a bolter "in the interest of F. M. Simmons."[25]

Many supporters of L. J. Moore refused to endorse either Cheatham or Mebane, raising hopes among the Democrats that they would vote for Simmons. The Kinston Free Press editor said "one or two" of the Moore leaders in the convention had told him "that the convention was nothing but a mob, that they were thoroughly disgusted and would not

23. Raleigh Signal, August 30, 1888.
24. Ibid., July 12, 1888.
25. Ibid., August 16, 30, 1888.

support either of the nominees." Moore quickly denied reports that he or his friends were planning to aid Simmons, though he admitted in the Raleigh *Signal* that he was "disgusted at the manner in which the Weldon convention was conducted."[26]

Moore's friend F. B. Loftin of Lenoir abandoned the Republican party, motivated partly by his anger over Republican congressional politics. A former senator from the Lenoir-Greene district, Loftin joined the Kinston Cleveland-Fowle club in July with the declaration that he had fallen out of sympathy with the attitude and goals of the Republican party. He mentioned the antisouthern tone of many northern Republicans, the party stand on the tariff, and "the feeling which the negroes of this Congressional district seemed to manifest against the white Republicans." He complained that in black counties Negro Republicans were determined to rule, and as evidence of antiwhite feeling he pointed to the treatment of Moore in the district convention. His friend "had a clear majority of the regularly chosen delegates, and yet some of them were unseated and Mr. Moore's claims ignored."[27]

As Republicans fiercely battled each other, Furnifold Simmons continued his remarkably low-key approach to racial issues. His comments before a convention held to reorganize the district committee, choose a presidential elector, and elect delegates to the national Democratic convention went about as far as any Democrat would go in opposing the extremist style of a "Buck" Kitchin. Speaking in Weldon a week before the Republicans' disorderly session, Simmons "said he was as much a white man as any who sat before him. He would not consent for colored men to rule this country; but he had all sympathy for them and believed it to be the duty of every one . . . to treat them fairly, justly and considerately and recognize their rights." His audience applauded, and Simmons reminded them of the support some blacks had given him two years earlier.[28] He left unsaid just what he considered the "rights" of Negroes. Later in the summer, after he had been formally renominated, Simmons told a Democratic rally in Kinston "that he considered it his duty to attend to the interests of the Republicans as well as Democrats. . . . He said that though he was a thorough Democrat

26. Kinston *Free Press,* June 7, 28, 1888. Raleigh *Signal,* July 5, 1888.
27. Kinston *Free Press,* July 19, 1888.
28. Weldon *News* quoted in Henderson *Gold Leaf,* June 7, 1888.

he asked the votes of the Republicans as well as Democrats, colored as well as white voters."[29]

Simmons was one of a few Democrats who hesitated to draw the color line in 1888. Most Democratic candidates throughout the state became harsher and more militant in their racist appeals as the campaign progressed, fearing that the Republicans were close to capturing the governorship. The GOP gubernatorial nominee, Oliver H. Dockery, was a member of the Farmers' Alliance and did his best to take advantage of the growing power of the order in his contest with conservative Democratic lawyer Daniel G. Fowle. As a strong vote-getter who had come within a hairsbreadth of carrying the state in 1882 as a candidate for representative-at-large, Dockery tried to neutralize the race issue by pointing to President Cleveland's overtures to the black vote. The North Carolina secretary of state, William L. Saunders, complained privately: "Our greatest trouble in North Carolina,—certainly one of the very greatest—comes from what I suppose may be called the exigences of Northern politics. I mean in plain words the necessity that has been upon Mr. Cleveland as to negroes. This I affirm unhesitatingly, has weakened us in our strongest point, that is to say, the race question."[30]

So Democrats repeatedly reminded voters of the threat to white supremacy in a Republican victory. "Shall the white man or the black man hold supremacy in the State is the overshadowing question," said the Warrenton *Gazette*. The more fanatical Democrats demonstrated a rising impatience with Negro voters and a willingness to follow "Buck" Kitchin in writing off the black vote. "Colored voters at the North are flocking by clubs to Cleveland's standard," noted the Tarboro *Southerner*. "They are not doing it here and no one cares the speck on the skin of a dried apple if they don't. . . . They have been argued with, coaxed and persuaded for the last time." The Wilson *Advance* condemned the "spirit of sycophancy that some Democrats exhibit when dealing with the negroes concerning their votes" and warned its readers: "The question is whether white men or negroes shall controll [*sic*] the state."[31] Although every postwar political campaign in North Carolina had been marked by some color-line rhetoric, the threats, demands, and appeals of

29. Kinston *Free Press*, September 20, 1888.
30. W. L. Saunders to M. W. Ransom, September 20, 1888, in Ransom Papers.
31. Warrenton *Gazette*, July 20, 1888; Tarboro *Southerner*, August 2, 1888; Wilson *Advance*, August 2, 1888.

1888 were the most intense and reckless since the early Reconstruction years. Remembering the Republican surge of two years earlier and fearing that their party was teetering on the brink of defeat, Democrats desperately clung to the one issue that might unite white voters.

One place in the second district where Democrats felt particularly anxious was Lenoir County, described in early July by local leader Jesse W. Grainger as "in desperate bad condition." The Democrats' effort to stay in power in Lenoir illustrates well the character of the statewide campaign in this twenty-third year since the end of the Civil War. Plagued by determined prohibitionists and discontented Alliance men, weakened by Governor Scales's unpopular railroad policy (which slighted Lenoir according to some local patriots), the party leaders were ready for strong measures to avoid defeat. Grainger wrote Senator Ransom two letters in two days, suggesting first that the party would gain 50 votes if two Lenoir men convicted of moonshining were pardoned, and pointing out the next day that Democrats in Lenoir and neighboring Greene needed a five-hundred-dollar campaign fund or else "we will be badly left." The party in the two counties was in a "worse condition than it has been *since the War*," averred Grainger.[32]

The Kinston *Free Press*, always fiercely partisan, sought to discourage Lenoir voters from supporting the state and national prohibition tickets by noting the female suffrage plank in the national prohibition platform. The editor invoked the frightful possibility of white women being forced to crowd against Negroes at the polls. The newspaper kept up a persistent barrage against two popular white Republican candidates, appealing to Democrats who had previously supported the men to vote the straight party ticket. "Can any truly WHITE man vote for Benj. Sutton?" asked the *Free Press*, referring to the Republican legislative candidate. Again and again readers were told that the two white Republicans were "politically black," reminded that the two had supported Negroes in the past, and exhorted "to stick to the white Democratic party."[33]

Such shrill appeals to white solidarity were sometimes matched by Republicans' fervent calls to Negro voters, if the partisan Democratic

32. J. W. Grainger to M. W. Ransom, July 4, 5, 14, 1888, Fabius H. Busbee to M. W. Ransom, August 27, 1888, all in Ransom Papers.
33. Kinston *Free Press*, September 27, October 4, 1888. See also November 1, 1888.

press is to be believed. Henry Cheatham, for example, was accused of delivering an "inflammatory" speech in Kinston, in which "he raised his eyes toward Heaven and swore that he wished God would strike him dead if he didn't honestly believe that if the Democratic party was successful in the coming election the negroes would be put back in slavery in less than 10 years." Like many a perspiring demagogue on the other side, Cheatham declared that any man of his race who voted for the wrong party was a "scoundrel." This language was out of character for Cheatham, and it is likely that his statement was exaggerated by the biased and irresponsible Kinston *Free Press*. Two weeks later a newspaper in Cheatham's home reported his speech to the Vance County Republican convention, describing it as a "much more sensible and conservative talk than some of the papers in the lower part of the district credit him with having made," though perhaps marked by some hyperbole.[34]

The prospects for a Republican victory in the congressional contest were greatly enhanced when Mebane pulled out of the race in the last part of September. Cheatham had gained the endorsement of the county conventions in Bertie and Lenoir, two areas that had originally refused to back him, and it may have been obvious to Mebane that he could not win. Many Democrats claimed Mebane withdrew because he had been bought off, and they accused a national tariff lobby, the Protective Tariff League, of supplying the money.[35] After the campaign a Republican campaign worker admitted that Mebane had been paid twenty-five hundred dollars to drop out of the congressional campaign. In February, 1889, Frank W. Leach, an aide to Pennsylvania Senator Matthew Quay, wrote an article for the Republican Raleigh *Signal* describing his covert efforts at unifying Republicans and ensuring an honest count of their votes. Leach said that Mebane had come to the Republican state committee with an offer to withdraw if he were given twenty-five hundred dollars for expenses. As Leach saw it, Mebane was less bought off

34. Kinston *Free Press,* September 6, 1888; Henderson *Gold Leaf,* September 20, 1888.
35. For Mebane's withdrawal statement, see Raleigh *Signal,* October 18, 1888. On the Bertie and Lenoir conventions, see Windsor *Public Ledger,* August 22, 1888; Kinston *Free Press,* September 6, 1888. For accusations regarding the "buying-off" of Mebane, see Wilson *Advance,* September 27, 1888; Wilson *Mirror,* October 3, 1888.

than bought back, since he had already been paid four thousand dollars by Democrats who hoped to divide the black vote.[36]

Assuming Leach's charge is accurate, the likeliest person to bankroll Mebane's insurgency was Simmons' former father-in-law, disaffected white Republican Lotte W. Humphrey. After word got out that Mebane was planning to step down, Humphrey wrote a long, revealing letter to Senator Ransom, asking for financial aid for Simmons and reporting on the state of the Democratic campaign in surrounding counties. "Mebane's withdrawal had not affected [Simmons] seriously as I thought it would," Humphrey wrote. "The prejudice against Cheatham caused by Mebanes candidacy is very great & will not down; the buying Mebane off by Cheatham, as they say, provokes greater feeling & the Mebane followers, leading men whom I have seen & heard from will vote for Mr. Simmons." Humphrey said a Tarboro black leader "regarded as Cheathams best man in Edgecomb [sic]" had been sent to see him by two Edgecomb [sic] white Democrats and would ("on account of local complications") support Simmons.

Humphrey was in touch with several other Republicans in Edgecombe who, because of a bitter, complicated party division over legislative candidates, were willing to support Simmons. "I have better co-operative help in Edgecomb [sic] than ever before," he said, and he noted encouraging reports of Simmons' strength in Jones, Craven, and Halifax as well. Humphrey appealed to Ransom: "I have no doubt that if Mr. Simmons could get the help he asks for he will be elected and in a legitimate way." Ransom's help was needed because Simmons and Humphrey had already "exhausted" themselves.[37]

A letter to Senator Ransom from a Craven Democratic leader provides further support for the idea that some Simmons supporter, not necessarily Humphrey, had financially aided Mebane. John D. Whitford commented: "There is much regret expressed respecting the run against Simmons. But it is truly said 'a dog that will fetch will carry.' A negro that can be bought will sell certain, therefore, I have feared all the

36. Raleigh *Signal*, February 14, 1889. Shortly after Mebane's withdrawal, E. R. Dudley, a black political veteran from Craven, charged that Mebane had "sold out for $3,000." Dudley announced that he would vote for Simmons. Raleigh *State Chronicle*, October 12, 1888.
37. L. W. Humphrey to M. W. Ransom, September 27, 1888, in Ransom Papers.

time such would be the final result of this presidential year."[38] But though the sources on this aspect of the campaign are frustratingly limited, it can be said with assurance that the Republicans did pay a substantial sum to Mebane, that many Republicans believed Mebane was cooperating with the other side, and that Humphrey spent a good deal of money in the effort to elect Simmons.

There is evidence that Humphrey was not the only former candidate for the congressional nomination who influenced the campaign with his money. Colonel R. E. Young, a wealthy leader in Vance County who had been a congressional aspirant in 1886, was said to have given important help to Cheatham. "His influence mainly nominated and elected Plummer Cheatham," reported a Democratic newspaper after the election. "But for his shrewdness in counter-acting certain influence favorable to the return of . . . Hon. F. M. Simmons that gentleman would doubtless have been reelected." The statement is vague, but it appears to refer to the Mebane candidacy. Young may have provided some of the money the Republican organization needed to "buy off"—or buy back—Mebane. A few days after the election the Gold Leaf, a newspaper published in Young's hometown of Henderson, observed darkly: "Had not Mebane been bought off the gallant Simmons would have succeeded himself. And it is alleged that it was not all 'Tariff League' money that got him out of the way, either."[39]

Whatever Young did for Cheatham, after the election Cheatham sought to have him appointed to a district collectorship in the Internal Revenue Department, an important post which Young's older brother Isaac had parlayed into considerable political power. When Cheatham first went to Washington, Young was said to be his "most efficient guardian."[40] Young and Humphrey were the sort of men who, under different circumstances, would be seeking the congressional nomination themselves. In the situation of 1888 such men were forced to choose between working outside the party or exercising political power in the background, from nonelective patronage or party positions.

For the next ten years no white candidate would come within striking

---

38. J. D. Whitford to M. W. Ransom, September 24, 1888, in Ransom Papers.
39. Raleigh State Chronicle, March 15, 1889; Henderson Gold Leaf, November 15, 1888.
40. Raleigh State Chronicle, March 15, 29, 1889.

distance of the second district Republican nomination. The era of
Bourbon equilibrium had trained a second generation of black political
leaders, men who had much greater mass appeal than the white leaders.
Henry Cheatham's generation had taken little part in Reconstruction,
was far better educated than the Negro leaders of the 1870s, and had
numerous, even expanding, opportunities to participate in local politics
or hold public service jobs in the postal service, internal revenue, public
school system, and elsewhere. Little did such men realize that political
opportunity would soon constrict; indeed, last year's state senator might
be next year's spittoon-cleaner in the District of Columbia. At any rate,
the intense competition among experienced black politicians made unlikely the success of a white candidate, however prominent.

Mebane's decision to drop out of the congressional race, for whatever
reasons, obviously limited Simmons' chances for victory. The divide-and-
conquer strategy of 1886 simply would not work again. Only if a significant number of Negro voters were persuaded to vote for Simmons—
or if he condoned vote fraud—could the Democratic candidate hope
to win. Both methods would be tried.

In the final weeks of the campaign it did seem that many black
voters were attracted by Simmons. When he spoke at the Vance courthouse, "among the crowd were many negroes who paid strict attention
to all the speaker said and many times he was heartily applauded on
that side of the house." In Enfield "not under 500" of an estimated 2,000-
person audience were Negroes and a colored brass band serenaded
Simmons, an apparently unprecedented event. When Simmons spoke
at another Halifax County town, Scotland Neck, a crowd of 700 or 800
included "about 250 colored men," according to the local newspaper.
Simmons told this group of blacks that he could do more for them in
Congress than could Cheatham.[41]

Republican state chairman John B. Eaves moved energetically in the
last few days of the campaign to discourage any black defections from
Cheatham. In a strongly worded circular to GOP workers he said:

I beg to advise that you see and send word to all the colored Preachers whom
you can reach, urging them to instruct the members of their churches to vote
and work for Professor Cheatham, without fail.

41. Henderson *Gold Leaf*, October 18, 1888; Scotland Neck *Democrat*, October
18, 25, November 1, 1888; Wilson *Advance*, October 25, 1888.

Tell them the Democratic managers are determined to elect Cheatham's opponent, by fair means or foul, and that Cheatham's defeat, in the largest Negro District in the United States, will be an everlasting disgrace to the Negro race.

Get them to advise their people to be sure to vote for Professor Cheatham and the whole Republican ticket, and not take their ballots from rascally negroes who have sold out their party and race for Democratic money.

. . . Ask these ministers to go to the polls and work for the election of Professor Cheatham, and for the uplifting of the colored race. THIS IS A RELIGIOUS DUTY. . . .

We must not allow Professor Cheatham to be defeated. WE ARE VERY MUCH AFRAID HE WILL BE! HEROIC MEASURES ARE DEMANDED TO SAVE HIM! The Democratic managers are determined to elect Simmons, if fraud, bribery and corruption will accomplish their purpose.

ACT AT ONCE![42]

On election day Cheatham led Simmons by a margin of several thousand votes, retaining the loyalty of the vast majority of Negroes, despite the confusion and bitterness of the long campaign and despite Simmons' appeals. Cheatham carried Craven, Edgecombe, Greene, Halifax, Northampton, Vance, and Warren, and only dishonest counting of the ballots made his victory seem a narrow one. "Official" returns had Simmons only 645 votes away from victory.

Cheatham's largest electoral hemorrhage occurred in Edgecombe County, where the Tarboro *Southerner* reported just after the election that he had received 3,196 votes to 1,775 for Simmons. The county canvassing board was able to eliminate much of this 1,400-vote margin when, according to the *Southerner*, "returns from several precincts were not counted because they were defective, and the Cheatham vote in some other townships were [sic] not counted because of alleged device on the ballots cast for him."[43] As a result the official returns listed 1,578 votes for Cheatham, only 200 more than Simmons' revised figure.

The canvassing board in Warren rejected the vote in seven precincts, reducing Cheatham to only 865 votes in a county that would give him nearly 1,900 two years later. The United States attorney for eastern North Carolina later sought indictments in twenty-seven "perfectly plain" cases of election law violations, including the canvassing boards in Warren and Northampton among the accused. After some difficulty

---

42. J. B. Eaves circular letter, October 31, 1888, in Hawkins Papers.
43. Tarboro *Southerner*, November 8, 15, 1888.

with Democrat-dominated grand juries, the Warren election case came to trial in 1891, but a jury "composed almost entirely of democrats" acquitted the defendents by ignoring what the prosecutor termed "overwhelming" evidence.[44]

All in all, according to the estimate of Daniel L. Russell, a prominent Republican attorney who helped prosecute the Warren case, the Republicans were defrauded of about 5,000 votes in the second district congressional race. The United States attorney was less definite, but he assured the attorney general that Republican congressional candidates ("especially in the Second Dist.") had been cheated out of "thousands of votes."[45] In spite of this, Republicans carried three of the state's nine congressional districts, the party's best showing since 1872.

In the legislative races second district Republicans suffered several sharp setbacks. In Bertie, Jones, and Halifax, Democratic candidates claimed victory, though the Republican nominees insisted that *they* had really won and vainly pursued election contests before the general assembly. As usual, the Democrats carried Wilson and, aided by the bruising journalism of the *Free Press*, won the house seat in Lenoir. Craven Republicans reelected their senator and representative, and the Republican nominees won in Edgecombe, Northampton, Vance, and Warren. A Republican was elected to the Lenoir-Green senate seat.

Elections for local offices showed a similar Republican contraction. For the first time in years Halifax elected a Democratic sheriff and register. In areas where Republicans held their own, three black registers of deeds were elected: Frank M. Hines in Edgecombe, Mansfield Thornton (for his sixth term) in Warren, and Thomas Eaton succeeding Cheatham in Vance.

Democrat Fowle defeated Republican Dockery in the gubernatorial election 148,000 to 134,000—or so the official returns said. Seven years later Dockery was telling people that two leading Democrats (by 1895 turned Populist) had told him "that he was really elected governor in

---

44. Charles A. Cook to Attorney General, December 11, 1889, March 24, June 9, 1890, June 9, 1891, in Department of Justices Files, Year Files, Record Group 60, National Archives. Raleigh *State Chronicle*, June 9, 1891. Compare A. W. Shaffer, "A Southern Republican on the Lodge Bill," *North American Review*, CLI (November, 1890), 605.

45. D. L. Russell to W. E. Chandler, February 25, 1890, in Chandler Papers. C. A. Cook to Attorney General, March 24, 1890, in Department of Justice Files, RG 60, NA.

1888, but was swindled out of it." Dockery's informants were Spier Whitaker, Democratic state chairman in 1888, and Whitaker's friend "Buck" Kitchin, both of whom had experience in dubious election practices from their activities in the second district. Josephus Daniels, who talked often with Whitaker during this campaign, remembered him as "cynical and sarcastic," a man who "thought it not wrong but smart to suppress the Negro vote," an art he had "mastered . . . in the Black District."[46] If many other counties followed the example of Edgecombe and Warren, it would be quite easy to believe that Dockery's claim was accurate.

The intense antiblack emotions aroused by the 1888 campaign did not fade quickly after the election. North Carolina Democrats seemed unwilling to face such a strong challenge again, and they adopted an aggressive and uncompromising attitude, born of a determination to disable the Republican party as the vehicle of black political aspirations. In the aftermath of the 1888 election, North Carolina politics would operate under ground rules far different from those of the decade following 1876.

A good illustration of this new ruthlessness was the matter of bonding local officers-elect. North Carolina law required that various elected officials post bonds to help insure honest execution of their duties, the size of the bond varying with the financial responsibilities of the position. The office of sheriff entailed the largest bond, since in most counties the sheriff had tax collection duties. For example, when Vance County officers renewed their bonds in 1887, Sheriff W. H. Smith presented three bonds (covering several aspects of his job) exceeding fifty-three thousand dollars, whereas Treasurer Robert Young's bond was eighteen thousand dollars, and Henry Cheatham's bond as register of deeds was only five thousand.[47] Whether the bond was satisfactory was left to the discretion of the nonpopularly elected county commissioners. If they found some defect in the bond or believed that the bondsmen had insufficient assets, they could reject the officer-elect's bond, declare the office vacant, and fill that office with another man.

The system of bonding hurt a party made up primarily of poor men. If, as a matter of party loyalty, Democrats refused to stand surety for any Republican elected to office, Republicans would soon find it very difficult to hold certain major offices such as sheriff or clerk of the superior court. The bonding system increased Republican dependence on the party's white members of means, for political success was impossible without men who either had the personal financial resources to underwrite party officeholding or the business connections and friendships to persuade nonparty members to do so. Moreover, since few Negroes were wealthy, or influential in business, the large bonds required for some offices had the effect of keeping such offices in white hands.

If Democrats were determined and disciplined enough, the bonding system could be used to undo the results of an election. Up to 1878 Democratic strategy was limited to pressuring party members not to sign Republicans' bonds. Designed to counteract Republican numerical superiority, such a political embargo was suited to the overheated mood of Reconstruction. Despite frequent exhortations from zealous editors, however, some Democrats ignored party lines and helped friends or relatives who had been elected on the GOP ticket. For instance, after the 1874 election in Edgecombe, the Tarboro newspaper campaigned strenuously against Democrats signing the bond of any "Civil Righter," but these appeals did not prevent several Democrats from acting as sureties for the Republican sheriff and register of deeds. One of those Democrats declared: "I signed the bond because [the editor] has been making such a fuss about it in his paper and I was determined he should not control me in my action."[48]

Democratic boards of county commissioners sometimes used the bonding system to frustrate majority will in "Negro counties." The Warren County commissioners used their discretionary power over bonds to foil Henry H. Falkener, a Negro who had won election to the position of clerk of the superior court in 1886. The board rejected Falkener's bond (according to one source "the chairman giving as his reason for his vote, that [Falkener] was a colored man an[d] he was opposed to his holding the office"), declared the office vacant, and elected the Democratic incumbent to another term. In 1882 the bonding system kept the Republicans who were elected Edgecombe's sheriff, clerk, and register

48. Tarboro *Enquirer-Southerner,* July 31, September 11, 1874. A year later the same newspaper, under a new name and editor, said that public opinion "winked at" the course of W. T. Cobb, who stood surety for his radical brother, Joseph Cobb. Tarboro *Southerner,* September 3, 1875.

from serving, and the commissioners installed Democrats in their places.[49]

Extreme views on bonds and politics became more popular in the period after the bitter 1888 election. The Kinston *Free Press* urged Democrats to refuse to go on the bond of any Republican for the federal position of postmaster "or any thing else." In Craven County, where the New Bern *Journal* had been advocating a moderate policy of coalition with dissident Republicans, the victory of the regular Republicans discredited the compromise policy. Taking a new hard line "straight out" approach, the *Journal* called on those Democrats who had in previous years signed the bonds of Republican officers to cease doing so: "Now Democrats, if you want to aid in keeping up the organization of the party which is endeavoring to poison the minds of these colored people against you, why go to work and sign the bonds of Hahn, Hancock and Berry. The money they make out of these offices will enable them to keep up their organization."[50] For over a month, readers of the Windsor *Ledger*, published in Bertie's county seat, debated the issue. A reader who signed his name "Abram Pristus" asked: "Why are there so many men that claim to be Democrats, yet, at the same time who are bonding Radicals in office; when they well know that the only hope of the Democrats getting in office in Bertie county is the failure of Radicals and negroes to give the bond?" According to this reader it was worse to bond a Republican than to vote for one. But another participant in this discussion observed that "weak kneed Democrats" were better than "strong kneed" Republicans and deprecated agitation of the bonding issue. Finally, after the election, the editor closed the debate by supporting the position that no Democrat ought to sign the bond of a Republican. Since a white Republican was simply a representative of Negroes, he maintained, could "any Democrat afford to assist in the continual defeat of his party?"[51]

49. Raleigh *Signal*, November 10, 1887. The quotation is from a card by M. M. Furgerson, a young white man who joined the GOP as a result of the Falkener affair. Tarboro *Southerner*, December 7, 1882. The Republican candidate for register, John C. Dancy, had run unopposed! During the 1882 campaign a white Republican aspirant for office had warned a Republican convention: "You all must nominate men who can give the bonds, there's no use talking about a Republican giving a bond unless the Democrats stand it, so you must nominate men who can get the Democrats to stand their bonds." Tarboro *Southerner*, September 21, 1882.

50. Kinston *Free Press*, November 15, 1882; New Bern *Journal* quoted in Kinston *Free Press*, November 15, 1882.

51. Windsor *Ledger*, October 3, November 7, 14, 1888. See also October 10, 17, 1888.

Inspired by such attitudes, Democrats in several second district counties reversed election results. In Green County, Republican R. D. S. Dixon had defeated Democrat John Sugg for sheriff, but when Dixon was unable to give a satisfactory bond Sugg took the office. Craven County had been under Republican rule since the start of congressional Reconstruction twenty years earlier, but the county commissioners refused to accept the bonds presented by the men elected sheriff, register, and treasurer, and put three Democrats in their places. Among the Edgecombe Republicans elected in 1888 only two Negroes, George Lloyd, a township constable, and Register of Deeds Frank Hines were able to give bond. The bonds offered by the sheriff-elect and the treasurer-elect, among others, were rejected. "Whether the result pleases every Democrat or not," said the Tarboro *Southerner*, "one thing should. Monday was a bad day for Edgecombe Republicans. They are left without a white leader in the county."[52]

The cautious, moderate spirit of Furnifold Simmons' term as representative of the second district was disappearing quickly. It had been undermined by the excesses of other Democrats, by Simmons' own willingness to use corruption and fraud, and by the tepid response of black voters. Changes on the national scene made North Carolina Democrats, like all southern Democrats, uneasy. For the first time in eight years there was a Republican president, a Republican House, and a Republican Senate, and some politicians were talking of new federal legislation to regulate southern elections and protect the Negro.

The next step for North Carolina Democrats was statutory restriction of the Negro vote and intensified social and political pressure on white Republicans in the black belt—a return, in short, to the Reconstruction-era politics of intransigence. A few weeks after the election the editor of the Tarboro *Southerner* commented: "If we take our own observations, right here in Edgecombe county we should say that the two races are drifting further apart, socially, religiously and politically."[53]

---

52. Kinston *Free Press*, December 6, 20, 1888; Tarboro *Southerner*, December 6, 1888.
53. Tarboro *Southerner*, January 31, 1889.

Chapter 9

A HARD ROW TO HOE

FROM THE START of his term Henry Plummer Cheatham had little chance of being reelected. Even as he took his seat in Washington in December, 1889, thousands of Negroes, including many from the second district, were migrating from North Carolina in a sensational "exodus." Fleeing hard times more than political oppression, these sharecroppers and laborers hoped to find economic opportunity in Arkansas, Texas, and Mississippi. Each family that boarded a Southwest-bound train represented several potential votes lost for Cheatham's party.

By mid-January, 1890, about sixteen hundred Negroes had left Edgecombe County and many more were thinking of leaving. "Temporarily, probably, but labor is more demoralized than it has been since the months just succeeding the downfall of the Confederacy," complained a Tarboro editor. The Kinston *Free Press* reported in March that Lenoir had lost one fifth of its black population. The whites who had welcomed the migration when it began early in 1889 had second thoughts a year later, and in several cases mobs obstructed the activities of labor agents promoting migration.[1]

Many of the black men who did not emigrate found their right to vote in jeopardy as a result of the general assembly's revision of the state election law. In an attempt to reduce the Negro vote, the law had increased the power of the overwhelmingly Democratic election officials and county canvassers. Republican leaders especially feared the mischief-making potential of one section of the law: "No registration shall be valid unless it specifies as near as may be the age, occupation, place

1. Tarboro *Southerner*, January 16, 2, 1890; Kinston *Free Press*, March 27, 1890; Anderson, "Race and Politics," 472, 476–80.

of birth and place of residence of the elector, as well as the township or county from whence the elector has removed—in the event of a removal—and the full name by which the voter is known." Applied with single-minded legalism, this provision could disfranchise many careless or ignorant voters.[2] Other features of the law made it difficult for illiterate voters to cast their ballots and easier for election officials to tamper with the count. If the election law of 1889 were rigidly enforced, Cheatham's position could be greatly weakened.

Little in Cheatham's background suggested that he would be able to overcome the odds against his reelection. He had been born a slave thirty-two years earlier, the child of a house servant, and he had spent his boyhood near Henderson. Better educated than his predecessors Hyman, Brogden, Kitchin, Hubbs, and O'Hara, Cheatham had graduated with honors from Shaw University in 1882 and served as principal of the Plymouth State Normal School for Negroes from 1882 to 1885. When the white Republican incumbent declined to be renominated and retired from politics, Cheatham was chosen as the Republican candidate for Vance County register of deeds, an office he won in 1884 and 1886.[3] Among his white neighbors, Cheatham had a reputation as "one of the most intelligent and responsible colored men in the county," a man "quiet in his demeanor, polite, courteous and dignified in his bearing." The Henderson newspaper said after his election: "While the GOLD LEAF regrets the defeat of Simmons, if a Republican and a colored man has to succeed him, we know of no one we envy the position and honor less than we do Plummer Cheatham. He has our respect and confidence to a degree few negroes have—because he merits and deserves such." In appearance Cheatham was tall, "quite stout," and fair skinned.[4]

2. North Carolina's early efforts at suffrage restriction are neglected in J. Morgan Kousser, *The Shaping of Southern Politics: Suffrage Restriction and the Establishment of the One-Party South* (New Haven, Conn., 1974), a valuable work arguing that scholars have overlooked the importance of statutory suffrage restrictions and overemphasized constitutional changes. *Laws and Resolutions of the State of North Carolina Passed by the General Assembly at Its Session of 1889* (Raleigh, 1889), Cpt. 287, p. 289.
3. *Congressional Directory*, 52nd Cong., 1st Sess., 78; Smith, *Negro in Congress*, 121. Warrenton *Gazette*, September 12, 1884, notes John W. Nicholson's refusal to accept renomination as Vance register.
4. Henderson *Gold Leaf*, March 31, 1887; November 22, 1888; Wilmington *Messenger* quoted in Henderson *Gold Leaf*, November 22, 1888. The biographical sketch in the *Congressional Directory* described Cheatham as a "bright mulatto" in appearance.

Well before Congress convened, Cheatham set to work on the problem of federal patronage for his district. Any congressman desiring reelection knew, of course, that the appointments he controlled must be made with care. For an inexperienced representative with a divided and declining political base, the subject was even more vital. Patronage, even more than eloquence on the floor of the House, would decide his fate. When a representative was of the same political party as the national administration, it was customary to allow him to dictate federal appointments within his district. Positions in the post office were the bulk of Cheatham's patronage, but his recommendation also carried weight in filling places in the customs, internal revenue, and judicial departments in eastern North Carolina, though he could not dictate a major appointment like collector of internal revenue for the eastern district. He worked as well to place deserving constituents in jobs in the District of Columbia.

There had never been more than two or three Negro postmasters in the towns of the second district, but in the first fifteen months of the Harrison administration black postmasters were appointed in at least nine places. The most important of these towns were Rocky Mount, Wilson, Windsor, and Halifax, the last three being county seats. Cheatham apparently followed sound political practice in making these appointments. His appointee at Wilson, Samuel H. Vick, was described by one local resident as an "active political worker," to whom Cheatham owed a "political debt." Former legislator Augustus Robbins became postmaster at Windsor, according to a Democratic newspaper, because he had "held the Bertie county Republicans for Cheatham." In Rocky Mount, after his first choice was charged with embezzling $693 and his second appointment was unable to give bond, Cheatham appointed W. Lee Person, the man who led the disruption of the 1888 convention on Mebane's behalf and served as chairman of the Mebane district committee.[5] Patronage could placate enemies as well as reward friends. Cheatham's influence brought the appointment of other blacks as postal clerks in the Railway Mail Service, census enumerators, and laborers and clerks in Washington, D.C. All of this convinced some Democrats that

5. John E. Woodard to M. W. Ransom, April 14, 1889, in Ransom Papers. Windsor *Ledger*, March 18, 1891. On the troubles of Cheatham's first two Rocky Mount appointments, see Tarboro *Southerner*, March 27, April 3, 1890.

they were being engulfed in black power. Harrison had been in office less than six weeks before the Kinston *Free Press* was ready to draw a moral: "The people now again are seeing what radical rule means—It means negro domination in the South."[6]

Cheatham's appointees varied widely in ability and performance. Several proved to be failures as public servants and provided grist for the antiblack propaganda mill. Henry W. Williams, postmaster at Tillery, was arrested for defrauding a fellow Republican; Weeks Armstrong was removed from the Rocky Mount postmastership after being charged with embezzlement; and Cora Davis lost her position at Halifax for the same reason.[7] How much of the financial difficulty of the post offices was the result of incompetent accounting and how much the result of intentional fraud is not clear. Several other Negro postmasters were exemplary officers, however, and even political foes were sometimes willing to concede it. A Rocky Mount banker said in 1898, in a private letter, that W. Lee Person had given "good service" as postmaster under the Harrison administration. In the same year a leading Wilson Democrat was willing to sign an endorsement of Samuel Vick as an intelligent, responsible man who had given "highly satisfactory" service in his tenure as postmaster.[8]

Despite the howls of partisan Democrats, Cheatham's richest patronage plums did not, in fact, go to Negroes but, as usual, went to white Republicans. The post office at Tarboro, county seat of politically turbulent Edgecombe, was awarded to Joseph J. Martin, former district solicitor, former congressman from the first district, and Republican candidate for presidential elector in 1888. The postmaster at New Bern was William E. Clarke, a four-term state legislator. In Kinston, Cheatham rewarded Republican leader W. W. N. "Nick" Hunter by securing the appointment of his wife Ada as postmaster. For the position of U.S. attorney in eastern North Carolina the administration chose Charles A.

---

6. Kinston *Free Press*, April 18, 1889. For complaints on Cheatham's having replaced white census enumerators with blacks, see Tarboro *Southerner*, June 5, 1890.

7. Scotland Neck *Democrat*, January 16, 1890; Tarboro *Southerner*, March 27, 1890; Wilson *Advance* quoted in Kinston *Free Press*, January 22, 1891. A reader of the Raleigh *News and Observer* (December 6, 1890) said of Cora Davis: "Not a white person in town believes her guilty; she can give the very best recommendation for honesty."

8. T. H. Battle to Marion Butler, April 16, 1898, J. E. Woodard to Whom It May Concern, March 16, 1898, both in Butler Papers.

Cook, a rival of Cheatham at the nominating convention who had given him strong support in the subsequent campaign. According to Josephus Daniels' *State Chronicle*: "Cook was backed by Cheatham, the colored Congressman, whose endorsement seemed to be the most potent power in Washington." This was stretching things a bit since Cheatham, along with North Carolina's two other Republican congressmen, had recommended Robert E. Young for collector of internal revenue and another man had been appointed.[9]

Most North Carolina black leaders were angry at the Harrison administration's appointment policy, and Cheatham's local success in securing offices for his black constituents went unnoticed. The general Negro discontent resulted in a meeting of two hundred delegates from around the state in Raleigh, August 26, 1890, to discuss the unequal distribution of federal patronage and other grievances. Speaker after speaker demanded just recognition of Negro voters, the backbone of the Republican party. The reputation of a discreet administration supporter like Cheatham could not have been high at such a gathering; indeed, according to one report, there was "much opposition" to Cheatham among the delegates, and one unnamed "leading negro" predicted his defeat at the next election.[10]

Cheatham was the only black member of the House when Congress convened. (Not until the first session was nearly over, months later, would John Mercer Langston of Virginia and Thomas E. Miller of South Carolina take their seats after successful election contests.) Cheatham would make very few speeches in his four-year congressional career. In fact in the first session of the Fifty-first Congress the youthful representative said nothing at all; his only "remarks" are in the appendix of the *Congressional Record*, where undelivered speeches were printed.[11]

A member of the Education Committee, Cheatham introduced a bill

9. Record of Appointments of Postmasters, Vols. 49, 69, RG 28, NA. For a response to Mrs. Hunter's appointment, see Kinston *Free Press*, October 3, 1889. Raleigh *State Chronicle*, October 18, 1889; New York *Times*, September 1, 1889.

10. New York *Times*, August 27, 1890; Raleigh *News and Observer*, August 27, 1890; Kinston *Free Press*, September 4, 1890. Compare George Sinkler, "Benjamin Harrison and the Matter of Race," *Indiana Magazine of History*, LXV (September, 1969), 197–209.

11. On the authority of a personal interview he had with Cheatham, Samuel D. Smith maintained that Cheatham "sought to do more in the committee room and by personal contact than in set speeches on the floor." Smith, *Negro in Congress*, 124.

for federal aid to common schools which embraced "the chief features of the Blair Bill," including an appropriation of about eighty million dollars over a number of years. The Education Committee reported the bill favorably, but it got no further than that. Cheatham proposed two other bills that received favorable committee reports but never reached the floor for debate—one a bill for the erection of a public building in Henderson, his home, and another to provide relief to black hero (and former congressman) Robert Smalls and his associates in the Civil War capture of the Confederate ship *Planter*. Like Simmons and O'Hara, Cheatham advocated relief for the depositors in the defunct Freedman's Savings and Trust Company, but his bill died in committee.[12]

In a rare dissent from party policy, Cheatham took a strong stand against the Conger lard bill, a measure to tax compound or artificial lard. Seeing the bill as an attempt by pure lard manufacturers to curb the production of cheap imitation lard from cottonseed oil, Cheatham could not approve. "I do not like . . . to differ with the leaders of my own party, but I am compelled in this case, representing the constituency I do on this floor, to raise my voice against the adoption of this measure," he declared in a printed speech. In the name of impoverished southern farmers, white and black, he objected to a tax that would raise the price of food supplies, finding himself allied with many southern Democrats in futile opposition to this bill. Cheatham supported the McKinley tariff and the Lodge election bill, two major House Republican measures of the session, but he did not speak in behalf of either. A caucus of southern Republican congressmen elected him to a committee charged with representing the interest of tobacco growers before the House-Senate conference committee on the tariff bill.[13]

As Cheatham gravely played his modest role in Congress, the second district was being shaken by an economic debacle, and the agricultural depression, in turn, intensified demands from farmers for more political influence. The cotton crop of 1889 was no more than half the average

12. *Congressional Record*, 51st Cong., 1st Sess., 248, 6901; Salisbury *Star of Zion*, July 17, 24, 1890; *Congressional Record*, 51st Cong., 1st Sess., 248, 269, 3700, 6652.
13. *Congressional Record*, 51st Cong., 1st Sess., appendix, 624–27. For his votes on the tariff and elections bills, see *Congressional Record*, 51st Cong., 1st Sess., 6940, 10641. Baltimore *Sun* quoted in Raleigh *News and Observer*, September 24, 1890. Cheatham did address the House Republican caucus on behalf of the Lodge bill. New York *Times*, June 11, 1890.

in the second district, and the corn was reported only slightly better. In some local areas the situation was even worse. A biracial committee of citizens in Warren estimated that the cotton crop was at least 75 percent below normal levels, and unless something was done "there would be starvation, the poor house or moving away for many," as the Warrenton *Gazette* put it. Mass meetings in Halifax and Northampton asked Governor Fowle to call a special session of the general assembly so that county commissioners in areas suffering from short crops could be empowered to issue bonds to raise money for relief. The editor of the Kinston *Free Press* disapproved of this economically unorthodox idea, but he was forced to adjust in his own way to hard times. Readers were told that they could pay for their subscriptions in yams, wood, or turkeys. "In fact if you are behind for your subscription and can't pay any other way at once, we could take eggs, fresh pork, corn or anything in that line at market prices."[14]

Economic distress hurt Cheatham in a very obvious way, of course, because it encouraged the migration of his black constituents. In the early months of 1890 Democrats were already calculating how much they had been helped by the decline in black population, and many looked to the election with confidence. With victory possible, the Democratic nomination in the second district had suddenly become a more valuable prize. But if it was more valuable, perhaps it was also worth squabbling over, for the depression in agriculture had not worked to unify the Democracy. The question of what to do about the farmer's plight provoked widely differing answers, with many traditional party leaders, such as lawyers and county editors, uneasy with the proposals of the aggressive and well-organized Farmers' Alliance. With a relatively united Republican organization and confusing strife in the Democratic camp, the 1890 campaign would be the reverse of most previous campaigns in the "black second."

The president of the North Carolina Farmers' State Alliance was Elias Carr, a gentleman farmer in Edgecombe County. During 1890 he carried on an extensive correspondence with Alliance leaders throughout the second district, and these letters reveal much about Democratic

14. Kinston *Free Press*, November 7, 1889; Raleigh *State Chronicle*, November 29, 1889; Warrenton *Gazette*, December 13, 1889, January 24, 1890; Kinston *Free Press*, December 19, 1889.

divisions in this election. For many Alliance men, Carr would have been the ideal choice for the Democratic congressional nomination. In March, he received a letter from James M. Mewboorne, business agent for the Lenoir Alliance, pointing out that a Democrat had a good chance to carry the district because of the black exodus and urging Carr to allow his name to be quietly promoted. If Carr would let his friends work for him, Mewboorne said, "in the next election it will be Carr the Laborers friend and brother instead of Cheatham his pretended friend."[15] Carr declined to follow this advice, but the talk of him for Congress would not go away.

Seemingly oblivious to the strong grass-roots demand for a farmer nominee, other editors suggested the familiar names of two lawyers. The Scotland Neck *Democrat* proposed William H. "Buck" Kitchin, the town's most famous citizen, and the Kinston *Free Press* supported Furnifold Simmons for a third nomination. Doubting that enough Negroes had left the district to make it safely Democratic, the *Free Press* said the former congressman "is in all probability the only man that can be elected in the 'black district', as he is the only one who can carry any considerable number of negro votes, which he did in both elections—and it takes some negro votes to elect a Democratic representative in this district."[16] But the trouble with nominating Simmons, as Mewboorne told Carr in a letter May 25, was that many Alliance men would not support him even if he were nominated. Others thought Simmons was a good man but that the three hundred lawyers already in Congress were enough, according to W. H. Worth, state business agent of the Alliance. Mewboorne again pressed Carr to run, adding that if Carr would not carry the Alliance demands to the people, Mewboorne himself "would bear them aloft and bid the lovers of these grand principles to follow," though he preferred for Carr to do the job. But despite appeals from Mewboorne, Worth, and others Carr declined to seek the nomination.[17]

15. J. M. Mewboorne to Elias Carr, March 4, 24, 1890, D. H. Rittenhouse to Carr, April 15, 28, 1890, all in Carr Papers. Tarboro *Southerner*, April 10, 1890. Mewboorne's name is often spelled "Mewborne." The correct form is not clear, though the man's own stationery was imprinted with "Mewboorne."
16. Scotland Neck *Democrat*, April 24, 1890; Kinston *Free Press*, May 1, 22, 1890.
17. J. M. Mewboorne to Elias Carr, May 25, 1890, W. H. Worth to Carr, May 28, 1890, W. B. Fleming and W. R. Wiggins to Carr, June 7, 1890, E. H. E. F. Perry to Carr, July 9, 1890, all in Carr Papers.

Many Lenoir Alliance men promoted Mewboorne as the farmer's candidate and at least half of the thirty-two Lenoir delegates to the district convention were his supporters. Those who favored a farmer for Congress were determined not to be deterred by "butter and honey words of the so called party leaders." But by mid-summer Furnifold Simmons seemed to be moving irresistibly toward another nomination. In a widely publicized letter to the secretary of the Greene County Alliance, a letter that helped him win the unanimous endorsement of the county Democratic convention, Simmons attempted to appease farmer discontent. Avoiding a specific endorsement of the subtreasury plan, he praised the Alliance's objectives and insisted that all the laws of which the Alliance complained were the work of the Republican party: "The Republican party is and has been the enemy of the farmer." He attempted to blunt the prejudice against his being a lawyer by declaring that his father was a farmer "and so were all his ancestors before him." He insisted that he shared farmers' interests, since he was himself "born and raised on a farm."[18]

Reports began to spread that Alliance man Mewboorne was not a staunch Democrat, that he had voted for Garfield in 1880 and Dockery in 1888 and frequently split his ballot in local elections. Carr asked Mewboorne for an explanation and received in reply an earnest epistle flavored with crusaders' clichés. "I am now and have been a lifelong Democrat," affirmed Mewboorne, asserting that he had never voted for a candidate for president, governor, other state officer, congressman, or even legislator who was not a Democrat. He did say he had voted twice for a Republican for sheriff because the Democratic candidate was a "great drunkard" who had treated the local option law with contempt. And he had also voted for one of his best friends for county treasurer, even though he was a Republican, and had declined to support the county's Democratic register of deeds for a third term "when I thought he ought to have gotten out." All this he had done openly—as he put it, "every man in the county knew it." But if any sincere Alliance men were afraid that Mewboorne was a crypto-Republican, let such a person support Captain William J. Rogers of Northampton, another agrarian aspirant, and Alliance principles would triumph just the same. The stories

18. W. H. Worth to Elias Carr, June 30, 1890, J. M. Mewboorne to Carr, May 25, 1890, both in Carr Papers. Kinston *Free Press,* July 3, 1890.

that Mewboorne was not a good Democrat were started for the purpose of discrediting the Alliance, Mewboorne was sure, and he was ready to answer any charges at the district convention.[19]

As farmers' efforts to nominate a tiller of the soil faltered, Simmons' strength grew. Party conventions in Jones and Craven endorsed him and former congressman Kitchin withdrew from the race for the sake of unity. At the same time Simmons deplored "class prejudice," saying that he would not accept the nomination unless it came to him "with something like practical unanimity." All vocations had suffered with farmers in the agricultural depression and he refused to bow before an irrational antilawyer sentiment. "I want it understood that I am neither a farmer's, a lawyer's, a mechanic's, a doctor's nor a merchant's candidate; but a Democratic candidate."[20]

Simmons realized that the nomination would be useless in the second district if any sizable group of Democrats were not totally committed to the candidate; lukewarm support would be as good as none in such a close district. Even though he seemed to have a good chance for the nomination, he apparently doubted that he could win in the general election. Accordingly, on July 27 he announced his withdrawal from the contest, giving as reasons the desire among many Democrats for a farmer nominee and his own refusal to sign the Alliance "demands" (though he said he backed the *principles* of the demands). Also, since the nominee for judge of the Second Judicial District was a Craven man, it might seem unfair to Democrats in other parts of the district if Craven County took the congressional nomination too. In short, Simmons presented himself as a loyal Democrat subordinating "all personal considerations" in favor of party success. Neither Simmons' friends nor the Alliance men took his withdrawal as final or permanent. Mewboorne privately regarded it as a "feint," and the Kinston *Free Press* expressed the hope that Simmons would yet be the Democratic candidate if the nomination were tendered him by a united convention.[21]

19. J. M. Mewboorne to Elias Carr, July 15, 1890, in Carr Papers.
20. Kinston *Free Press*, July 10, 17, 1890; Tarboro *Southerner*, July 17, 1890; Scoltand Neck *Democrat*, July 17, 1890.
21. Kinston *Free Press*, July 31, 1890. According to the Scotland Neck *Democrat*, July 31, 1890, the letter first appeared in the New Bern *Journal*, July 27, 1890. J. W. Mewboorne to Elias Carr, August 6, 1890, in Carr Papers. Kinston *Free Press*, July 31, 1890.

Mewboorne's alleged party irregularity became a more urgent issue in the wake of Simmons' withdrawal. Mewboorne "is no Democrat and it would be a disgrace to nominate him," the Wilson *Advance* declared bluntly. "We want a straight Democrat," said Tarboro's *Carolina Banner*; "He has badly split his ticket in the past." When Democrats in Mewboorne's home county of Lenoir met to choose candidates for the county offices and the legislature, the convention passed a resolution endorsing Simmons for Congress.[22]

Despite their imperfect unity, Democrats were confident of victory when their convention met September 3 in Kinston. One speaker said Democratic chances were much better than in 1888 thanks to the work of labor agent "Peg Leg" Williams "and his emissaries," and delegates had a hearty laugh when someone suggested a round of three cheers for "Peg Leg." (In the fall of 1890 the Tarboro *Carolina Banner* estimated that the second district had lost twenty-five hundred voters.)[23]

Alliance delegates to the district convention met the morning before the main meeting to lay their plans. It quickly appeared that William J. Rogers of Northampton had greater support than Mewboorne, so all agreed to back Rogers. Mewboorne's name would not be put in nomination.

Divided as they were, the Democrats had no embarrassing credentials contests of the sort that graced Republican conventions. The sign of the dominant faction in their convention was found in the ink and paper of the platforms and resolutions, not in the turmoil of broken furniture or brawling delegates. The political language adopted by this meeting condemned monopolies, the force bill, "the tyrannical . . . usurpation of authority by the Speaker of the House," alien land ownership, national banks, insufficient volume of currency, and the single gold standard—indicating clearly that the farmers were having an impact. Only Simmons and Rogers were nominated for Congress. Simmons' friends said their man was not seeking the office but they were nominating him anyway, and one speaker tried to show "that it was the farmers

---

22. Wilson *Advance*, July 31, 1890; Tarboro *Carolina Banner*, August 1, 1890; Kinston *Free Press*, August 14, 1890. The Tarboro *Southerner*, which had defended Mewboorne, changed its view August 14, 1890, after the action of this Lenoir convention.

23. Kinston *Free Press*, September 4, 1890; Tarboro *Carolina Banner*, October 17, 1890.

who were bringing forward Mr. Simmons' name before the convention."
For a man who said he did not want the nomination, Simmons made a
remarkable showing. Craven and Greene supported him unanimously and
Jones's delegates voted for him 13–2. He carried Wilson by 1 vote and
split Bertie's delegates with Rogers. Northampton, Vance, and Warren
went for Rogers by overwhelming margins, whereas Simmons did somewhat better in Lenoir, Halifax, and Edgecombe, receiving at least a
third of the votes. The final vote, ignoring marginal ballots, was 200 for
Rogers and 149 for Simmons.[24]

Although the farmers had pressed their candidate upon party leaders,
William J. Rogers was not an uncouth, militant hayseed; he was, in
fact, little different from previous winners. A native of Northampton, a
graduate of the University of North Carolina, and a former Confederate
officer, he was fifty-two in 1890. "He has been a life-long Democrat
of the Jeffersonian school," reported one journalist with optimistic vague-
ness.[25]

The campaign for the Republican nomination had little of the flair and
drama of the Democratic one, Cheatham being renominated in the midst
of his legislative labors, August 14, in Henderson. To counter any discontent against the incumbent, Cheatham had enrolled the help of J.
Willis Menard, former black congressional aspirant from Louisiana. In
a public letter urging Cheatham's renomination, Menard noted that a
congressman cannot accomplish much during his first term. Considering
this, he said, "it is not strange that dissatisfaction has been created among
some of the constituents in regard to the distribution of patronage." One
term was not sufficient for a fair trial of a representative's talents,
especially of one whose success was important to Negroes throughout
the nation. "A colored man has a hard row to hoe," wrote Menard,
"whether he be in or out of Congress. What he gets, is but little, and
he has hard work to get that."[26]

On more than one Sunday morning, certainly, Baptist Henry Cheat-

24. Kinston *Free Press*, September 4, 1890.
25. *Ibid.* Rogers was elected Northampton register of deeds in 1880. Northampton
County Record of Elections, 1878–1906 (microfilm), in North Carolina Department
of Archives and History.
26. Salisbury *Star of Zion*, July 31, 1890. The Kinston *Free Press*, August 14,
1890, noted publication of a pamphlet by R. M. Johnson, a Greensboro black, that
"savagely attacked" Cheatham, but I have been unable to discover any specifics
of Johnson's criticism.

ham had been told that a soft answer turneth away wrath. The proverb seemed particularly apt in a time of political turmoil when old systems and loyalties were weakening; in its spirit Cheatham conducted a cautious campaign to win white farmers' votes and reassure Negro supporters.

When he delivered a campaign speech in Wilson, at least a third of his audience was white. Avoiding comment on the force bill or the tariff, Cheatham "devoted himself mainly to the ills from which the agriculturists were suffering" and spoke of a congressional bill to stop speculation in cotton. He condemned that great monopolist Andrew Carnegie "for importing laborers and refusing to hire negroes" and called for a large national appropriation for education. Carefully avoiding losing black voters, he "proudly boasted that he had put more negroes in office than any man on earth." Toward his opponent he showed no bitterness, assuring his hearers that he expected a fair election and victory. In summary, the hostile report in the Wilson *Advance* conceded: "His speech was a politic one. He was careful not to offend or arouse the feelings of white men present, nor did he play upon or excite the prejudices of the negroes."[27]

Cheatham made a similarly mild speech in Kinston, where he opened his remarks "by saying he came with no harsh words, he was not here to stir up any ill-feeling or animosity towards any man or party of men." Again he said nothing about the tariff or the elections bill, instead speaking on subjects more popular among Alliance men, such as the compound lard bill, the measure to reduce the hours of government employees to eight hours a day, and the Sherman Silver Purchase Act. "The speech was altogether different from the one he made two years ago," observed the Kinston *Free Press*. "Then he made almost an incendiary speech; this time he urged harmony between the races."[28]

As Cheatham appealed to white farmers, Alliance strategists were confident that they could draw a significant number of Negroes to their side. An Alliance man in Lenoir had written Elias Carr in the spring reporting that black voters were restive. "A very prominent" Negro clergyman of Lenoir had told him recently "that his people had lost confidence in the leaders of both of the old parties," and if the Alliance

27. Wilson *Advance*, October 20, 1890.
28. Kinston *Free Press*, October 30, 1890.

would nominate a "good honest" farmer or working man, blacks would give "liberal" support. An Alliance leader wrote to Mewboorne in August: "If Cheatham is nominated I have a good Negro allianceman here [District of Columbia] that will come down into Halifax and Warren and beat him there." The Alliance business agent in Craven thought local Negroes were "delited [sic] to think that we have an Alliance man for Congress" and promised to hold them together if he could have some money to quiet some of the "mouthy" ones.[29]

The small, but highly significant white contingent in the district Republican organization was in considerable confusion during this campaign summer of 1890. Before either party had nominated its candidate, New Bern attorney Leonidas J. Moore wrote to the chairman of the Democratic state executive committee, announcing the end of his twenty-year relationship with the Republican party. Moore had been an active participant in congressional politics, having been an aspirant for the nomination in 1886 and 1888; in 1882 he had backed James O'Hara against the white incumbent from his own county, Orlando Hubbs. Moore's letter explained his political conversion by pointing to the "legislation of the present Congress," which he considered antisouthern. Apparently he had been shaken by the elections bill, the tariff, and the methods of "Czar" Thomas B. Reed, Speaker of the House: "I know many men who, like myself, have for years acted with the Republican party, and who have felt obliged to change their political relations . . . by the violent and unlawful legislation of the present Congress." He did not mention his own disappointed ambitions. Francis D. Winston, a talented young Republican from Bertie, also left the Republican party during this campaign and he too cited national issues as being responsible for his decision. The leaders of the GOP, he complained, had abandoned the "wise, liberal and progressive" policies carried out by Garfield, Arthur, and Cleveland. Within eight years he would be a leader in his new party, a militant white supremacist helping write legislation to disfranchise the North Carolina Negro, but in 1890 Winston still saw himself as "a friend of the negro."[30]

29. B. F. Scarborough to Elias Carr, May 19, 1890, D. H. Rittenhouse to J. M. Mewboorne, August 4, 1890, J. M. Mewboorne to Carr, August 6, 1890, H. H. Perry to Carr, September 22, 1890, all in Carr Papers.
30. Kinston Free Press, July 31, 1890; Raleigh News and Observer, October 7, 1890.

In Edgecombe long-time Republican officeholder Joseph Cobb retired from politics after the county Republican convention endorsed the Democratic candidate for county treasurer. The office was one of those usually held by a white Republican, mainly for economic reasons, and by conceding the place to the opposition Edgecombe's black politicos expressed a total unconcern for men like Cobb who had so long been important in party councils. The Negroes seemed interested only in offices black candidates could plausibly seek. It is also quite possible that the party chairman had been bribed to secure Republican support for selected Democrats. Cobb had been the GOP candidate for sheriff, but he withdrew from the race, telling his party colleagues in farewell "that whenever the Republican party turned its back on the white Republicans, the party was soon gone." He predicted, "You may succeed this year, but it is the last time."[31]

The poor health of the Democrats' congressional nominee, W. J. Rogers, made it difficult for them to take advantage of the divisions among their political enemies. Earlier in the summer, before the convention, Rogers had come close to dropping out of the congressional race because of illness, and now, as the campaign moved into its final month, he was not well enough to canvass the district.[32] He therefore resigned and set in motion a confusing series of events.

After failing to reach a quorum October 8, the executive committee for the second district met October 14 to consider the new situation. They accepted Rogers' resignation but decided that a replacement was "inadvisable" in view of the lateness of the date. Still determined to advance Alliance principles, James Mewboorne declared himself an unofficial Democratic candidate several days later. The Warrenton *Gazette* and Kinston *Free Press* endorsed him as the only remotely Democratic candidate available, and the *Gazette* condemned the executive committee's course as either cowardly or stupid. Others would not

31. Tarboro *Southerner*, September 25, 1890. Partly in protest of these endorsements, another GOP ticket came out before election day. See Tarboro *Southerner*, October 16, 1890. According to the 1895 testimony of Frank L. Battle, a minor black politician in Edgecombe, from 1888 on it was routine for Republican chairmen to receive a "bonus" for having Republican conventions endorse certain Democrats. U.S. Congress, House, *Contested Election Case of Henry P. Cheatham v. Frederick A. Woodard from the Second Congressional District of the State of North Carolina* (Washington, D.C., 1896) 172–73.

32. W. J. Rogers to Elias Carr, July 7, 1890, in Carr Papers.

accept Mewboorne even under these circumstances. "There is a very good chance for a Democrat in this district," said the *Carolina Banner*, "but many around here say they cannot vote for such a self made candidate and we are compelled to say please excuse us."[33]

Mewboorne was unaware that his action had upset the secret plan of a few party leaders. According to Y. T. Ormond, executive committee chairman, the real reason for the decision not to nominate a replacement for Rogers was not shortness of time. Instead some committee members believed that the Democratic legislative tickets in Halifax, Northampton, and Vance, as Ormond remembered it, would have a better chance of being elected if there were no Democratic nomination for Congress. Presumably if Cheatham ran unopposed fewer Negroes would bother to register, and it was better, they assumed, to lose the congressional race than to risk losing control of the state legislature, as had nearly happened in 1886. Ormond was not present when this decision was made and he opposed it. After consulting with the state chairman, he decided that the committee ought to put a congressional nominee in the field at the last minute after the registration books had been closed. In this way, Democrats would have a man to vote for in the congressional election, and the legislative candidates would profit, too.[34]

More specifically, the plan was to distribute W. J. Rogers' ballots even though he had not campaigned and to elect him in a coup that would surprise everybody. Mewboorne's independent announcement ended this scheme and provoked an angry letter to him from Elias Carr, who had been aware of the plan. Mewboorne wrote back: "In reply would say that surely I meant *good* if harm as you predict may come." Mewboorne said his actions had been dictated by zeal for Alliance principles, not personal ambition. He had been urged to act by local Democrats, including some who had opposed him before, but had he known of Rogers' plan he would not have announced himself a candidate. "I did it . . . because no one was out and as I understood it no one was to be put out" as a candidate.[35] As he was writing to Carr,

33. Kinston *Free Press*, November 20, 1890; Wilson *Advance*, October 16, 1890; Kinston *Free Press*, October 23, 1890; Warrenton *Gazette*, October 24, 1890; Tarboro *Carolina Banner*, October 22, 1890.

34. Kinston *Free Press*, November 20, 1890.

35. W. J. Rogers to Elias Carr, October, 1890, Carr to J. M. Mewboorne, October, 1890, W. S. Barnes to Carr, October 2, 1890, J. M. Mewboorne to Carr,

Mewboorne had already been formally endorsed by the district executive committee. Meeting October 27, the committee first voted 5–4 against a motion for dropping every name that had been mentioned and selecting "some good farmer and Alliance man." In a second vote Mewboorne became the party's official nominee, the committee having no real choice since the state secretary of the Alliance had three days earlier issued a letter calling upon all Alliance men to support Mewboorne.[36]

Still, only with reluctance did some Democrats accept Mewboorne. The *Carolina Banner* editorialized: "Yes, Mewborne [*sic*] is to be preferred [*sic*] to Cheatham and now should receive the undivided support of his party. Our interests demands [*sic*] that we throw aside all prejudice and unite on him." The Wilson *Advance* agreed, saying, "The only way to vote against Cheatham is to vote for Mewborne [*sic*]." The Kinston *Free Press* editor feared that there were a "good many" Democrats who were thinking of not supporting Mewboorne, however, and warned such men "of the danger of their course." Mewboorne attempted to reassure Democratic critics. "While I am a farmer and a member of the Farmers' Alliance," he wrote in a letter published in the *Free Press*, "and would do all I could to build up the interest of farmers, yet in doing so, never should I consent to anything else but the upbuilding of all other interests."[37]

Belated attempts at unity were ineffective, for Mewboorne lost by about 1,200 votes to a Republican who had seemed such an easy mark months before. One Democratic newspaper had taken to calling the Negro candidate "Cheat'em" in the last days of the campaign, but the epithet now had an ironic ring since Democrats had "cheated" themselves out of victory by bungling and disunity.[38] Cheatham received 16,943 votes, carrying Craven, Edgecombe, Halifax, Northampton, Vance, and Warren, whereas 15,713 voters supported Mewboorne, who carried Bertie, Greene, Jones, Lenoir, and Wilson.

Considering the controversy surrounding his name, that many Demo-

---

October 29, 1890, W. J. Rogers to Carr, November 22, 1890, all in Carr Papers. The Kinston *Free Press,* October 30, 1890, refers to rumors about a last-minute candidate.

36. Wilson *Advance,* October 30, 1890; Warrenton *Gazette,* October 31, 1890.

37. Tarboro *Carolina Banner,* October 31, 1890; Wilson *Advance,* October 30, 1890; Kinston *Free Press,* October 30, 1890.

38. Tarboro *Southerner,* October 2, November 6, 1890.

crats "when voting for Mr. Mewboorne were taking a bitter, bitter, bitter dose," the last-minute Democratic candidate did rather well, especially for one running in an off-year election. In fact, his vote total was the second highest for any Democrat in the fourteen elections between 1872 and 1898. Only his immediate predecessor, Simmons, had garnered more votes. In Lenoir, his home county, where there was an abnormally low turnout, he defeated Cheatham almost two to one, increasing the Democratic margin of victory by over 100 votes. The Kinston *Free Press* conceded that in a "few townships some of the white Republicans and a few negroes voted for him."[39] Mewboorne was the first Democrat in the history of the "black second" to carry Greene County, winning by 290 votes in a county Simmons had lost by 34 votes two years earlier. But in some other areas his performance was disappointing. The Republican majority in Craven, Simmons' home, grew from 646 votes to 788, and Mewboorne fell nearly 700 votes short of Simmons' 1888 figure in Halifax.

Many Democrats expressed frustration with the results. "If we had had the noble Simmons as our leader this time," wrote one editor, "we could have elected him by an overwhelming majority." The *Carolina Banner* commented: "There is no doubt but that the right man could have carried this district by a good majority. . . . North Carolina no longer has a black district if the Democrats work, and work right." W. J. Rogers privately expressed the opinion that he could have been elected "by at least 3000 majority had I continued in the canvass."[40]

The congressional race was one of the few Republican successes in the second district, for after more than twenty years of domination, the GOP lost disastrously in the eleven counties' legislative and local elections. Of the fourteen representatives the district elected to the state house, only two were Republicans, and for the first time since 1868 the black strongholds of Edgecombe and Warren sent white Democratic legislators to Raleigh. In Edgecombe two Republican slates appealed for votes, and by their division allowed a Democratic senator and two

39. Kinston *Free Press*, November 6, 1890.
40. *Ibid.*, Tarboro *Carolina Banner*, November 14, 1890; Wilson *Advance*, November 20, 1890. W. J. Rogers to Elias Carr, November 22, 1890, in Carr Papers. Rogers' claim was based on the assumption that he could have carried his own county by 1,200 to 1,500 votes. This seems unlikely since there were no more than 2,418 potential voters in the county, a majority of them black, and Republicans had carried the county in eight previous congressional elections.

representatives to go to the general assembly supported by a minority of voters. Democrat W. W. Long defeated a black Republican for Warren's house seat with the aid of hundreds of Negro votes. Said the Warrenton *Gazette* of colored voters: "This shows that they are beginning to think and act for themselves and will no longer submit to being led by the nose."[41] Republicans did win the senate seat in Warren, as well as the one in Craven, and George H. White was reelected solicitor of the Second Judicial District.

According to at least one report, Cheatham (or his friends) had some responsibility for the massive Republican losses. "There was considerable swapping of votes," said the Raleigh correspondent of the Wilmington *Messenger*, "so that the Democrats gave Cheatham votes [in exchange] for votes for Democratic candidates for legislature. This was notably the case in Halifax, Northampton and Edgecombe." The Tarboro *Southerner* cited this report and denied that it was true as far as Edgecombe was concerned, but election returns in the county can be interpreted as giving indications of "trading." Mewboorne ran over 100 votes behind his party's legislative slate, whereas Cheatham ran about the same margin ahead of the combined votes of the two leading men on the respective Republican tickets. Cheatham got more votes than any other Republican office seeker; in fact, with the exception of the minor positions of coroner and surveyor he was the only Republican to carry Edgecombe County. Mewboorne, on the other hand, got fewer votes than any other Democrat, trailing behind the Democratic candidates for county treasurer, sheriff, clerk, register, representative, surveyor, coroner, and senator, in that order. In Northampton County the figures also suggest some kind of arrangement to Cheatham's benefit. He defeated Mewboorne, 1,756 to 1,607, even as the two Democratic house candidates received 2,316 and 1,985 votes against their opponents' 1,176 and 834. Cheatham was more that 1,000 votes ahead of Mewboorne in Halifax, yet the Republicans lost the legislative raees; and the Republican candidate for sheriff, who lost by 27 votes, ran 500 votes behind Cheatham.[42]

41. Tarboro *Southerner*, November 6, 1890; Warrenton *Gazette*, November 7, 1890.

42. Tarboro *Southerner*, November 13, 6, 1890; Northampton County Record of Elections, 1878–1906; Halifax County Record of Elections, 1878–1896.

In the elections for local offices Democrats won almost everywhere in the district, even in places long known as strongholds of black power. A few Republicans survived, like black Registers Mansfield Thornton in Warren and Thomas Eaton in Vance, and white Clerk of the Superior Court William L. Lyon in Bertie. John T. Gregory, Republican clerk in Halifax, was reelected without opposition. In general, however, Democrats controlled the offices by one method or another. The winning Republicans in Craven were replaced by their unsuccessful opponents when the board of county commissioners refused to accept their bonds and declared the positions vacant.[43]

The resounding failure of the Republican party in these elections was the result of changes in the black vote: fewer Negroes in the district, fewer eligible voters, and weakening black political unity. "More Negroes voted the Democratic ticket Tuesday than ever before in this section," reported the *Gold Leaf.* "And by this we do not mean that they scratched their tickets and voted for certain Democrats, but that they voted the entire ticket, State and County. Time was when they would not do this." At the same time the Republican party in the second district was becoming more exclusively black, as pressure intensified against whites who continued to support the GOP. The editor of the Kinston *Free Press* cruelly pilloried, by name, a "promising" young man who had voted Republican, actually casting a ballot for Henry Cheatham. "It is a pity to see any young white man sink so low as to vote for a negro." The editor hoped other youth would take note of this bad example.[44]

In the state as a whole, the 1890 election was also a Republican disaster. The suffrage restriction measure of the previous year had its intended result, as GOP strength in the general assembly was cut in half to only 24 members out of 150. Outside the second district, Democrats were victorious in every congressional race. The rich and inconsistent polity of the 1880s was being transformed, it seemed, into a rational, consistent, and barren one-party system. Cheatham's narrow victory had been greatly assisted by division among his opponents. The best hope for his party after 1890 was that the Democrats' struggle to contain the agrarian revolt within the "white man's party" would fail.

43. Kinston *Free Press*, December 4, 1890.
44. Henderson *Gold Leaf*, November 6, 1890; Kinston *Free Press*, November 6, 1890.

Chapter 10

THE COLLAPSE OF THE BLACK SECOND

FOUR MONTHS AFTER CHEATHAM was narrowly re-elected to the House of Representatives, the North Carolina General Assembly contrived a way to prevent such a thing from happening again. In redrawing the boundaries of the state's nine congressional districts in 1891, the legislators "tried to make compact districts, and also to make them all Democratic," as one candid senator put it.[1] The changes definitely diluted the "blackness" of the second district, long known for its large Negro majority. Jones, Craven, and Vance counties were removed and Wayne County reentered the district after an eight-year absence. A look at the 1890 census illustrates the political effect of these new borders. In the three counties taken out of the district, black adult males outnumbered white adult males by 1,354, whereas Wayne had a white majority among voting-age males of 1,414. In the reapportioned district as a whole, if all black men met voting requirements the Negro majority was little more than 400.[2] In practical terms, the "black second," as a district of overwhelming Republican, black strength, had been destroyed.

Rejoicing that the "cloud of blackness which has hovered over this section for so long" had been lifted, the Tarboro *Southerner* saw a fighting chance for Democrats in the next election—if they were united and chose the right candidate. The editor thought the black exodus, which had continued into 1891, had probably given Democrats an effective majority in the district.[3]

For Henry Cheatham the reapportionment had personal significance, since Vance, his home county, was now outside the second district. If

1. Raleigh *Daily State Chronicle*, March 7, 1891.
2. *Eleventh Census* (1890), Vol. I, Pt. I, pp. 775–76.
3. Tarboro *Southerner*, March 19, 1891.

he were to continue to represent the district, he would have to find a new political base. He chose for this purpose the town of Littleton, straddling the Halifax-Warren county line. Whatever the intentions of the Democratic strategists in Raleigh, Cheatham was weakened by being forced to move away from his native ground.

In the lame duck second session of the Fifty-first Congress, meeting at about the same time as the North Carolina legislature, Cheatham did little worthy of note. He attempted but failed to get his education bill to the floor, and he submitted no speeches, delivered or undelivered.[4] His prospect of influencing legislation was even less in the Fifty-second Congress, in which he was the only Negro in a strongly Democratic House. Only one of the bills he introduced was even reported out of committee, and that was a private bill. He again introduced bills to provide relief to depositors of the Freedman's Savings and Trust Company, to "aid in the establishment and temporary support of common schools," and to provide relief to the pilot and crew of the *Planter*. He asked for a public building for Goldsboro and for the preparation of statistics on the progress of the "colored race." A resolution calling for the printing of the history of Negro soldiers and a bill relating to the American exhibit at the World's Columbian Exposition were also introduced by the lone black Republican. In view of his legislative interests, he must have been pleased with his committee assignments: agriculture, education, and expenditure on public buildings.[5] Cheatham's first actual statement from the floor came early in this session, in a speech eulogizing east Tennessee Republican Congressman Leonidas C. Houk. Claiming to speak in behalf of Negroes in Houk's district, in his state, and in the country as a whole, Cheatham mourned the death of this "lover of right and justice," noting especially Houk's support of education to elevate poor whites and blacks and his backing of the bill to reimburse Freedman's Savings depositors.[6]

Cheatham made the most successful speech of his congressional career on May 25, 1892, about six weeks after he had been nominated for a third term. Apparently at his request, New Jersey Congressman C. A.

4. *Congressional Record*, 51st Cong., 2nd Sess., 234, 1874, 2830.
5. *Ibid.*, 52nd Cong., 1st Sess., 213, 134, 212, 4740, 5974, 4695, 103, 104. The bill for the relief of John D. Thorne was the only Cheatham bill to emerge from committee (p. 876).
6. *Ibid.*, 703.

Bergen proposed to amend an appropriation bill to provide up to a hundred thousand dollars for a Negro progress exhibit at the World's Columbian Exposition, and a sharp debate broke out on the subject of the South's abuse of the Negro. Finally Cheatham rose to regret that the measure had "assumed a hot political phase." "It seems to me," he said, "that whenever the colored people of this country ask for anything, something unfortunate intervenes to hinder their getting what they ask." He appealed to congressmen to "lose sight of party feeling in the matter; lose sight of all race feelings, and give us this appropriation which is so much needed." These conciliatory remarks inspired compliments even from the opposition press. The correspondent of the Wilson *Advance* commented:

A remarkable scene greatly to the credit of a North Carolina member and in marked contrast with some of his Republican colleagues, occurred . . . during the debate on the World's Fair. . . . The amendment not being in order was ruled out, but Representative Cheatham . . . made an eloquent, manly and sensible appeal to the house to grant the appropriation. There was no demagogy in it. Not only was the speech loudly applauded all over the chamber but he received a perfect ovation at his seat at its conclusion from the Democrats. . . . Among those who shook his hand were some of the oldest and ablest Southern Representatives on the floor. Cheatham has made a fine impression here for character and good sense.

Cheatham offered a similar motion later in the session, but it was again ruled not in order. An attempt to secure unanimous consent for later consideration failed when a member from Kentucky objected on the ground that the law ought not to recognize color.[7]

In an undelivered speech on the "anti-option" bill, Cheatham expressed sentiments that even the most racially prejudiced Alliance man in his district could strongly endorse. The bill was directed against one of the evils frequently condemned by angry agrarians, futures speculation in agricultural commodities. "The very fact that farming has not prospered as other business," declared Cheatham, "is beyond any doubt attributable to the unfair and fraudulent methods by which farmers' products are bought and sold in the markets in the United States." In taking this position, Cheatham aligned himself with the 1892 North Carolina Democratic platform which, in an effort to appease the Alliance, demanded

7. *Ibid.*, 4683, 4684; Wilson *Advance*, June 2, 1892; *Congressional Record*, 52nd Cong., 1st Sess., 6824–25.

"that Congress shall pass such laws as shall effectually prevent the dealing in futures of all agricultural and mechanical productions."[8]

A crucial vote involving the silver issue was the occasion of Cheatham's most notable departure from his party's line and, like the anti-option speech, was probably motivated by a desire to appeal to politically conscious farmers. Nevada Senator William Stewart had introduced a bill for the free coinage of gold and silver, and when an attempt was made to bring the bill to the House floor, the entire North Carolina delegation voted in favor of consideration. Only eight other Republicans (out of eighty-eight) joined Cheatham in supporting the motion, which was voted down 136–154.[9]

Cheatham conducted his congressional activities with one eye on the bewilderingly volatile political situation in North Carolina, and several times during the spring and summer of 1892 he left Washington to participate in political conventions or to campaign. The Republican district convention met April 7 in Littleton, earlier than usual and on Cheatham's ground. Cheatham was renominated by acclamation in a session attended by six hundred people, and for once reporters could write that "good order prevailed." Harmony was less than complete, however, as a contesting delegation from Warren left the convention when they were not seated and together with "a great many negroes from Warren, Halifax, Edgecombe and other counties" met in another hall in an alternate convention. Denouncing Cheatham and declaring that "the time had come when they could no longer be driven by the party lash," this rump convention nominated William W. Long, a thirty-one-year-old white Democrat from Littleton who had, thanks to a large number of black votes, represented Warren in the 1891 general assembly. The Warrenton *Gazette* commented on Cheatham's nomination: "If a republican is to have it; we would as lief, it be he as any body. But any republican in the district can be beaten: if the Democrats put up the right kind of a man." A week later the *Gazette* suggested that Long might be the right man.[10]

8. *Congressional Record*, 52nd Cong., 1st Sess., appendix, 508. Tarboro *Southerner*, June 9, 1892.

9. *Congressional Record*, 52nd Cong., 1st Sess., 6133; New York *Times*, July 14, 1892.

10. Raleigh *Signal*, April 7, 1892; Raleigh *Weekly State Chronicle*, April 12, 1892; Windsor *Ledger*, April 13, 1892; W. F. Tomlinson, *Biography of the State*

Another sign of discontent within Cheatham's party was a conference of "leading white Republicans" from eastern and southern North Carolina which offered an "address" to Tarheel Republicans in the April 7 issue of the Raleigh *Signal*, a Republican weekly published by J. C. L. "Loge" Harris. "The Republican party in all the negro belt is weaker today than it has ever been since the day of its birth on Southern soil," the document began. "It is hard to find one young white man of ability and promise in all the black belt who admits himself to be a Republican." The address was written by three veterans of Reconstruction, R. M. Norment of Robeson, Daniel L. Russell, a weighty, witty lawyer from Wilmington (and future governor), and George W. Stanton of Wilson, former legislator, former candidate for secretary of state, and one-time aspirant for Congress from the second district. They complained that "many of the best Federal offices have been given to colored men," and although it may have been "simple justice" to recognize "all elements in the distribution of party rewards," the administration had been misled by "unscrupulous politicians" into appointing "black men whose conduct makes them offensive to the white people of their communities."

The authors of the address seemed unable to understand the changes in black leadership since Reconstruction. "Until recently . . . the colored people have been disposed to invite the leadership" of respectable white men. "But now the tendency is towards the elevation of the most corrupt negro element to control of the party in the black counties." In places the GOP was nothing more than a Negro party and "there is scarcely a precinct in the black belt where you can find active white Republicans enough to obtain even the semblance of a fair election." (Democratic schemes of fraud could not be stopped, they assumed, without the financial strength, legal skill, and perhaps even social status of prominent white Republicans.)

The only policy offering escape from "this dismal outlook" was one of nonaction—a Republican attempt to break the solid white vote by not contesting local elections in the Negro counties or nominating a state ticket in 1892. Instead Republicans should restrict their political involvement to national issues and allow the North Carolina Democratic

Officers and Members of the General Assembly, 1893; Other Interesting Facts (Raleigh, 1893), 116–17. Warrenton *Gazette*, April 8, 15, 1892.

party to break into factions. Speaking for those who had attended the conference, the signers of the address said: "We are Republicans as we have been through all the years of disaster and defeat. Our adherence to the fundamental principles of Republicanism cannot be weakened by the conduct of corrupt and venal upstarts who want to keep honest white men out of the party." Besides Norment, Stanton, and Russell, twenty listed white Republicans, as well as "various other prominent Republicans who have been the recognized leaders of the party," were said to endorse the manifesto.[11]

The restiveness of these white leaders was related to a bitter factional fight in the state party organization between state chairman John B. Eaves and his supporters and a group of dissidents led by former chairman John J. Mott and including Russell and editor Harris. Eaves's enemies accused him of taking an extreme pro-Negro stand to preserve his own position in party affairs. Personal antipathy fueled the feud, as Mott had helped bring about Senate rejection of Eaves as internal revenue collector for western North Carolina. The Mott-Eaves rivalry had marred the Republican state convention in 1890 and broke out with fresh vigor in the 1892 convention.[12]

Eaves opened the convention with a speech calling for Republicans to stand firm and to contest the Democrats at every level, a policy he predicted would bring victory in this year of political crisis. "He announced as the basis of Republicanism the absolute freedom and equality of white and black" and suggested a five-year Republican moratorium on the word "nigger." As if in answer to the Norment-Stanton-Russell address, he reminded the delegates that corrupt politicians were not all of one color, and in closing he asked James H. Young, Negro customs official, to serve as temporary chairman.

While waiting for the credentials committee to report—the anti-Eaves faction complained that none of their men was appointed—the convention heard speeches from several party orators, including Congressman Cheatham, George White, and John C. Dancy. Cheatham spoke hope-

11. Raleigh *Signal*, April 7, 1892. Only two counties in the second district, Wayne and Wilson, were specifically mentioned as represented in the group. Most of the men identified came from southeastern North Carolina.

12. New York *Times*, August 29, 30, 31, 1890, January 5, 1891. Joseph F. Steelman, "Vicissitudes of Republican Party Politics: The Campaign of 1892 in North Carolina," *North Carolina Historical Review*, XLIII (October, 1966), 430–42.

fully of change in the South, "condemned party quarrels, and confessed that he was at sea in talking politics in North Carolina." Solicitor White made a vigorous, partisan speech, warning Democrats who thought the Republican party was dead that in November "they would find it the 'liveliest corpse' they ever saw." He said Republicans should not yield an inch nor heed "overtures by other parties." John Dancy, collector of customs at Wilmington, ridiculed the Democrats as unwilling wearers of the Alliance yoke.

After the convention resolved credentials disputes and elected a permanent chairman, the Eaves forces attempted to make the first order of business the election of a new state chairman, although the convention had been called to choose delegates to the national convention. This provoked a tremendous uproar, punctuated with complaints of "bossism" and denunciation of the "officeholders." The convention was by no means divided into two clear factions, one for Mott and the other for Eaves. Many delegates contributing to the tumult no doubt agreed with Edgecombe black politician George Lloyd, who shouted: "We want a third man. Down with the bosses!" Finally, after a private conference between the Eaves men and the Mott supporters, a compromise was arranged, the motion to elect a state chairman withdrawn, and the meeting moved to the election of delegates-at-large to the national convention.

The first delegate selected was Henry Cheatham, elected by acclamation after a Charlotte white Republican described him as a man who had never lost an election, "the equal politically, morally and socially of any man in the State." The convention filled the remaining positions by the more prosaic method of balloting, choosing three men from the five who were suggested. John C. Dancy was among the winners and George White was one of the two losers. As finally constituted, the delegation to the national convention included two Negroes and two whites. For presidential electors-at-large the convention chose two white men, one from the mountains and the other from the coastal plain. George White was nominated for the position, but withdrew his name, saying "that he had encountered Uncle Sam's Boys . . . and had been defeated, and that he did not care to be slaughtered a second time." He was referring to the influence of federal officeholders.

At this point the Eaves faction renewed the motion to elect Eaves to a third term as chairman of the executive committee. As the Mott faction bitterly objected, the convention was several times on the verge of chaos, with delegates shouting, cursing, hooting, and ignoring the chairman's effort to control the proceedings. Eaves's foes excoriated him as a traitor to the party and charged that he had been responsible for multilating party tickets in 1890. They said in his home county Eaves had arranged to have the name of Charles Price, a personal enemy who had been the Republican nominee for chief justice, cut off the ballots before they were distributed. Eaves did not answer this accusation, and after considerable confusion he was reelected by a better than three-to-one margin. The drama of the convention passed, the delegates selected an executive committee and adjourned.[13]

Cheatham spoke for many men when he said he was "at sea" in discussing North Carolina politics. Democrats were as disunited as Republicans, and both old parties faced the challenge of a new, third party. The sweeping Democratic victory of 1890 produced an Alliance-dominated "farmers' legislature" of 1891, which expanded public educational facilities, established a railroad commission, and reelected Senator Zebulon Vance. But the triumph disintegrated as conservative Democrats, including Senator Vance, resisted the more radical demands of the Alliance, particularly the subtreasury scheme, a plan to provide federally underwritten credit on crops deposited in public warehouses. In North Carolina, as well as across the South, the attempt to contain and absorb the Alliance within the old political system had failed by the beginning of 1892. Led by a North Carolina man, southern Alliance President Leonidas L. Polk, militant agrarians were ready to organize a new party to achieve enactment of the subtreasury plan, government ownership of railroads, and other goals. Polk presided at the St. Louis convention of the Confederation of Industrial Organizations in February, a group dominated by southern Alliance delegates, and was generally expected to head the national ticket of the new party as a nominee for president. A mass

13. Raleigh *Signal*, April 14, 1892. McKinney erred when he wrote: "Blacks were excluded from North Carolina Republican state conventions as early as 1888." Gordon B. McKinney, "Southern Mountain Republicans and the Negro, 1865–1900," *Journal of Southern History*, XLI (November, 1975), 511.

meeting after the convention had adjourned, endorsed the idea of a third party, and called for it to organize in Omaha in July.[14]

Adding to the lure of a third party was the intense distaste many North Carolina Democrats felt for Grover Cleveland, whose conservative economic policies made him seem a symbol of the power of Wall Street. "Buck" Kitchin, as usual, put it more strongly than anyone else. Several years earlier he had told Senator Vance: "I would prefer the Devil himself for President to Cleveland, provided he was not a Republican."[15] If the national Democratic party nominated Cleveland again, it might well be the last straw for many who had hesitated to leave the old party of states' rights and white supremacy.

The second district provides a microcosm of the political upheaval that subsequently shook the entire South. Living in a district represented by a black congressman and populated with many Negroes, white Populists had to resolve doubts about the danger of "Negro domination," answer taunts about disloyalty to their race, and consider with care political alliance with blacks. Democrats in the second district struggled to contain the agrarian uprising at the same time as they sought to complete the district's "redemption" from Republicanism. Even as they denounced black political power in an effort to hold whites together, they were forced to use the black vote to stave off defeat. Republicans argued about cooperation with the third party, wondering if the crisis of 1892 portended the total collapse of the GOP or its new vitality in three-party contests.

Weeks before a third party (soon to be known as Populist) candidate for governor or president was in the field, there was a third party congressional nominee in the second district. Meeting June 16 in Rocky Mount, about fifty third party delegates selected Edward Alston Thorne as their candidate for the House of Representatives. A Halifax man who had been active as an Alliance lecturer, Thorne apparently had a good reputation among Negroes. One Warren Alliance leader had suggested Thorne as a good replacement for Rogers in 1890, describing him as a "strong candidate" who could "poll more *honest* negro votes than any

14. Hugh T. Lefler and Ray R. Newsome, *North Carolina: The History of a Southern State* (Chapel Hill, N.C., 1973), 546–48. Woodward, *Origins of the New South*, 235–42.

15. W. H. Kitchin to Z. B. Vance, [December, 1887], in Vance Papers.

other man in the district." Democrats accused the third party men of aiding Cheatham at a time when a united opposition could have defeated him. "All chance of [defeating Cheatham] is now at an end, and Cheatham should feel as grateful to the third party people as he does to his own avowed supporters," said the Tarboro *Southerner*. "In effect they are identical."[16]

This was partly campaign bluster, for the number of Democrats anxious to be the party nominee for Congress indicated a rising confidence that Cheatham could be beaten. At the July 27 district convention eight men were nominated, including "Buck" Kitchin, W. J. Rogers, Frederick A. Woodard, and W. W. Long. The Scotland Neck *Democrat* observed: "Heretofore the nomination for Congress in this district has gone for the asking, and very frequently for the begging." Now Democrats were confident that "the black district" was "just on the eve of a perfect redemption."[17]

Although he led from the start, Frederick Woodard was not nominated until the ninth ballot, and at several points it seemed another man might win. On the fourth ballot he had 121 votes to Rogers' 84, with 136 votes divided among three other candidates. Kitchin did well, despite his public denunciations of Cleveland, the probable party nominee for president, and the Tarboro *Southerner*'s criticism of his habit of "intemperately abusing those who differ with him." He received 99 votes on the third ballot, and on the seventh ballot Woodard led him 123 to 109, as four candidates split the remaining 104 votes. Long, who had the support of some dissident black Republicans, particularly in Warren County, came within 23 votes of Woodard on the eighth ballot.[18]

Frederick Augustus Woodard was a thirty-eight-year-old Wilson lawyer who had been the Democratic congressional nominee ten years earlier in a hopeless battle against James O'Hara. A native of ever-Democratic Wilson County and a friend of Josephus Daniels and Henry

16. Tarboro *Southerner*, June 23, 1892. The Kinston *Free Press*, March 12, 1891, lists Thorne as Alliance district lecturer for the second district. John Graham to Elias Carr, October, 1890, in Carr Papers (letter badly damaged).
17. Scotland Neck *Democrat*, July 28, 1892.
18. *Ibid.* Tarboro *Southerner*, June 9, 1892. (See Kitchin's response in the June 16 issue.) The Tarboro *Southerner*, May 26, 1892, printed resolutions adopted at a pro-Long Republican meeting in Warrenton, May 14. Cheatham was described as "a man who has betrayed not only his trust, but his race," whereas Long was praised for his support of Negro education.

G. Connor, Woodard had never held public office, his political experience being limited to party posts such as chairman of the congressional district executive committee. He was the sort of candidate who might have been rejected in 1890, but now, with many dedicated agrarian advocates out of the party (including 1890 nominee James Mewboorne), a more traditional type of candidate could be nominated.[19]

Woodard was running against an incumbent who appeared full of honors and at the peak of his political prestige, despite his problems with reapportionment and rebels. The Raleigh Signal, for all its complaints of Eaves's pro-Negro policy, praised Cheatham as a "faithful public servant," entitled to the "active support" of all Republicans. "During his four years in Congress he has reflected great credit on his race, the Republican party and himself," the Signal said. At the Republican national convention Cheatham had the honor of seconding President Harrison's nomination in a brief speech.[20]

Cheatham was influential enough that one angry Republican called him "the actual leader of the party in the State." Denouncing Eaves and the "revenue gang," Daniel Russell ventilated his vigorous opinions in an interview published in the Signal and noticed around the state. In the past, he said, black voters in the second district had been willing to elect "white men of character and capacity" to Congress. But now "none but a negro" would be considered for the nomination, "and the more incompetent and treacherous he is the more certain he is to get the prize." If a Republican hero like James Blaine, Speaker Reed, or Judge Tourgée lived in the second district, he could not secure the nomination "unless he bought it at a good round price." According to Russell, Cheatham was the "real Boss" of the state Republican organization, having "put his corrupt cronies in office about as he pleases," where they stay "until they break into the penitentiary." In bitter scorn of Eaves and his supporters, Russell suggested that the "revenuers" run Cheatham for governor. "HE CAN read and write and DOES wash his face at least once a week," he sneered.[21]

19. Congressional Directory, 54th Cong., 2nd Sess., 98. The Raleigh Signal, August 4, 1892, noted that Mewboorne had joined the People's party. (This issue of the Signal is misdated, on various pages, August 3, August 5, and July 7.)

20. Raleigh Signal, April 21, 1892; Proceedings of the Tenth Republican National Convention; Held in the City of Minneapolis, Minn., June 7, 8, 9 and 10, 1892 (Minneapolis, 1892), 127.

21. Raleigh Signal, August 4, 1892. See Raleigh News and Observer, August

Many of these comments can be dismissed as the product of Russell's overheated imagination. Cheatham had considerable influence in the disposal of patronage in the second district and adjoining areas and he had received significant recognition in being elected delegate-at-large by acclamation, but by no means was he the "real Boss" of North Carolina Republicans. And it soon became apparent that he was not even strongly committed to the policies of John B. Eaves. As for any hint that Cheatham was crude or obnoxious, a violator of southern etiquette, it is only necessary to turn to the Democratic newspaper published in his hometown for rebuttal. "Congressman Cheatham, of this district, is a resident of our town," noted the Littleton *Courier*. "He is a polite, genteel man and is thought well of by everybody. Some of our colored citizens should take pattern after him. We wish we could speak as complimentary of all of his color who hold federal offices in this State."[22]

The Republican state convention on September 7 demonstrated clearly that Cheatham did not control the GOP nor was he a tool of chairman Eaves. The Republicans were the last of the three major parties to hold a state nominating convention in 1892. In an attempt to hold as many Alliance voters as possible, the Democrats in May had nominated for governor Elias Carr, one of the more conservative Alliance leaders, and adopted a platform that echoed many agrarian demands.[23] The Populists met in August, selecting for their standard-bearer W. P. Exum of Wayne County. An articulate minority of Republicans, including the anti-Eaves faction, thought the party should not field a state ticket at all, since doing so would only divide the anti-Democratic vote. With no Republican ticket in the campaign, the Democrats would be unable to raise the race issue and would be ousted from power by the Populists.[24]

Cheatham took no significant part in the convention proceedings, and, in fact, there is no definite record that he was a delegate. Although

---

10, 1892. Russell's remark about appointment of Cheatham's "corrupt cronies" is reckless and inaccurate. The *Signal*, October 15, 1891, praised postmasters S. H. Vick and W. F. Young as "colored men of excellent character," good education, and "gentlemanly deportment."

22. Littleton *Courier*, September 1, 1892.

23. See Tarboro *Southerner*, June 9, 1892.

24. For example of such thinking, see J. J. Mott's "Address to the Public" in the Raleigh *Signal*, July 21, 1892. The editorial policy of the *Signal* generally reflected this point of view.

most black Republicans favored a state ticket, the New York *Times* reported that Cheatham, along with George White and James O'Hara, opposed the idea. The night before the convention opened, a caucus of delegates debated for three hours the expediency of running a state slate. Many western delegates desired a ticket; J. C. L. Harris, George White, and another eastern Republican did most of the speaking in opposition.[25]

The next day the convention began with a noisy fight over the credentials of the New Hanover County delegation. James O'Hara loudly denounced the officeholders' ring when an attempt was made to curb debate. "If the Wilmington custom house and the Charlotte postoffice are to rule this convention, let it be known," he shouted. Insisting that there be no "gag law," he agreed that "if there were free and fair discussion of matters, he and others would abide by the decision of the convention." George White also spoke in favor of full discussion.

J. C. L. Harris presented resolutions declaring the inexpediency of nominating a state ticket, urging Republicans to support their candidates for Congress and president and recommending "sound discretion" in voting for other offices, with a view of destroying the Democratic party. But despite his hour-long speech, Harris' resolutions were tabled by "a very large majority," and the convention went on to adopt a traditional platform and nominate a full slate of candidates for the state offices. Former judge David M. Furches, a western white Republican, headed the ticket as gubernatorial nominee. The only second district man nominated was Hiram L. Grant of Wayne, candidate for auditor, and he had been one who questioned the wisdom of contesting the state offices.[26]

The three-way split of state politics was now complete. Voters had a choice of three presidential candidates: Republican Harrison, Democrat Cleveland, and Populist James B. Weaver (selected after Polk died on the eve of the People's party convention). Carr, Exum, and Fuches competed in the gubernatorial race, and in some congressional districts, including the second, there were also three candidates. Indeed, in certain localities the division extended to county and legislative tickets.

As election day approached, the second district Republican organiza-

25. New York *Times*, September 7, 8, 1892.
26. Raleigh *Signal*, September 15, 1892.

tion lost supporters to each of the other parties. Populists gave proof of the sincerity of their appeal to black voters by offering a few offices to Negroes in several of the black counties. In Edgecombe one of the People's party nominees for the house was a Negro; in Warren the Populists nominated Harry B. Eaton, Vance representative in 1883 and 1885, for the Vance-Warren senate seat. Warren black Republican Hawkins W. Carter, a man who had served five terms in the general assembly, announced that he was working for the Populist candidates for state, local, and legislative offices. Tom Hawkins, another Warren black, was the Populist nominee for register of deeds against Mansfield Thornton.[27]

Two important Republican local officials defected to the Democrats during this campaign. John T. Gregory, Halifax clerk of the superior court for over twenty years, resigned his position as county Republican chairman and left the party. He took the step because the Republican party, "once national, powerful and great," was becoming narrowly sectional, and he cited "the reckless and revolutionary policy of the late House of Representatives" as an example of this declension. The white Republican clerk in Bertie, William L. Lyon, also announced that he was severing his relation to the GOP:

The party as conducted in Eastern North Carolina has become a byword and reproach. Their conventions have become howling mobs and nominations are put up to the highest bidder. Ignorant, incompetent and corrupt negroes have taken complete control of the political machinery and have nominated for positions of profit, honor and trust most incompetent and corrupt men, while men of respectability who served the party faithfully for years are allowed no voice in the deliberations of the party. They have driven away from the party nearly every white Republican and hundreds of the best colored people are disgusted. I can no longer stay with a party managed by such men.

Lyon declared that he would vote for Cleveland "and the balance of the Democratic ticket at the coming election."[28]

---

27. Tarboro *Southerner*, September 8, 1892; *Vance County Farmer* quoted in Raleigh *Signal*, October 27, 1892; Raleigh *Signal*, October 6, 1892; Warrenton *Gazette*, November 4, 1892. On Carter's Populist activity, see also Warrenton *Gazette*, September 9, October 14, 1892.

28. John T. Gregory to Whit Hardee, J. H. Hannon, M. M. Furgerson, and other members of the Executive Committee of the Republican party of Halifax County, October 22, 1892, in John T. Gregory Papers, North Carolina Department of Archives and History. Windsor *Ledger*, September 7, 1892.

Even some black Republicans were thinking of aiding the traditional enemy, the Democracy. If the Republican party was in a process of decline and fall, a prudent person would make what arrangements he could. A young man named James E. Shepard, later famous as a Negro educator, dispatched a letter in June to Senator Calvin S. Brice of the Democratic national committee. Shepard had been a Republican, had even written a political broadside for Henry Cheatham in the 1892 campaign, praising Cheatham as an exponent of protectionism and urging "all classes, both white and colored," to "rally to his standard." Now, however, he wanted to travel North to lecture in behalf of the Democratic party. "You see if I was to lecture up North this would have some weight, a colored young man from the South once a Republican but now a Democrat." He advised Brice that the Democrats could carry the second district "if Money was wisely spent." Without a doubt, Democrats were relying on black votes to remain in power in North Carolina. Former governor Thomas J. Jarvis wrote to the state's leading editor, Samuel A. Ashe, September 26, 1892, warning that the Democratic party was not "out of danger." "The 3rd Party will poll a much larger white vote than our friends think and I really fear that it is *absolutely necessary* for us to get many negro votes to get through."[29]

Men of both races were willing to consider alternatives, to think about voting a new way. A contributor to the Lasker *Patron and Gleaner* thought he detected a different spirit in the town of Rich Square, Northampton County. There seemed "to be right much division among the negroes," who were attending the meetings of all parties, listening with care. A large number of white Democrats turned out to hear Cheatham speak in Kinston, and he was careful to make his remarks conciliatory. ("It was a milk and cider speech," snorted the Kinston *Free Press.*) Saying "nothing to disturb the peaceful relations between the two races," Cheatham assailed cotton speculators for causing the poverty of the South. His opponents Woodard and Thorne were good men, he said, but "he could accomplish more than they because he had four years experience in congress, while they had done."[30]

29. J. E. Shepard to C. S. Brice, June 15, 1892, with broadside "Vote for the Good of Your District!" enclosed, in Ransom Papers; T. J. Jarvis to S. A. Ashe, September 26, 1892, in Samuel A'Court Ashe Papers, North Carolina Department of Archives and History.

30. Lasker *Patron and Gleaner,* October 27, 1892; Kinston *Free Press,* October 27, 1892. Cheatham's speech in Tarboro was described as "quite creditable" by a

On election day the three-way division of congressional votes enabled Frederick Woodard to win, although he was more than 3,000 votes short of a majority. The Democratic candidate carried six of the nine counties of the district, including, for the first time since the start of congressional Reconstruction, Edgecombe County. Woodard received 13,925 votes to Cheatham's 11,812 and 5,457 for Thorne. Cheatham carried only the three counties closest to his home in Littleton—Halifax, Warren, and Northampton—and even in these heavily black counties his vote was smaller than two years earlier. In Warren, for example, Cheatham's vote was down about 200 from 1890, the Democratic vote was over 400 smaller, whereas the Populist total was 681 votes. Woodard came within 65 votes of a plurality in Northampton. The Populists' strongest showing was in Wilson, where 32 percent of the voters supported Thorne, as opposed to little more than 10 percent for Cheatham. Obviously, in this case hundreds of Negroes were supporting the third party; Cheatham received 422 votes in a county that had about 1,400 black men of voting age.

Dismal as Cheatham's performance was, he received more votes than either President Harrison or gubernatorial aspirant Furches. In the nine counties of the second district, only 9,338 men voted for Furches, approximately 2,500 fewer than the number who voted for Cheatham.[31] Cheatham's performance seemed to have little relation to the success or failure of local and legislative tickets. Every legislator elected from the district, save one, was a Democrat, and that one, a Negro from Warren, was later unseated in an election contest. The other two counties Cheatham carried sent purely Democratic delegations to Raleigh.

Democrats won in several counties because Republicans and Populists did not cooperate. In Edgecombe's senate race, a Democrat defeated a black Republican, 1,866 votes to 1,706, but fell far short of a majority as the Populist nominee won the support of 515 voters. A similar situation existed in the Warren senate race and in the Northampton

---

partisan antiblack editor. "He never alluded to Harrison." Tarboro *Southerner,* October 13, 1892.

31. Compiled from Donald R. Matthews (ed.), *North Carolina Votes: General Election Returns, by County, for President of the United States, 1868–1960, Governor of North Carolina, 1868–1960, United States Senator from North Carolina, 1914–1960* (Chapel Hill, N.C., 1962), 119, 144, 151, 153, 165, 177, 204, 207, 209.

legislative elections. Even where fusion did take place, however, Democrats were somehow able to win. The Democratic candidate for sheriff of Wayne narrowly defeated the fusion candidate 2,193 to 2,086. Halifax Sheriff B. I. Allsbrook, who had been 27 votes ahead of Republican James T. Dawson in 1890, now defeated Dawson by a two-to-one margin, despite the fact that Dawson had been endorsed by the Populists.[32]

Time and again in this year of political realignment the election results were curiously quirky. Cheatham, Grover Cleveland, and Elias Carr were the winners in Northampton, for example. Although 1,472 Northampton voters were willing to cast ballots for Cheatham, 1,360 supported Harrison, and only 1,027 voted for the Republican gubernatorial nominee. Over 800 men voted for Populist Exum for governor but only 457 voted for Populist presidential nominee Weaver.[33] Halifax, with its long record of tainted elections, produced even odder results. A county that listed only 2,261 whites of voting age in the 1890 census, Halifax went for Carr by a huge margin. According to the returns 3,328 voters supported the Democrat for governor, as against 1,124 for the Republican and 593 for the Populist.[34] Yet at the same time Cheatham carried the county over Woodard and Thorne, though election returns indicate that 600 fewer voters participated in the congressional election than in the gubernatorial.

Most Negroes continued to vote the Republican ticket, though significant numbers voted for Populist or Democratic candidates. From Halifax County a Democrat wrote state supreme court Justice Walter Clark, reporting that in the town of Weldon "the negroes voted with us in droves." The major Democratic newspaper in Bertie, noting that "a very considerable number" of black voters supported the Democratic county, legislative, and congressional nominees, thanked Negroes for their support and assured them they had nothing to fear from the Democrats.[35]

32. A letter from Donnell Gilliam published in the Tarboro Southerner, October 18, 1894, cites the Edgecombe official vote for 1892. For some reason this information is not in the Edgecombe County Record of Elections, 1880–1894 [sic], North Carolina Department of Archives and History.

33. Lasker Patron and Gleaner, November 17, 1892.

34. Eleventh Census (1890), Vol. I, Pt. I, pp. 775–76; Matthews (ed.), North Carolina Votes, 153.

35. W. E. Daniel to Walter Clark, November 15, 1892, in Clark Papers. Windsor Ledger, November 16, 1892.

The legislators elected from the second district showed that a political shift, beyond a simple Democratic landslide, had occurred. In some counties, of course, there was nothing new about Democratic victories. For years Democrats had been winning regularly in Wilson and Wayne; the last Republican house member from Lenoir had been elected in 1880. And since 1888 Democrats had represented Bertie and Halifax. What was remarkable about the victors of 1892 was that only three of the seventeen Democrats elected had any prior experience in the general assembly, and most had little political experience of any kind. Phrases like "lived a quiet life on the farm and never held any position," "never engaged actively in politics until the late campaign," and "followed farming all his life," run through their biographies.[36] By any reckoning these were new men. Despite the People's party defeat, the agrarian insurgency had transformed politics in the second district.

In the state returns, Elias Carr received 135,519 votes, more than 40,000 ahead of Furches, but even the most jubilant Democrat could not help but notice that Furches and Exum together were 8,000 votes ahead of the Democratic nominee. Cleveland captured the state's electoral votes and the Democratic candidates were victorious in every congressional district except the fifth, which elected young Republican Thomas Settle, son of the famous Judge Thomas Settle of Reconstruction days.

The passions unleashed by this campaign were to be renewed in the next four elections, reaching greatest intensity in the "white supremacy" campaign of 1898 and the disfranchisement election of 1900. An incident in Goldsboro typified the vicious tactics increasingly employed against the foes of the Democratic party, particularly white men who "betrayed" their race. The day after the balloting, the Goldsboro *Daily Argus* published a sensational front-page attack on Hiram L. Grant and other Wayne Republicans, arraigning them "before the bar of public opinion." The *Argus* said that large numbers of black women had gathered at the courthouse the day before, browbeating in a "disgraceful" way Negro men who showed any disinclination to vote for the fusion county ticket and Republican candidates for national and state office. The "brazen impudence" of these women was the "insidious work" of Major Grant, who had stirred up Goldsboro's black women in an "incendiary"

36. Tomlinson, *Biography of State Officers and Members of the General Assembly*, 24, 20, 119, *passim*.

speech the night before the election in a meeting at the colored public school. Readers were reminded that Grant's first appearance in Goldsboro, nearly three decades earlier, had been as the commander of a company of Negro soldiers, "that he lead [sic] against the white people of the South." Warning that local whites were "determined that no inferior race nor invading Radical office seekers nor depraved white supporters of local renown, shall dominate our people," the article frantically declared: "What we have written we have written as the righteous expression of an honest, high-toned, long patient, law-abiding people, who . . . have . . . determined that if it has come to the survival of the fittest they will do the surviving."

In a few days the outrage exposed by the *Argus* dwindled into an insignificant event. Grant announced that he had had nothing to do with the calling of the meeting, that it was not held in the public school, and that he did not counsel black women to attend the polls for any purpose. As for his brief speech, "I did not say one word . . . that I would not have said in the court house or public square in the presence of any of the citizens of Goldsboro." Five days after the election the principal of the colored public school confirmed Grant's statement that no political meeting had been held at the school, stating that the meeting in question had convened at another place. After the local Cleveland-Carr club held an indignation meeting and passed resolutions against Grant and Faircloth, two Democrats wrote to the *Argus* disassociating themselves from the action.[37] A minor incident, yet this Goldsboro affair would find many echoes in the next eight years.

As Representative Cheatham served out the last weeks of his term, making no speeches and introducing no bills in the second session of the Fifty-second Congress, he gave consideration to a new career. The defeated politician decided that lecturing in the North seemed attractive, and he dispatched a letter to another retired North Carolina politician and experienced public speaker, Albion W. Tourgée. His letter asked for suggestions on lecturing and revealed that he was considering two topics: "The old and New South," and "The Condition of American Laborers and how to improve it." In the second lecture he hoped to bring in "the discrimination against the Negro of America in almost every avenue."[38]

37. Goldsboro *Daily Argus*, November 9, 10, 12, 18, 22, 1892.
38. H. P. Cheatham to A. W. Tourgée, February 6, 1893, in Tourgée Papers.

As he considered this adjustment to private life, the black congress-man was not yet thirty-six years old. Well-educated, discreet, and diplomatic, Henry Cheatham had given his best efforts to conciliating white voters and building a personal machine—practicing policies later perfected by Booker T. Washington. By all indications, his relative lack of legislative achievement was due less to his own shortcomings than to the disinterest of his colleagues. In the section of eastern North Carolina he represented, Cheatham's hold on black voters weakened, and he did not receive the full potential strength of his own group. More importantly, his efforts showed how difficult it was for one candidate to succeed without a strong partisan base, how important the health of the local and state Republican party was to second district congressional aspirants. In a larger context of the confusing agrarian revolution, with new men and new issues shaking both old parties, a strategy like Cheatham's had little chance to succeed.

Chapter 11

SPLITS AND BOLTS

> It is well to speak plainly. There may have been election frauds in a very few counties in North Carolina ever since they were inaugurated by the Republicans, when ballots were carried to South Carolina to be counted and when the Republicans stole the State from Merrimon in 1872. In a few negro counties it may be that the negro vote has sometimes been partially suppressed. But it has never occurred in more than eight or ten counties.
>
> —*News and Observer*, August 18, 1894

EARLY IN 1894 GEORGE H. WHITE, solicitor of the Second Judicial District, moved his home from New Bern to Tarboro with the purpose of seeking a seat in Congress.[1] For almost eight years he had regularly appeared at court week in Bertie, Northampton, Halifax, Warren, Edgecombe, and Craven, gaining the admiration of most blacks and the respect of many whites. To fulfill his ambition he needed, of course, to reside in the Second Congressional District, which no longer included Craven.

A native of southeastern North Carolina, the forty-one-year-old lawyer was well qualified for a place in the House. After graduating from Howard University in 1877, he had served as principal of the colored graded school, Presbyterian parochial school, and state normal school, all in New Bern, also finding time to study law under former judge William J. Clarke, earning his law license in 1879. His career as an educator and lawyer was interrupted by service in the state house in 1881, an unsuccessful campaign for the state senate in 1882, and a term in

---

1. Tarboro *Southerner*, February 15, 1894; Richmond *Times* quoted in Kinston *Free Press*, March 29, 1894.

the general assembly's upper house in 1885. In 1886 White won his first four-year term as district solicitor in a three-way race with black incumbent John H. Collins and a Democrat. Since the office paid well— three thousand to four thousand dollars a year—White was a man of modest wealth by 1894.[2]

White's skill and ability were so marked that even Democrats occasionally praised him. "He is probably the best colored lawyer in the State and is a man who sustains a good moral character in this city where he lives," said the New Berne *Weekly Journal* upon his nomination in 1886. A correspondent of the *News and Observer* described him as a "first-rate" speaker in his official duties, adding, "So far I can judge he has more ability than any other negro in the State." Another Democratic source conceded that white was "impartial in his work, showing neither favors to his own race, nor bitterness towards whites."[3]

On the other hand, the indignity of a black prosecutor questioning "pure and refined white ladies" in court had been cited in the Wilson *Advance* during the campaign of 1888 as a demonstration of the evils of "Negro rule." The editor said of White: "A more presumptuous, disgustingly would-be familiar negro does not draw the pure atmosphere of North Carolina." The general assembly of 1891 tried to prevent future black solicitors by approving a constitutional amendment providing a statewide vote for solicitors, in the same way superior court judges were selected, but the voters rejected the idea in the election of 1892.[4]

In entering the second district, White was entering a political atmosphere of intense corruption. For many politically active citizens of the district—white and black—dishonesty had become standard procedure.

2. New York *Freeman*, February 5, 1887. The *Freeman's* biographical sketch does not mention the 1882 race. See New Bern *Daily Journal*, September 3, 1882. White was defeated by the son of his law tutor, William E. Clarke, 1,503 votes to 771. Two other candidates received a total of 725 votes. Craven County Election Returns, 1878–90, Abstract of Votes for General Assembly, 1882, North Carolina Department of Archives and History. White did not read law with Democrat Walter Clak, later North Carolina chief justice, as Frenise Logan claims. Logan, *Negro in North Carolina*, 28.
3. New Bern *Weekly Journal*, August 26, 1886; Raleigh *News and Observer*, October 7, 1890; Scotland Neck *Democrat*, November 22, 1894.
4. Wilson *Advance*, October 25, 1888. In the debate on the solicitors amendment, the Craven white Republican senator praised White as a "good man," "loved" by his constituents. Raleigh *Daily State Chronicle*, February 6, 1891.

It was a common thing to speak of a man's political character as opposed to his character in general. A man could be "a Judas . . . whenever any cash is floating around," and yet an opponent might say: "His character is good, but his political character I can not vouch for."[5] A white man who stole votes or bribed Negro politicians did not lose his standing in his community, nor did a black leader automatically forfeit respectability for disrupting a convention, organizing false and flimsy challenges to legitimately elected delegates, or buying a convention. Some elements of corruption had been present in the "black second" from its formation —as in any political system. Turbulent conventions, stolen votes, corruptly inspired "bolts" were not new in 1894. What distinguished the early 1890s from previous years was the degree of corruption, its widespread and powerful influence. Corruption grew from being a secondary characteristic of a basically healthy system to being the essence of a decaying political life. As early as 1886 John C. Dancy's *Star of Zion* had said of the district: "It takes ability, political shrewdness, sometimes a profuse scattering of 'filthy lucre,' and even a resort to 'ways that are dark and tricks that are vain,' to obtain a nomination there, and even then one must take his chances to gain victory."[6] His description was even more accurate eight years later.

As a man who had not been wounded in earlier congressional battles, a popular officeholder who had shown integrity and independence, White was in a promising position to revive Republican strength in the district. New leadership and electoral success might deliver the GOP from the most debilitating forms of corruption.

White's main rival for the nomination was former congressman Henry P. Cheatham. The two men's wives were sisters (daughters of Henry Cherry, Reconstruction legislator from Edgecombe), and their political competition was to have a sharp, unpleasant character. In fact, Cheatham later claimed: "White moved into this district to give me trouble on purely personal grounds."[7] Cheatham and White have usually been described in terms of marked contrast. Historian Samuel D. Smith, for

5. *Contested Election Case of Cheatham v. Woodard*, 229–30. For similar distinctions between "political character" and character in general, see 508, 164.
6. Salisbury *Star of Zion*, August 20, 1886.
7. Henry P. Cheatham to Thomas Settle, July 17, 1894, in Settle Papers. On the two men's wives, see Maurine Christopher, *America's Black Congressmen* (New York, 1971), 161.

example, drew a strong distinction between Cheatham, a man who "always identified himself with the better class of white people," and the "aggressive," "race-conscious" White, who gained the detestation of white North Carolinians as a "venemous," "incendiary politician." At the close of a long career in Democratic politics and journalism, second district scion Josephus Daniels recalled: "At least one Negro Congressman elected won the confidence of people of both races—Henry P. Cheatham. . . . I have always regarded him highly and our relations were friendly." White, on the other hand, was "the most militant of the Negroes elected to Congress," a man who "demanded office and equality for members of his race" and sometimes made "bitter and vicious speeches."[8]

Smith and Daniels wrote more than thirty years after Cheatham and White retired from politics, and as they looked back their assessments were unavoidably colored by the bitter events of 1898 to 1900. Contemporary observers, though they noted definite differences between White and Cheatham, did not always place them in such clear-cut categories. Before the storm, White was not seen as so fierce or offensive as later; and perhaps in the terms of 1894, Cheatham did not appear entirely reliable or harmless. How else can one explain the comment of a Northampton County Democratic newspaper: "Solicitor Geo. H. White, colored, is a candidate for the Republican nomination for Congress in this district. He is undoubtedly the ablest man in the party who has been mentioned in this connection, and the Republicans of this county could do no better than instruct their delegates to vote for him in the nominating convention. . . . We want to see good men nominated by all parties."[9]

For the first time since 1888, there were white Republicans actively seeking the congressional nomination. Joseph J. Martin, former postmaster at Tarboro, and D. W. Patrick of Greene controlled several delegates by the time of the district convention. Neither man had broad support, however, and could only hope to be nominated in case of a deadlock.

Delegates and would-be delegates from every county gathered in

8. Smith, *Negro in Congress,* 125, 127, 133, 143; Daniels, *Tar Heel Editor,* 177, 167; Josephus Daniels, *Editor in Politics* (Chapel Hill, N.C., 1941), 336.
9. Lasker *Patron and Gleaner,* June 21, 1894.

Weldon on June 27, with most political omens in White's favor. But as so often before in the second district, the meeting ended in furious division and disorder. When the session "broke up in a row" at 3:00 A.M. after thirteen ballots, the Republican organization was burdened with two intransigent "nominees": Cheatham and White. "The democrats will have a 'walk in,' without the necessity for fraudulent counting," commented one bitter Republican.[10]

Each side issued its own version of what happened, and the conflicting reports are not easy to disentangle. An immense credentials dispute, involving six of the nine counties in the district, magnified the existing hostility between Cheatham and White. After the convention Charles A. Cook, former United States attorney for eastern North Carolina, explained the matter in a letter to Congressman Thomas Settle: "Bogus contests were made in the interest of Cheatham from Warren and Edgecombe (of my personal knowledge), and I am informed and so believe, also from Bertie and Wilson." Following custom, the committee on credentials was selected from the three uncontested counties, Wayne, Lenoir, and Greene. According to Cook, the committee "proved to be very partizan in Cheatham's favor. But the convention was really for White."[11]

White himself told much the same story, claiming that if all the delegates from counties whose conventions had endorsed him had voted for him, he would have had 18 of the 24 possible votes. "But, according to an expressed plan several weeks before any county had held a convention, each county that instructed for me was contested," he charged. Although the credentials committee rejected seven of his delegates, White led the other candidates from the start, on each ballot falling only 1 or 2 votes short of the 13 needed to nominate.[12]

According to one report, the two white candidates threw their strength behind Cheatham on the final ballot, enabling him to win. A witness friendly to Cheatham said that as the chairman was announcing the result, W. W. Watson ran onto the stage to create a disturbance, much as he had done in 1888, and a half hour of uproar ensued. At some point White made a speech claiming that the convention had been

10. Raleigh *News and Observer*, July 1, 1894; C. A. Cook to Thomas Settle, July 7, 1894, in Settle Papers.
11. C. A. Cook to Thomas Settle, July 7, 1894, in Settle Papers.
12. New York *Times*, August 2, 1894; Raleigh *News and Observer*, July 1, 1894.

conducted unfairly and denouncing a few hundred white Republicans of "Lenoir, Wayne, and other counties" for stifling the will of the vast black majority. (His remarks, if accurately quoted, probably referred to the Wayne-Lenoir-Greene credentials committee or Martin's and Patrick's cooperation with Cheatham. The pro-Cheatham chairman, John Fields of Lenoir, may also have borne some of his ire.)[13]

Since each man insisted that he had been nominated, Cheatham producing a statement signed by the chairman, White citing another signed by the secretary, it is impossible to say precisely how the convention ended. Perhaps "broke up in a row" is as good a description as any. C. A. Cook thought that no legitimate nomination had been made: "The declarations of a mob should not be noticed by civil people."[14]

Whoever had the best claim to being the convention's choice, White appears to have been the more popular man with the masses of black voters. Incumbent Congressman Frederick Woodard had expected his opponent to be White and told a Warren County Democratic leader, "I think Cheatham is not as strong in the District as White." Although Woodard no doubt welcomed the turn of events at Weldon, many Republicans who had expected to be represented by White delegates were angry. A mass meeting in Bertie, responding to the call of the Republican county chairman, denounced the two Cheatham supporters who had been seated at Weldon for "misrepresenting the wishes of the Republicans of Bertie" and affirmed that White was the "Regular nominee."[15] For the rest of the summer, influential Republicans attempted to resolve the White-Cheatham feud, realizing that continuing division "simply means the return of Woodard or some other Democrat to the next Congress." Some party leaders hoped that the dispute might be arbitrated by the Republican national congressional committee, a group of representatives who coordinated and assisted Republican congressional campaigns. As a member of this committee, Tarheel Congressman Thomas Settle received advice from all sides.[16]

13. Tarboro *Southerner*, July 5, 1894; *Contested Election Case of Cheatham v. Woodard*, 75, 79; Raleigh *News and Observer*, July 1, 1894.

14. C. A. Cook to Thomas Settle, July 7, 1894, in Settle Papers. See *Contested Election Case of Cheatham v. Woodard*, 37–38.

15. F. A. Woodard to M. J. Hawkins, June 28, 1894, in Hawkins Papers. "To The Public" (broadside), 1894, in Settle Papers.

16. W. T. Faircloth to Thomas Settle, July 4, 1894, W. E. White to Settle, July 13, 1894, both in Settle Papers.

Hiram L. Grant, white Republican of Wayne, told Settle that "in the event the committee decide to act they will find Mr. White favorable to me as the compromise man." Grant pointed out that he had not been present at the chaotic district convention, "so both [Cheatham and White] seem friendly towards me." After consulting with Populist chief Marion Butler, Grant reported that the People's party was willing to delay choosing a congressional candidate in order to give the Republicans time to overcome their problems. The Populists were prepared to endorse Grant if he were the Republican candidate, or make no nomination if another "not too objectionable" man were selected. "I do not flatter myself with even a hope of success in this Dist. even with White & Cheatham out of the field and Woodard the Candidate on the Democratic ticket with his manipulations of the machinery for counting[,] unless the People['s] party made no nomination," said Grant.[17]

Charles Cook told Settle, "White is truly loyal to the party, but would not yield to Cheatham." In such circumstances, "the only way to restore harmony" was for both men to withdraw—"and I even then doubt our ability to redeem the District." Cheatham had a much cheerier view of the situation: "The party is so determined to elect a Rep. member of Congress I believe I shall be elected with White bolting." He suggested that Cook and Grant were disappointed at not being chosen for the nomination themselves, and that when they got over their "sourness" enough to "speak out for the party," White would "stop his foolishness." The former congressman told Settle of White's criticism of white Republicans, though in the retelling the speech became a broader-gauged attack, aimed at more than just a few local white Republicans. "After White saw that he was defeated and that the white Republican brethren nominated me he (White) made a mean speech against the white Republicans of the state," asserted Cheatham.[18]

Eventually Cheatham and White allowed the national congressional committee to arbitrate their claims, and on September 24 the committee decided in Cheatham's favor. After nearly three months of strife, the Republican party in the district could enjoy having only one GOP congressional aspirant for the final six weeks of the campaign. At least two

17. H. L. Grant to Thomas Settle, July 2, 11, 1894, both in Settle Papers.
18. C. A. Cook to Thomas Settle, July 21, 1894, H. P. Cheatham to Settle, July 17, 1894, both in Settle Papers.

Democratic editors expressed disappointment in the committee's decision. "As one [or] the other was to run, we would have been glad to hear of White's victory," said the Tarboro *Southerner*. "He is a courteous darky, especially in his official duties. He was by far the strongest man in Edgecombe," said the newspaper, in an admission it might not have made if White had indeed been the victor. The Lasker *Patron and Gleaner* regarded White as the more capable of the two men, and thought he would have given Woodard "a close race."

White is undoubtedly the ablest man of his party in East Carolina now in public life. But there is no comparison between Cheatham and Woodard, and there ought to be no doubt as to the result of the election. Cheatham is said to be a man of excellent character; but we need a man of energy and ability to represent us in Congress. During Cheatham's four years in Congress he did not seem to learn anything except to draw his salary. . . . Even a postal card request to Congressman Woodard receives courteous and immediate attention, while Cheatham paid no attention to anyone except his political henchmen.[19]

In the meantime the Democratic party had not been entirely free from dissension. Although Congressman Woodard had shown considerable skill in balancing the demands of his southern regional loyalty and his responsibility as a Cleveland administration supporter, he had disappointed some of his constituents, particularly in the matter of patronage. The Democratic chairman in Warren County noted privately the existence of "pronounced dissatisfaction with the course pursued by Mr. Woodard in the distribution of the patronage which is supposed to pass through his hands" and charged that Woodard had surrendered in this matter to Senator Ransom. Ransom was not a good patron for Woodard to embrace, since the senator's popularity was under strain in the 1894 campaign. Former governor Thomas J. Jarvis, appointed to an unexpired Senate term on Vance's death, was seeking to unseat Ransom in 1895 and gain for himself a full six-year term. As both camps worked with determination to elect Democratic legislators favorable to their man, Woodard's reelection effort would have been stronger if his name had not been linked to either man.[20]

19. Raleigh *News and Observer*, September 27, 1894; *Henry P. Cheatham v. Frederick A. Woodard*, House Report 1809 to accompany House Resolution 337, 54th Cong., 1st. Sess., 1896, p. 1; Tarboro *Southerner*, September 27, 1894; Lasker *Patron and Gleaner*, September 27, 1894.

20. John A. Collins to M. J. Hawkins, August 4, 1894, in Hawkins Papers. The editor of the Goldsboro *Argus* warned Ransom that anti-Ransom feeling was strong

Counting on support in Warren, Northampton, and Halifax, state Senator William H. Day considered a race against Woodard. Day "has people in all the other counties telling the people that the Democrats in [Halifax] will not support Woodard if nominated," wrote Robert Ransom to his father. Another Halifax man, attorney W. A. Dunn, was cautiously endorsed by the Scotland Neck Democrat—if there was to be a contest for the nomination.[21]

Before the district convention met on August 22 in Rocky Mount, Day abandoned the idea of challenging Woodard, but opposition to the incumbent continued to smolder ineffectively. The discontent did not extend to all parts of the district, however, and Woodard was easily renominated. The entire Edgecombe delegation and the majority of the Halifax delegation supported Richard Speight for the nomination, a few Edgecombe delegates being so adamantly opposed to Woodard that they voted against the customary motion to make the nomination unanimous. This recalcitrance prompted a reproachful editorial in the Democrat: "There have gone out some rumors that the Democrats of Edgecombe are growing lukewarm, and some of them are positively indifferent, because their man was not nominated." One of the Edgecombe leaders of the opposition to Woodard explained that he was angry because Woodard had relied on a rival in making all appointments of Edgecombe men.[22]

The local skirmishes of Cheatham, White, Woodard, and associates were overshadowed by the issue of Republican-Populist state fusion, which threatened to end twenty-five years of Democratic legislative control and a dozen years of one-party judges. After an intense debate, North Carolina Republicans agreed to cooperate with the Populists to discomfit their mutual foe. The two out-of-power parties had little in common except for their determination to defeat the Democrats, their promise to restore county self-government, and their protest against dis-

---

in Northampton, Halifax, and Edgecombe. Joseph E. Robinson to M. W. Ransom, August 26, 1894, in Ransom Papers.

21. Robert Ransom to M. W. Ransom, August 4, 1894, in Ramson Papers. Scotland Neck Democrat, July 19, 1894.

22. Robert Ransom to M. W. Ransom, August 15, 1894, in Ransom Papers. Scotland Neck Democrat, August 30, 1894; Tarboro Southerner, September 6, 1894. See also Contested Election Case of Cheatham v. Woodard, 166, 176, 455, on Democratic discontent with Woodard.

honest elections, but these were the essential issues in 1894.[23] As in the 1882 to 1884 Liberal movement, the two parties meeting in separate conventions produced a single ticket. A Republican was the fusion nominee for chief justice, and a Populist, Democrat, and Republican the nominees for associate justices. The Republicans and Populists shared the six superior court nominations, and William H. Worth, a Populist, was the candidate for state treasurer.

In the face of this combination, Democratic strategists realized, in the words of state Senator Benjamin F. Aycock of Wayne: "Our only hopes to carry this state . . . is by using the *Negro*." Aycock urged Senator Ransom to secure the appointment of E. E. Smith, a prominent North Carolina Negro, as minister to Liberia. The appointment of Smith, a Democrat, "at this particular time would be worth a great deal to the party in this state," said Aycock. Nor was patronage the only way to appeal to black voters. Senator Jarvis advocated a strong Democratic stand in favor of increased educational expenditure, for "we must have some of the negro vote and such action will lay the foundation for work among the negroes."[24]

Democrats devoted a good deal of energy to weakening fusion by criticizing the Populists as insincere friends of the Negro and attempting to persuade Negroes that electoral cooperation with the third party was against their best interests. The Tarboro *Southerner* accused Populists of telling white voters "We've nominated a good ticket this year; there is no negro on it" and scattered the statement (in italics) across the pages of the last two issues before election day. Less prophesying than whistling in the dark, the Warrenton *Gazette* announced that the colored people would "vote to suit themselves" and had no idea of "being sold out" to the Populists. In another issue the *Gazette* asked: "Now, where is the Third Party's love for the negro? It simply uses them when it can and gives them nothing."[25] Such arguments did not interfere with

23. Joseph F. Steelman, "Republican Party Strategists and the Issue of Fusion with Populists in North Carolina, 1893–1894," *North Carolina Historical Review*, XLVII (July, 1970), 244–69; Lefler and Newsome, *North Carolina*, 548–49.

24. B. F. Aycock to M. W. Ransom, August 1, 1894, in Ransom Papers. T. J. Jarvis to S. A. Ashe, August 2, 1894, in Ashe Papers.

25. Tarboro *Southerner*, October 25, November 1, 1894; Warrenton *Gazette*, October 12, 26, 1894.

simultaneous Democratic criticism of white Populists for cooperating with black politicians.

Democrats knew what they were about when they attacked the bond between Republicans and Populists, for in practice the alliance was often frail. A few Republicans refused to tolerate any compromise of party principles. In a reversal of his attitude during the Liberal movement, James O'Hara condemned coalition with the new party, which he saw as a group of office-seeking former Democrats. Now practicing law in New Bern, O'Hara returned to his old home, Halifax County, on an antifusion speaking tour. "The Populists said he [in a speech in Scotland Neck], are like Jack-o-lanterns in the swamps and marshes, they spring up and shine but when you go to find them they are not there. O'Hara said that if you will take the idea of office out of the Populist party there will be nothing left." He urged Halifax Negroes to vote the straight Republican ticket "and take no part in fusing with the Populists." Most second district Republicans were not prepared to follow this advice, though they were concerned to maintain the strength and identity of their party. "Nearly all Republicans were in favor of fusion," said McMurray Furgerson, youthful white chairman of the Halifax GOP, after the election. "The only difference was as to terms." He reported that black voters were "extremely bitter" against any arrangement that looked like "unconditional surrender to the Populists."[26] In several legislative and county races around the district, the Populists and Republicans were unable to reach agreement on fusion.

One of the failures of the fusion policy was in the congressional race. Populist leaders told Hiram Grant that they would make no nomination if the Republicans chose a "not too objectionable" man, meaning, perhaps, a white candidate. When the Cheatham-White feud finally ended late in September, the Populists faced a Hobson's choice. No matter what they did the Democrats would accuse them of aiding the black Republican candidate. When it seemed the third party would make no nomination, Populist voters were warned that "not voting is equivalent to a vote for Cheatham." Democrats took a different tack, however, after a People's party convention less than a month before the election decided to nominate for Congress Howard F. Freeman, former state senator

26. Scotland Neck *Democrat*, October 25, 1894. *Contested Election Case of Cheatham v. Woodard*, 73–74.

from Wilson. The Freeman nomination was "simply for the express purpose of defeating Mr. Woodard and thereby elect[ing] Cheatham." According to the *News and Observer*, "Every vote cast for [a Populist nominee] is in effect giving support to Cheatham."[27]

The charge that Freeman's nomination would help Cheatham ignored the fact that Freeman appealed to hundreds of Negroes who could not bring themselves to vote for a Democrat. In a year when many Republicans were angry at their official candidate, Freeman might well hurt the GOP as much, or more, as he hurt the Democracy. Cheatham's supporters had hoped for a Populist endorsement, or failing that, no nomination.[28]

In the final days of a very confusing campaign, political currents pulled voters and candidates in several directions. A Warren white Democrat, for instance, hoped to defeat the black Republican incumbent register of deeds, Mansfield Thornton, with help from the Negro nominee for Congress, whereas Thornton had the endorsement of the Populists and quiet help from some Democrats. J. Gilliam Newsom, the Democrat who would be register, wrote to the Democratic county chairman that the Republicans of Judkins, Fishing Creek, and Littleton precincts were engaged in "bitter warfare," with "Chas. Cook [as a candidate for the state senate] & Mansfield Thornton fighting Cheatham[,] each arraying their forces against each other & in my opinion very equally divided." Newsom later wrote that he was confident of a "full vote," though he knew some Democrats were planning to vote for Thornton. He did not explain how he was going to receive this "full vote," but Congressman Woodard knew. "Gilliam Newsome [*sic*] is doing all he can to trade with Cheatham," complained Woodard, who did not appreciate the effort to "trade me off" in Littleton.[29]

H. A. Foote, editor of the Warrenton *Gazette*, suggested in a letter to

27. Tarboro *Southerner*, October 4, 1894; Warrenton *Gazette*, October 19, 1894; Raleigh *News and Observer*, October 10, 1894.
28. Former state senator Albert Alston, a Warren black leader, told Democrat J. Gilliam Newsom "that if the Populist convention . . . failed to endorse Cheatham for Congress, & put up a candidate, that the . . . republicans would not support the combination tickets with the Pops." In Newsom's opinion, if Cheatham were not endorsed by the Populists, "it assures Woodard's success." J. G. Newsom to M. J. Hawkins, October 9, 1894, in Hawkins Papers.
29. J. G. Newsom to M. J. Hawkins, October 9, 25, 1894, F. A. Woodard to Hawkins, November 3, 1894, all in Hawkins Papers. Warrenton *Gazette*, September 21, 1894, notes Populist endorsement of Thornton.

Woodard that bribery might be a promising tactic: "Meade Burchett the negro leader of Smith Creek [township] was in my office a few days ago. . . . I asked him if they would vote for Cheatham since White had withdrawn: he said no 'under no circumstances'—I then asked him if they would vote for you & he said he did not know." Foote offered Burchett and another Negro twenty-five dollars if they would carry the township for Woodard. He advised Woodard not to use general canvassers, but instead to "deal directly with the leaders of each township—It can be easily arranged[.] I am told that the republican chairman is not averse to an 'approach' now." Woodard may have been impressed with this advice, for in the last few days before the election he discussed with the Democratic county chairman payments of this sort for two townships.[30]

In Halifax County some black voters believed Cheatham had "traded off" the black Republican nominee for solicitor in return for votes for himself. Cheatham gave the story credibility after the election by asserting that in Weldon precinct "there was agreement made for the exchange of votes for Cheatham for Congress in return for votes for Daniels [Democrat] for solicitor and for the county ticket."[31]

Halifax Populists provided another illustration of the complicated calculations that prevailed in the climax of this most unusual election. For the best of reasons, they decided that not voting at all would be the best way to bring Populist control of North Carolina, and four days before the balloting they withdrew their entire ticket. Thoroughly familiar with Democratic methods of fraud—W. H. Kitchin, after all, had joined the local party—Halifax Populists "thought the more votes polled, the more would be counted for the Democratic State ticket."[32] They feared, in other words, that the Democrats would not be content to suppress their vote, but would go on to count it for the other side.

Bribes, voting strikes, and intricate bargains were all signs of a polity in disarray. Familiar expectations were no longer reliable as voters and leaders tried to create a new order from the fragments of the system

---

30. H. A. Foote to [F. A. Woodard], October 10, 1894, F. A. Woodard to M. J. Hawkins, November 3, 1894, both in Hawkins Papers. Compare Walter B. Faulcon to Hawkins, November 3, 1894, in Hawkins Papers. Cheatham carried Smith Creek by a comfortable margin, despite Foote's efforts.
31. Contested Election Case of Cheatham v. Woodard, 242, 8.
32. Ibid., 73. Compare 54–59.

of the 1880s. Black political power had been reduced—but not eliminated—as Negroes showed less unity, as the Republican party declined,
and as Democrats increased their control of electoral machinery. The
basic decision to restrict black voting, made at the state level in 1889,
had been imperfectly implemented, however, because both Populists
and Democrats appealed for black votes in the turmoil of the early
1890s—though neither side allowed Negroes a significant role in their
party machinery. Less predictable than previously, black voters were
not powerless, even in this period of defeat.

On the first Tuesday in November, Democratic chicanery and Republican disunity produced an electoral disaster for Cheatham. He carried
only Warren County, and that by less than a majority (he lost Northampton after the county canvassers rejected three precincts in which
he led Woodard by 416 votes).[33] Once again Woodard was a minority
victor with 14,721 votes to Cheatham's 9,413 and Freeman's 5,314. The
Populist candidate made his strongest showing in Wilson, where 40
percent of the voters supported him, and in Warren, which gave him 34
percent of the congressional vote. "Our district could have been made
a close one," claimed a Warren Populist in a letter to one of the party's
state leaders, "if Dr. Freeman had canvassed thoroughly. I do not think
he made a single speech. Cheatham is very unpopular in Warren &
Halifax. Woodward [sic] received many negro votes that Dr. Freeman
could have gotten."[34]

Cheatham thought otherwise. In his view, his defeat was not the result
of Republican factionalism or of poor cooperation with the Populists, but
was caused by wholesale Democratic vote-stealing. Securing as his
counsel a well-known Democratic attorney, John W. Graham, Cheatham
sought to overturn Woodard's victory in an election contest before the
House of Representatives. On the assumption that black voters outnumbered white voters in the district by more than 5,000, and that
almost all Negroes supported him, Cheatham claimed that instead of

33. *Ibid.*, 2–3, 15. Woodard carried Bertie by a 131 plurality after the canvassers
rejected a precinct Cheatham carried by 15 votes and refused to accept 124 Cheatham ballots for being in the wrong box at another precinct. Forty-eight Cheatham
supporters at a third precinct were not allowed to vote under an extreme interpretation of the registration law, (pp. 9, 10).

34. John Graham to Cyrus Thompson, November 15, 1894, in Cyrus Thompson
Papers, Southern Historical Collection, University of North Carolina, Chapel Hill.

trailing Woodard by 5,308 votes he had actually defeated the Democrat by 6,672 votes.[35]

The Republican-controlled House Committee on Elections sifted through voluminous testimony—in printed form the depositions and documents presented by the two sides ran to more than five hundred pages—and concluded that, even giving Cheatham the benefit of doubt, the evidence did not support his claims. As a result of the bitter rivalry between Cheatham and White, the committee reported, "a very great many of the colored Republican voters refused to vote for Mr. Cheatham, a few of them even preferring to vote for Mr. Woodard, Democratic candidate, and a great many of them voting for H. F. Freeman, the Populist candidate." Cheatham had not shown that there was a black majority of registered voters or that "the colored vote was solid for him." The *Daily Charlotte Observer* quoted a member of the committee as saying, "If there had been no division of the Republicans shown the contestant would have won the seat."[36]

Thus Cheatham failed to prove that he had been cheated out of a seat in Congress, although the evidence he presented did suggest strongly that vote fraud was frequent, if not extensive enough to account for his defeat. Democratic magistrates often appointed ignorant and pliable men to represent Republicans and Populists at the polls, instead of those requested by opposition party leaders. Cheatham's witnesses told of other techniques to discourage black registration, miscount votes, intimidate voters, or take advantage of their ignorance.

But it is also clear, from the precincts where Cheatham did not allege fraud, that many Negroes simply refused to support him. According to the poll book in township number nine, Edgecombe County, 116 whites and 51 blacks voted on election day, yet Cheatham did not receive a

35. *Contested Election Case of Cheatham v. Woodard,* 14.
36. *Henry P. Cheatham v. Frederick A. Woodard,* 1–2; *Daily Charlotte Observer,* May 15, 1896. The committee presented the report May 14, 1896—the day after George White was nominated for Congress in the second district convention. One wonders if the report would have been delayed if Cheatham had been nominated for a fifth time. The Republicans on the committee may have been disinclined to help Cheatham, at any rate, after learning of his "trade" arrangements. The Washington correspondent of the Scotland Neck *Democrat* informed readers on July 18, 1895: "A few weeks ago a Republican who stands high in the National counsels [*sic*] of his party told me the National Republican Committee had knowledge of the existence of a compact between Plummer Cheatham . . . and certain small democratic leaders which militates against ex-Congressman Cheatham's fealty to the Republican party."

single ballot as Populist Freeman carried the precinct 88 to 78. In township number thirteen, 97 blacks and 71 whites voted, but Cheatham came in last in the three-way congressional race: 77 men voted for Freeman, 47 for Woodard, and 44 for Cheatham. There were exactly 110 registered voters of each race in Ormundsville precinct, Greene County, but Freeman easily defeated Woodard 123 to 70, with but 1 voter supporting Cheatham.[37]

The returns in Warren, a county Cheatham carried by a comfortable plurality, are particularly revealing. The voting statistics in four townships are strong evidence that the rumored Newsom-Cheatham "trade" was real. At Cheatham's home precinct, Littleton, the Democratic candidate for register received 256 votes—94 more than the total number of registered white voters—whereas only 21 men cast ballots for his Negro opponent. At the same time Cheatham had the aid of 20 or 30 whites—assuming that the Negro turnout was less than 100 percent and a handful of blacks voted for Woodard and Freeman. Friends of Cheatham and Newsom had a similar understanding at Fishing Creek, where the oddly matched Republican-Democratic pair swept the township.

Negroes had a 34-voter advantage in Judkins township, yet Cheatham lost the precinct to Woodard, illustrating the other side of the matter. State senate candidate Charles A. Cook, Thornton's ally in the Republican internal strife, received 107 votes at the same polling place, overwhelming his Democratic opponent's 58 votes. Obviously some men who voted for Cook also voted for Woodard. Cheatham claimed that fraud was the only explanation for his miserable performance in Warrenton, which Woodard carried by an absolute majority, though 65 percent of the voters were black. But it is more reasonable to assume that Republican voters rejected Cheatham through the influence of his rivals. Cook and Thornton amassed over 400 votes for their respective offices. Newsom trailed far behind Woodard on the Democratic side.[38]

A Halifax Negro who admitted during the investigation of the election

37. *Contested Election Case of Cheatham v. Woodard*, 147, 448. Greene County Record of Elections, 1878–98, North Carolina Department of Archives and History. York D. Garrett, Cheatham supporter and Republican legislative candidate, admitted that there were many black Populists in townships nine, ten, and thirteen. *Contested Election Case of Cheatham v. Woodard*, 478.

38. Warren County Record of Elections, 1878–96, North Carolina Department of Archives and History.

Table 4   Selected Returns, Warren, 1894[a]

| | PRECINCTS | | | |
	Fishing Ck.	Judkins	Littleton	Warrenton[b]
REPUBLICAN				
Cheatham (Congress)	170	77	194	72
Thornton[c] (register)	13	75	21	447
DEMOCRAT				
Woodard (Congress)	58	79	71	261
Newsom (register)	226	88	256	177
POPULIST				
Freeman (Congress)	19	7	11	181
REG. VOTERS				
Negro	182	124	182	513
White	89	90	162	273

[a] *Contested Election Case of Cheatham v. Woodard,* 449–50. Warren County Record of Elections, 1878–96.
[b] fraud alleged by Cheatham
[c] endorsed by Populists

that he had voted for Woodard spoke for many black voters. "Is it a custom for the colored people of this township to vote the Democratic ticket?" asked one of Cheatham's attorneys, attempting to corner the man. Exaggerating a bit, the witness replied: "It has been a custom since there has been so much trading in our party, now they are voting to suit themselves."[39] George White also viewed Cheatham's defeat as a case of blacks voting to suit themselves. He told a Democratic journalist two months after the election "that Cheatham's contest was preposterous and had no foundation in fact to sustain it before an . . . impartial investigating committee." White added: "Even with Freeman . . . out of the field, Mr. Woodard would have carried the district as the slump in this district was on a par as the slump in the State against the Democracy."[40]

As White suggested, the second district was one of the few bright spots for North Carolina Democrats in the 1894 elections. Republicans and Populists captured six of the state's nine congressional districts and gained a seventh seat in a contested election. The fusion ticket for state

39. *Contested Election Case of Cheatham v. Woodard,* 250.
40. Goldsboro *Daily Argus,* January 4, 1895.

and judicial offices also triumphed, adding to the disaster for Democrats. The Republican-Populist alliance dominated the state senate forty-two to eight and controlled the House by a seventy-four to forty-six margin. If their cooperation continued, the fusionists could elect their own men to the United States Senate. Of the total of eight Democratic state senators, three came from heavily black counties in the district—a circumstance that would have been incredible six years earlier. Bertie, Edgecombe, Halifax, Northampton, Wayne, and Wilson sent Democrats to the house, whereas Warren, Lenoir, and Greene elected Populists.[41] James Mewboorne won the Lenoir-Greene senate seat and another Populist represented the Wilson district in the senate. The only successful Republicans were senate candidates Charles A. Cook and Hiram L. Grant.

In the county elections Democrats maintained control of almost all local offices in the district. An occasional fusion candidate succeeded, such as Thornton in Warren, but Lenoir was the only county to reject the entire Democratic slate. At first it appeared that the Lenoir fusion ticket had lost, for the county canvassers gave the Democratic candidates a narrow victory by throwing out the returns from two townships for alleged irregularities. But the Democratic aspirants declined to accept the offices after they realized that there was "wide sentiment" among Democratic voters for a counting of the two townships. The Democratic candidate for solicitor in the Third Judicial District also refused to accept office on a technicality, saying that his opponent had really won.[42]

The Democrats' local successes made little difference. The fusion state victory was certain to produce major changes, and a few legislators, sheriffs, and registers of deeds could not halt the process. The fusionists had promised to overturn the old centralized county government system and to rewrite the partisan election law—reforms that would increase the influence of black voters and make it difficult for the Democratic winners of 1894 to be reelected.

The Republican party in the district had survived the discouraging years from 1887 to 1894, weakened and disorganized, but still a biracial organization in an increasingly segregated society. The natural friction between white Republicans and a new generation of black leaders, as

41. The Populist House candidate in Greene was seated after an election contest.
42. Kinston *Free Press*, November 8, 15, 1894. Rocky Mount *Argonaut*, December 20, 1894.

each side sought to adjust to the maturation of the black community, was exacerbated by Democratic propaganda, social pressure, and antiblack legislation. It is not surprising that many white Republicans surrendered to a racist environment and left the party, or that those who remained often faltered in their application of the principles of racial equality. What was remarkable was that any locally prominent white men continued to collaborate with a party dominated by Negroes, despite the inducements to do otherwise. As Carl N. Degler has noted: "It is not given for many men and women to transcend their history; most are lucky if they can make even a few changes in their vast and varied inheritance from the past. The Populists and Republicans of the South were among those exceptions."[43]

Despite the reelection of Frederick Woodard, second district Negroes could look to the future with hope. If reapportionment, corruption, suffrage restrictions, and migration had killed the "black second" in 1891, in the fusion victory of 1894 was the promise of resurrection.

43. Carl N. Degler, *The Other South: Southern Dissenters in the 19th Century* (New York, 1974), 357.

PART FOUR

George H. White and the Triumph of Extremism 1896–1901

Chapter 12

THE REVIVAL OF THE SECOND DISTRICT

JUST AS THE "BLACK SECOND" was created in Raleigh in 1872, so it was a decision of the general assembly that revived it in 1896. A liberalized election law enacted by the fusion legislature made possible once again the election of a black congressman. North Carolina was the only southern state at this time to tolerate so great a degree of black participation. Indeed, by 1896 two states, Mississippi and South Carolina, had already disfranchised most Negroes.

Designed to correct the abuses of two decades, the new law removed many obstacles to Negroes' registering and voting and attempted to insure an honest counting of ballots. The Populist and Republican legislators made certain that no one party could control the electoral machinery by requiring a Populist, Democrat, and Republican election judge and registrar at each precinct. The old Democratic practice of appointing unlettered men to "represent" the opposition was forbidden by a provision that the party representatives be appointed by the clerk of the superior court "upon the written recommendation or approval" of the party's state chairman and also that all registrars and election judges be literate.

The legislators closed several loopholes in the old law that had been used on many occasions to "count out" Republican or independent candidates. "Any ballot found in the wrong box," the new law ruled, "shall be presumed to have been deposited there by mistake of the officers of election, and unless such presumption shall be rebutted, the ballot shall be counted." The prohibition against symbols or "devices" on the ballot was dropped; in fact, the law permitted party tickets of various colors. The general assembly ordered the secretary of state, in canvassing the presidential returns, "to disregard any . . . apparent clerical error as may not render it reasonably uncertain who was the person intended to be designated as voted for." The law abolished the old county board of canvassers, a body with broad, vague powers, and gave the responsibility for counting the vote to the clerk of the superior court in each county.[1]

Other decisions, made in Washington and elsewhere, contributed to the resurrection of the black district. The matter of Henry Cheatham's contested election case was a most important outside influence upon district affairs, for Cheatham harbored hopes of another nomination and his chances depended to a great degree on the decision of the House Committee on Elections. He contended that if he were seated early in 1896, his candidacy would be much stronger. A decision in favor of Cheatham would also certainly divide the Republican party in the district.

Cheatham and his friends allied themselves with Congressman Thomas Settle, a leader in the North Carolina faction that favored Thomas B. Reed for president and opposed the gubernatorial ambition of Daniel Russell. The Cheathamites counted on Settle's influence to aid them in the election contest, and again and again his black associates in eastern Carolina expressed their hopes. "If the party will assist me and seat Cheatham we will controle [sic] the next State Convention," wrote R. H. W. Leak, an important Raleigh clergyman, late in 1895. "I am determined to capture the 'East' for our side," Cheatham told Settle on February 6, 1896. "Just think of it, if I was seated or if I could be within the next two weeks—I would be able to carry this whole Eastern Country with a [w]hoop! Why the prestige would cause all the colored people everywhere to stand by me." By the end of the month W. Lee Person was writing: "C must be seated at once to help us any." James E. Shepard, his 1892 flirtation with the Democracy long forgotten, made a similar appeal to Settle: "If he is seated then we can safely count on this District for Reed in the State Convention." Shepard clearly hoped that Settle would see political advantage in aiding Cheatham and not be too fastidious about details: "It is circulated here that you have written personal letters of inquiries concerning the Cheatham case. This caused some uneasiness but I have disapproved the statement. I hope you will see Mr. Reed, & members of the committee, warning them against the

1. *Public Laws and Resolutions, 1895* (Raleigh, 1895), Cpt. 159, pp. 211–36.

letters that may come from this District in opposition to our candidate."[2]

As in 1894, Cheatham's main rival for the nomination was his brother-in-law, George H. White, a fact that made the outcome of the contested election doubly important. If the committee on elections seated Cheatham, he could interpret the action as proof of his claim that black voters had been solid for him, whereas if Woodard won it would be difficult to deny that black voters had been divided in 1894. Goaded by their grudges, Cheatham and White would each strive mightily to avoid losing the nomination to such a particular foe. In this atmosphere political tactics could be unsavory. W. Lee Person of Edgecombe revealed the uncompromising attitude of one Cheatham operative when he wrote to Congressman Settle: "I have done all a man can do with what has been furnished me and my County Executive meets on tomorrow[.] [I]f they spring a resolution on me have not a dollar to oppose them with and you know [Edgecombe] cost more money than any County in the East."[3]

The other side was using equally rough tactics, according to Person. When the district executive committee met to set a date for the district convention, Hiram L. Grant (now secretary of the United States Senate) allegedly proposed a deal with the Cheatham forces. "He says he will take his hands off of Mr. Cheatham & Let him be seated also renominated if we will pledge ourselves to send him to the National Convention from this Dist," Person told Senator M. S. Quay. "We cheerfully declined then he got around through the crowd and said he would fight us as he would see to it the Case should be defered or not tried at this session." The executive committee called the convention to meet in Weldon May 12 and endorsed Cheatham for the nomination.[4]

The convention that assembled May 12 had as much potential for disaster as the 1894 meeting. Once again a majority of the delegations

2. R. H. W. Leak to Thomas Settle, November 22, 1895, H. P. Cheatham to Settle, February 6, 1896, W. L. Person to Settle, February 29, 1896, J. E. Shepard to Settle, March 10, 1896, all in Settle Papers.

3. W. L. Person to Thomas Settle, March 26, 1896, in Settle Papers.

4. W. L. Person to M. S. Quay, March 24, 1896, Person to Thomas Settle, March 26, 1896, both in Settle Papers. In the end, the district convention selected Grant as a delegate to the GOP national convention and the report of the election committee was not delayed, though it was not issued until after the district convention. Cheatham had tried to prevent Grant's appointment as Senate secretary. See New York *Times*, July 29, 1895.

(Bertie, Edgecombe, Halifax, Northampton, and Warren) faced challenges to their seats. Chairman John Fields, the pro-Cheatham presiding officer of two years earlier, provoked an "uproar" when he tried to appoint a "Cheathamite" credentials committee, the tactic that had been so successful in 1894. The convention took a recess to iron out the problem. As the unsympathetic *News and Observer* reported: "During the recess Cheatham lost ground, and before the convention reassembled it was whispered around that Fields had been bulldozed by the White faction." After the recess Fields named a new committee more friendly to White, "and the Cheathamites wilted." Defeat in the credentials battle clearly doomed Cheatham's hopes. When White was overwhelmingly nominated, the former congressman "took his defeat quietly," though he claimed he had been "cheated out of the nomination." The exhausting session, which dragged on past midnight, also endorsed Daniel Russell for governor and Republican Senator Jeter C. Pritchard for a full term in the Senate.[5]

Less than forty-eight hours later, Republicans convened in Raleigh to choose a state ticket. With victory in the air, the meeting "brought together the largest number of people that has attended a convention of this party in twenty years," according to the Populist *Caucasian*. The two leading contenders for the gubernatorial nomination, Daniel L. Russell and 1888 nominee Oliver H. Dockery, had nearly equal support and the outcome depended on thirty-four contested delegates from ten counties. State chairman A. E. Holton, an ally of Speaker Reed, appointed a nine-man credentials committee which was said to be heavily weighted in Dockery's favor. After deliberating for fourteen hours, the majority of the committee voted to award eighteen of the contested seats to Dockery and sixteen to Russell. A lone Russell supporter on the committee issued a minority report which recommended that Russell get thirty delegates and Dockery only four. Although the Populist reporter thought "it was a disgraceful and dirty job," the convention accepted this minority report, after four hours of debate. Russell subsequently won the nomination on the seventh ballot, defeating Dockery by the narrow margin of 119 3/7 to 104 4/7, with a third candidate receiving 13 votes.

The Republicans nominated an incomplete ticket, choosing candidates for governor, auditor, attorney general, and one of the two associate

5. Raleigh *News and Observer*, May 14, 1896; New York *Times*, May 14, 1896.

supreme court justices to be elected in 1896. They hoped the Populists would cooperate with them in the state election, and so the Republican state committee was authorized to complete the ticket at its discretion. If the People's party agreed to another fusion campaign, the Republican ticket would incorporate the Populist nominees for lieutenant governor, secretary of state, treasurer, superintendent of public instruction, and the other associate justice.

The party platform criticized Democratic tariff policy, endorsed bimetalism, advocated nonpartisan management of the public school system, and called for change in North Carolina tax law. But "the paramount issue for North Carolinians in this campaign," maintained the platform, was the preservation of the reforms of the last general assembly which produced honest elections and local self-government. "No differences as to questions of currency or questions of tariff" should overshadow the basic right "to vote and have that vote honestly counted. We warn our voters that if the Bourbons once more gain control of the State we may bid a final farewell to this, the greatest right of freemen, and expect that the South Carolina or Mississippi plan of heartless disfranchisement of the poor and uneducated will be incorporated into the organic law of North Carolina within sixty days after the return of the Bourbons." George White's new position of importance in Republican affairs was underlined in his selection as a delegate-at-large to the national convention.[6]

As the Republicans' odd skeleton ticket suggests, 1896 was to be a year of complicated bargains. Should men who agreed on the "money question" cooperate regardless of party labels or was reform in state government really the "paramount issue"? Until the three parties had resolved such questions, politics in the second district was bound to be confused.

In the congressional race, for Democrats to insure that the district would be represented by a free-silver advocate, they needed to move cautiously in making a nomination, wooing Populist support. Northampton state legislator Robert B. Peebles advised such a policy: "In my opinion it is very important not to nominate a candidate for Congress [at the district convention] on the 23rd [of June] but to appoint delegates to Chicago & to adjourn to a day in July & invite all silver men to

6. Raleigh *Caucasian*, May 21, 1896; New York *Times*, May 17, 1896.

unite with us in nominating a candidate to beat the Gold Standard candidate of the Republicans. In this way I think White can be beaten." But the party ignored such counsel and pushed ahead with the re-nomination of incumbent Democratic Congressman Frederick Woodard. Perhaps many Democrats shared the fatuous confidence of the Golds-boro *Headlight*, which found Woodard's nomination "equal to an elec-tion," though the newspaper did recognize the need for every Democrat "to go actively to work from now until November." Populists were forced to weigh the unpleasant alternatives: an unpopular Democrat or a Negro "gold bug."[7]

Of course the Populists could always nominate their own man and go "in the middle of the road," in the current political slang. One aspirant for the Populist nomination thought he could be elected with the help of Henry Cheatham and his disappointed followers. Five weeks after George White's nomination, D. Schuyler Moss of Littleton wrote to the state's Populist leader, Senator Marion Butler, asking for a private conference on a matter "of importance to myself and the Populist party of the 2nd Congressional District." He had, he said, "been furnishing a little money for Cheatham's (ex congressman) leaders in Warren, Halifax, Bertie, and Edgecomb [sic], counties to organize secetly [sic] their leaders in my favor for Congress as they say they are determined to beat White (the Republican nominee) if they have to go to the Democrats to do it. Cheatham is a personal friend of my father and he can turn this tide to me and says he will if I get the nomination from my party." Moss informed Butler that he could tell "a great deal more" if he could meet the senator. "I have had Bowers the chairman of P. P. of Halifax Co. and other leading Populist [sic] in the co. in a private conference with Cheatham and his friends." Before he went any further, Moss wanted Butler's view of whether there was wisdom in the scheme. "If there is any thing in it I can by the use of a little money sement [sic] the larger percentage of the Cheatham vote to me." If a meeting with Butler could be arranged, Moss wanted "no one to know about it unless you think otherwise."[8] There is no record of

7. R. B. Peebles to Edward Chambers Smith, June 14, 1896, in Edward Cham-bers Smith Papers, Duke University. Goldsboro *Headlight*, June 25, 1896.

8. D. S. Moss to Marion Butler, June 20, 1896, in Butler Papers. Moss said W. H. Kitchin was "not on to the plans" as "we think he is leaning towards the Democratic party or trying to disorganize the populist party . . . at least we can't tell where he is going to take his stand."

what became of the Moss-Cheatham negotiations. It is likely that Butler and the Populist leadership were not yet ready to make firm commitments in the second district. Before they decided whether to make a strong effort in this race, they needed a better sense of how state politics would develop. But a plan like Moss's could not wait in limbo for two or three months, of course, and probably the opportunity for collaboration with Cheatham simply faded away.

The events in Raleigh were certainly intricate enough to keep Butler and associates busy. The state Democratic convention met June 25, nominating a full slate of candidates, with Cyrus B. Watson the gubernatorial nominee. After the Democratic and Populist national conventions met in Chicago and St. Louis and selected the same man, William Jennings Bryan, for president, but chose different vice-presidential candidates, Butler proposed to the North Carolina state Democratic chairman that the Populists and Democrats cooperate on all levels. (In the proposed division of offices, the second district congressman would go to the Democrats.) This offer the Democrats ignored.[9]

The last of the three parties to hold its state convention, the Populists gathered in Raleigh August 13 and, amid occasionally heated discussion, selected a not-quite-complete ticket. For governor they chose Durham lawyer William A. Guthrie and matched him with Oliver H. Dockery, defeated aspirant for the Republican nomination now calling himself a "silver Republican," for lieutenant governor. The Populists put forward men for all other state offices except attorney general and one associate justice of the supreme court, which were to be named later by the party's state committee. An anti-Butler faction, loudly represented by convention chairman Congressman Harry Skinner, opposed the nomination of Dockery and Butler's suggestion that the convention nominate the Republican nominee for attorney general. Skinner complained that Butler was acting as convention boss and that his policy had "caused our party to be a harlot between the old parties." He also revealed the very limited commitment of many Populists to racial justice when he warned delegates: "But whatever we do we must recognize that the white man must rule in North Carolina. The time has not come for the

---

9. Raleigh *Caucasian*, August 20, 1896. See also, on this campaign, Edmonds, *The Negro and Fusion Politics*; Robert F. Durden, *The Climax of Populism: The Election of 1896* (Lexington, Ky., 1965).

negro to rule and govern the white people of the state. He is not qualified for that great work, and if he should undertake it he would even endanger his own liberties."[10]

All of this was relatively simple compared to the maneuvering that followed in September and October. After lengthy consultation the Republican and Populist state committees agreed to work together to maintain the "free and honest elections" and local self-government promoted by the legislature of 1895. On the face of it, the agreement gave the Populists more than the Republicans. The Republicans conceded the Third, Fourth, Sixth, and Seventh Congressional Districts and promised to support the Populist nominees for secretary of state, treasurer, superintendent of public instruction, and associate justice. The Populists, on the other hand, reserved the right to name candidates in the Second, Fifth, and Ninth Congressional Districts (fusion having been locally arranged already in the first and eighth districts) and agreed to support the Republican candidates for attorney general, associate justice, and judge of the superior court in the Fifth Judicial District, but made no commitment to vote for Daniel Russell or the Republican candidate for auditor. The two parties agreed also to "equitably cooperate" in the legislative races.[11]

Privately Populists thought the Republicans were unbeatable in the second and fifth districts, where White and Settle were running. "It is not at all certain that the Democrats and Populists combined could elect Congressmen from the Second and Fifth Districts," said state chairman Hal W. Ayer, in an attempt to explain the complex fusion arrangement to local leaders. "The Republican nominees in these districts are almost certain to be elected against any opposition that can be thrown against them."[12]

George H. White urged Populists to support him, though everyone realized that Frederick Woodard's financial views were much closer to People's party doctrine. In a speech in Wilson, White told Populists that they held "the outcome of his election in their hands." Avoiding the

10. Raleigh *Caucasian*, August 20, 1896.
11. *Ibid.*, September 17, 1896.
12. "Confidential" duplicated letter from Hal W. Ayer, 1896, in Butler Papers. The letter was apparently sent to influential Populists around the state. The Raleigh *Caucasian*, October 15, 1896, complained of the public use of such a circular by a dissident Populist.

silver issue, he attacked the old Democratic election law and emphasized what Republicans and Populists had in common. The Wilson *Advance* seemed to fear that some of his white listeners were influenced: "His argument proving their near relationship was disgusting and should be condemned by every man who believes in white supremacy." An observation the *Advance* made about Wilson County was true for most of the district: "Fusion on the county ticket has put the Populists under obligations to White and his crowd." As Edgecombe Populist James B. Lloyd admitted in a letter to Senator Butler, many of his associates feared "that it would endanger the success of the Legislative tickets in this Dist to antagonize White with a candidate who would make an aggressive campaign." Second district Populists therefore took the unusual step of nominating a candidate, D. S. Moss, but refusing to allow him actually to run unless the district executive committee decided he should. Lloyd had been hoping for the nomination himself, but his friends "did not think that there was any chance to defeat White" and did not want him "sacrificed."[13]

North Carolina fusion plans reached their full Byzantine splendor about the same time, as the Populists and Democrats perfected a way to share the state's 11 electoral votes. According to the agreement, five of the electors were to be Populists, five Democrats, and one a member of the splinter National Silver party.[14] In this way, no one lost face, and William Jennings Bryan lost no electoral votes. The Populists were in the peculiar position of working with the Democrats to elect a president, while simultaneously helping the Republicans elect judges, legislators, county officers, and state officials—though three candidates for governor remained in the field.

These arrangements were not without their friction, and Populists felt the strain of coordinating contradictory goals. As the party's official organ described McKinley as a "Slave of the Money Power," loyal Populists were planning to assist in the election of gold bugs and Negroes and supporters of "Mark Hanna The Oppressor" to the general assembly, where they would vote, without doubt, for the reelection of Senator

13. Wilson *Advance*, September 17, 1896; J. B. Lloyd to Marion Butler, September 19, 1896, in Butler Papers.
14. Raleigh *Caucasian*, September 24, 1896.

Pritchard.[15] As Populists worked with Democrats for the election of Bryan, the new election law they had helped enact made it possible for thousands of black admirers of McKinley to register in preparation to vote for the wrong man. Could either set of allies be trusted?

Two letters Senator Butler received from Edgecombe lieutenants in the last month of the campaign reveal the anxieties of black-belt Populists. On October 6, William E. Fountain, fusion candidate for county treasurer, wrote that the Republicans must not be allowed to take advantage of local fusion to carry the state for McKinley, as Bryan's victory was more important than cooperation with the Republicans in local races. Registration in heavily black counties like Edgecombe was not simply a matter of law, a self-enforcing procedure. Like voting itself, registration was full and fair only when enough courageous men insisted that the law be followed. Familiar with the old election methods, Fountain knew that the Republicans were "relying upon the local fusion in counties to influence our people in getting out a full Republican registration." There was more than a trace of the old ways in his comment to Butler: "We have the chairmanship of the Registrars & in these eastern counties it is a leverage. We can in ten days instruct our people & can make the Republicans understand that they are more dependent upon us than we are upon them." James Lloyd was also suspicious of the Republicans. "I understand their little game," he told Butler. "They want the Pops in the East to get their voters registered, and now that they have cooperation on County offices here, they think that we will be active in getting out their vote for our men, when as a matter of fact they are more anxious to secure the Legislature for Sen Pritchard and the State for McKinley. They are dependent on us to get their voters out, and if they then see they can 'stand alone' I would not be surprised if more independence were not shown by them toward us."[16]

The cooperation between Republican and Populist was difficult enough, even without the fears expressed by Lloyd and Fountain. Democrats delighted in reminding Populists of unpleasant and inconsistent aspects of fusion. How is it, asked a Goldsboro newspaper, that

15. The descriptions of Hanna and McKinley are from headlines in the Raleigh *Caucasian*, October 15, 1896.
16. W. E. Fountain to Marion Butler, October 6, 1896, J. B. Lloyd to Butler, October 10, 1896, both in Butler Papers.

Populists have agreed to support Republican John I. Mozingo for Wayne sheriff, when Mozingo has admitted that he is going to vote for George White? "No more bitter and vindictive color line speeches have ever been made than by George White, the negro candidate for Congress in this district," the newspaper claimed, though it cited no specifics and there are no other reports of reckless speeches by White.[17]

Second district Populist leaders agonized over the question of Moss's candidacy until the last days of the campaign. District chairman J. T. B. Hoover wrote to Butler on October 21 asking for advice, since the executive committee was divided with a majority of the members in favor of Moss's making the race. "The matter stands this way, if he runs it will only draw many of the Pop. votes from the Silver man, without a ghost of a chance of his Election. If he does not run it might be possible for Woodard to pull through and thereby defeat the negro Gold bug." The fact that Woodard was "a very unpopular man in the Dist" did not make the decision any easier. "But as between him and White I shall vote for Woodard," said Hoover. "If our man makes the race I shall vote for him even though I know (as I do) that my vote is lost." He added that Moss did not care to run "if by running he will elect White." It is not clear what decision the Populists finally reached, but on the thirtieth Moss sent a letter of withdrawal to Hoover. As there "is no chance for me to be elected," he urged "our friends" to vote for Woodard to prevent White, a supporter of gold, from winning.[18] But his last-minute effort to drop out of the campaign did not prevent Moss tickets from being distributed in every county of the district on election day. Chairman Hoover may have found it too late (or inexpedient) to notify county leaders of Moss's wishes.

The fears about drawing votes away from the silver candidate proved unnecessary on election day as George White won an absolute majority (51.6 percent) in the three-way race. More than 37,000 voters turned out to vote in the congressional race, the highest number since James O'Hara's victorious campaign of 1884 and almost 8,000 more than in 1894. White overcame Woodard by 19,332 votes to 15,378, and a miniscule total of 2,738 men (7.3 percent) cast their ballots for Populist

17. Goldsboro *Daily Argus*, October 19, 1896.
18. J. T. B. Hoover to Marion Butler, October 21, 1896, in Butler Papers; Goldsboro *Daily Argus*, October 31, 1896.

Moss. The Republican candidate carried Bertie, Edgecombe, Halifax, Northampton, and Warren counties and fell only 25 votes behind Woodard in Greene County. In Halifax, where the Democrats had claimed suspiciously huge numbers of votes two years earlier, White polled nearly 4,000 votes, rolling up a plurality of approximately 1,900. Warren County gave White 64.6 percent of the vote, his biggest victory in the district.

Although he did not receive full party strength, the Populist candidate for governor ran more than 900 votes ahead of Moss. At the same time the Democratic gubernatorial hopeful ran 746 votes behind Woodard, suggesting that many Populists reluctantly voted for Woodard as the only silver man with a chance to win. There were about 600 men who voted in the McKinley-Bryan presidential contest who abstained from voting in the congressional race.[19]

In the legislative races, Republicans and Populists did exceedingly well. Only one of the twelve house members elected from the district was a Democrat, and of the ten senators elected from senatorial districts wholly or partially within the Second Congressional District, all were either Populists or Republicans. Seven black men were among those elected to the general assembly.[20]

Fusion arrangements brought county offices into the hands of Republicans and Populists everywhere except in Wayne County. In Lenoir County, Bruton L. Taylor, defeated for register of deeds in 1884, came back to office in 1896. James T. Dawson was elected sheriff of Halifax County—his first successful campaign since 1880. Henderson R. Deloatch, a Republican, became Bertie register of deeds, a position he had last won in 1882. For the first time since 1876, voters had a chance to choose county commissioners and magistrates, and these offices, too, fell to the fusionists.[21] Every one of the Edgecombe justices of the peace elected in 1896 was a Negro, and Bertie had sixteen black magistrates when the

19. The figures for president and governor are from Matthews (ed.), *North Carolina Votes.*
20. The seven Negro legislators were Representatives E. E. Bryan and Jordan H. Dancy of Edgecombe, Scotland Harris and J. H. Arrington of Halifax, Edward R. ("Ned") Rawls of Northampton, and Senators W. Lee Person and W. B. Henderson.
21. The information on Negro magistrates is from Raleigh *Gazette*, November 21, 1896; Windsor *Ledger*, September 8, 1898. See *Congressional Record*, 56th Cong., 2nd Sess., appendix, 304, for a list of black magistrates in Edgecombe.

voting was over. No wonder Democrats uttered dark prophecies about a renewal of Reconstruction.

Daniel Russell became the first Republican governor in twenty years, winning with 46.5 percent of the vote and an 8,500 vote plurality over Cyrus Watson, the Democratic nominee. William Guthrie was a remote third, with less than 10 percent of the vote. The Republican candidate for lieutenant governor, a late entrant into the race when the Populists and Republicans could not agree on complete fusion, and the GOP nominee for auditor were also successful. Where Republican-Populist cooperation had been arranged (in the elections for the other state officers, two associate justices, and one superior court judge), the fusionists won by a wide margin. In the presidential balloting Bryan received more than 175,000 votes—20,000 ahead of McKinley, though the Republican presidential candidate ran slightly ahead of Russell.[22]

The Republicans elected three members of Congress—White in the east and two candidates in the far western part of the state—whereas the Populists won five seats and the only successful Democrat was W. W. Kitchin, who defeated gold bug Thomas Settle in the fifth district. So North Carolina emerged from the 1896 election with a Republican governor, a Populist-dominated congressional delegation, a mixed state administration, a fusion legislature, and a unanimous electoral vote for William Jennings Bryan.

For once the election was characterized by full participation and honest counting, and for this reason the results deserve careful attention. Voters who were used to casting a straight party ticket showed remarkable skill at supporting the complicated alliances entered into by their leaders. One way to understand how voters reacted to the choices of 1896 is to look at the returns in a small area. In Lenoir County, for example, there were perhaps 100 men who voted a Bryan-Russell ticket.[23] The returns in Table 5 also suggest that a small number of Populists wielded an immense amount of influence as a result of their balance-of-power role. Based on the vote for McKinley and White, there were about 1,400 Republican voters in the county, and judging

22. Matthews (ed.), *North Carolina Votes*, 6, 111.
23. James Mewboorne, Lenoir Populist and former state Alliance president, told secretary of state-elect Cyrus Thompson that he had voted for Russell "and more than an hundred others did likewise." This statement confirms what the statistics suggest. J. M. Mewboorne to C. Thompson, November 11, 1896, in Thompson Papers.

from the vote for Watson and the losing candidate for register about 1,600 men could be expected to cast straight Democratic tickets. This leaves about 350 Populists, who by shifting their influence from one side to the other helped elect Bryan, shared control of the county government, and gained a member of the state house.

White's victory, like the fusion sweep of the district, rested on a narrow base. It would have been difficult, first of all, for such a large number of Negro voters to participate without the active support of Populists in the registration process. The Republican-Populist local alliance meant that in each county significant groups of white men would resist attempts to prune the number of black voters by technicalities or trickery. In such circumstances, disagreements over methods of registration and voting would be *political* conflicts, and the potential for an explosive *racial* confrontation would be reduced. Also, white men were essential in the actual balloting. Subtract the small group of white Republicans, estimated at no more than 2,000 by one source, from George White's vote and add the approximately 2,700 Moss voters to the Democratic column, and White's victory evaporates.[24]

Although there was no avoiding the "central theme" of southern history—white supremacy—the election of 1896 was basically a debate over ordinary civic issues. How should local government be constituted? How should elections be conducted? Ought the incumbents to be retained in office? In a district that cast the majority of its vote for a Republican governor and president, it was not surprising for a popular leader and effective organizer like George White to be elected to Congress.

But if a frightening race rivalry became the theme of the next election, the Populists and white Republicans would be in a vulnerable position indeed. For this reason White's triumph was less substantial than it seemed; a crucial part of his support (direct and indirect) came from groups that were very susceptible to pressure. All that was needed to activate such pressure was a distinct increase in black political power and influence. By labeling it "Negro domination," Democrat propaganda could use rising black political importance to demoralize white Republi-

24. The New York *Times*, November 1, 1896, estimated that "not more than 2,000" white Republicans resided in the second district. This may be an underestimate, since the article was emphasizing how few white Republicans remained in the party in the face of alleged Negro misconduct.

Table 5 Lenoir Election Returns, 1896, Selected Offices[a]

Office	Winner	Party	Vote	Vote for Loser(s)
President	W. J. Bryan	Dem.-Pop.	1,966	1,410—Rep.
Register	Bruton Taylor	Rep. (fusion)	1,754	1,596—Dem.
Congressman	F. A. Woodard	Dem.	1,662	1,395—Rep.
				291—Pop.
Governor	C. B. Watson	Dem.	1,598	1,501—Rep.
				260—Pop.

[a] Based on Lenoir County Record of Elections, 1880–1900; Matthews (ed.), *North Carolina Votes*, 60, 165.

cans and neutralize the Populists. Blacks are advancing at our expense, Democrats could say, and how can you be a traitor to your race?

In the days that followed the victory of 1896, some members of the coalition were already faltering. Three months after the election, a Populist former legislator from Warren observed privately: "The Negros [*sic*] are fussing for rule and power and must be put into subjection, and any course we may persue [*sic*] that does not lead in that direction consistently will divide the majority of Pops, or make democrats of them."[25]

25. W. B. Fleming to Marion Butler, February 11, 1897, in Butler Papers.

Chapter 13

INSULTING OUR PEOPLE

"BUCK" KITCHIN WOULD HAVE BEEN embarrassed if a letter he wrote in March, 1882, had been published fifteen years later. When Congressman Orlando Hubbs appointed a "wild Irishman" who had lived in the community only a few years as postmaster at Scotland Neck, Kitchin wrote Senator Ransom protesting the elevation of a "dirty grog-shop keeper." "He is totally unfit to make a postmaster. If Hubbs knew the character of his appointee *he* would recoil in disgust and horror," declared Kitchin. He urged Ransom to use his influence to have the old postmaster retained, adding "if you find that impossible for gods sake have some decent colored man appointed."[1] Such a statement, so reasonable in the context of 1882, would have been inconceivable in 1897—especially from Kitchin.

When Congressman George White attempted to place a Negro in the Scotland Neck post office, local whites reacted angrily. "If the Administration deliberately sought to insult our people, it could not better succeed than by making these [postal] appointments," wrote W. A. Dunn, a Democratic attorney, "and if it was the purpose to create race prejudice and set back the Negro it could not better succeed than by placing him where he is regarded as an insult to our people." A Negro as postmaster was highly "objectionable" because the post office was bound to become a "loafing place" for the local black politicos. Dunn deluged Senator Butler with evidence that White's man was lacking in character, but a Scotland Neck Populist was more straightforward:

1. William R. Woods to M. W. Ransom, March 18, 1882; W. H. Kitchin to Ransom, March 18, 1882. Another of Ransom's correspondents called Hubbs's appointee a "professed Democrat." Richard H. Smith to Ransom, March 18, 1882; all in Ransom Papers.

"I have no charges to make against the applicant—he is a good man—but the people here do not want a colored P. M."[2]

One of the reasons people in Scotland Neck, and all around the district for that matter, were so sensitive on the subject of black postmasters was that Negroes were being appointed to such positions in unprecedented numbers in 1897 and 1898. In the eyes of many whites, the black man in charge of the local post office was not merely an individual, who might be polite or obnoxious, efficient or incompetent, honest or corrupt, but he was a symbol, a manifestation of a pervasive black assertiveness that was deeply disturbing. The party of white supremacy was unable to control local, state, or national governments, and second district whites could ponder, if they chose, the brooding words of Governor Russell's inaugural: "There is retribution in history."[3]

As soon as his party's president was inaugurated, George White set to work securing patronage for his constituents—like any congressman seeking to consolidate his hold on a district. His Republican supporters, mostly Negroes, behaved remarkably like other politically minded citizens at the changing of administrations, eagerly awaiting as clean a sweep of the federal offices as the civil service law allowed. If Democrats denounced the appointment of blacks, White had to reckon with a pressure from the other direction, which insisted that his political friends be rewarded. "Hon. George H. White will make postmasters hum for the next sixty days," commented the Rocky Mount correspondent of the black Raleigh *Gazette* on March 13, 1897. "Let Rocky Mount be first to receive the plum." Within six months White had secured the appointment of more than twenty black postmasters.[4] Some of them were put in charge of obscure and unprofitable places like Lawrence (Edgecombe County) or Ridgeway (Warren County), but others served in major towns and county seats. Negro postmasters managed the post offices in Littleton, Rocky Mount, Halifax, and Windsor by August, 1897, and by the spring of 1898 the list included Wilson and Weldon.

White Democrats (and some Populists) reacted strongly against

2. W. A. Dunn to Marion Butler, March 16, 1898, A. A. White to Butler, March 21, 1898, both in Butler Papers.
3. For the complete text of Russell's speech, see the Raleigh *Gazette*, January 23, 1897.
4. *Ibid.*, March 13, July 31, August 14, 1897.

White's policy. The Tarboro *Southerner* thought Negro postmasters were an inevitable result of the fusion victory and said: "Let the black white folks enjoy their vote." The paper later elaborated: "We believe that the white man who allies himself with the negro in politics makes a serious mistake. No question can be made of his legal right to do so and his convictions are entitled to respect if they are honest. But, having chosen his course, he cannot complain if it leads him into subjection to his political associates and places above him a negro official." A Rocky Mount postal patron complained that "white ladies have to file in a booth built in front of the delivery window, in order to be waited on. [T]he booth is always crowded with negroes large and small male and female, at mail time." The "bull pen arrangement," according to another citizen of Rocky Mount, resulted "in practical prohibition to ladies," and a petition from Rocky Mount postal patrons said white ladies were put to "great inconvenience" by the "idlers and loafers" who lounged around the office.[5]

The most successful objections came from Scotland Neck, where White had arranged the appointment of C. P. Anthony, a black Halifax county commissioner. Although Halifax's Populist state senator, Edward T. Clark, described Anthony as "a manly well behaved colored man," and leading local white Republicans certified his good character, Anthony came under attack as an objectionable, immoral person. He had been the keeper of a colored bar, said a relative of the Democratic incumbent. Lawyer Dunn produced evidence that Anthony had fathered two illegitimate children, though what this had to do with selling stamps and delivering the mail was unclear. However, Scotland Neck was an important enough office to require senatorial advice and consent, and in the end the Senate did not confirm Anthony's appointment.[6]

Not all of the Negroes who managed second district post offices were capable officers. At least two of White's appointees, the postmasters at

5. Tarboro *Southerner*, April 1, October 7, 1897; John R. Underwood to Marion Butler, December 15, 1897, T. H. Battle to Butler, April 16, 1898, Petition from Citizens and Patrons of the Rocky Mount Post Office to Butler, April 9, 1898, all in Butler Papers.

6. Edward T. Clark to Marion Butler, April 4, 1898, R. J. Lewis to Jeter C. Pritchard, May 3, 1898, Statement by M. M. Furgerson, May 3, 1898, F. H. Busbee to Butler, March 17, 1898, W. A. Dunn to Butler, April 19, 25, 27, 30, 1898, all in Butler Papers. See also affidavit of Robert Wilkens, April 14, 1898, in Butler Papers. Record of Appointments of Postmasters, Vol. 69, RG 28, NA.

Rocky Mount and Tillery, went to jail for dishonest or incompetent stewardship of government money. Local Democrats played up such incidents as typical of the dangers of black officeholding, just as they had done several years earlier during Cheatham's tenure in Congress. In fact, of course, many whites objected to any Negro postmaster on purely racial grounds and loudly opposed extremely capable blacks like Wilson Postmaster Samuel H. Vick, "whose character was beyond reproach"—as Josephus Daniels admitted years later.[7] The black postmasters were particularly irritating to whites because they were so visible and unavoidable. Unlike a Negro legislator or congressman, a black postmaster was in daily contact with the whites of his community. This fact, more than any real power wielded by the postmaster, provoked white criticism. When Democrats complained of "Negro domination," they often had in mind relatively minor officials necessary to the transaction of ordinary business.

The postmasters were part of a larger change. For six years black officeholding in the second district had been minimal, but now suddenly there were hundreds of Negro public officials, both elected and appointed, ranging from constable to congressman. In the minds of Democrats the change seemed more sweeping, no doubt, because black participation had been so sharply reduced in the years after the enactment of the 1889 election law. In 1896 a Democrat in Edgecombe or Halifax or Northampton felt like a man who had gone to sleep by a dim, guttering fire, only to awake in a house ablaze.

It is not clear how many blacks held office during the fusion renaissance, since the contemporary evidence is scattered and incomplete. At the climax of the heated 1898 campaign, Democratic state chairman Furnifold Simmons issued a public letter to Senator Pritchard specifying the number of Negro officers in many counties, and at the state and federal level, but mentioning only one such official by name. For some positions and localities Simmons gave exact numbers, whereas in other cases he made only general estimates. His letter lists sixteen black magistrates in Bertie, thirty-one in Edgecombe, and twenty-nine in Halifax, but gives no figure for heavily Negro Warren and Northampton.

7. Raleigh *News and Observer* quoted in Goldsboro *Daily Argus,* June 9, 1900; Daniels, *Tar Heel Editor,* 208. C. W. Battle, Nash postmaster recommended by White, also went to prison.

Table 6   Partial List of Negro Postmasters, Second District, 1897–1901[a]

County	Post Office	Postmaster	Date Appointed
Bertie[b]	Windsor	Lewis T. Bond	May, 1897
	Lewiston	Daniel W. Baker	June, 1897
Edgecombe	Rocky Mount	Israel D. Hargett	July, 1897 (replaced Feb., 1899)
	Lawrence	Ada Dickens[c]	
Halifax	Halifax	Edward Cheek	April, 1897
	Scotland Neck	C. P. Anthony[d]	September, 1897
		Thomas Shields[e]	July, 1898
	Tillery	J. M. Pittman	April, 1897 (replaced Oct., 1898)
	Weldon	John H. Howard	January, 1898 (replaced June, 1902)
	Littleton	Henry D. Mayo	May, 1897
Warren	Ridgeway	Stuart Wortham[f]	ca. April, 1897
	Arcola	Henry Watson[g]	ca. November, 1897
Wilson	Wilson	Samuel H. Vick	May, 1898

[a] Based on Record of Appointments of Postmasters, Vol. 69, except where noted otherwise.

[b] The postmasters at Kelford (Edward D. Clark) and Drew (James D. Cherry) were probably Negroes, though I have been unable to identify definitely the race of the two men. The Atlanta *Constitution*, October 2, 1898, claimed that there were black postmasters at Kelford, Lewiston, Drew, and Windsor. Several other blacks served at small offices in Bertie County. The Windsor *Ledger*, September 8, 1898, said there were nine black postmasters in the county, and on March 8, 1900, stated "about a dozen" Negroes served as Bertie postmasters.

Several other Negro postmasters are not listed in this table. Edgecombe politician Clinton W. Battle was the postmaster at Battleboro in Nash County, but he is not included because he was appointed outside the district. The Raleigh *State Journal* said Mt. Olive (Wayne) and Kittrell (Vance), among other places, had black postmasters (quoted in Littleton *News Reporter*, June 1, 1900).

[c] Tarboro *Southerner*, October 7, 1897.

[d] not confirmed.

[e] removed.

[f] Warrenton *Gazette*, April 23, 1897.

[g] *Ibid.*, November 19, 1897.

Simmons claimed the total number of black magistrates "in the various Eastern counties" was "nearly three hundred." He apparently had only the vaguest idea of how many blacks served as school committeemen, simply asserting that there were "several hundred" of them. His letter emphasized most strongly the power of Negroes in Craven and New Hanover counties and the cities of New Bern, Wilmington, and Greenville. As far as it goes, Simmons' manifesto seems to be accurate. His claim of "15 to 25 negro postmasters in Eastern North Carolina" is not at all exaggerated, for example, whereas the sixteen black magistrates he claimed for Bertie are listed by name in an issue of the Windsor *Ledger*. If anything, Simmons underestimated the real extent of black officeholding. He noted the black registers of deeds in New Hanover and Craven, but did not mention those in Warren and Vance. He counted a black county commissioner in Craven, but was apparently unaware of the Negroes elected to the Warren and Halifax county commissions in 1896.[8]

In her pioneering study *The Negro and Fusion Politics in North Carolina, 1894–1901*, Helen G. Edmonds responded to the charges of Simmons and others by arguing that many of the offices held by Negroes were unimportant, and by noting that Simmons objected as strongly to black candidates as to black officials. The scope of her work precluded an extensive examination of local sources and compilation of a more accurate inventory of Negro officers. Indeed, in several ways *The Negro and Fusion Politics* also underestimated the number of black officeholders. Edmonds noted only five black members of the 1897 legislature, ignoring completely six Negro representatives from Edgecombe, Halifax, Northampton, and Vance.[9]

The most prestigous black officeholders are easy to enumerate: Congressman White, Wilmington customs collector John C. Dancy, and James H. Young, Wake legislator and commander of a Negro regiment during the Spanish-American War. These men, Young and White especially, were frequently the whipping boys of white supremacy propa-

8. Quoted in Edmonds, *The Negro and Fusion Politics*, 234–36; Windsor *Ledger*, September 8, 1898.
9. Edmonds, *The Negro and Fusion Politics*, 84–135, 219–20. The Negro legislators Edmonds failed to mention are E. E. Bryan and Jordan H. Dancy of Edgecombe, Scotland Harris and J. H. Arrington of Halifax, Edward R. ("Ned") Rawls of Northampton, and Moses M. Peace of Vance.

ganda, and subjects of misquotation and caricature. An influential advisor to Governor Russell, a state fertilizer inspector, and a director of the state blind asylum, Young was the only one of the trio whose position was in any way novel. Dancy had served as Wilmington collector in the Harrison administration. And, of course, there had been a Negro in the House of Representatives from 1875–1877, 1883–1887, and 1889–1893.

It is also not difficult to measure the increase in black officeholding in the North Carolina legislature. The eleven black legislators in the 1897 general assembly matched the total number of Negroes in the three previous sessions.[10] In this respect, fusion politics had returned North Carolina to the conditions that had prevailed before 1890—not to the state of affairs in 1868, as Democrats often suggested. The legislatures of 1876, 1879, 1883, and 1887 each had fifteen or more black members.

On the local level, it is somewhat harder to measure and assess black officeholding. Little information is available on many of the lesser officers who provided so great a day-by-day irritation to rank-and-file Democrats. Moreover, if the second district is any example, Negro officeholding in local affairs was quite different in the fusion years than earlier.

The most important local office, the only one with power over county financial policy, was that of county commissioner, a position very few Negroes held. In the second district, C. P. Anthony served as a commissioner in Halifax and W. E. Hall was a member of the county board in Warren—until he fled the county to escape prosecution on a bastardy charge. Hall was replaced by another Negro, John Wright, described by the local Democratic journal as "a man of good sense." The paucity of Negro commissioners was in marked contrast to the numerous black commissioners in Reconstruction county government. In 1876 one or more black commissioners had been elected in six second district counties, and Halifax, Edgecombe, and Jones had black majorities on their county boards. James O'Hara had been chairman of the Halifax commissioners.[11]

In ending the centralized Democratic system of county government, the fusion legislature of 1895 had shown great sensitivity to Democratic

10. I have not included J. H. Wright of Warren in the number of Negro legislators in the sessions of 1891, 1893, and 1895 because he was unseated after an election contest. See North Carolina *House Journal*, 1893, pp. 202–203.

11. Warrenton *Gazette*, April 16, 1897. On Negro commissioners in 1876, see Chapter 2 herein.

fears of misrule and extravagance in eastern counties. The revised county government law provided for minority party representation on the board of commissioners under certain conditions and, when minority members were added to the board, required more than a simple majority for actions involving money. This same fear of criticism—as well as the need for cooperation with Populists—led Republicans to nominate few black commissioners. Even Governor Russell, in his inaugural address, had seen a "danger of misrule by propertyless and ignorant elements" in local affairs.[12]

In the second district, almost all the important executive positions in county government, such as sheriff, clerk of the superior court, and register of deeds, were held by white men. During the 1880s several blacks in Edgecombe, Warren, Halifax, Northampton, and Bertie had won election as registers of deeds. (The office was not regarded as more honorary than remunerative," as one historian has claimed. According to the Tarboro *Southerner*, "The office is a fat one in fees and is easily attended to." The Halifax register collected about twenty-five hundred dollars in fees during 1882–1883.) One black was elected clerk in Warren County in 1886, though the Democratic county board refused to accept his bond and seated the losing Democrat. All this was very different from the elections of 1894 and 1896, in which Negroes were seldom even nominated for a major executive post. The only second district black elected to such a position in 1896 was Mansfield Thornton, register of deeds in Warren since 1878; strong black counties like Edgecombe and Halifax elected white Republican registers. The Republican-Populist triumph in 1896 produced not a single Negro sheriff or superior court clerk in the second district, or for that matter in all of North Carolina.[13]

Political expediency (and, in the case of an office like sheriff, Negro

12. Edmonds, *The Negro and Fusion Politics*, 119; Raleigh *Gazette*, January 23, 1897.

13. Edmonds, *The Negro and Fusion Politics*, 122; Tarboro *Southerner*, May 8, 1890; *John H. Hannon v. James M. Grizzard, et al.*, 96 NC 293, February, 1887, in North Carolina Department of Archives and History. (These supreme court papers involve a case in which a Negro candidate was denied office on a technicality. After the supreme court decided in his favor in an 1883 case, he sued the county commissioners for damages, pointing out that the man who had unfairly held the office collected about twenty-five hundred dollars in fees from December 13, 1882, to November 6, 1883.

It should be noted that in Vance and Craven, counties that had once been part of the second district, Negroes did successfully seek the position of register of deeds in the fusion era.

poverty) limited the number of major local offices held by Republican black politicians. Offices that blacks had frequently sought during Reconstruction and the Bourbon equilibrium were now monopolized by Populists and white Republicans. With the basic policy-making and executive positions in white hands, blacks turned to other positions to fulfill their civic ambitions—offices that sometimes entailed honor, sometimes money, but seldom a great degree of power.

The large number of black postmasters appointed in the second district illustrates this shift in black participation. Before 1889 there had never been more than one or two Negroes in charge of post offices in the second district. After 1897 one might find half a dozen or more in a single county. Although a postmaster exercised little autonomous authority, he did represent an essential service, and whites found themselves regularly exposed to a situation in which a Negro was in charge. Nor was the financial compensation of a major post office insignificant. Samuel H. Vick earned eighteen hundred dollars a year managing the Wilson office, and the Scotland Neck postmastership paid eleven hundred dollars.[14] Being a postmaster could be far more profitable than being a state legislator or county commissioner—or a small farmer.

Many Negroes won election as magistrates (justices of the peace), a position that had been dominated by whites even during Reconstruction. In 1875 a black Edgecombe legislator said that it had been customary for a majority of magistrates in the county to be Democrats, and they were elected by Republican votes. There were in Warren County, in the same year, seventeen white Democratic justices of the peace, five black Republican justices, and a lone white Republican magistrate. Northampton County elected seventy-eight magistrates from 1868–1874, but forty-six of them were Democrats, although Republicans invariably carried the county in national and state elections.[15]

Now in several of the black counties of the district, such as Bertie or Edgecombe, numerous black magistrates dispensed crossroads justice, judging neighbors who committed petty thefts, participated in affrays, went on drinking sprees, or committed some other misdemeanor. A small claim between a white farmer and his black tenant or laborer might be

14. See *Official Register*, 1899, II, 252–68, for North Carolina postmasters and their compensation.

15. Raleigh *Era*, March 18, 1875; Raleigh *Signal*, June 28, 1888 (reprinting a letter written to the Charlotte *Observer* in 1882 by C. A. Cook); Washington (D.C.) *National Republican* quoted in Wilmington *Post*, September 24, 1882.

tried before a Negro, himself a poor schoolteacher or landless farmer. Even in a white county like Lenoir a handful of Negroes served as magistrates. A militant Democratic editor complained that one of the county's four black justices earned more money in fees than any other magistrate and noted angrily cases in which the Negro man had "issued a civil warrant . . . against as respectable a white lady as there is in Lenoir county," ordered a white potato peddler "to appear before him and answer the charge of not having his measure examined and stamped" by the official standard-keeper, and issued warrants against five white country boys upon the request of a black constable.[16] The editor's objections were petty, even ridiculous, yet his ire shows that the proximity of power, more than its magnitude, fueled white supremacists' fears of black officeholding. A dozen magistrates (or constables, or postmasters) were far more provocative than one or two county officers or a state legislator.

Blacks in the second district did not start at the top, as Booker T. Washington charged Negroes in politics did. Their problem was that they started at the bottom. Unable, for various reasons, to seek the most significant local jobs, invariably passed over for statewide offices, those black politicians who were not powerful enough to win election to the state or national legislature crowded into federal patronage posts and lesser local offices, serving as postmasters, magistrates, county coroners or surveyors, constables, town policemen, or as deputies to the major officeholders. After 1896 Negroes filled some of these positions in unprecedented numbers—though never in proportion to their population strength. Democrats in Halifax, for instance, complained of twenty-nine black magistrates, about twenty black township school committeemen, twelve Negro postmasters, five black constables, a black jailer, and a Negro deputy recorder of deeds.[17]

Democrats recognized a substantial increase in Negro influence, of which black officeholding was but one aspect, and realized that fusion rule meant a reversal of the trend of the early 1890s. They assumed that the situation following the election of 1896 was only the beginning of black reinvolvement in politics. As the election of 1898 approached, therefore, many whites were in an explosive and fearful frame of mind.

16. Kinston *Daily Free Press*, October 1, 1898.
17. Scotland Neck *Commonwealth* quoted in Goldsboro *Daily Argus*, October 8, 1898. There was a total of thirty-one postmasters in the county. *Official Register, 1897*, II, 240–55.

Chapter 14

THE MEANING OF WHITE SUPREMACY

Criminal means once tolerated are soon preferred.
—Edmund Burke

AFTER IT WAS OVER, the rival parties offered sharply differing interpretations of what had happened. According to Democrats, the "white supremacy campaign" of 1898 was just what it appeared to be—a furious popular rejection of the increased black political power fostered by fusion politics. According to Republicans and Populists, race became an issue because cynical Democratic leaders conjured up an imaginary threat of "Negro domination" in order to return their party to office. Populists, in particular, saw economic motives behind the campaign and repeated their preelection charges that "the Democratic 'machine' and railroad monopolists" were insincere in their "howling lustily about 'negro domination.' "[1]

Recent historians have tended to support the Populist interpretation. Joseph F. Steelman, in a carefully researched doctoral thesis, argues that the conservative "Matt W. Ransom faction of the [Democratic] party was in the ascendancy in 1898." He maintains that "the economic policies of the Fusionists, particularly the aggressive record of the Railroad Commission" led Democrats to use "drastic" measures to regain control of the state. "Conservative interests were in the vanguard of the white supremacy campaign," in Steelman's version of events. Hugh Lefler and Ray Newsome present the 1898 campaign as more than simply a struggle for white supremacy, noting "heavy financial support from business interests" for the Democrats and citing the claim of the conservative Charlotte *Observer* that "the business men of the State are

1. Raleigh *Caucasian*, September 1, 1898.

largely responsible for the victory." A recent student of the process of suffrage restriction, J. Morgan Kousser, views the 1898 election in a similar light. Accepting J. G. de Roulhac Hamilton's claim that the menacing "Red Shirt Clubs" were primarily composed of the "respectable and well-to-do," Kousser suggests that the campaign was designed to protect upper class economic interests as well as to insure white rule.[2]

There is no question that nonreformers had strong influence in the Democracy of 1898, and the choice of Furnifold Simmons as state chairman was a sign of this. As for the role of "business interests," Simmons himself later admitted that he had passed the word to the state's major corporations that their taxes would not be raised in the next legislature if the Democrats were victorious.[3] Yet it would be a mistake to conclude that white supremacy was a contrived issue, that Democratic leaders were not genuinely concerned about increasing black political influence.

The main leaders of the white supremacy campaign, Josephus Daniels, Charles Aycock, and Simmons, were second district men, and their actions may be understood in light of their heritage. Three times Furnifold Simmons was a serious contender for the Democratic congressional nomination in the "black second." In 1886 and 1888 he attempted to accommodate Democratic politics to the presence of a large, active Negro voting bloc—a task he found frustratingly difficult, requiring the occasional aid of corruption and miscounting to succeed. In 1890 the activities of the Farmers' Alliance showed him how division in the white man's party could allow the black candidate of the "Negro party" to win an unexpected victory. The Democrats' most potent orator, Charles B. Aycock, was a native of Wayne County. Although Republicans seldom won in this county, they offered the Democrats strong opposition and occasionally elected a county officer or legislator. Twelve years before the white supremacy campaign, when Democrats faltered in the state election, Aycock attributed the party's poor showing to hard times,

2. Joseph F. Steelman, "The Progressive Era in North Carolina, 1884–1917" (Ph.D. dissertation, University of North Carolina, 1955), 168, 714; Lefler and Newsome, *North Carolina,* 558; Kousser, *Shaping of Southern Politics,* 187–89. Robert H. Wooley's "Race and Politics: The Evolution of the White Supremacy Campaign of 1898 in North Carolina" (Ph.D. dissertation, University of North Carolina, 1977), takes issue with this view, offering evidence that "the White Supremacy campaign . . . was aptly named after all" (180).
3. Rippy (ed.), *Furnifold Simmons,* 29.

over-confidence, and "failure to draw the color line."[4] Josephus Daniels, the Democrats' most effective journalistic propagandist, used inflammatory cartoons, angry editorials, and often inaccurate news reports in the Raleigh *News and Observer* to preach a philosophy he had learned in the Second Congressional District. As early as 1882 Daniels was promoting white supremacy in the Wilson *Advance*. After one disorderly Republican convention, the teen-age editor declared that the confusion at the session "clearly demonstrated that the negro was unfit for self government." Five years later the *Advance*, now co-edited by Daniels and his brother, announced that it had "no faith in the negroes voting the Democratic ticket," since blacks would simply become purchasable voters when they abandoned their loyalty to the Republican party.[5] Daniels received a personal lesson in the perils of "Negro domination" when his mother was removed as postmaster of Wilson at the behest, so her son believed, of black politician James O'Hara.[6]

No one learning his politics in the "black second" could imagine that race was a secondary issue. In counties where Negroes were 40 percent, 60 percent, even 70 percent of the population, the question of the black man's role in civic life never faded. For a time, it is true, the majority of eastern Democrats accepted Negroes as a permanent part of the voting population, opposed political violence, and showed some toleration of officeholding by black Republicans. Yet even when tensions were at their lowest level and political life operated most "normally," a white Republican was in an equivocal position and genuine Democratic-black cooperation (as distinct from "trades" and deals) was rare. Democratic orators seldom let a campaign pass without warning white voters of the danger of renewed Reconstruction (and "Negro domination") if the Republicans captured the state once more.

"White supremacy," the dogma that the white community must always be able to control relations between the races, held the Democratic organization together. As Aycock himself observed, "We have fought for tariff and against tariff; we have fought for internal improvements and against them; for a tax on liquor and against it. We have fought for this issue and against that policy, but everywhere and all the time we

---

4. Raleigh *State Chronicle* quoted in Goldsboro *Messenger*, November 15, 1886.
5. Wilson *Advance*, July 21, 1882, November 10, 1887.
6. Daniels, *Tar Heel Editor*, 208.

have fought for white supremacy and the right to govern ourselves."[7]

Whatever hopes of railroads and other businesses were threatened by Populist economics, no matter the factional disputes within the Democratic party, regardless of the narrow partisan maneuvers of Democratic leaders, the "real issue" of the 1898 campaign was "Negro domination." It is not enough to demonstrate, as Helen Edmonds does in her *Negro and Fusion Politics*, that black political power was far below black numerical strength, that Negroes did not actually control any level of government.[8] Democratic propaganda asked white voters different questions. Is the present level of black influence acceptable? Can the majority of white voters tolerate a situation in which the overwhelming majority of black voters, allied with a minority of white voters, are able to choose the state administration? Is the current *trend* of increasing black political influence a dangerous one? If conditions remain unchanged, will blacks and whites soon negotiate as equals in *some* areas? In short, what is the black man's place in our political system? "Negro domination" was partisan shorthand for the notion that the interests of white men were threatened by the improving political status of blacks, and to men like Simmons, Daniels, and Aycock there could be no more important issue.

George White expressed well the basic issue of the 1898 campaign in a speech to the House of Representatives a few months after the election. American Negroes, he noted, were going through a "peculiar crisis."

It is not necessary . . . to enter into any explanation as to what brought about this crisis. I may say, however, in passing, that possibly more than by any other one thing it has been brought about by the fact that despite all the oppression which has fallen upon our shoulders we have been rising, steadily rising, and in some instances we hope ere long to be able to measure our achievements with those of all other men and women of the land. This tendency on the part of some of us to rise and assert our manhood along all lines is, I fear, what has brought about this changed condition.[9]

Simmons, Aycock, Daniels, and their associates saw the same process at work and responded with angry and distorted language. At bottom,

7. Quoted in *ibid.*, 180.
8. Edmonds, *The Negro and Fusion Politics*, 84–135, *passim*.
9. *Congressional Record*, 55th Cong., 3rd Sess., 1124.

drained of invective, "Negro domination" meant the same thing as asserting "our manhood along all lines."

The centrality of the race issue is shown clearly in the words and actions of white Republicans and the Populists—the primary targets (if not the ultimate victims) of the white supremacy campaign. A white "fusionist" living in eastern North Carolina faced exceedingly difficult choices. Motivated by his fear of ostracism, his hatred of ruthless foes, his racial prejudice, his sense of order and purpose in history, he was forced to make a decision as agonizing as the one that confronted the men of 1861. Democrats relentlessly repeated the message that "Negro domination" had been "brought about through a division of the white men at the ballot box," and if white men had remained united "these things could not have been."[10]

Even before intense campaigning began, some eastern Populists were having second thoughts. "I was one of the first in this section to join the Populist party and supported it in the thickest of the fight," wrote an Edgecombe man to Senator Butler. "And have been abused and lied about as much if not more than anyone in this section. And I do not know now what part I shall take in the coming fight but of one thing I am almost sure I shall not take the same course under similar circumstances that I did in the last campaign." Cooperation with either the Democrats or the Republicans would destroy the People's party, he feared, whereas a three-way fight would lead to a Republican victory. A Littleton Populist in the spring of 1898 expressed his fear of Negroes' wielding too much power. "In the eastern counties of N.C. the question of the black man ruling our state and county government is getting to be a serious matter with us just now. Unless the white people take some steps to call a halt to the manner in which things have been managed, they will soon have entire controll [sic] of the eastern counties, and too great a hold on our state and national government."[11]

If Butler and other Populist leaders had had their way the 1898 campaign would have been fought on the issue of "white metal" rather than on "white supremacy." Collaboration with the Republicans had never been easy, and Butler was determined to attempt once again fusion with

10. Goldsboro *Daily Argus*, October 28, 1898.
11. John D. Mears to Marion Butler, February 16, 1898, J. J. Williams to Butler, May, 1898, both in Butler Papers.

reform-minded Democrats. Meeting in mid-May, before either the Republicans or Democrats, the People's party state convention overwhelmingly endorsed "honorable and harmonious co-operation of all who oppose the domination of gold and monopoly, and who favor the overthrow of the National bank and railroad influence in controlling legislation." A conference committee was established to negotiate with any party "or faction of a party" that might desire a coalition of "reform forces" to elect nine "free silver and anti-monopoly" congressmen, an "anti-monopoly" legislature, and nonpartisan judges. The delegates rejected the proposal of Butler's rival, Congressman Harry Skinner, that the party simply reaffirm its basic principles and "make no proposition to any party."[12]

Although some Democrats found the idea of a free silver united front attractive—the Northampton county convention voted 50–9 in favor of cooperation with the Populists, for example—the Democratic state convention brusquely turned down the Populist offer. Meeting May 26 in Raleigh, the convention also instructed the state executive committee to ignore any future proposals for fusion.[13] It was politically unwise to risk splitting the party over economic policy when the Democrats might find unity in the basic issue of "good government" and white supremacy. And as if the Democratic position were not clear enough, the election of Furnifold Simmons as state chairman a month later reemphasized the Democratic strategy for 1898. It was Simmons, after all, who had directed the uncompromising, victorious Democratic campaign of 1892. He was chosen for the chairmanship by a slim margin, defeating another former second district congressman, Frederick A. Woodard.[14]

Although some Populists talked boldly of an independent campaign against both the old parties, political realism pushed the People's party toward a third conservative election in tandem with the Republicans. The large number of Populist legislators and local officials who had been elected from eastern North Carolina faced certain defeat without the aid of Negro Republican voters. On their own, how could the Populists hope to produce winners in places like Northampton and Halifax? And unallied, the few hundred Populists in Lenoir would never

12. Raleigh *Caucasian*, May 26, 1898.
13. *Ibid.*, May 26, June 2, 1898.
14. Tarboro *Southerner*, June 30, 1898.

have boasted of a Populist clerk of the court, legislator, and chairman of the county board. Democrats wanted to make an issue of the record of fusion, to ask the voters, in the words of the Tarboro *Southerner*, "Shall North Carolina have another legislature as the last two were?"[15] Such rhetoric also tended to bind the fusion partners together once more, destroying any chance for a campaign based upon clearly articulated economic issues.

The Democratic effort to exploit race prejudice gave special prominence to the shrewd, eloquent black man who was a representative of North Carolina in Congress, and the heightened visibility of George White often made fellow fusionists uncomfortable. As the campaign intensified in the summer of 1898, White was firmly in control in his own district. He had been renominated by acclamation in an early district convention in Warrenton May 10, turning aside with apparent ease the effort of W. Lee Person to oust him. At the state Republican convention on July 20 he made a speech that instantly became famous and eventually cost the party thousands of votes.[16]

White and his Republican audience probably regarded the speech as purely routine. Just before adjournment, in a talk that was not one of the major addresses of the convention, White promised support for the party platform and leaders. He also delivered a mild but cogent attack against the white supremacist spirit building among Democrats. (Perhaps he had read the comments of his hometown newspaper the week before. "It is time that the color line should be drawn. Those who are not with us are against us," declared the Tarboro *Southerner*. "In politics the negro has nothing in common with the whites, and the sooner he is out of politics the better it will be for Edgecombe county.")[17] White discounted Democratic fears of "social equality," saying, "No white man dares enter my home unless invited there, and I dare not enter any white man's home unless invited there. The laws of the land do not regulate social equality. Man regulates the social problem for himself. There's nothing in this social equality plea. It's a scheme to get in on."

15. *Ibid.*, July 14, 1898.
16. Washington (D.C.) *Colored American*, May 14, 1898; Resolutions from Rocky Mount Township, April 11, 1898, and "That Wanton Attack: By the (Seven) Migrators," by W. Lee Person (campaign pamphlet), both in Butler Papers. Charles Aycock claimed White's speech lost thousands of votes for the Republicans. Oliver H. Orr, *Charles Brantley Aycock* (Chapel Hill, N.C., 1961), 121.
17. Tarboro *Southerner*, July 14, 1898.

Turning to the political side of race relations, White added, "The Democrats are going to say that I am a negro office holder. Yes, and there are going to be more just like me. The Constitution gives me the right to vote and this gives me the right to hold office."[18]

By inaccurate, sensational reporting Josephus Daniels' *News and Observer* gave White's words a belligerent, swaggering tone. "You dare not enter my door to *enjoy social equality*," the newspaper had the black congressman saying, "unless I invite you there." The report completely ignored the second half of White's formula, in which he declared he had no right to enter a white man's home "unless invited." According to the *News and Observer*, on the subject of Negro officeholding White said: "I am not the only negro who holds office. There are others. There are plenty more being made to order to hold offices. We are the modestest people in the world and don't hold as many offices as we will. I invite the issue. If you will come into my district we will have a joint debate." But the *News and Observer*, though it was enraged by White's attitude, was casual and inconsistent in reporting the offending remarks. In another place on the same page a different version of White's comments was reported. "Oh yes I am a negro office holder, and there are many other negroes that are going to hold office. They are being built to order. I want to invite *the issue of the white man against the negro*. I want to meet it in the black belt, and whether they meet me or not, I am going to have them hear me."[19]

Later in the campaign White told a Democratic reporter that his speech had been misquoted and that he did not favor raising the race question. Fusion campaign literature denied that White made some of the statements attributed to him by the *News and Observer*, even producing affidavits from White's hearers, but the report proved impossible to counteract. The Democratic press was furiously promoting the notion that blacks were the aggressors in North Carolina racial conflict, that, in the words of the Wilmington *Star*, "the negro was never as assertive as he is now," and the remarks attributed to White served to illustrate this contention.[20]

18. Raleigh *Morning Post*, July 1, 1898.
19. Raleigh *News and Observer*, July 21, 1898 (emphasis added). For yet another version, see Daniels, *Editor in Politics*, 285.
20. Raleigh *Morning Post*, September 2, 1898; Kinston *Free Press*, September 2, 1898; Raleigh *News and Observer* quoted in Kinston *Free Press*, August 13, 1898; Wilmington *Star* quoted in Kinston *Free Press*, July 23, 1898.

Even if White had not become notorious in this way, Populists in his district would have been uncomfortable with his House voting record, which revealed his conservative view of economic problems and his rejection of the free-silver panacea. In a maneuver designed to force second district Democrats to vote for a Populist or risk charges of insincerity, the Populist district convention met July 29, before a Democratic candidate had been chosen, and nominated Tarboro Populist James B. Lloyd for Congress. Another Tarboro man, former Populist state chairman W. E. Fountain, was chosen as district chairman.[21] Unless Democrats supported Lloyd, a man who believed in Bryan-style reform, they could be blamed for dividing the white vote and facilitating the reelection of a Negro.

But the Populists themselves were less than unanimous in their support of Lloyd, a close associate of Senator Butler. One member of the state executive committee gave his opinion that second district Populists would divide their votes between Lloyd and White. As late as two months after Lloyd's nomination, the News and Observer reported: "The minority Populists in his district are opposed to him and declare that White has kept the fusion agreement, is entitled to a re-election and that they will vote for him."[22]

Democrats met the Populist challenge in their district convention August 31 in Wilson. Benjamin F. Aycock, brother of the future governor, opened the meeting with a "ringing speech" comparing the task of overthrowing Republican-Negro rule in 1898 with the American fight for independence from England and the effort against Reconstruction in 1868. With Northampton and Greene unrepresented, the delegates passed resolutions affirming their support of the 1896 Democratic platform and declaring "that the white race must administer all the laws in North Carolina." To show their sincere devotion to white supremacy, the assembled Democrats voted to adjourn (subject to the call of the district chairman) without making a nomination. The convention did not formally endorse Lloyd, but as the Kinston Free Press put it, the action left "the race open between the negro congressman, White, and Mr. J. B. Lloyd, the Populist nominee." "The color line has been drawn,"

21. Raleigh Caucasian, August 11, 1898.
22. Kinston Free Press, August 17, 1898; Raleigh News and Observer, September 8, 29, 1898.

commented the Democratic Wilson *News*. "It is now a case of the survival of the fittest."[23]

The *News and Observer* praised "our friends" in the second district for their "giving up of party advantage" in order to elect a "free silver white man to Congress," at the same time making clear that Democratic support for Lloyd was contingent upon his support of white supremacy. "Congressman White is at the head of the black column. Will Captain Lloyd place himself at the head of the white column?" asked an editorial. "Let us wait and see if he will do it."[24]

The military metaphor was appropriate, for Democratic journalists and organizers were by this time busily drilling the "white column," attempting to overcome the demoralization of the previous four years. Their efforts were to be more and more effective as the campaign progressed. In a county where Democrats were "lifeless and hopeless" at the end of July and a Democratic newspaper admitted that "politics is more a side line this year than ever," white voters were roused to a fever pitch by October and fusionists were apprehensive about rumors of violence.[25]

Democratic editors, Josephus Daniels chief among them, found readers receptive to reports of uppity blacks, and they eagerly rushed into print choleric comments on any obnoxious or illegal Negro action that came into their ken. A minor incident could provoke the most sweeping conclusions. "Elevated Their Feet" was the headline over the story of one outrage, telling how "seven or eight negro politicians" riding in the first class coach to the Republican state convention had pulled off their shoes and put their feet on top of the seats, "some of their rusty toe nails sticking up in plain view." The action of these men was "a natural result of Rep.-Pop. fusion rule in North Carolina" and if white men were united "rule by such indecent elements" would not continue.[26]

Press propaganda was supplemented by a special white-only organization, the brain child of former Republican Francis D. Winston. The Kinston *Free Press* introduced the White Government Union to its

23. Wilson *News* quoted in Kinston *Free Press*, September 3, 1898; Kinston *Free Press*, September 3, 1898; Wilson *Advance*, September 1, 1898.
24. Raleigh *News and Observer*, September 2, 1898.
25. J. B. Lloyd to Marion Butler, July 22, October 14, 1898, both in Butler Papers. Tarboro *Southerner*, July 21, 1898.
26. Kinston *Free Press*, July 23, 1898.

readers in early August: "The sentiment in favor of white rule in North Carolina is growing. The presence of negroes in important offices they cannot fill, the growing assertiveness and impudence of negro politicians, and the infamous speech of Congressman White in the Republican State convention have aroused and alarmed the white people of the whole State." Any white man who was willing to join the Democrats in the fight for "white supremacy," regardless of previous party affiliation, was eligible to join the union. The plan was to have a White Government Union organized in every county by the end of August, according to chairman Simmons. "Our state," he explained, "is the only community in the world, with a majority of white voters, where the officers to administer the government are the choice of negroes, and not of the whites. This condition has been brought about by an unfortunate division among the white people, and it is likely to continue until that division is removed, and unity again prevails among them as it did prior to 1892." Simmons promised that only "honorable, legitimate and proper" methods would be employed in the White Government Union's effort to restore white supremacy.[27] Obviously the first purpose of the new organization was to overawe and discourage those white men who had cooperated with Negroes in an anti-Democratic coalition.

Assuming that Democratic propaganda was aimed at western white counties, not all eastern Populists immediately realized how serious the Democratic challenge was. As Edgecombe Populists negotiated with Republicans in early August for a combined local and legislative ticket, some argued that if Populists supported black Republicans for the legislature "it would be thunder for the Democrats in Western counties." Edgecombe Populist leader W. E. Fountain complained, "Republicans would yield only one member [of the general assembly] in face of the danger in Western counties."[28] Fountain and the Edgecombe Populists would realize before the campaign was over that the real thunder was not in the west, but that white supremacy extremism was most intense in the east.

Fountain wrote a "strictly confidential" letter to Senator Butler on August 9, 1898, which revealed important hidden weaknesses in the Populist ranks. Illustrating how heavily Republicans depended on their

27. *Ibid.*, August 10, 1898.
28. W. E. Fountain to Marion Butler, August 9, 1898, in Butler Papers.

allies, the Edgecombe leader noted that local Populists insisted on a favorable division of offices with the Republicans—"otherwise it would be difficult to get them to take the interest in election necessary to secure an honest count." Fountain was not disturbed by the anti-Negro tone of the Democratic campaign, convinced as he was that "we have nothing to loose [sic] even should there be a change in election law whereby negroes would be disfranchised." Democrats had kept Negroes a factor in politics even when the Democracy was in control "for the sole purpose of demoralizing and corrupting them" and using them as a "bug bear to scare ignorant white men, thereby solidifying them in the perpetuation of Democratic machine rule." Populists ought to call their opponents' bluff: "I believe the time has come to force the white man idea in such a way as to compel the Democrats, should they be successful in securing the legislature, to disfranchise the negro as Tilghman [sic] has done in South Carolina." Fountain, who owed his office to substantial Negro support, concluded, "If it is to be a fight between white men, we can next time . . . beat the gold men, leaving us the dominent [sic] party in the state."[29] That Fountain could be unperturbed by the Democratic onslaught, unwilling to defend Negro allies, and confident that the Democrats were falling into a trap—that any major eastern Populist could take such a view of matters goes far toward explaining the Democratic triumph of 1898.

During September and October, Lloyd and White waged an oddly quiet congressional campaign—in the eye, as it were, of the white supremacy hurricane. Neither man made personal attacks upon his rival or resorted to fanatical rhetoric. Lloyd "confined his speeches to national issues" and privately negotiated for a Democratic endorsement.[30] White visited Republicans around the district, urging caution and determination and asking the support of Populists.

In the Northampton County GOP convention the Negro representative "counseled harmony and deliberation and urged the convention to stick to the Populists and give them a fair division of the offices," according to a remarkably fair Democratic newspaper, the Rich Square *Patron and Gleaner*. White expressed an eminently moderate view of North Carolina race relations: "Congressman White said that he was opposed

29. *Ibid.*
30. Charlotte *Daily Observer*, October 12, 1898.

to negro supremacy and that the effort of the politicians to make people believe that the negro was seeking to control the government was a slander upon the race. He said that all the negro wanted was an equality before the law and a fair division of the offices." To refute the charges of "Negro domination" he pointed to the eastern counties where blacks were in a large majority "and could elect a negro to every office" yet had never done so. Furthermore, the congressman "advised his people not to undertake to do so at this time." This statement echoed what White had told the Raleigh *Morning Star*: "No eastern counties are dominated by negroes."[31]

It was a difficult time to preach restraint. One second district newspaper published a story headed "Nigger! Nigger! Nigger!" which listed the black officials in numerous counties and towns. The New Bern *Journal* noted with deep indignation that a white man in Craven County was forced to go to a Negro officeholder for a marriage license, for registration of a deed, for the autopsy of a loved one. A white man might be arrested by a Negro and tried before a black magistrate. The Kinston *Free Press* declared that North Carolina was the only state "in all the Union" that held out to the Negro "the inducement to enter her citizenship and seek her political honors. . . . Let it be proclaimed to the world, after this fierce conflict that the white people of North Carolina have endorsed this Republican policy and that this party is now firmly intrenched in power, and does any one doubt, can any one doubt, that there will be an influx of negroes into North Carolina from Virginia, South Carolina and other southern states that will soon give the negroes the majority in many counties where they are now in the minority?" "Who shall say," asked this sensational piece of journalism, that when Colonel James H. Young "returns as conquering hero" he may not summon "his race to join him in making North Carolina the San Domingo of the Union."[32]

Former Republican congressman Curtis H. Brogden, now past the age of eighty, denounced White in a letter to the Goldsboro *Daily Argus* as "an unprincipled, swaggering demagogue . . . who delights in all his speeches to harp on the negro, negro, negro, while at the

31. Rich Square *Patron and Gleaner*, September 1, 1898; Raleigh *Morning Post*, September 2, 1898.

32. Kinston *Free Press*, September 3, 1898; New Bern *Journal* quoted in Kinston *Free Press*, September 3, 1898; Kinston *Free Press*, September 7, 1898.

same time intending an insidious . . . disparagement of the white race."
Brogden said he understood some Populists intended to vote for White
instead of Lloyd—a fact that "passeth all my understanding." White
favored gold, monopoly, and high taxes, and the aged statesman thought
him "the most objectionable negro in the State as a politician," citing as
evidence the famous convention speech.[33] As an experienced politician
in the second district, George White was well aware that Brogden was
prone to explosive invective when he became agitated, and he may have
remembered with a wry smile the former congressman's attacks on
Humphrey and Hubbs in 1880. Yet it was tragic that a man who had
risked something for equal rights during Reconstruction now stood on
the other side of the issue.

Keeping his head while all about him others gave way to extremism,
White worked to maintain the discipline and morale of his supporters.
At the Edgecombe Republican convention he "warned the Democrats
against interfering with the ballot." Denying that he meant any threat,
only a statement of facts, he declared "he had as much right to fight
for his ballot as he had to protect his home." The extremely partisan
correspondent of the Charlotte *Daily Observer* admitted: "I saw from
the way the crowd of gaping negroes listened to and cheered White's
speech that he could make them do anything. But his speech was not
vindictive. It was conservative and full of Republicanism. He did not
draw the color line, as he is reported to have done at other places."
The Tarboro *Southerner* gave a somewhat different version of the
speech, saying White was "cheered often and long" as he "drew the
color line, but put the blame on the Democrats for doing so." The *Southerner* simultaneously recognized the Negro congressman's talent and expressed contempt for white fusionists: "In White we recognize a man far
above the average of his race and by long odds superior to the whites
who took part in the convention."[34]

There was a less favorable reaction when White warned an audience
in Kinston of the danger of disfranchisement if the Democratic party
were returned to power. The speech was basically "a string of lies and
perversions of fact," according to the Kinston *Free Press*. White's calm

33. Goldsboro *Daily Argus*, September 13, 1898.
34. Charlotte *Daily Observer*, September 20, 1898; Tarboro *Southerner*, September
22, 1898.

address to the Bertie Republican convention surprised the Windsor *Ledger,* though one discreet speech was not enough to convince the editor that White's image as a fiery militant was inaccurate. His speech "was just the reverse nature as the one he made at the Republican State Convention. Undoubtedly he has been advised along that line." When White spoke at the Goldsboro courthouse the local newspaper observed: "His speech was moderate in tenor—surprisingly so for White, and was respectable and decent in tone: every word of it could be given in type without reservation." (This was in marked contrast, alleged the report, to a "vile" and "vulgar" speech by a white Republican candidate.) One of the major themes of White's speeches was a denial of the Democratic charge of "Negro domination." As one correspondent noted, "Congressman White tells the negroes that inasmuch as he is the only negro Congressman in the United States the cry of the white people about negro domination is an empty sound."[35]

The anger and fear set loose by the white supremacy campaign frequently made it impossible for White to express his message effectively. The owners of a vacant lot in Rich Square refused the congressman permission to speak there, "believing that the speech would be devoted largely to the abuse of white men." Rumor quickly created a wildly distorted version of the incident, compounding the misunderstanding. A Raleigh newspaper quoted an unnamed gentleman, "whose veracity and integrity cannot be questioned," claiming "that White counselled the negroes . . . to get their guns and ammunition ready" immediately in order to "demand their rights" at the polls. According to the gentleman informant, as soon as White made these remarks the owner of the land on which he was speaking ordered him to leave.

White quickly denied that he had used any such language, and since he was dealing with the Raleigh *Morning Post* instead of the *News and Observer* his response was treated with a modicum of fairness. In a published letter to the editor he said: "I counselled the people to be forbearing, law-abiding, and to avoid everything that might lead to disorder, riot or bloodshed. . . . I made the same speech there that I made in Kinston, Windsor, Goldsboro, Wilson, Tarboro and other points

35. Kinston *Free Press,* September 21, 1898; Windsor *Ledger,* September 22, 1898; Goldsboro *Daily Argus,* September 23, 1898; Charlotte *Daily Observer,* September 23, 1898.

in my district, which have [sic] been pleasantly noticed by the honest Democratic editors of this district." The *Post* accepted White's statement, saying that the original report attributing "incendiary language" to him had been surprising, "for he is a man of more than ordinary intelligence, and must know that . . . results naturally consequent upon such [language] falls [sic] most heavily upon his own race." White's record was enough to "unite all white men against him, without violent speeches," concluded the *Post*.[36]

James B. Lloyd devoutly wished that all white men would unite against George White, but his campaign was forced to seek success by delicate indirection. Lloyd was unwilling to win a seat in Congress by accepting the Democratic issue of "Negro domination" or by surrendering all local fusion arrangements with Republicans. In Lloyd's own Edgecombe County, the fusion agreement entailed tacit Populist aid for two Negro gold bugs for the legislature, since Populists nominated only one legislative candidate. The cooperation arrangement left open to individual Populists the matter of actually voting for a Negro, but the distinction between this and an outright endorsement was difficult for many voters to see. The final result was certain to be the election of two black legislators—as well as one Populist member the Populists could never have elected on their own—and Populist control of certain key county offices. Democrats refused to allow Lloyd to have it both ways. "You must either renounce your promise to vote for negro legislators from Edgecombe or sit back in silence and see White walk away with the pie," warned the Tarboro *Southerner*.[37]

Undeterred by public criticism, Lloyd worked in private to secure assistance from Democratic leaders. Chairman Simmons passed word to Lloyd, through an intermediary, that the Democrats would not nominate their own congressional candidate—"provided Lloyd remains in the field and makes the fight." He made no promises about printing Lloyd's name on the Democratic ballot, however. In a September 24 letter to Senator Butler, Lloyd explained another approach to the opposition. The Democratic candidate for solicitor of the Second Judicial District told Lloyd

36. Rich Square *Patron and Gleaner*, September 28, 1898; Raleigh *Morning Post* quoted in Kinston *Daily Free Press*, October 6, 1898; Raleigh *Morning Post*, October 7, 1898.

37. J. B. Lloyd to Marion Butler, September 19, 1898, in Butler Papers. Tarboro *Southerner*, September 15, 1898. See also September 8, 1898.

that if the black Republican candidate for solicitor "could be forced to withdraw," leaving the Democrat no opposition, "he would guarantee that I would get the solid vote of this Dist." Lloyd attempted to get the Negro candidate to drop out of the race, but his efforts were unsuccessful.[38]

In the final weeks of the campaign emotions ran high—practically out of control—among white voters. The politicians had "stirred the minds and feelings of the people more deeply than they intended," as one perceptive and cautious white supremacist remarked after the election. Just as few heeded or understood George White's appeals for calm, so many white men were impatient when Lloyd devoted his stump speeches to national matters, preaching the familiar doctrines of silver and reform. "He did not refer to State politics at all," noted the report of a Lloyd speech in Warrenton, as if there were something wrong in a candidate for the national legislature "confining" himself to national issues. "He only referred to his running against White one time, and said he was a white man, a W. J. Bryan man and a silver man, and that the people of the district ought to vote for him, because he represented their interests." Such routine, uncharged rhetoric failed to persuade in the highly emotional climax of the white supremacy campaign. Thanks to the effective work of men like Simmons, Daniels, and Aycock, political discourse was dominated by sensation and vituperation.[39]

"I do not think it advisable for you to make a speech here," Lloyd wrote Senator Butler in mid-October, "or in any of the 'black' Counties —Threats are daily made here of trouble. They are saying that Mr. Fountain will be killed, and if trouble comes all the Pop leaders will be the first to suffer. The feeling here is intense." A correspondent of the Charlotte *Daily Observer*, issuing firsthand reports from the "Negro-dominated" east, had several weeks earlier characterized Fountain, the Populist treasurer of Edgecombe, as "the most unprincipled, mean white man in this section of the State." Although Fountain had been elected mayor of Tarboro eight times and was active in promoting the town's cotton factory and the Bank of Tarboro, the "decent white people" of

38. J. B. Lloyd to Marion Butler, September 19, 24, 29, 1898, all in Butler Papers.
39. H. G. Connor to George Howard, November 25, 1898, in Henry G. Connor Papers, Southern Historical Collection, University of North Carolina, Chapel Hill. Raleigh *Morning Post*, October 6, 1898. See also Charlotte *Daily Observer*, October 12, 1898.

the town were now said to "look upon him as they would a midnight houseburner." The reporter added, in words that Lloyd echoed: "And, should a riot ever occur, he would be the first man to suffer."[40]

A fire-breathing editorial in the Kinston *Daily Free Press* made clear the frightening position of white fusionists: "If there must be race conflicts, the real white men should select prominent renegade whites, who are inciting the negroes to cause trouble, for proper and sure treatment. They are meaner than the negroes. But for them there would be no danger of race conflicts." Only if Negroes tried to "force matters," to "intimidate the white people," would there be danger of racial strife. "The negroes will not do this unless they are encouraged by their mean renegade white leaders. Any white man who would thus encourage negroes to conflicts with the whites is too mean to live and richly deserves death at the hands of the whites."[41]

Democratic newspapers continued to play up incidents of Negro "insolence." Three traveling salesmen signed a letter complaining about a "young buck negro" who cursed an "elderly white man" and kicked over another man's valise and a "young half-blood" who crowded next to a white man in order to get a window seat. "Is a Race Clash Unavoidable?" asked the headline over a September 21 article reporting cases of Negro bicyclists refusing to yield the right of way to white female pedestrains, drunken blacks resisting arrest, and Negroes in other ways demonstrating "impudence." "Such exasperating occurences [*sic*] would not happen but for the fact that the negro party is in power in North Carolina," maintained the newspaper, "and that there are negro magistrates and other negro officials in office, which emboldens bad negroes to display their evil, impudent and mean natures." The patience of "true white men" was near the breaking point and they were on the verge of taking the law into their own hands to "make negroes behave themselves" by use of "organized force." It made little difference that some of the Negro "outrages" had little basis in fact. After reporting that a black woman

40. J. B. Lloyd to Marion Butler, October 14, 1898, in Butler Papers. Charlotte *Daily Observer*, September 20, 1898. Fountain served as mayor of Tarboro 1887–1889, 1891–1895. Tarboro *Southerner*, April 26, 1900. On his business activities see Raleigh *Caucasian*, January 21, 1897. An influential businessman who could have easily assumed "the role of oppressor," Fountain chose instead to join the Populist attack on "monopolistic rapacity," according to the *Caucasian*.

41. Kinston *Daily Free Press*, October 26, 1898.

had "whipped one of Dr. Faulkner's little boys . . . with a buggy whip" and that Dr. Faulkner was "awfully mad," the Kinston *Free Press* had to retreat slightly two days later. It turned out that Dr. Faulkner had not been told about the incident by his wife, and that the "mean negro woman" struck the boy only once before being stopped by a "good old negro woman." Even so the incident showed "the necessity of downing the fusion party . . . the success of which encourages negroes to commit outrages."[42]

The most sensational "outrage" of the campaign involved the second district's Negro representative and his conduct at a circus performance in Tarboro on October 8. According to white witnesses, White, "in company with six or eight colored women and children," sat in the section of the tent reserved for whites, even though "there were other seats, abundant in number and equally comfortable," set aside for Negroes. In response to white complaints, a circus employee asked the congressman to move to the black section, but White said "he had paid his money, and was as good as the white people up there." He even refused to move when a town policeman requested it. After a second policeman told White to move he and his party walked out of the circus.[43]

Democrats reacted angrily to this incident, seeing in it a powerful argument for white solidarity. "This 'big, black, burly' leader of the fusion forces in North Carolina not only favors negro domination," charged the *Free Press*, "but is now demanding social equality. . . . Will not the white men of North Carolina resent this insult and vote to forever quell such negro insolence and arrogance[?]" White well knew that southern social practices condemned actions such as his, declared the Goldsboro *Daily Argus*, and the incident illustrated the Negro's seeming "hunger for an elimination of all lines of separation." Indeed, the article continued, "When an educated negro, a graduate of a college of some standing, one who has attained to a position of some importance, must be forced by a policeman to keep within the bounds set for his race . . .

42. *Ibid.*, October 19, 1898; Kinston *Free Press*, September 21, 1898; Kinston *Daily Free Press*, September 23, 1898. For further examples of "Democratic lies," see the Raleigh *Caucasian*, October 6, 1898.

43. Kinston *Daily Free Press*, October 15, 1898. Tarboro *Southerner* quoted in Goldsboro *Daily Argus*, October 14, 1898; Charlotte *Daily Observer*, October 12, 1898.

what may we not expect of the ignorant and more vicious of the race?"
White's behavior made clear "the necessity for the absolute and un-
qualified domination of the white people in all the departments of
government. Nothing but a thorough realization of this complete domination will end such conduct, and the friction tending to serious and
dangerous disturbances. . . . A great, a living, an ineradicable truth is
involved in this conflict . . . and it must be settled . . . once and for all.
In all that involves power, authority or privilege, concerning the affairs
of the people and the relations of the races, the white people will rule
this State. The necessity for this is but increased by the bad conduct
of the colored leader at Tarboro."[44]

The affair revived old resentments against the talented and proud
black man, resentments that had been present long before Democrats
pilloried White as a symbol of fusion. J. P. Caldwell, editor of the
Charlotte *Daily Observer*, said he was not surprised by White's action at
the circus. "Quite ten years ago a judge, who had just finished riding the
circuit of which White was then solicitor, and telling of the insolence
of this worthy, said to the writer, that the white members of the bar were
compelled to address him as 'Mr.,' adding, if 'You should address him
as "White," he would call you "Caldwell." ' "[45]

The circus incident greatly agitated White's rival for Congress, Populist nominee Lloyd. "Such conduct as this the Pops can not stand," he
wrote to Senator Butler, noting that there were Negroes on the Republican-Populist cooperative ticket for Edgecombe County. White's action
at the circus was "*exceedingly* embarrassing," said Lloyd, "and since
White has made himself so obnoxious I have advised Mr. Fountain to
notify the County Rep Ex Com that unless they remove all the negroes
from the ticket we would have nothing to do with the election." If the
Populists ran an independent slate, cooperating with neither of the
old parties, "the negroes might elect everything and then we would be
held responsible for it." In Lloyd's opinion a Democratic victory in the
county would not be worse. "If we attempt to carry the present burden
since White's escapade it will destroy us." Unless the blacks were

44. Kinston *Daily Free Press*, October 15, 1898; Goldsboro *Daily Argus*, October
14, 1898.

45. Charlotte *Daily Observer*, October 16, 1898. An October 14, 1898, report
claimed White had insisted on sitting in a white railroad waiting room during the
"past fall."

dropped from the fusion ticket "we are defeated, for in two large townships we have not sufficient force to hold the election—and the Dems threaten, and I believe, will take these townships if they are necessary for them to carry the county. By continuing the fight now with the negroes we will, I very much fear, destroy our party in the county." Lloyd noted threats against county leader W. E. Fountain and expressed the fear that "some fiend may assassinate him." "The conservative anti-machine Dems are not giving us any moral support as they did two years ago, and the feeling is extremely bitter." Not one word did Lloyd write about his own campaign for Congress, indicating perhaps that he had given up hope of being elected.[46]

It is not possible to know for certain if the circus segregation "outrage" actually occurred as Democratic sources describe it. An intriguing bit of evidence suggests that the event was greatly exaggerated and distorted in the retelling. Two years later the *Free Press* alleged that George White and his private secretary, a Negro, had taken seats in the white section of a railroad car on a recent trip, refusing to move when the conductor told them to go to the Negro compartment. Only when a group of white men announced that they "would take pleasure in throwing the scamp off the train," did the two black men gather up their luggage and retreat, according to the newspaper.

"This impudent negro, it seems will never learn his place," commented the *Free Press*. "He tried to sit with whites at a circus at Tarboro a year or so ago. He is a mean negro." White wrote to the editor two days after the story appeared, insisting that "your editorial does me, inadvertantly [sic], perhaps, a grave injustice." "At least a dozen" men of both races could prove that the facts of the case were far different. White and his secretary had gotten on the train at Goldsboro and sat on the Negro side of the partition. No whites were present in this section of the car. When the train stopped at New Bern, White and the secretary got off to speak with friends but left their satchels and umbrellas in their seats. They returned to the Jim Crow compartment on the return trip only to find it filled with whites. The conductor advised them to move to the rear car, but "I thereupon remonstrated upon the humiliation of going through several crowded cars when I was already riding in the compartment provided by law for colored people." The conductor made

46. J. B. Lloyd to Marion Butler, October 15, 1898, in Butler Papers.

a lame remark about not liking to ask people to move, and the two Negroes moved to the car in the rear. White said he heard no remarks about throwing him off the train. "I have never had, have not now, nor do I ever expect to have any hankering to push myself among any class of people where I am not wanted. The circus incident to which you allude was started in much the same way as the incident now under discussion and had no foundation in truth."[47]

A few days after the circus incident, another sensational story involving George White appeared in the press. The Wilmington *Messenger*, citing the word of "a gentleman who arrived in this city last night," claimed that White had been met by "about one hundred and fifty of Lenoir county's 'Rough Riders' " when he arrived in Kinston to deliver a speech. Upon being informed that he "couldn't slander and vilify the white race at Kinston without being put under the sod," White quietly went on to the next station "where he was not booked to speak." White responded by publicly denying "that he had been intimidated at Kinston," and the *Free Press* branded the report of "Kinstonians stopping White" a "fake." "The Messenger has been imposed upon by a liar."[48]

If this particular report were false, there were many other examples of closed minds, plugged ears, and vile tactics as election day drew near. The editor of the Tarboro *Southerner* urged town authorities to refuse Negroes permission to use the town commons for a "big political meeting" just before election day. "The negro has more than his right in this county," reasoned the editor, "and it is high time they [sic] were taught their place." A week before the election the *News and Observer* employed large type and a front page box to charge that Mrs. George H. White had received an express package containing rifles and that the congressman's daughter was circulating a petition "asking all colored people to refuse to work for white people."[49]

As the campaign entered its final days, the Populist congressional campaign fell into complete disorder. A reluctant, discouraged candidate, Lloyd spent most of the last three weeks before election day in Raleigh.

47. Kinston *Daily Free Press*, July 23, 30, 1900.
48. Wilmington *Messenger* quoted in Kinston *Daily Free Press*, October 25, 1898; Raleigh *News and Observer*, October 26, 1898; Kinston *Daily Free Press*, October 25, 1898.
49. Tarboro *Southerner*, October 20, 1898; Raleigh *News and Observer*, November 1, 1898.

On October 21 the Populist district committee met in Rocky Mount to consider an offer from the Democrats which entailed the withdrawal of Lloyd and selection of a candidate who could unite white voters. Despite the urgings of district chairman Fountain, the committee decided to defer action until Senator Butler and state chairman Cyrus Thompson could be present. Lloyd wrote to Butler the next day requesting that he come to Raleigh for a meeting with Fountain. "I can not write the situation as it is too serious," he said. A newspaper man noted Lloyd was "remarkably reticent" that day, and Lloyd told another reporter: "The charge that the East is under negro domination is not true."[50]

Democratic strategists planned an immense mass meeting for October 28 in Goldsboro as the high point of their effort to suppress political diversity among white men, particularly those in eastern North Carolina. Convening just a day after the chairman of the Populist and Republican parties had warned that "the adoption of South Carolina methods is in the event of Democratic success to be followed by a system of government under which only the machine and the bosses are to exercise power," the meeting showed the power of the white supremacy theme. William A. Guthrie, Populist nominee for governor in 1896, and Furnifold Simmons were among the speakers who addressed the group. Former governor Thomas J. Jarvis introduced a set of resolutions declaring that conditions had become intolerable in those communities where local offices were held by Negroes, that such "deplorable conditions were brought about through a division of the white men at the ballot box," and appealing to all honest white men to unite in peacefully ending "negro domination." Republican Senator Pritchard's published suggestion that federal troops be sent to the state to preserve the peace was roundly denounced.

In a dramatic turnaround W. E. Fountain announced his support of the white supremacy movement. Both speaker and audience seemed to forget the heated abuse and threats of violence that had recently been directed toward Fountain, as he told the mass meeting that there was indeed "negro domination in Eastern North Carolina." This man, who had been state chairman of the Populist party and was now sup-

50. Raleigh *Morning Post*, November 5, 1898; J. B. Lloyd to Marion Butler, October 21, 22, 1898, in Butler Papers. Charlotte *Daily Observer*, October 23, 1898; Raleigh *News and Observer*, October 23, 1898. For F. M. Simmons' version of events, see the Kinston *Daily Free Press*, July 10, 1900.

posed to be directing Populist efforts in the second district, declared that he had made his decision because present conditions in the state drove away outside business investment. "As chairman of the Populist Congressional Committee in the Second district, I want to say that I have for a week or more been negotiating and devising plans whereby Geo. White, the negro Congressman, might be defeated and a white man elected to succeed him. I say to you that George White must be defeated and I will leave nothing undone to accomplish this."[51]

Lloyd sent a telegram to Senator Butler the next day: "Wire your advice withdrawal defeat White great responsibility on me prefer that course answer here immediately." Both men realized that if Lloyd endorsed white supremacy it could well cost the party legislative seats and local offices throughout the district—especially in places like Northampton and Halifax where the fusion ticket included Negroes.[52] Lloyd's refusal to endorse white supremacy angered many Democrats. "He has acted in a way most calculated to drive Democrats from voting for him," complained the *Free Press* on November 2, 1898. "We suppose most Democrats will vote for Lloyd anyway, rather than not vote at all against the negro, but it is a bitter pill." If Lloyd were not a tool of Butler, if he had had the "manhood" to withdraw in favor of "a true white man like Fountain," the *Free Press* thought there would be "some hope of defeating the negro."[53]

The next day, less than a week after the Goldsboro mass meeting, Fountain took matters into his own hands and announced himself a candidate for Congress, citing Lloyd's failure "to meet the overshadowing issue of white supremacy" as the reason for his course. Fountain accused

51. Raleigh *Caucasian*, October 27, 1898; Goldsboro *Daily Argus*, October 28, 1898; Kinston *Daily Free Press*, November 1, 1898; Raleigh *Morning Post*, October 29, 1898.

52. J. B. Lloyd to Marion Butler, October 29, 1898 (telegram), in Butler Papers. In Halifax the Populists had agreed to support two black legislative candidates and a black nominee for county commissioner—and even this did not satisfy a Republican faction led by John H. Hannon. See J. T. Pope to Marion Butler, September 24, 1898, in Butler Papers. In Northampton Populists allowed a Negro legislative candidate on the fusion ticket, much to Butler's distress. The local Populist leader explained to the senator that "of course we do not want a Negro to Represent us in the next legislature but had rather have him than a Dem because he will not kill us and the Democrat will." See Marion Butler to G. [sic] S. Garner, October 8, 1898, C. S. Garner to Butler, [probably October, 1898; filed under November], both in Butler Papers.

53. Kinston *Daily Free Press*, November 2, 1898.

Lloyd of offering to resign and then preventing action by the district committee, and he assured his fellow Populists that "by this conduct Mr. Lloyd has released us from any obligation to vote for him." Lloyd wrote bitterly to Butler that he considered Fountain a Democratic candidate and complained: "Mr. Fountain did not state that the Committee declined to allow me to withdraw." But Fountain's announcement had come too late to change the outcome of the election. In the five days remaining before election day he could do little more than notify voters that he was running and make certain that his ballots were available in the precincts. Even this limited campaign was incomplete by November 8, as two precincts in Lenoir reported that they did not receive any Fountain tickets.[54]

In spite of all the excesses of the white supremacy campaign, George White was able to win a second term in Congress. More than 35,000 voters turned out to cast ballots in this off-year election and nearly half of them voted for White. The Negro incumbent's 49.5 percent of the vote comfortably outdistanced Fountain's 42.1 percent and Lloyd's hard core of 6.9 percent. White carried the district's four northern counties, Bertie, Northampton, Halifax, and Warren, amassing landslide margins of 65 percent in Warren and 67.9 percent in Halifax. Fountain carried all of the counties with white majorities and captured Edgecombe County by a 13-vote plurality. The Republican failure in Edgecombe, a predominantly black county, can be attributed to the complete collapse of the local Republican-Populist alliance in the final week of the campaign —the result, partly, of the Lloyd-Fountain feud.[55]

Considering the unmeasured denunciations that had been visited upon him by Democratic propagandists, White did remarkably well. Only in Wilson County did he fall below 40 percent of the total vote for the three major candidates. In three of the four white counties he received more votes than he had in the presidential year of 1896. At the same time his vote declined in four of the five black counties of the district, falling over 1,300 votes in Halifax alone, despite the fact that he carried the county by a huge percentage. Perhaps pressure against black registration and voting was weaker in areas with safe white majorities.

54. *Ibid.*, November 5, 1898; J. B. Lloyd to Marion Butler, November 4, 1898, in Butler Papers; Kinston *Daily Free Press*, November 9, 1898.
55. The percentages are my own computation. See Raleigh *News and Observer*, November 1, 2, 1898, on the confusing denouement in Edgecombe.

The primary goal of the 1898 campaign had been the election of a Democratic legislature, not the defeat of a lone Negro congressman, and in this objective Democrats gained a tremendous success. The twelve Republican legislators elected in 1896 dwindled to three—all Negroes—in 1898; and the Populists virtually disappeared as nine representatives and senators in 1896 became only one two years later. Eighteen Democrats represented the second district in the 1899 general assembly (after an election contest in Greene was resolved in the Democrats' favor), as opposed to one in the session of 1897.

Democrats also triumphed in most of the local races, winning even in Halifax, a county White carried. The Republican sheriff was reelected in Northampton, and by a margin of less than 40 votes a Negro, E. E. Roberts, won the registership of deeds. Warren County's perennial register, Mansfield Thornton, was reelected to another term, and Bertie elected seven black magistrates and two constables. Robert W. Williamson, Negro Republican candidate for solicitor of the Second Judicial District, lost by an extremely narrow margin after the county clerks in Halifax and Northampton rejected 427 votes Williamson claimed were due him. The *Caucasian* found it peculiar that "the Democrats carried the district by a big majority, yet permitted the negro congressman to be elected when they easily could have prevented it. Did they want the negro elected so as to leave them seed to cry 'nigger' two years from now?" The Democratic victories in Edgecombe and Halifax need not be explained by a conspiracy theory, however. As the editors of the *Caucasian* knew, the fusion forces were badly divided in both counties. Populists in Edgecombe were totally demoralized, and Halifax Republicans split into two factions over local offices.[56]

All in all, despite White's reelection, the white supremacy campaign in the black belt had been a sweeping success. Hundreds of white men who had voted against the Democracy in 1894 and 1896 were lashed back into the "white column." "A large part of our Populist[s] went to the Dems in this County," wrote an eastern Populist leader, explaining "they could not stand the Negro Racket. I tell you it was bad down

56. Windsor *Ledger*, November 24, 1898; Goldsboro *Daily Argus*, November 18, 1898; Raleigh *Caucasian*, November 24, 1898. Lloyd received only 87 votes in Edgecombe, his home, down from 370 two years earlier. On Republican factionalism in Halifax, see Charlotte *Daily Observer*, September 21, 1898; Raleigh *News and Observer*, September 22, October 26, 1898; Kinston *Free Press*, September 14, 1898; J. T. Pope to Marion Butler, September 24, 1898, in Butler Papers.

here." Over the state the Populist party was reduced to ruins, electing only 6 members to the 150-member general assembly, plus 1 congressman. After an election contest in the ninth district was resolved in the spring of 1900, there were 3 Republican representatives and 5 Democrats. The 134 Democrats in the legislature were nearly three times the number the party had elected in 1896.[57]

Two conservative second district lawyers, fancying themselves men of honor, reflected on the state of things in North Carolina in the days following the election. "The campaign was in many ways distasteful to me," wrote Henry G. Connor, soon to preside over the North Carolina house, "altho', as I saw the state into which we were drifting I felt more strongly the necessity for pressing it to a successful termination." Although he had recognized the need to "destroy the local conditions here," Connor did not make "incendiary" speeches. "The crop of fools and knaves always flourishes under such conditions as we have been dealing with. I could not stand Fountain and many of us refused to vote for him. I think his attempt to fasten himself on us was an outrage." Writing to his Tarboro friend George Howard, Connor declared: "I dread the work before me. . . . The situation is far from pleasant and the problem full of complications."

"I suppose anything must be justifiable to preserve a woman's virtue, a man's honor, and our Christian Civilization," wrote Howard in reply. "I have just read again [Benjamin] Kidd's Social Evolution (the most comforting book to me outside of the Bible) and in its light, the 'late unpleasantness' was simply Providential natural evolution—an evil preventing a much greater evil."

Two and a half weeks after the election Connor wrote again to Howard. "I am determined that, with my consent, no law shall be passed, having for its purpose or permitting frauds," he said. Connor was prepared to place "every possible constitutional restriction" upon registration, "but when the vote is cast it must be counted, and honestly returned." If possible, the Wilson representative hoped to "secure the permanent and undivided political supremacy of the white man" through a constitutional change. "We must take the responsibility and must have

57. C. S. Garner to Marion Butler, November 10, 1898, in Butler Papers. Lefler and Newsome, *North Carolina*, 558.

the power. . . . As a doctrinaire, I may not have reached my present state of mind, but dealing with 'a condition and not a theory' it seems to me this is the only solution of the problem."[58] The "problem," as seen by these two men of substance, was not Populistic economic radicalism, unsound fusion railroad policy, or anything else save the "political supremacy of the white man."

58. H. G. Connor to George Howard, November 11, 1898, Howard to Connor, November 14, 1898, Connor to Howard, November 25, 1898, all in Connor Papers. Richard Hofstadter has described Kidd's *Social Evolution* (1894) as "a peculiar mixture of obscurantism, reformism, Christianity, and social Darwinism." Richard Hofstadter, *Social Darwinism in American Thought* (Boston, 1955), 100–101.

Chapter 15

LEADER OF THE BLACK PHALANX

NONE OF THE MEN WHO REPRESENTED the "black second" from 1872 to 1897 had a greater gift for oratory than George H. White. Charles R. Thomas, John Hyman, Curtis Brogden, Orlando Hubbs, and Henry Cheatham all had been virtually silent members of the House. William H. Kitchin's speeches had a tone of windy bombast, as if he could never outgrow the stump ranting in which he was so skilled. James O'Hara and Furnifold Simmons were capable speakers, but their language was not, in the words of St. Paul, "seasoned with salt." George White, the veteran prosecutor, spoke with vigor and wit, undeterred by the most controversial topics.

He had a strong feeling that he spoke for all the nation's Negroes, not just the people of the Second Congressional District, and he was prepared to respond spiritedly to racist pronouncements by southern colleagues. Although his defense of his race was strong and direct, his words were never unrestrained and irresponsible—as the language of some Negrophobic House members was. It is quite inaccurate to suggest, as Samuel D. Smith did, that White was a hypersensitive and bitter man, taking affront at the slightest hint of racial discrimination. During White's tenure in Congress, southern white zealots, in many cases young men with no memory of the Civil War, frequently expressed the most thoroughgoing extremism on the subject of race relations. White rebutted these attacks with courage—and moderation—sensing no doubt that he lived in a time that was out of joint.[1]

As a lawmaker White was unremarkable, accomplishing no more than

1. Smith, *Negro in Congress*, 125–27; Frenise Logan, "Influences Which Determined the Race-Consciousness of George H. White, 1897–1901," *Negro History Bulletin*, XIV (December, 1950), 63–65.

an average representative who sought favors for his constituents and occasionally secured the passage of a bill or resolution. Under the circumstances it was difficult for him to do more. When he did propose an important and far-sighted measure for federal action against lynching, Congress was not prepared to consider the idea. The greatest significance of this last black congressman from North Carolina, then and now, is as a spokesman and symbol.

Congressman White delivered his maiden speech on March 31, 1897, demonstrating none of the traditional unobtrusiveness of a new member attending his first session. He entered the debate of the Republican tariff bill to praise the measure as a benefit to the lumber industry of eastern North Carolina and the black laborers of the nation. White ridiculed the Democratic free trade "yarn": "Why, they have from time to time advocated 'free whisky' also; and in the last campaign their shibboleth was 'free silver.'" Repeating a familiar jibe of North Carolina Republicans, White added: "In fact the Southern element of the Democratic party has advocated 'free' everything except free ballots and free negroes." This remark, the *Record* notes, was greeted by "laughter and applause on the Republican side and in the galleries."[2]

A South Carolina Democrat had charged that North Carolina Republican R. Z. Linney did not represent the South when he advocated a protective tariff. "I think . . . that it comes with bad grace from the gentleman to talk of misrepresentation of the Southern people," said White, "when he considers the fact that 130,000 voters in his State are not allowed to vote at all." At the end of his brief speech, which closed with an appeal for protection of American industry and labor from "the pauperism and cheap labor of foreign countries," White was "vociferously applauded" by the Republicans. "He bore himself admirably, and is regarded as the most capable man of his race now in public life," stated the Republican *Daily Raleigh Tribune.*[3]

The only bill White introduced in this first, special session was one for

2. *Congressional Record*, 55th Cong., 1st Sess., 550. The Goldsboro *Daily Argus,* October 5, 1896, quoted a Republican campaign speaker who said the Democratic party "was in favor of everything being free except the ballot and the negro." Although White's speech in the *Congressional Record* uses the phrase "free negroes," other reports attribute to him the expression "free niggers." *Daily Raleigh Tribune,* April 1, 1897; Troy (N.Y.) *Daily Times* quoted in Raleigh *Gazette,* April 10, 1897.

3. *Congressional Record*, 55th Cong., 1st Sess., 550–51; *Daily Raleigh Tribune,* April 1, 1897.

the relief of black Civil War hero (and former congressman) Robert Smalls, a proposal made earlier by O'Hara and Cheatham, which once again failed to pass. In the second session of the Fifty-fifth Congress, he introduced a resolution for relief of the family of the Negro postmaster murdered by a Lake City, South Carolina, mob. He first tried to secure unanimous consent to have the resolution immediately considered, but a Georgia member objected. Later his resolution received a favorable report from the Committee on the Post Office and Post Roads, but it was never adopted. The other measures he presented, a bill to incorporate the National Colored American Industrial Association and five private bills, also failed to pass.[4]

White revealed a reactionary streak in his political philosophy when he assailed the civil service law in a speech of January 11, 1898. The present civil service law was administered not as a merit system, declared White, a self-confessed believer in the principle that the spoils belong to the victor, but as a system of "life tenure" or "inheritance" of office. Gentlemen who believed that when a politician won an "honest victory" his friends were "not entitled to the emoluments that naturally ought to follow" would find themselves very unpopular if they lived in the second district, said White. In the course of his remarks he noted disfranchisement of southern blacks as another cause for alarm. "Will the American Congress sit supinely by," he asked, "and declare its inability to interfere . . . while our organic law, the Constitution of the United States, is being openly violated?"[5]

As war with Spain approached, White protested the absence of Negroes in the army artillery and used the occasion to make several general observations on the race problem. The federal government, he charged, was indifferent to outrages (including "even cremations") against southern blacks, but "if some half-breed foreigner claiming allegiance to our government is insulted by any foreign country, redress for him is at once demanded, and in most cases large indemnities given." White emphasized that he was not pleading for "special privileges" for

4. *Congressional Record*, 55th Cong., 1st Sess., 2427, 2516, 3153, 5669, 2214, 236, 1866. Ida B. Wells attempted to get White to withdraw his bill for relief of the Lake City postmaster's family and allow Illinois Senator W. E. Lorimer to introduce a stronger one that "would stand a greater show of being passed" because it came from a powerful northern senator. Alfreda M. Duster (ed.), *Crusade for Justice: The Autobiography of Ida B. Wells* (Chicago, 1970), 252–54.

5. *Congressional Record*, 55th Cong., 2nd Sess., 541–42.

Negroes, but simple justice—"all the privileges of an American citizen" —adding, "We will be content with nothing less." The Washington *Colored American* commended the "manly" tone of the address, as well as the "poise and dignity" with which it was delivered, and printed the speech in full.[6]

White took the floor again on April 22, 1898, during the debate on a Tennessee contested election case. Two Democrats each claimed to be the rightful representative, and much of the discussion centered around how the Negro vote was cast in the district in question. "Mr. Speaker," began the black congressman, "if half of what has been said against either of these gentlemen contending for a seat on this floor is true, I doubt very much whether either ought to have a seat in the Congress of the United States." This sally provoked merriment and applause among White's associates, as did his further description of the contestant as "the smaller of two evils presented to me" and his statement that he would "swallow him with my eyes closed."

Although it was not "exactly germane to the subject under consideration," White went on to raise the larger issue of disfranchisement, suggesting that Congress ought to consider whether a "republican form of government" existed in Mississippi, South Carolina, Louisiana, and other southern states. He said that 150,000 black votes were suppressed in Mississippi and insisted that low voter turnouts in the South were not the result of Negro apathy. Denying the black man his constitutional right to vote threatened the very foundation of the nation, he warned: "The lifeblood of the Union is being sapped . . . and one day or the other it will not be a Cuban question that confronts us; it will not be a question of standing by and putting down the Spaniards, but it will be a question as to whether or not the Federal Constitution in this great Republic of ours shall be perpetuated or not." Yet in spite of all this some members came to the House and spoke of the "darky" and told undignified dialect stories. White enlivened his rather somber remarks with a witty reference to his own lonely position. "I am easily the leader of one thing, and that is the black phalanx on this floor. [Laughter] I

6. *Ibid.*, 2556. Washington (D.C.) *Colored American*, March 19, 1898. White was "unavoidably absent" during the voting on the Cuban resolution, which empowered the president to use force to secure the independence of Cuba, but he took pains to make clear that he favored it. *Congressional Record*, 55th Cong., 2nd Sess., 4086.

have no rival, and I will not be disturbed in that leadership. [Laughter]"[7]

Apparently White's performance in Congress earned him good marks from other Republicans. New York Congressman George N. Southwick wrote of White: "Calm, courteous and conservative he is always ready to overlook, in his daily walk and conversation, the petty prejudices manifested toward him by his Democratic colleagues from the cotton belt, while winning the esteem, even the affection of his Republican associates." Southwick concluded: "He is a stalwart among stalwart Republicans."[8]

When the nation's only Negro congressman returned to Washington for the third session of the Fifty-fifth Congress, he had more reason than ever to defend blacks. White supremacists had just won a sweeping victory in North Carolina, after a bitter campaign based on race prejudice. The election had been followed by an anti-Negro riot and municipal coup d'etat in Wilmington.[9]

On January 26, 1899, White interjected the most extensive statement he had yet made on race relations into the debate on army reorganization. Perhaps because he suspected that he would not be reelected in 1900 ("I will sit here only two years longer, should I live," he told his colleagues), he spoke with greater force and candor than ever before. He began by expressing his complete support for the administration's war policy, though not without a touch of sarcasm. "It has been the province of the people of the United States at all times to extend a helping hand to the oppressed, to the outraged—I mean, of course, without the borders of the United States." White wholeheartedly endorsed the "acquisition of all of the territory that is within our grasp" as a result of the Spanish-American War, including the Philippines. Sharing the imperialists' assumption that expansion was a progressive, civilizing, Christianizing process, and recognizing the challenges of America's new course, he favored "the extension of our standing Army commensurate with our new conditions."

This much said, White digressed from the topic of debate to a "pos-

7. *Congressional Record*, 55th Cong., 2nd Sess., 4194.
8. Washington (D.C.) *Colored American*, June 11, 1898.
9. On the Wilmington riot, see Jerome A. McDuffie, "The Wilmington Riots of November 10, 1898" (M.A. thesis, Wake Forest University, 1963); Edmonds, *The Negro and Fusion Politics*.

sibly more vexing problem"—the plight of American Negroes. As "the only representative on this floor of 10,000,000 people," White felt called upon to answer slurs on black Americans made by racist colleagues, men who referred to Negroes "as savages, as aliens, as brutes, as vile and vicious and worthless." To such critics—and he mentioned specifically Congressmen John Sharp Williams and John M. Allen of Mississippi— White replied: "Yes, by force of circumstances, we are your inferiors. Give us two hundred and forty years the start of you, give us your labor for two hundred and forty years without compensation, give us the wealth that the brawny arms of the black man made for you, give us the education that his unpaid labor gave your boys and girls, and we will not be begging, we will not be in a position to be sneered at as aliens or members of an inferior race. Not at all."

Citing statistics, White again reminded the House of vote suppression in Mississippi and South Carolina and suggested that disfranchised voters "ought not to go into the representation of the district or the State." "It may seem a little strange to hear me speak," he said, "but nobody else has tackled this question because the boot does not pinch anybody else as it does me and my race. But it will come home to you. You will have to meet it." As much as White decried current conditions, he was not a pessimist. The black American, unlike the Indian, would not die out and be reduced to "a few mummies in the Smithsonian Institution." The Negro was "here to stay for all time to come" and was making remarkable progress in property, citizenship, and education. "I believe that the negro problem in less than fifty years will be a thing of the past," White said.

Blacks had no desire to be absorbed into white society like the thousands of immigrants streaming into the country—"the 'riffraff' of all nations of the earth," White called them. "We do not ask to be assimilated; we do not ask to be amalgamated; we do not ask for anything but to remain a distinct and separate race as we are, to be permitted to work out our own manhood and womanhood. We do not expect anything else."

To those who told blacks to bear patiently their lack of representation in the national government and remain silent in the face of lynching, White asked: "How long must we keep quiet, constantly sitting down and seeing our rights one by one taken away from us? As slaves it was to be expected; as slaves we were docile and easily managed; but as citizens

. . . we have a right to expect all that the law guarantees to us." In closing he declared: "It is well to stop and consider; you cannot always keep a free man down." White appealed to the representatives to "recognize your citizens at home" as they laid plans for Cuba, Hawaii, Puerto Rico, and the Philippines, and he sat down amid "prolonged applause."[10]

White's concern with national matters affecting his race did not cause him to neglect his local constituency. He attempted to get seventy-five hundred dollars in improvement funds for Fishing Creek, a waterway in his district, but the House was unwilling to appropriate such funds in addition to maintenance funds. As a North Carolinian, White spoke in support of a proposal for a public building in Durham made by Tarheel Congressman William W. Kitchin, like his father "Buck" Kitchin a racial extremist, but the bill was narrowly defeated 104–117, and Kitchin and White agreed on few things thereafter. Neither of the two minor bills White introduced in this session passed.[11]

The representative of the second district was very active in the first session of the Fifty-sixth Congress. Now a member of the District of Columbia Committee, he introduced a bill to prohibit bone or fertilizer factories in the district. Like O'Hara, Simmons, and Cheatham before him, White proposed relief for the depositors of the Freedman's Savings and Trust Company. He introduced bills to provide a Negro progress exhibit at the Paris Exposition of 1900, to pay certain colored War Department employees money they claimed due them from the Civil War, and to make lynching a federal crime. A joint resolution offered by White called for a home for aged and infirm blacks. Besides all these measures, he introduced seventeen bills, including one for the relief of Robert Smalls which finally passed both houses of Congress and was approved by President McKinley.[12]

Almost all of White's remarks in this session dealt with lynching. On January 31, 1900, he briefly commented on the relation of rape to lynch-

10. *Congressional Record*, 55th Cong., 3rd Sess., 1124–26. Although it regarded White's speech as a masterpiece, the Washington (D.C.) *Bee* objected to his proexpansion sentiments as unrepresentative of most blacks. February 4, 1899.

11. *Congressional Record*, 55th Cong., 3rd Sess., 1369–70, 2894, 1964, 2689.

12. *Ibid.*, 1963, 151, 373, 594, 791, 1021, 1108, 3549, 2867, 156, 889, 698, 596, 1373, 1323, 1427, 793, 3604. Smalls's most recent biographer was unaware that Congress finally rewarded the captor of the *Planter*. Okon Edet Uya, *From Slavery to Public Service: Robert Smalls, 1839–1915* (New York, 1971), 30.

ing, provoking abusive criticism in North Carolina. His statement was not part of a prepared address but was merely interjected into a speech against lynching and North Carolina election methods delivered by R. Z. Linney, Republican from western North Carolina. White said: "I have examined that question and I am prepared to state that not more than 15 per cent of the lynchings are traceable to that crime [rape], and there are many more outrages against colored women by white men than there are by colored men against white women." White's statement provoked vigorous applause from the public galleries, which "contained many colored people," according to the New York *Times*.[13]

The Associated Press reported what White said with significant revisions: "I have investigated lynching in the South and find that less than 15 percent of them are due to the crime of rape. And I desire to announce here, that if it was not for the assaults of white men upon black women, there would be less of the other class."[14] This version of the statement was particularly provocative because it could be construed as offering justification, if ever so slight, for black violators of white women.

The whole subject was so sensitive, however, that it is not necessary to look carefully at a turn of phrase or a shade of meaning to find what provoked bellows of rage from North Carolina Negrophobes. If some journalists cursed White for "justifying" rape, others thought the statement was an insult to virtuous white ladies because it placed them "upon the same level" with "virtue-selling and lewd black wenches."[15] The sexual implications of the race issue involved such a confused tangle of powerful fears, lusts, and stereotypes that few turn-of-the-century white southerners could discuss the topic coherently. George White committed unpardonable offenses against racial etiquette by assuming the honor of black women was as important as that of white women, by accusing white men of sexual hypocrisy, and by denying that lynching was a remedy for unspeakable crimes.

Josephus Daniels' *News and Observer* used White's statement as the occasion for an unrestrained attack on White and a call for "permanent

13. *Congressional Record*, 56th Cong., 1st Sess., 1365; New York *Times*, February 1, 1900.
14. Charlotte *Daily Observer*, February 1, 1900; Raleigh *News and Observer*, February 2, 1900. The New York *Times* version (February 1, 1900) is virtually identical.
15. Tarboro *Southerner*, February 15, 1900.

white rule in this State." White replied on the floor of the House, after asking the clerk to read the editorial, which began, "It is bad enough that North Carolina should have the only nigger Congressman." Daniels asserted that "White justifies assaults by negroes on white women by slandering white men" and used the congressman as an object lesson on the necessity of Negro disfranchisement. "Venomous, forward, slanderous of the whites, appealing to the worst passions of his own race, he emphasizes anew the need of making an end of him and his kind."

White told the House that he wanted wide publication of the *News and Observer* diatribe so that the world could see "what the poor colored man in the Southland has to undergo from a certain class." He was quick to add that there were many fine white people in North Carolina, "but unfortunately, men of the type of him who wrote the article are now in the ascendancy." White said that he had not justified black assaults on white women, he had simply said that not all rapes were committed by black men against white women. Some outrages were "committed by white men upon black women, as evidenced by the great numbers of mulattoes in the Southland." Rapists, said White, ought to be hanged, "but it ought to be done by the courts, not by an infuriated mob such as the writer of that article would incite." Finally White defended his own character: "I want my colleagues in this House, both Democrats and Republicans, with Populists thrown in, to judge my character and conduct for the last three years on this floor and say whether or not it has conformed to the description given by this fellow who edits the *News and Observer* and pollutes the country with such literature as has been read at the desk." The *Record* notes that applause greeted this personal appeal.[16]

Five days after White's defense, the *News and Observer* issued a new accusation, charging in a February 10 editorial and a news story that in order to lessen the political damage of his statement White had "doctored" his original words before they appeared in the *Record*. According to the news story, two unnamed North Carolina members of Congress had secured "the exact copy of what White really said" from the notes of the "official stenographer." This copy stated: "I have investigated the facts in regard to these lynchings, for the last two and a half years, and I say that less than seventy-five percent of the lynch-

16. *Congressional Record*, 56th Cong., 1st Sess., 1507.

ings which occurred in the United States were chargeable to the cause stated; and if there were not outrages and assaults committed—not upon white women by black men, but by white men upon black women, those lynchings would be less than they are now." Not only was the figure of 75 percent completely inconsistent with White's views on lynchings and rape expressed on several occasions before and after the January 31 remark, but this "undoctored" statement was confusing because it seemed to have White saying that there would be fewer lynchings—not rapes, but lynchings—if white men left black women alone.[17]

No North Carolina representative objected to the accuracy of the *Record* on the floor of the House, even though two of them replied to Linney's speech, during which White had made his comment. In May, W. W. Kitchin even quoted the section of the *Record* that included White's statement, but he made no mention of the doctoring charge.[18]

In the end, it made no difference whether the statement was doctored. All three versions of White's words were obviously repugnant to the editor of the *News and Observer*. On February 2 the newspaper denounced the Associated Press version of the statement; on February 8 a wrathful editorial quoted the *Congressional Record* version; and finally, on February 10, ten days after White had uttered the words, the "true" version was revealed to the readers of the *News and Observer*. The next day adjacent front-page articles attacked Linney and White, each employing a different version of the notorious statement![19] As in the case of the 1898 "invite the issue" speech, precise quotation was unimportant.

White was not afraid to broach the lynching issue again, for he delivered a major address on February 23, 1900, in support of his antilynching bill. He claimed that since emancipation "fully 50,000 of my race have been ignominiously murdered by mobs, not 1 per cent of whom have been made to answer for their crimes in the courts of justice." White devoted a portion of his speech to answering several congressmen who had "undertaken the unholy task of extenuating and excusing" and actually justifying various mob acts. One of these men was Congressman James M. Griggs of Georgia who had related to the

17. Raleigh *News and Observer*, February 10, 1900. In a speech the previous spring, White presented statistics "showing that only a very few [lynching victims] were even charged with rape." Washington (D.C.) *Bee*, May 13, 1899.

18. *Congressional Record*, 56th Cong., 1st Sess., appendix, 299.

19. Raleigh *News and Observer*, February 2, 8, 10, 11, 1900.

House the horrible crimes of one Georgia lynching victim, "a monster in human form," by way of explaining what drove white people to mob action. But Griggs had a very selective sense of outrage. As White pointed out: "He might have depicted also, if he had been so inclined, the miserable butchery of men, women, and children in Wilmington, N.C., in November, 1898, who had committed no crime, nor were they even charged with crime. . . . But this description would not have accomplished the purpose of riveting public sentiment upon every colored man of the South as a rapist from whose brutal assaults every white woman must be protected."

Noting other aspects of the plight of Afro-Americans, White quoted several paragraphs from a speech by Alabama Senator John T. Morgan which warned that placing Negroes and whites on a basis of political equality would only "clog the progress of all mankind in its march, ever strenuous and in proper order, toward the highest planes of human aspiration." The Negro representative replied: "It is easy for these gentlemen to taunt us with our inferiority, at the same time not mentioning the causes of this inferiority. It is rather hard to be accused of shiftlessness and idleness when the accuser of his own motion closes the avenues of labor and industrial pursuits to us. It is hardly fair to accuse us of ignorance when it was made a crime under the former order of things to learn enough about letters to even read the Word of God."

White devoted considerable effort to refuting the popular notion that rape was the "usual crime" punished by lynchings. Using statistics for 1898 and 1899, he showed that most lynching victims were not even accused of rape, but that a person could be killed for a variety of alleged offenses, ranging from murder and arson to "impudence." He read into the *Record* an editorial from the New York *Press* which praised the recent statements of Congressmen Linney and White and denounced the southern refrain "that every Southern family had a potential orang-outang in its woodshed in the shape of its black 'hired man.'" "The ravishers among negroes are almost literally one in a million," said the newspaper. White reminded the House that the *News and Observer* had "jumped" on him as a "slanderer of white men" when he had said that "this wretched crime" was not restricted to Negroes. With the bitter quip "out of their own mouths shall ye know them" he read an item from the *News and Observer* reporting the arrest of a white magistrate who was accused of raping a black crippled girl. The story had been published "but a few days" after the newspaper criticized White.

"I tremble with horror for the future of our nation," White declared, "when I think of what must be the inevitable result if mob violence is not stamped out." He then read a bill, which he had already introduced, providing for federal action against lynching. As the first bill presented in Congress to suppress lynching, the measure merits careful attention. White proposed to protect all American citizens "from being murdered, tortured, burned to death by any and all organized mobs commonly known as 'lynching bees,'" whether spontaneous or planned. Further, "whenever any citizen or citizens of the United States shall be murdered by mob violence in the manner hereinabove described, all parties participating, aiding, and abetting in such murder shall be guilty of treason against the Government of the United States and shall be tried for that offense in the United States courts." The penalty for participation in a lynching would be the same as for treason, thus making lynching a federal capital crime. The last section of White's proposed law repealed "all laws and parts of laws in conflict with this statute." The remainder of White's speech was devoted to arguments for the constitutionality of the bill. But despite his eloquence, despite the "prolonged applause" that greeted the speech, White's bill was never seriously considered.[20]

White's next effort was more successful. In the discussion of the bill for the government of the territory of Hawaii, he offered an amendment striking out the measure's universal poll tax. He said he could not support the bill if it included "this and other sections of the Mississippi election law." Although his amendment was voted down, the clause he had objected to was later removed in conference committee. A Democratic representative claimed that the Republicans dropped the clause because they had been embarrassed by the twitting they had received (from White and others) for supporting such a plan.[21]

---

20. *Congressional Record*, 56th Cong., 1st Sess., 2151–54. White's figure of fifty thousand dead in thirty-five years was wildly exaggerated. Lynchings, the most frequent and costly form of mob action, were at their peak in the 1890s and even in that period they averaged fewer than two hundred a year. In the Second Congressional District, mob violence of any sort was rare in the years 1872 to 1900. See National Association for the Advancement of Colored People, *Thirty Years of Lynching in the United States, 1889–1918* (New York, 1969).

21. *Congressional Record*, 56th Cong., 1st Sess., 3814; appendix, 636.

George White was the lamest of lame ducks by the time the second session of the Fifty-sixth Congress convened. Not only had he not run for reelection, but he had also decided to leave North Carolina and move to the North. In his final session, White introduced but one bill, a private pension measure which the House passed. He was also successful in his fight for passage of the bill providing a home for aged and infirm colored people, to be built and maintained with the unclaimed bounty money of black soldiers in the Civil War. The bill itself was introduced by Tennessee Republican Walter P. Brownlow, but White offered resolutions in support of it in both sessions of the Fifty-sixth Congress, and it was he who brought it to the floor on behalf of the Committee on Military Affairs.[22]

During the debate on reapportionment, White unsuccessfully tried to get time to reply to racial attacks by several southerners. In a short statement on January 8, 1901, he promised to reply at a later date, especially to the statements of three young congressmen, one of whom was North Carolina's W. W. Kitchin. Even under these frustrating circumstances he retained his sense of humor. "I am glad to state, however, that these three gentlemen are all young men, and as an extenuating circumstance for their vile words against my people I apply to them the statute of youth. They will know better when they get older. [Laughter and applause.]"[23]

White delivered his famous farewell speech on January 29, 1901. After a few perfunctory remarks on the topic under discussion, the agricultural appropriation bill, White turned to other matters, "matters of life and existence" to black Americans. "I would not thus digress from the question at issue and detain the House in a discussion of the interests of this particular people at this time but for the constant and persistent effort of certain gentlemen upon this floor to mold and rivet public sentiment against us as a people."

"Certain gentlemen" included Congressmen Oscar W. Underwood of Alabama, Stanyarne Wilson of South Carolina, and W. W. Kitchin of North Carolina, and White rebutted each in turn. No member of the House had more persistently tried to "bring the black man into disre-

22. *Congressional Record,* 56th Cong., 2nd Sess., 1875, 188, 1268–70. This bill was blocked in the Senate and failed to become law, 2504, 3499, 3503.
23. *Ibid.,* 737.

pute," said White, than Congressman Kitchin. "As an excuse for his peculiar notions" about the right to vote, the black legislator noted a "few facts and figures surrounding his birth and rearing." Kitchin was a product of Halifax County, a place that had produced very unusual returns in the recent balloting on North Carolina's disfranchising constitutional amendment. White charged that the Democrats carried the town of Halifax 990 votes to 41, or nearly 500 more votes than there were registered voters. In light of this, Kitchin's ideas on voting and counting were not surprising, "nor is it to be a wonder that he is a member of this Congress, having been brought up and educated in such wonderful notions of dealing out fair-handed justice to his fellowman."

White next attacked a speech by Oscar Underwood, which labeled the Fifteenth Amendment a "lamentable mistake," asked northerners to leave the race issue to the South, and deplored discussion of cutting southern representation under the second section of the Fourteenth Amendment. How could southerners openly violate the Constitution, asked White, and then demand that the law be not enforced? Reduction of southern representation meant little to White or his race, except as an issue of respect for law. If the South had fewer seats in the House it would mean the secure installment in power of "the great Republican party," but it might also increase the influence of the lily-whites, those southern Republicans "who, after receiving the unalloyed support of the negro vote for over thirty years, now feel that they have grown a little too good for association with him politically." Fortunately, he added, the lily-whites constituted "a very small percentage" of white Republicans. White heaped scorn on Underwood's description of Negroes as a race that had been "forced among" southerners, asking if the gentleman from Alabama had forgotten the slave trade, the middle passage, and the coerced labor of Negro slaves when he furnished this "startling information."

White criticized another southerner who had told the House that justice could exist only between equals, "among lions, but between lions and lambs, never." If Negroes were lambs and whites were lions, White observed that lambs were "innocent," "inoffensive," "useful," whereas lions were "clothed with great strength, vicious, and with destructive propensities." The metaphor created a problem for the southern member, noted White sarcastically: "What will he do with all the heterogeneous intermediate animals, ranging all the way from pure lion to pure lamb, found on the plantations of every Southern State in the Union?"

In response to Congressman Wilson of South Carolina, who had "dragged in the reconstruction days" by way of denouncing blacks in his state, White insisted that unscrupulous white carpetbaggers ought to come in for criticism too. He declared that "the musty records of 1868 . . . as to what the negro was thirty-two years ago, is [sic] not a proper standard by which the negro living on the threshold of the twentieth century should be measured," citing statistics indicating that blacks were advancing in literacy, refinement, and wealth. The advance of the Negro came "in the face of lynching, burning at the stake, with the humiliation of 'Jim Crow' cars, the disfranchisement of our male citizens, slander and degradation of our women, with the factories closed against us. . . . With all these odds against us, we are forging our way ahead, slowly, perhaps, but surely." He called attention to two of his bills still sleeping in committee, the antilynching bill and the bill to reimburse depositors of the Freedman's Savings and Trust Company.

White knew that his speech was the last a Negro would make in the House for some years. "These parting words are in behalf of an outraged, heart-broken, bruised, and bleeding, but God-fearing people, faithful, industrious, loyal people—rising people, full of potential force. . . . The only apology that I have to make for the earnestness with which I have spoken is that I am pleading for the life, the liberty, the future happiness, and manhood suffrage of one-eighth of the entire population of the United States." There was loud applause, and then an apologist for lynching and disfranchisement, Williams of Mississippi, continued the debate on the agricultural appropriation bill.[24]

One recent student of George White's career has concluded: "He served his people well, though his services would have been more effective had he refrained from vindictiveness." This scholar, describing White as "impetuous" and "belligerent," concluded that the black congressman was "overly concerned with race problems" and allowed himself "to speak without restraint" after he had given up hope of being

24. *Ibid.*, 1634–38.

reelected, responding "with equal intensity" to fierce white supremacy attacks.[25]

Nothing in White's congressional record supports the view that he was a fiery radical. Although he was not afraid to raise sensitive issues like lynching and rape, his language and ideas were always moderate yet forthright. His political philosophy advocated no revolution in American economic life, reflected no alienation from the basic values of American society and politics, urged no reckless or violent actions on the part of the oppressed. A middle-aged, prosperous lawyer, George White would likely have been a McKinley Republican even if he were not a southern black man. Compared to those who heaped abuse on him and his race, he was very restrained. In the bitter and ugly triumph of white supremacy in the years 1898 to 1901, George White was simply a useful symbol for the real fanatics.

25. Elmore, "North Carolina Negro Congressmen," 188, 189, 193, 196, 199. For a similar view, see Wooley, "Race and Politics," 181–83, 194.

Chapter 16

"I CANNOT LIVE IN NORTH CAROLINA
AND BE A MAN"

"THE LIE IS SO STUPID that it could not have been started and repeated but for the profound ignorance of the niggers generally," announced the Wilmington *Messenger* in the heat of the 1898 campaign. This "most stupid lie of the campaign" was the fusionist charge that "if the Democrats should carry the State they would disfranchise the negroes." The Democratic party line emphatically promised that the ballot would be denied no voter.[1]

Despite this commitment, a few months later the Democratic-controlled general assembly produced an amendment to the state constitution which, if ratified by the voters, would require literacy of all future voters except those who could qualify under a "grandfather clause." Since a majority of black voters were illiterate and few Negroes could claim direct descent from a man who had been qualified to vote on or before January 1, 1867, the effect of the amendment would be to disfranchise large numbers of unlettered blacks while allowing almost all native-born white illiterates to continue voting if they paid a poll tax.[2] To facilitate the success of the amendment, the legislature rewrote the election law for partisan advantage and required a complete new registration of the state's voters.

The question of the legality and wisdom of the amendment dominated

1. Wilmington *Messenger* quoted in Goldsboro *Daily Argus*, October 20, 1898; Lefler and Newsome, *North Carolina*, 557–59.
2. Kousser, *Shaping of Southern Politics*, 192, describes the North Carolina grandfather clause as "temporary," implying that it was a minor "concession to poor whites" by men who actually desired to disfranchise *all* illiterates. The grandfather clause was temporary in the sense that it expired in 1908, but all illiterates who registered under it before that date were permanently qualified to vote. Thus nearly all native white illiterates thirteen or older were untouched by the amendment's literacy requirements.

the election of 1900, turning the campaign into a passionate conflict like that of 1898. Since the legislature scheduled the vote on disfranchisement, as well as the state election, for August—three months before the regular national election—there were no national issues to distract the electorate. Disfranchisement was the overriding issue, and once it was resolved the matter of McKinley versus Bryan was anticlimactic.

Demoralized by the defeat of 1898, the anti-Democratic coalition never responded effectively to the renewed white supremacy cry. A group of eighty-nine Negro leaders, with George White presiding, met to discuss the impending danger even as the legislature was framing the amendment, but they did nothing more than issue a mild manifesto against suffrage limitation, concluding with an appeal to North Carolina whites "to continue your friendly aid toward us, which has so marked the good relations existing between the two races in our State in the past." White and other outspoken men were narrowly defeated when they proposed that the group use the threat of large-scale black emigration to halt disfranchisement plans. As if to underline the feebleness of fusionists, Senator Butler's *Caucasian* offered equivocating, racist criticism of the amendment. A March 2, 1899, editorial insisted that colonization (*i.e.* removal) was the only solution to the race problem, "preferable to simply disfranchisement."[3] The response of Negroes and fusionists in 1899 anticipated the weakness of the antiamendment forces in 1900.

As the beginning of the 1900 campaign approached, the incumbent second district congressman seemed to doubt that he could be reelected, given the conditions in the state. In the autumn of 1899 White purchased "an elegant three story brick dwelling" in Washington, D.C., to serve as his family residence when his wife and children were in the city. "Mr. White is warmly welcomed here as a quasi citizen," said the *Colored American,* "and as a valuable acquisition to the local bar." He had received his license to practice before the District of Columbia Supreme Court during the year. Early in 1900 the Washington *Bee* predicted that White would practice law in New York City at the expiration of his term, if he did not return to the South. "Of course the South is Mr. White's home; all of his interests are there; but from the present outlook the Democratic party South is against the Negro. A man of Mr.

3. Charlotte *Daily Observer,* January 19, 1899; Raleigh *Caucasian,* March 2, 1899.

White's attainments will be appreciated in a state where a man is recognized for his ability."[4]

Yet White may have still maintained some small hope of being reelected. At the end of January, 1900, Democratic journalists reported that unnamed white Republicans were profusely abusing the Negro representative, charging that he was "desirous of making any kind of a deal to get reelected," though it is not clear whether they feared deals within or without the GOP. White was still working energetically in the first few months of the year to secure patronage for his political friends, an effort perhaps indicating that he had not abandoned all hope for himself or his party. There was an air of politics-as-usual, for example, in his actions regarding census enumerators. Much to the embarrassment of the Populist district supervisor, White turned in a list of men he wanted appointed as enumerators in Warren County, and the list included some Negroes. Appealing to Senator Butler in his quandary, the supervisor (a former state senator from Wilson) expressed his deep opposition to recommending White's men. To "load the eastern counties with negro enumerators will blast our prospects (now so bright)," he felt, by providing "travelling object lessons." Furthermore, he believed that "it will be worth the life of any negroe [sic] (in the red hot condition that will prevail about June) to go nosing around among white people."[5]

The supervisor was typical of the weak, fading support White and other black officeholders could expect from the Populists. Most third party men agreed heartily with the census official's conviction that 1900 was a year for blacks to "stand aside," though they did not see the bright prospects he saw. "There is no use to nominate a ticket in this county," declared the former county board chairman in Lenoir. " 'Jess' Granger's [sic] gang will count us out if we were to get every vote but the poll holders in the county." The Wilson County chairman was equally depressed: "[I]t seem that two year ago all our populists turn Democrats and I have not heard much of Politics until the present."[6]

4. Washington (D.C.) *Colored American*, October 21, 1899; Washington (D.C.) *Bee,* January 13, 1900. "Hon. Geo. H. White has returned to the city for permanent residence," reported the Washington (D.C.) *Colored American,* October 14, 1899.

5. Charlotte *Daily Observer,* January 31, 1900; Wilmington *Messenger* quoted in Kinston *Daily Free Press,* February 1, 1900; J. T. B. Hoover to Marion Butler, March 14, 1900, in Butler Papers.

6. J. T. B. Hoover to Marion Butler, March 14, 1900, Robert B. Kinsey to Butler, February 19, 1900, George W. Green to Butler, April 5, 1900, all in Butler Papers.

The opposite spirit pervaded the Democratic camp. Several men were eager to capture the party nomination for Congress, an honor that had once seemed so questionable. The Wilson *Daily News* set forth the merits of former congressman Fred Woodard, arguing "now that victory seems certain it seems to us that the man who led the party under the adverse conditions of previous campaigns should be considered." The Tarboro *Southerner* said it was time for an Edgecombe man to get the nomination and began steady promotion of local white supremacy zealot Donnell Gilliam. "White supremacy clubs" were springing up across the district to promote the success of the amendment, and there were no doubt many sessions like the "good meeting" in Kinston March 16. One speaker, a former Alliance leader, said "it was a matter of history that the white race was the only race capable of self-government" and a local teacher "quoted a vile piece from George White."[7]

Over the years second district Republicans had frequently disagreed about the role of white leaders in a largely black party, with tension between white veterans of Reconstruction and rising black politicians intensifying after the late 1880s. Now, with the very existence of the party in jeopardy, the quarreling in some cases became extremely harsh, almost as though the generals of a vast, exhausted, retreating army had fallen to blaming each other for anticipated defeat. One of the most important white Republicans in the district was Hiram L. Grant, who had lived so long in Wayne County that people had stopped calling him a carpetbagger. A former Union army officer, then long-time postmaster at Goldsboro, Grant had helped engineer the Republican coalition with the Populists in 1894, serving in both fusion legislatures as a senator from the ninth district. At a factional convention of Wayne Republicans on April 3, 1900, Grant delivered a speech which showed that he could adapt to new conditions, that he accepted the future. After denouncing the black leader of the rival faction, "he declared himself as wholly opposed to the Amendment," but also opposed to Negroes holding office. In fact, he had always opposed black officeholding, "and when the test of his Republicanism was that he must vote for a negro then he was no

7. W. A. Dunn to Francis D. Winston, December 20, 1899, in Francis D. Winston Papers, Southern Historical Collection, University of North Carolina, Chapel Hill. F. A. Woodard to M. J. Hawkins, February 10, 1900, in Hawkins Papers. Wilson *Daily News*, April 3, 1900; Tarboro *Southerner*, January 25, 1900; Kinston *Daily Free Press*, March 17, 1900.

longer a Republican." He admitted that the Negro had an abstract right under the law to hold office, "yet public sentiment was stronger than law, and public sentiment was opposed to negroes filling offices over white people."

Of course most blacks—95 percent, he thought—were not ambitious to hold office. The problem arose only with the educated Negroes. "When you educate a negroe [sic], thereafter there are only three avenues he looks to—teaching school, preaching and politics. Give them a smattering of education and they are then ready for one or the other or all three of these roles." One troublesome educated Negro was the district's congressman, George White, whom Grant urged the colored delegates to avoid supporting. "You have not a worse enemy to your race—one who has done more to injure you as a race than the man who represents this district in Congress to-day. Geo. H. White has drawn the color line in this district. He has said that the negroes constitute the voters and that they must hold the offices."[8]

In claiming that he had always opposed black officeholding, Grant showed a selective memory of his long career in Republican politics. One could go as far back as Grant's 1882 support of James O'Hara in preference to a northern-born white man, though that would be unnecessary since more recent examples were readily available. The day after Grant's speech a Negro clergyman wrote the Goldsboro *Daily Argus* protesting the major's sentiments. Not only had Grant secured the appointment of five black magistrates for Wayne in the legislature of 1895, according to the Reverend C. Dillard, but "Mr. White would not have been in the American Congress today but for the ardent support of Maj. Grant." A delegate from Wayne to the 1896 congressional convention, Grant had there "championed the cause of Congressman White." As one who might be considered among "the 5 per cent of the race that has aspirations," Dillard resented Grant's remarks on educated Negroes and countered, "If it is right for the negro to aspire in politics, does it not show wisdom on his part that only 'educated negroes' aspire?" Dillard charged that the real reason Grant disliked educated blacks was because they refused to "be pliant tools in the hands of designing politicians."[9]

8. Goldsboro *Daily Argus*, April 3, 1900.
9. *Ibid.*, April 4, 1900.

Much the same complaint, only from the other side, came from an unidentified "prominent white Republican politician" quoted by an *Argus* columnist a month later. "This is the only district in the State in which the negroes are giving us any trouble by their 'uppishness,'" the man was reported as saying. "And that fellow White, d— him, is the cause of it. He has made the negroes in his district so 'uppish' that we can't make them stay in the background 'till the constitutional amendment is settled."[10]

Perhaps such remarks are worth noting only as an indication of the fretful confusion the race issue produced in many white non-Democrats. Surely it took a sensitive man to find "uppishness" in North Carolina black voters in the last year of the nineteenth century. The Edgecombe County Republican convention, meeting April 19, could serve as a synechdoche of the entire second district party organization. About twenty-five "forlorn" Negro delegates and no whites gathered to choose delegates to the state and district conventions, their deliberations somber as a funeral, according to the local newspaper. "There was no enthusiasm. The old scenes of noise and disorder were all lacking today." Although it was an all-black convention the delegates showed no disposition to reject all white leaders—two of the four delegates to the state convention were white men prominent in the party since Reconstruction.[11]

The incumbent and his cronies, as one might expect, had considerable influence in the district convention, held on April 26 in Tarboro, but that would not be considered "uppishness" except under the conditions of 1900. There was a consensus among the delegates before the meeting convened that they should make no congressional nomination at this time but should restrict themselves to the business of choosing delegates to the national convention. For the first time since 1880 both delegates to the national convention—Congressman White and his close ally Henry E. Hagans, Negro leader of the Wayne County regulars—were black. This was less a sign of black assertiveness than a mark of black retreat, however. Three black nominees in earlier years (O'Hara in 1884, Cheatham in 1892, and White in 1896) had been sent to the national convention as delegates-at-large, and White must have realized that it was unlikely the state convention would so honor him in 1900. On the

10. *Ibid.*, May 3, 1900.
11. Tarboro *Southerner*, April 26, 1900.

streets and in ad hoc caucuses several white delegates promoted the idea that a white man ought to receive the congressional nomination when it was eventually made. "White's friends hope to secure the nomination," asserted the Tarboro *Southerner*, "but the white members of his party are against him. . . . The negroes do not seem to know what to do."[12]

The Republican state convention showed the strength of the policy of deemphasizing the Negro. Fewer than 40 of the 240 delegates were black, a dramatic change from previous Republican conventions. Although he had addressed the conventions of 1892, 1894, 1896, and 1898, George White gave no speech this year. The Republicans seemed to think that keeping Negroes out of the limelight would break the force of Democratic charges of "Negro domination," that North Carolina voters would forget that the overwhelming majority of Republicans were black if white men graced the convention platform. For governor the delegates nominated Spencer B. Adams, who was subsequently accepted by the Populists as the fusion standard-bearer.[13] His Democratic opponent was to be Charles B. Aycock, the Goldsboro lawyer whose labors on behalf of white supremacy made him an inevitable choice.

If second district Republicans hesitated to select a congressional candidate before they knew the outcome of the disfranchisement voting, Democrats had no reason to delay. Meeting in Goldsboro on May 24, they produced a drawn-out nomination battle, unmatched even in the annals of Republican conventions. Although the convention was peaceful, with no contested delegations, the delegates took hours to choose a candidate, balloting all night long. Fred Woodard, Donnell Gilliam, R. B. Peebles, and Claude Kitchin, the son of W. H. Kitchin, all sought the nomination, and it was not until the 120th ballot, at five o'clock in the morning that Kitchin finally won. "To say that he will be elected in November is already a fact beyond the possibility of contravention," said the Goldsboro *Daily Argus*.[14]

Kitchin was soon out on the stump in behalf of the amendment, showing a bravado much like his father's. At the end of a two-hour-and-ten-minute speech in Goldsboro, he reached the peak of Negrophobic ora-

12. *Ibid.*, May 3, 1900; Goldsboro *Daily Argus*, April 27, 1900.
13. Goldsboro *Daily Argus*, May 3, 1900. Cyrus Thompson, the original Populist nominee for governor, became the fusion candidate for secretary of state under cooperation arrangement. Goldsboro *Daily Argus*, July 28, 1900.
14. *Ibid.*, May 25, 1900.

tory: "With his left arm lifted and his fist clinched [sic] he declared by the Eternal that white men shall rule; the negro shall not have domination over us and our loved ones."[15]

Such sentiments were stronger in the eastern half of the state, where most North Carolina blacks lived, than in the west. To insure the victory of the disfranchising amendment, ironically enough, Democrats needed to sweep the Negro counties. Much of their blustery fist-waving and rodomontade was aimed, as before, at white men who might interfere with their plans by breaking racial solidarity, for Democrats assumed that cheating and intimidating Negroes would be less difficult if the blacks were isolated. As the Tarboro *Southerner* said on election day: "If there were no white traitors in Edgecombe, the county would give the amendment 3000 majority."[16]

Morale among eastern fusionists, both white and black, was low enough to satisfy any Democrat as the amendment campaign moved to its climax in the summer of 1900. Senator Butler's eastern correspondents had nothing but discouraging news. "I have never seen so much indifference [sic] shown in an election by members of the Peoples Party since our organization," declared the Populist chairman in Greene County. "They seem to think it is useless to try to do anything." The party leader in Halifax reported: "We have Chmn in very few precincts & not enough to appoint Poll holders & distribute tickets." He had met only two Populists "who favor our making any move at all here." Former state senator Edward T. Clark felt he dared not take an active part in the campaign because he was in debt and the Democrats had the power to "crush" him. Two weeks before the election the Greene County chairman wrote again to accuse Republicans "all over the East" of apathy. Many of his own Populist township chairmen did not "realize the importance of this election." "In fact they all want the Negro out of polatics [sic] & think it would be better for our party in the future. It seems to me now that I am in the field fighting alone."[17]

All around them the fusionists saw overwhelming evidence that their

15. Clipping from Raleigh *Morning Post*, June 16, 1900, in Claude Kitchin Papers, Southern Historical Collection, University of North Carolina, Chapel Hill.

16. Tarboro *Southerner*, August 2, 1900.

17. W. E. Murphrey to Marion Butler, June 19, 1900, W. E. Bowers to Butler, July 11, 1900, E. T. Clark to Butler, July 7, 1900, Murphrey to Butler, July 18, 1900, all in Butler Papers.

opponents would carry the election even if dishonest methods were required. "If we could have a fair Registration & a fair count in our county (Lenoir) I feel sure we would have very little trouble to beat the Democrats," wrote a white Republican to state chairman A. E. Holton. But the local Democratic registrars were using various pretexts to keep Negroes from registering. "At this precinct they are refusing to Register over half the colored voters. *At this rate we are not in it.*" A registrar in Halifax County told a Negro who said he had been born in Warren County that he would have to go to Warren and get two witnesses to prove it before he could register! In Snakebite township, Bertie County, the registrar refused to register several Negroes because they could not tell the day and month of their birth—just the year.[18]

A more advanced form of fraud was to allow anybody to register, with the intention of counting as many votes as necessary for the Democrats—regardless of actual balloting. From the town of Halifax a badly educated farmer reported that "the Register dont try to keep any one from Registering[—]negroes and all can Register with out any trouble that I have been able to learn" and he expected all qualified voters to be allowed to vote. "In our county, there Is a large negro majority about four thousand & they want that vote and the last bit of It as a Rebuttal against the Western vote, If It is needed. If they find that they need several thousand votes from the negro Partie to carry things like they want them why all they have to do Is Just tel the boys to say that all the negroes voted the Democratic ticket & count them that way, and It is done." A similar complaint came from a Littleton Populist, who found no fault in the registration but feared the "desperately Democratic election Board" would take advantage of every "oppertunity [sic] to carry thier [sic] plans fair or foul." Former senator Clark found the poor whites almost all opposed to the amendment, but Democrats told him: "We dont care whether they vote or not we intend to carry it anyway." The Populist chairman in Warren said: "I[f] we can poll our votes and get them counted &ct [sic] we will carrie the Co by a good majority," but he expected the Democrats to cheat. They were threatening to shoot

18. James F. Parrott to A. E. Holton, July 6, 1900, S. L. Gibson to Marion Butler, July 17, 1900, E. T. Clark to Butler, July 7, 1900, J. R. Bynum to Butler, July 19, 1900, all in Butler Papers. See also S. H. Bright to Butler, July 12, 1900, S. K. Edwards to Butler, July 16, 1900, both in Butler Papers.

any white who tried to instruct Negro voters, saying "they have the negros [sic] where they want them if no white man interfers [sic]."[19]

The state Republican organization did little to help eastern blacks register and made few efforts to get out the vote, leaving these tasks to the Populists, who, it was assumed, could do them more expediently. Feeling deserted by their party, some blacks did not register and showed an unusual indifference to politics. George White took command of the local Edgecombe organization, maneuvering to elect the Populist or "independent" nominees for local office, as well as working against Aycock and the amendment. His policy was outlined in a speech he delivered at the June 30 Republican county convention, an address that even the Tarboro *Southerner* conceded to be "quite conservative." Declaring himself "out of politics so far as wanting office" was concerned, White "advised his race to register and to vote, but create no disturbance and to strive to cultivate harmony and good feeling between the races." Just before the election White was professing confidence that the amendment would be defeated by a large majority unless the Democrats employed fraud, in which case the courts would overturn the result.[20]

Most blacks were not as bold as the Edgecombe Baptist congregation which passed resolutions calling for Negroes to leave the state if they were "denied the right to vote hereafter" and "go to some state like Georgia" which had not disfranchised black voters. "We do not want to hold the offices or rule the white people," said the resolution. "We pay taxes and ought to be allowed to vote."[21]

The courage that inspired a country preacher to sponsor such a manifesto and send it to the fiercely prejudiced editor at the county seat was matched in other men here and there around the district. Often poorly informed and with flawed motives, these men faced defeat with courageous grace. George Shearin, a Halifax farmer, wrote to Senator Butler: "Mr. Butler Just a little longer & a fellow like myself will not be Saft [sic] here they will use Something worse than Rotten Eggs, for It Is *us*

---

19. George W. Shearin to M. Butler, July 10, 1900, Robert Fletcher to Butler, July 21, 1900, E. T. Clark to Butler, July 7, 1900, R. D. Paschall to Butler, July 21, 1900, all in Butler Papers.

20. A. E. Holton to Marion Butler, July 17, 1900, J. S. Basnight to Butler, June 26, 1900, both in Butler Papers. Tarboro *Southerner*, July 5, 1900; Washington (D.C.) *Colored American*, August 4, 1900.

21. Tarboro *Southerner*, June 28, 1900.

they are after & not the negro & Every man that they find that they cant fool nor force they make It hard & very hard for *him*." Shearin, believing the Populist propaganda that the amendment would allow literate Negro loafers to vote in 1908 while forcing white illiterates to "Stand a Side," added: "But let me tell you I may go to the bad place or I may be draged up to a limb like the cartoon In the News & Dissturber but I never will be draged In or forced In the Democratic Partie, nor I never be forced to vote a way the Rights of my four little Boys that Is at this moment at the plow handles plowing for Bread." On the eve of the election Shearin wrote again to the senator, reporting some of the people around him had "gone wile." "I cant tell Just what they wil do to me. . . . they seem to have lost Reason." A brave Northampton man, the only Populist in his precinct, had difficulty expressing himself on paper: "i have been insulted time and again because i would not joind the white suppremisay club some of the fools have carried it in our Sunday school and left the class because i would not joined the club." The Populist chairman in Warren thought of the current Boxer Rebellion as he considered his besieged, isolated party men: "Think our people here need protection as well as in China or any other Heathern [*sic*] nation."[22]

No one was surprised when Aycock and the amendment won an overwhelming triumph on election day. Aycock was elected governor by a majority of more than 60,000 votes, defeating his opponent 186,650 to 126,296. The amendment trailed slightly, with a victory margin of just under 54,000 votes. In the second district the Democrats appropriated thousands of Negro votes. Halifax was perhaps the most glaring example, since election officials counted 7,495 votes in a county that had only 7,249 adult males according to the 1900 census, and Aycock won 88.3 percent of the vote in a county that had given Russell more than 60 percent in 1896. Edgecombe claimed 3,758 votes (90.7 percent) for Aycock—more than twice the party's total in any previous election— even though there were only 2,369 white registered voters in the county. The vote for Aycock exceeded the total number of white men of voting age by 500 in Bertie, by 250 in Northampton, and by over 700 in Warren. The 18,333-vote majority Aycock received in the nine counties of the

22. G. W. Shearin to Marion Butler, July 10, 1900, Shearin to Butler, July 30, 1900, John W. Knight to Butler, July 17, 1900, R. D. Paschall to Butler, July 28, 1900, all in Butler Papers.

district was more than 30 percent of his statewide margin of victory, illustrating just how important the black belt was to the Democrats.[23]

There was abundant testimony that the election was grossly fraudulent, that, as one Populist put it, "really there have been *no election* held—It was a complete robbery & every honest man knew it." A man in Whitaker's township, Edgecombe County, said the election in his precinct had been "farcical," an "outright steal," and that the Negroes had voted "solidly" against Aycock and the amendment. "I believe better element of Dems. at heart are against such, but are afraid to denounce it," he said. At one Warren precinct 27 more votes were returned than polled and at another there were 7 more votes for the amendment than there were voters. More than 2,000 Negroes had voted in Warren, and, according to a Populist leader, not more than a dozen had voted for the Democratic ticket, yet Adams received only 1,063 votes for governor. Warren Populist John B. Powell accused Democratic-controlled election officers of depositing Democratic tickets in place of the Republican or Populist ballots handed them. Unfortunately there were no witnesses to most incidents of ballot-box stuffing or ticket changing since Democrats did their best to keep voting and counting out of public view. As an Edgecombe man wrote to Senator Butler: "It is poor play to stand by a Simmons Bull Pen in Edgecomb [*sic*] an tell what is being done on the inside."[24]

In unguarded moments even the Democrats admitted what had happened. About six weeks after the election the Windsor *Ledger* condemned the political purists who were "willing for the State to be carried by any means" but objected to party rewards for those who had been "guilty of 'election methods.' " "The men who carried this election, the men who wore red shirts, the men who construed the election law stringently, the men who held the polls, the men who planned the campaign, all these Democrats, are the peers of any man who complains and good enough to be given the best that the party which they put in

23. Lefler and Newsome, *North Carolina*, 561–62; Matthews (ed.), *North Carolina Votes*, 11, 119, 144, 151, 153, 165, 177, 204, 207, 209; *Twelfth Census* (1900), Vol. I, Pt. I, pp. 992–93; Tarboro *Southerner*, August 9, 1900.
24. John B. Powell to Marion Butler, August 6, 1900, Cullen G. Battle to Butler, August 3, 1900, Powell to Butler, August 9, 1900, A. J. Willliams to Butler, August 13, 1900, all in Butler Papers. See also Stephen O. Holmes to Butler, August 6, 1900, W. E. Murphrey to Butler, August 5, 1900, R. Liles to Butler, August 3, 1900, C. A. Cook to Butler, August 3, 1900, all in Butler Papers.

power has to give." On October 11, 1900, the *Ledger* continued its argument: "If votes have ever been counted unfairly, there was justification for it in the awful and horrible conditions that surrounded them, and the wives of those, who did the counting." It was a revealing comment —and hardly the quality of writing one would expect from an advocate of literacy tests.[25]

George H. White reacted to the success of the disfranchisement amendment by deciding to leave his native state. "I cannot live in North Carolina and be a man and be treated as a man," he said in a widely reprinted interview. "In my intercourse with the bar of North Carolina in the past, I have never been made to feel that I was on a different plane with any one else because I was a colored man, but I know I cannot be so any longer." Consequently, White planned to practice law in New York or elsewhere when his term expired.

He made the final decision not to seek reelection sometime about August 20, 1900, giving the press three reasons. His wife's health, he said, had been ruined by the vicious political attacks that had been made upon him. "I have been made the target for those who have been fighting against the negro race in North Carolina, and nothing has been too hard to say of me." White was also certain that the Democrats would deny him a certificate of election even if he were elected, and he did "not care to have a contested election case," knowing, as he did, what that involved. Finally, he said he did not have sufficient means "to carry on a political fight that can only prove expensive."

In renouncing his North Carolina political career, White offered several observations on Negroes in the state and nation. The disfranchising amendment, he said, was "not really political," but rather part of a process of "general degradation of the negro." He predicted that North Carolina would lose fifty thousand black residents in the "next eight or ten years." Although he realized that "the bulk of the colored people" would remain in the South and he disapproved of all-black colonization schemes, he declared: "I advise and encourage the immigration of the negroes of North Carolina to the West and North, but especially to the West." Systematic, prudent migration might make the black population less concentrated, allowing Negroes to "lose themselves among the people of the country" as they acquired farms and homes in the "vast

25. Windsor *Ledger*, September 13, October 11, 1890.

West." A black imperialist, White also saw hope for the Negro in America's expansion: "I believe the conditions of the South will eventually cause many of our people to go to Cuba, Porto Rico, Hawaii, or the Philippines."

The retiring politician expected no salvation for his race in politics. "I do not believe the black man has much relief in any political party. He must paddle his own canoe. He must think for himself and act for himself. Legislation will not help him." He noted a recent speech by Senator Pritchard expressing acceptance of white rule in Negro counties and accused Tarheel white Republicans of wanting the votes of black men but opposing their holding office.[26] Although he was discouraged, White did not renounce the Grand Old Party. Less than a month after his announcement he was campaigning in Ohio for the reelection of William McKinley.[27]

The New York *Times* described White's announcement as "one of the most significant results of the race trouble in North Carolina." White was said to be one of the "best known figures in the Fifty-fifth and Fifty-sixth Congresses," a "good speaker," and the "leader of the colored Republicans of North Carolina." "Some of his speeches during the last session attracted considerable attention, notably one on the lynching question."[28]

The triumph of extremism was virtually complete. Eight members of the Republican district committee—five black and three white—met on September 14 for the futile task of choosing a congressional nominee. Joseph John Martin, sixty-six-year-old Tarboro postmaster, won the nomination on the second ballot without receiving a single white vote— as the Democratic press was quick to note. The choice had been between Martin and another white man; George White did not even attend the committee session. A genial, popular man, Martin had been active in Republican politics since Reconstruction, serving two terms as district solicitor in the Second Judicial District, as well as representing

26. New York *World* quoted in Charlotte *Daily Observer*, August 28, 1900; New York *Times*, August 26, 1900.

27. Washington (D.C.) *Bee*, September 15, 1900.

28. New York *Times*, August 26, 1900. "Now let M. Butler follow the example of White," said the Tarboro *Southerner* in response to White's decision. The *Southerner* (August 30, 1900) denied that abuse of White had anything to do with his wife's illness.

the First Congressional District in the House for most of the Forty-seventh Congress. The Tarboro *Southerner* greeted Martin's nomination with the comment that the committee had "probably selected the best man in [the] party. But Kitchin will beat him all the same."[29]

Claude Kitchin went through the motions of a vigorous campaign, though he did not expect large crowds to turn out to hear him, with the disfranchisement question settled and the November congressional result a foregone conclusion. He showed not the slightest consciousness of contradiction as he alternated appeals for freedom and white supremacy. In a major speech in Wilson, he devoted the first portion of his remarks to the district's Negro postmasters, "as one of the terrible evils of the McKinley administration." He then denounced imperialism, pleading "for human liberty wherever the American flag floated." According to a journalist's summary "he said he would stand by Bryan in hurling down the flag where it covered depotism, oppression, subjection." Speaking of events in the Philippines (but not North Carolina) he said: "You may call it imperialism, subjection, manifest destiny, or anything else you want to, but it is this: Government without consent of the governed."[30]

George White's last word to his constituents was a circular addressed to "The Executive Committee and Republicans in and for the Second Congressional District" which he issued in the first part of October. Exactly what the circular said is uncertain, for of the three reasons he gave for not running Democratic newspapers noted only the third. This one the opposition played up because White said if he ran again he would not have the "hearty cooperation of many of the white Republicans in the State." He noted that his recommendations regarding second district census officers had been ignored and that no colored enumerators were appointed in the district thanks to Senator Pritchard. In light of the recent state convention, which had "almost entirely ignored" the Negro, and the statements of Pritchard, chairman Holton, H. L. Grant, and others who had suggested legislation preventing Negro officeholding in black counties, White could no longer support the party's state leaders: "I wish

29. Kinston *Daily Free Press*, September 17, 1900; Wilson *Daily News*, September 20, 1900; Tarboro *Southerner*, December 20, September 20, 1900.
30. Claude Kitchin to M. J. Hawkins, September 19, 1900, in Hawkins Papers. Clippings from Raleigh *Morning Post*, October 31, 1900, Wilson *Daily Times*, October 30, 1900, Wilson *Times*, November 2, 1900, all in Kitchin Papers.

to state here and now that I will never follow such leadership again. . . .
I have lost all faith in . . . so-called Republicans that we have at the
head of affairs in our State at this time."[31]

Election day was quiet. Although the Republicans were utterly demoralized and neither candidate had campaigned vigorously, the returns
alleged that as many voters turned out to vote as in the exciting election
of 1898. For the first time a Democrat claimed to have carried the full
potential white vote, as Kitchin defeated Martin 22,901 votes to 12,521.
The Democratic vote was 6,000 ahead of any previous year and in some
counties soared far above the registered white vote. Martin's best performance was in heavily Negro Warren County, where he received 43.2
percent of the vote. These implausible returns were never challenged.
Martin weighed the prospects of an election challenge but it is not
known if he reached a decision before his death December 18, 1900.
The local newspaper suspended politics long enough to describe him as
"kind-hearted" and a "model postmaster."[32]

At the end of twenty-eight years of struggle, peace had come to the
"black second." The district had been redeemed, and the congressman-
elect was the son of old "Buck" Kitchin, the blustery Rebel captain who
had vainly sought the office in 1872. "Yet the price of peace had come
high," wrote Judge Robert W. Winston years later, speaking of the
"peace" that followed disfranchisement. The brother of the creator of
the White Government Unions added: "It cost bloodshed and rioting—
the usual price of white supremacy, whether in Ethiopia or Egypt, in
South Africa or in the Southern states."[33]

Perhaps the old judge was too melodramatic. In the second district,
at least, the suppression of Negro voting was accompanied by very little
violence, though potential violence was an important part of the process. But damage to a community is not measured only in corpses and
gunfire. It costs something for a community to honor men who have
justified systematic lying, who owe their success to fraud. H. G. Connor
wrote to his friend George Howard in the first few days of the new
century, observing that it did not require "much acumen" to perceive
that the struggle for white supremacy had not brought forth "an over-

31. Clipping from the Scotland Neck *Commonwealth*, October 11, 1900, in Kitchin
Papers. Windsor *Ledger*, October 25, 1900.
32. Tarboro *Southerner*, November 15, December 20, 1900.
33. Robert W. Winston, *It's a Far Cry* (New York, 1937), 238.

abundant supply of political saintliness." "Yet I think there are true, faithful men who hope and work for better and higher things," he wrote optimistically.[34]

A sensitive, responsible, well-intentioned man who might have done much to seek better, higher things had already resolved to leave the state, and his life is a symbol of more than the tragedy of early twentieth century southern Negroes. "I cannot live in North Carolina and be a man and be treated as a man," he had said. An era—an entire age—of retreat and accommodation could only reply that his definition of manhood must have been wrong.

34. H. G. Connor to George Howard, January 15, 1901, in Connor Papers.

PART FIVE

Conclusions

Chapter 17

SCHOOLS, COURTS, AND WHITE SUPREMACY

THE "WHITE SUPREMACY" EXCITEMENT cost second district Negroes more than their votes. Although Democratic orators had denounced the corruption, ignorance, and insolence of black voters and leaders, the basic issue went beyond electoral behavior. In effect, North Carolina's ratification of the disfranchising amendment validated a general process of Negro degradation already underway. The political life of the "black second," in other words, was not an isolated charade with little significance for ordinary people. The same themes that animated the political arena, with its patronage wrangles, chaotic conventions, and complicated bargains, were reflected in other areas ranging from religion and agriculture to railway travel. The practical implications of the electoral struggles are nowhere clearer, perhaps, than in the routine business of punishing crime and educating school children.

The district's two most important public institutions were the court and the school. Even the most ill-informed citizen, who cared not at all about the tariff, civil service, railroad rates, or even the party label of the local postmaster, sensed the significance of the legal system, with its promise of security and just deserts, and of the schools, the most visible of local expenses. The justice and education systems illustrated the substantial stakes of power in the "black second"—and the relevance of politics to the general pattern of race relations.

The two systems were alike in several ways. Both courts and schools were locally centered institutions, with many basic decisions made at the county or district level. Congressional politics had little direct connection to the functioning of these systems, though second district representatives did seek federal aid to education and, in one case, federal action against lynching. But indirectly the congressional district had

315

important ties to local government, especially to the courts and schools. One connection was through the political leaders of both parties who emerged from the legal system. Of the ten men who served in the House from 1870 to 1900, five were lawyers (including one prosecuting attorney), one was a judge, and another a sheriff. Three of the four black congressmen had been teachers, though James O'Hara and George White subsequently turned to law. For the Republicans especially, with their limited pool of experienced leaders, courthouse and classroom served as essential minor leagues, supplying the candidates for wider arenas. If the normal functioning of either the congressional polity or the lower-level education and justice systems was disrupted, the results could not be isolated. Thus it is no surprise that both education and administration of justice follow the pattern of congressional politics, with sharp contractions of Negro opportunity in each area at the end of the Bourbon equilibrium, followed by brief revivals of influence in the fusion era.

The legal system in the Second Congressional District had three tiers, the highest being more democratic and open to black influences than the two lower levels. Superior court judges, presiding over multi-county judicial districts, served eight-year terms and depended upon popular election for their positions. During Reconstruction each district elected its own judge, but as part of the Democratic undoing of Reconstruction, superior court judges were elected on a statewide basis after 1876. In this way, Republican districts would have Democratic judges as long as the Democracy was able to control the state as a whole. (There was no abrupt Democratic sweep of the judgeships, however, as the Republican judges elected in 1874 continued in office until 1882.) The state prosecutor also owed his place to an election but, unlike the superior court judges, was chosen by the district in which he served. Thus, Democrats were not able totally to exclude Republicans from this important office in the period from 1882 to 1894.[1]

Much less subject to popular control was the lowest level of the judicial fraternity, the local magistrate. An elected official during Reconstruction, the magistrate (justice of the peace) was appointed by the state legislature in the nearly two decades from 1877 to 1896. Besides

1. Henry G. Connor and Joseph B. Chesire, *The Constitution of the State of North Carolina Annotated* (Raleigh, 1911), liii, liv.

judging minor civil and criminal cases, the magistrates, as a board, elected the county commissioners under the Democratic system of centralized local government. Armed with a post-Reconstruction legislative authorization, the board of magistrates also sometimes created an intermediate county court, the inferior court, between the magistrate's court and the superior court. This court was one step further removed from the electoral process, for it was established (or abolished) at the will of the board of magistrates, who also chose its judges.[2]

The courts had the assistance of a number of law enforcement officials, ranging from the county sheriff to township constables. In the region's few towns a handful of policemen, often poorly paid and ununiformed, also attempted to restrain lawbreakers. Even after Reconstruction the voters continued to select the sheriff and local constables. Town police were appointed by the town commissioners.

Judged by the standards of the nineteenth-century South, the legal system allowed a remarkable degree of black participation, especially in the Second Judicial District, which included Warren, Halifax, Northampton, Edgecombe, Bertie, and Craven. For sixteen years, from 1878 to 1894, Negro Republicans served as district solicitor, one of the most significant judicial positions held by any black American of the time. When John H. Collins first won the post, white Democrats were shocked by the victory of an obscure, inexperienced Negro, but by the time George H. White had reached the end of his second term, in 1894, many whites were ready to admit that a black man could be a competent solicitor.[3]

Collins may have been something of a figurehead, guided by a white lawyer who helped him capture the Republican nomination. "He makes the bills and Mr. [J. C. L.] Harris does the pleading," reported a Raleigh Negro in 1880. On his first official visit to Warrenton, the local newspaper described Collins as "a young man of quiet manners" but noted that Harris "transacted most of the business for him." When Collins took matters into his own hands he did not do well, if an 1881 comment in the Kinston *Journal* is reliable: "The colored solicitor is not a competent prosecutor. He is slow and inaccurate, and not able to compete

2. *Laws and Resolutions of the State of North Carolina, 1876–77* (Raleigh, 1877), 250–55, 562.
3. See 64, 207 herein.

either in scholarship or piney woods sense with [other] members of the bar."[4]

George White was occasionally described as "insolent" or "familiar" but never incompetent. "Solicitor White says that notwithstanding his color and his politics have been different from most of the lawyers and all the Judges in the courts, his associations with them have been of the most pleasant character," said the Scotland Neck *Democrat* at the end of White's tenure in office. "He has been impartial in his work, showing neither favors to his own race nor bitterness towards whites."[5]

Negroes served on juries throughout the period, though even during Reconstruction they were seldom represented in proportion to their numbers in the population. For the superior court's 1873 spring term in Edgecombe, ten of the thirty-six jurors drawn for the first week were black, whereas half of the eighteen for the second week were Negroes. The next year the Tarboro newspaper complained that the Republican judge had pressured county authorities to put more blacks on the jury lists and that the county faced the "disgrace" of a grand jury that was five-eighths Negro. Only eleven of the thirty-six men on the Warren jury list for the 1874 spring term were black, and six of the eighteen jurors for the second week were black, despite the fact that Negroes constituted 70 percent of the county's population. Low as these figures may seem, they were infinitely better than the records of some North Carolina counties. In Carteret County, adjoining Jones and Craven counties to the south, no Negro had ever served on a jury as late as 1877, and when a Republican judge compelled the sheriff to call a few black men for jury duty, the grand jury indicted him for "malfeasance and corruption in office."[6]

Strangely enough, as more and more blacks acquired education and property, the number of Negroes on juries declined. At one term of the superior court in 1879 in Lenoir only two of the thirty-six men on the jury list were black. The jurors for the August, 1880, term of the Edge-

4. *Exodus Report*, 251; Warrenton *Gazette*, September 13, 1878; Kinston *Journal*, June 16, 1881. A correspondent of the Wilmington *Post* (January 17, 1879) said Collins showed "much ability in drawing out bottom facts in the examination of witnesses."

5. Scotland Neck *Democrat*, November 22, 1894. On White's career as solicitor, see Chapter 11.

6. Tarboro *Southerner*, March 20, 1873; Tarboro *Enquirer-Southerner*, May 1, 1874; Warrenton *Gazette*, July 24, 31, 1874; Wilmington *Post*, November 2, 1877.

combe inferior court included only six Negroes from a total of twenty-nine. Vance County's Negro majority was represented by five men on the list of thirty-six jurors for the first week of the October, 1887, term of the superior court. After the late 1880s, as race relations deteriorated rapidly, black jurors became even fewer. Only one of the fifty-four jurors for the two weeks of an 1892 superior court session in Northampton was a Negro, and this was at a time when George White prosecuted state cases. Twenty-five men and four blacks were jurors for the January, 1893, session of the Warren inferior court.[7] When fusion politics revived black influence in civic life, jury service was affected along with more political offices. "We have a jury box that seems to be crowded with negroes," complained a Kinston editor in 1898. "We have the humiliating spectacle of negroes sitting around the court room to be called into the box as talismen [sic] and of seeing their expectations gratified."[8]

Black magistrates, after being a significant minority during Reconstruction, virtually disappeared between 1880 and 1895, only to reach their greatest number during the fusion years. The first session of the general assembly after constitutional changes ended the popular election of justices of the peace did appoint some Republican magistrates, both black and white, in Republican counties. At least eight Negroes, representing the counties of Warren, Halifax, Edgecombe, and Craven, were appointed to two-year terms as magistrates by the legislature of 1876–1877. The only black justices appointed after that received office at the hands of Republican clerks of the superior court, who had the power to fill vacancies among the magistrates. Between 1882 and 1886, for example, the Republican clerk in Lenoir appointed three black magistrates.[9]

In the Bourbon equilibrium years, a few Democrats supported the value of black representation among the magistrates. When Frank

7. Kinston *Journal*, March 13, 1879; Tarboro *Southerner*, July 15, 1880; Henderson *Gold Leaf*, September 22, 1887; Goldsboro *Headlight*, September 16, 1891; Lasker *Patron and Gleaner*, November 10, 1892; Warrenton *Gazette*, November 18, 1892.

8. Kinston *Daily Free Press*, October 1, 1898.

9. I am aware of the following black magistrates appointed by the Democratic legislature in 1877: W. A. Boyd, Wilson Hicks, and Mansfield Thornton (Warren); J. A. White and J. T. Reynolds (Halifax); Frank Whitted (Edgecombe); Willis D. Pettipher and E. R. Dudley (Craven). For the three blacks appointed by W. W. Dunn in Lenoir between 1882 and 1886, see Kinston *Free Press*, November 1, 1888.

Whitted was appointed a magistrate in 1877 it was with the endorsement of the whites of Lower Conetoe township in Edgecombe, including leading Democrats. They felt no threat to the social pattern, apparently, in having a black as one of the township's three justices. Twenty-one Warren County Democrats petitioned the legislature in 1881, requesting that ten Negro justices be appointed in order to maintain the "most friendly relations" that existed between colored Republicans and the county's Democrats in local affairs. The petitioners asserted "that we the Democrats shall feel injured in our County interests" if the legislature excluded blacks as magistrates.[10]

Similar pragmatic considerations governed the employment of Negro policemen. As late as 1883 half of Tarboro's four-man force was black, and in the 1890s Populists attempted to blunt the force of Democrats' race appeals by reminding voters of the fact. In response to a question from a third-party man, the editor of the Tarboro *Southerner* admitted that Democratic boards of town commissioners had employed Negro policemen for many years, but he argued that there had been ample justification: "Their reason for doing so was the large negro population of the town made it necessary for the proper policing of the town. A negro could get about among his fellows, spy upon the haunts of the lawless with greater effectiveness than a white man."[11]

The most glaring shortcoming of southern legal systems in the late nineteenth century was the existence of frequent and rarely punished mob actions against Negroes accused of crime or misbehavior. If the counties of the Second Congressional District are judged by the frequency of lynching within their borders, the area's system of justice appears reasonably good—again, in comparison with other parts of the South. But although lynchings seldom occurred in the second district, public opinion grew more comfortable with the notion that certain circumstances justified lynch law, and it is no coincidence that such opinions grew with the increasingly severe racial tension of the later years of the period. There was no consensus in favor of lynching, even in the late 1890s, however, as many people were ambivalent and incon-

10. Tarboro *Southerner*, April 6, 1877; N.C. General Assembly, Legislative Papers, 1881, Petition for colored magistrates from twenty-one Warren County Democrats.
11. Tarboro *Southerner*, March 29, 1883, September 1, 1892. See also May 14, 1875.

sistent on the subject, condemning mob law in the abstract but condoning specific, close-at-hand examples of it.

Thus the Henderson *Gold Leaf* offered qualified criticism of lynching on April 14, 1887: "The pulpits and common schools, as well as the courts, must teach respect for and submission to the law, and then lynch law must follow the code duello into oblivion." But the same newspaper, a few months later, reprinted the comment of a Piedmont newspaper which defended the lynching of a Negro "for one of the most heinous of all crimes." In 1888 the *Gold Leaf* reported the death of three Negroes in Oxford (none of them accused of the unnameable crime) at the hands of a mob that included blacks and seemed to offer an excuse for vigilantism: "The laxity of the law, the various technicalities by which the ends of justice are defeated, are more responsible for the lynchings that occur than anything else."[12]

The killing of Ben Hart, a "half-witted, ignorant boy" from Edgecombe, was the most publicized example of lynch law in the twenty-eight-year history of the "black second." His death in 1887 elicited comment from a number of prominent men in the district, both black and white, including Josephus Daniels, James O'Hara, and John C. Dancy. According to the report Daniels wrote for his newspaper, the *State Chronicle*, Hart attempted to rape a beautiful fifteen-year-old white girl, a member of a highly respected Edgecombe family. Hiding in a "piece of woods" about a mile from Tarboro, Hart had waited for the girl to come by, then rushed out naked with a bag over his head "and grasped her in his arms." A child who was walking with the girl ran for help as the victim screamed and scratched and succeeded in tearing the bag from her attacker's face. "Some negroes near by heard the cries, ran to the rescue, and saved the young lady, although she was badly choked and bruised, with her clothes torn into rags." Hart was arrested and incarcerated in the Tarboro jail to await trial, but the superior court judge, learning of lynching threats, ordered him quietly moved to the jail in the nearby town of Williamston. What followed was "the coolest, most deliberate, daring and well-planned expedition for lynching a scoundrel known in the annals of the State," as Daniels put it.

12. Henderson *Gold Leaf*, April 14, September 22, 1887, September 6, 1888.

Several hundred disguised, masked men, using a commandeered railroad construction train for transportation, rode to Williamston, broke into the jail, and seized Hart. After taking him back to the scene of the incident, the mob hanged him ("Who will say that it was not the work of patriots and true husbands, fathers, and brothers?" asked Daniels.), and someone attached the following message to the Negro's corpse: "We hang this man, not in passion, but calmly and deliberately, with a due sense of the responsibility we assume. We take executive power in this case and hang this man in accordance with the unwritten law of the land, because the written law provides no penalty adequate to the crime. And be it understood, we who have done this act will repeat it under similar circumstances." The statement was signed "People's Committee."[13]

Daniels said the lynching was "endorsed on all sides" (meaning, of course, among white people) and joined in the endorsement himself. "It is always . . . to be regretted," he said, "when men take the execution of the law in their own hands," since the "safety of society" depended on "standing by law." "But we also know that there is no protection for our women unless summary justice follows upon all violations, or attempts, of their persons," he added. "There is no man in North Carolina who surpasses me in love of law, or who deplores resorts to violence more. I think that a mob can rarely be trusted to do a wise thing. . . . I have never in my seven years experience in journalism known a case of lynching which has met my approval except this one."[14]

Under the heading "And You Too Edgecombe," John C. Dancy published an editorial in the Star of Zion expressing deep regret for the lynching. Edgecombe had had a good reputation among North Carolina counties, Dancy said, never having suffered from Ku Klux Klan activi-

---

13. Raleigh State Chronicle, May 12, 1887. I know of only two other cases of lynching in the second district during this period. In 1883 a Negro who allegedly attempted to rape a white girl was lynched in Windsor by an interracial mob. Warrenton Gazette, April 20, 1883. A Negro accused of a Bertie County murder was lynched in 1890 in the neighboring county of Hertford. Windsor Ledger, December 24, 1890. In the year after disfranchisement there was a lynching near LaGrange (Lenoir) and another in Jackson (Northampton). See Walter S. Lockert II, "Lynching in North Carolina, 1888–1906" (M.A. thesis, University of North Carolina, 1972), 128. Northampton County Miscellaneous Records ("Lynching of Jeter Mitchell" File), North Carolina Department of Archives and History.

14. Raleigh State Chronicle, May 12, 1887.

ties or political murders. "But new blood has gone into the county during the past few years," lamented Dancy, a native of the county, "and incited the populace to deeds of violence . . . hitherto unknown." The editorial noted that the Tarboro *Southerner* condoned the crime and had warned the Negroes to keep quiet about it. The *Star of Zion* offered other advice: "We say, colored men, speak out and denounce the atrocity, and if you die, die like men."[15]

Since the killing of Hart was the "first case of the kind that had ever occurred in the county," Edgecombe's Negro state Senator R. S. Taylor devoted considerable effort to seeking punishment for the lynchers. He assisted the county coroner in a three-day public examination of witnesses—proceedings attended by hundreds of blacks—but they were unable to discover the identity of the culprits. More than two months after the death of Hart, Taylor received a threatening letter which ordered him to cease discussing the lynching or meet the same fate himself. The anonymous writer told the black legislator he ought to approve of the lynching, rather than condemn it.[16]

James O'Hara's Enfield *Progress* thought "the good people of Edgecombe" would regret the lynching "when reason resumed her sway." He warned that blacks might respond in kind to white lawlessness. "There is always great danger that the calling into action [of] unlawful methods as a remedy to existing evil will give rise to greater evil. This appeal to lynch law may lead to incendiarism, or other great crimes. Then those who sowed the wind will reap the whirlwind."[17] A white editor replied that the hanging of Hart was not an attack on Negroes in general, "but merely a prompt and sure death to despoilers." "As for the consequences . . . the good people of the county are prepared for whirlwinds, incendiarism or anything of the kind."[18]

Yet at other times second district newspapers issued clear, strong attacks on lynch law. After a white man was lynched in the western part of the state the Kinston *Free Press* commented: "Some cases of crime are very aggravating . . . but it is murder to lynch a man, therefore the lynchers are themselves criminals. . . . It is better that

15. Salisbury *Star of Zion,* May 26, 1887.
16. Raleigh *Signal,* July 28, 1887.
17. Enfield *Progress* quoted in unidentified clipping in James O'Hara Papers.
18. Unidentified clipping in O'Hara Papers.

many guilty men escape rather than one innocent man be punished." The same incident, little more than two years after the Hart murder, elicited an editorial in a Tarboro newspaper entitled "Lynch Law a Menace." When a Negro was lynched in Asheville in 1891, the *Free Press* denounced the action as "not at all warranted by the circumstances" and "murder."[19]

But the image of a Negro raping a white woman could set ordinarily reasonable white men raving. "There will be no lynchings of colored men if they do not commit crimes," wrote Kinston journalist W. S. Herbert in 1892, "but if colored or any other men commit outrages upon the pure white women of the glorious south the true men of this sunny clime will not wait the law's delay for the punishment of such brutes." An 1897 editorial suggested that Negro rapes of white women were on the increase and asked "Is not the prompt lynching of the rapist, whether white or black, the best method of lessening this horror?"[20]

The lynching-rape hysteria was another sign of the general white fear, in the last decade of the nineteenth century, of improving Negro status, a fear that manifested itself in increasing hostility to black participation in politics and civic life and, occasionally, in outright communal violence. Certainly the frenzied dedication to swift, summary justice for violators of white female purity was seldom present in earlier years. No one was lynched, for example, in the sensational 1878 Worley murders case in Wayne County, although the crime involved rape and multiple murders and the victims were white. The Negroes accused of this atrocity were defended by Swift Galloway, a leading white lawyer and active Democrat, and George T. Wassom, a black Republican politician and attorney. Two white Republicans and Goldsboro's most distinguished Democratic attorney prosecuted the case. In later years there might have been talk that black "brutes" ought not to benefit from the "law's delay," but such thinking did not prevail in 1878.[21]

Twenty-four years later, after a black alleged rapist had been killed in Wayne County, the coroner's jury issued a verdict that illustrated the shift in opinion. They declared that the Negro had come to his death "by gun shot wounds, inflicted by parties unknown to the jury, obviously

19. Kinston *Free Press*, October 24, 1889; Tarboro *Southerner*, November 7, 1889; Kinston *Free Press*, October 1, 1891.
20. Kinston *Free Press*, June 9, 1892, August 14, 1897.
21. Goldsboro *Messenger*, May 6, 9, 1878. See also *Exodus Report*, 137–38.

by an outraged public acting in defense of their homes, wives, daughters and children." The jurors added: "In view of the enormity of the crime committed by said Tom Jones, alias Frank Hill, we think they would have been recreant to their duty as good citizens had they acted otherwise."[22]

If lawlessness was the enemy of the legal system, the public schools were combating ignorance. The task was simply immense, even compared to the job of securing law and order. To make a rough comparison, it was as if the courts had to deal with a massive crime wave in which Negro brigands or white vigilantes dominated most neighborhoods, and elderly, half-armed constables struggled to contain them. For widespread, persisting illiteracy was the fundamental problem confronting the district's public schools, and a poorly equipped and inadequately staffed system made slow headway toward a solution.

In nine of the twelve second district counties, the majority of black men could not read in 1900. The illiteracy rates for Negroes of voting age exceeded 62 percent in Edgecombe and Halifax. White illiteracy, which could not be explained by the heritage of slavery, ranged from 13 to 26 percent. (The corresponding figures for Ohio, a representative northern state, were 3.2 percent for whites and 22 percent for blacks.)[23]

The depth of the educational poverty, even after considerable advance, is suggested by the fact that North Carolina's educational expenditure for 1900 was only $1.65 for each school-age child. In testimony before the Industrial Commission in 1900, Congressman George H. White noted that the average public school term in North Carolina was sixty-two days, a figure that obscured the full weakness of the schools at the bottom of the scale, the small rural schools. Attendance was not compulsory and the average child attended school little more than four weeks per year, according to Louis Harlan's *Separate and Unequal*, a study of racism and public education in the South Atlantic states. The average annual salary for all North Carolina teachers was $82.87; for Negro women the average dropped to less than $65.[24]

---

22. James Elbert Cutler, *Lynch-Law: An Investigation into the History of Lynching in the United States* (New York, 1905), 264.
23. Computed from *Twelfth Census* (1900), Vol. I, Pt. I, pp. 992–93.
24. *Report of the Industrial Commission*, X, 424; Louis R. Harlan, *Separate and Unequal: Public School Campaigns and Racism in the Southern Seaboard States, 1901–1915* (New York, 1968), 9–10, 13.

It was not that blacks were apathetic toward education. The Warrenton *Gazette* observed in 1882 that, "relatively speaking," the Negroes were "taking more interest in education and surpassing us in gaining the rudiments of an education. They go to school every chance they get and shell out their money freely to pay the teachers." A survey of landlords, tenants, and laborers taken in 1886–1887 found similar opinions. "The colored take more interest in education than the whites," observed a Vance County man, and a Jones landlord said: "The parents of white children are oftentimes very negligent about the education of their children, and do not take advantage of even the poor opportunities that they have."[25]

Despite this black enthusiasm for learning, however, educational progress remained unsatisfactory. A local perspective vividly demonstrates the reasons for frustration. In 1881 in Warren County, where blacks constituted more than 70 percent of the population, there were ten school-houses for whites and twenty-one for Negroes. Most buildings for either race were "miserable log huts," generally not county owned, and on the average valued at under $50 each. As part of an upgrading program, many schools were suspended in 1883 so that operating expenses could be devoted to building new schoolhouses. The county superintendent of education reported fifty schools in that year, with an average value of $151 for white schools and $144 for black schools. In 1884 the county boasted thirty-one schools for each race, though a number of black schools were unable to find teachers and nearly half the children in the county did not attend school at all. The Warrenton *Gazette* noted that the local authorities had voted money for ten more schoolhouses, and when these were constructed all but three of the county's school districts would have a county-owned building. All this was "gratifying and wonderful progress" in the free school system.[26]

Education actually retrogressed in Edgecombe, another heavily black county. Under the leadership of William P. Mabson, a black teacher-politician serving as county school examiner, the public schools enrolled

25. Warrenton *Gazette*, January 13, 1882; N.C. Bureau of Labor Statistics, *First Annual Report*, 136, 100.

26. Warrenton *Gazette*, February 22, 1884; North Carolina, *Biennial Report of the Superintendent of Public Instruction, 1883–84* (Raleigh, 1885), 211, 215. The Superintendent's Report and this issue of the Warrenton *Gazette* give slightly different figures for the number of schools in 1884.

55 percent of the school-age children in the 1876–1877 school year. Thirteen years later, in 1890, fewer than 40 percent of the potential students attended school, even for a few days, and the absolute number of students was lower than in 1877. Black education suffered in particular. Although per capita expenditure for white teachers was markedly higher than for blacks in 1877, Negroes could at least find comfort in the fact that the bulk of funds went to them. In 1890 blacks received less than half the school fund, though Negro students were twice as numerous as white students. Per pupil expenditure on teacher pay was $4.67 for whites and $1.59 for blacks.[27]

Most counties, however, could report better progress than Edgecombe, and across the district the number of students, teachers, and schoolhouses definitely increased. Whereas only 45 percent of the district's school-age children attended school in 1883, 65 percent had some exposure to public schools in 1901. But the group most in need of educational services, blacks, did not share evenly in this advance, as shown by Table 7. In the nine counties for which there are complete statistics, expenditures for black teachers' salaries rose from $24,000 in 1877 to $36,000 in 1901, but at the same time the money spent for white teachers increased at a rate three times faster. By the first year of the new century, black teachers received less than 40 percent of the salary funds, though 53 percent of the public school pupils were black.[28]

Negroes were often so determined to get an education for their children that they turned to private schools to supplement or replace the meanly funded public schools. "I have never sent one of my children to a public school in North Carolina in my life," said Congressman White, explaining that blacks in many towns had established private schools. In New Bern, the congressman had been principal of a Presbyterian parochial school as well as the public school, and, later, the state normal school. Like prosperous whites, many Negroes did "not care to have their children go into the public school and be mixed up with the kind

27. Computed from *Report of the Superintendent of Public Instruction, 1877*, 50, 53, 56, 59; *Report, 1889–90*, 68, 71–73. The main reason for the wide difference in per pupil expenditure between black and white teachers was the heavier teaching load of black teachers. Almost half the teachers in Edgecombe in 1890 were white, although more than two thirds of the students were Negroes and whites did not teach in black public schools. *Eleventh Census* (1890), Vol. I, Pt. II, p. 83.
28. *Report, 1883–84*, 112–18; *Report, 1900–1901 and 1901–1902*, 90–97.

Table 7   Expenditure for Teachers' Salaries in Nine Counties[a]

	1877	1884	1892	1901
Black	$24,038.50 (55.0%)	31,064.23 (52.2%)	31,997.40 (49.8%)	36,329.00 (39.9%)
White	19,693.12	28,499.91	32,284.98	54,732.60
Total	43,731.62	59,564.14	64,282.38	91,061.60

[a] Figures for Bertie, Craven, Edgecombe, Greene, Halifax, Jones, Northampton, Wayne, Wilson, from *Report of the Superintendent of Public Instruction, 1877*, 49–52; *1883–84*, 206–208; *1891–92*, 27–32; *1900–1901 and 1901–1902*, 85–89.

of pupils that are there." The second district provides a number of examples of private black schools in towns, including Edgecombe Normal School (Tarboro), Baptist-sponsored Shiloh Institute (Warrenton), Goldsboro Normal and Classical Institute, Eastern Academy (New Bern), the A.M.E. institution Kittrell College, with its emphasis on manual training, and many other schools, parochial and nonsectarian, successful and short-lived.[29]

In some cases it is not easy to draw a clear distinction between public and private. Congressman White told the Industrial Commission that in rural areas, "You will find cases where a teacher may teach a school for two months, and the people will feel that they have not done justice to their children, and they may have a little money, and they will run it as a subscription school for a month or two." In other words, any rural private school was "a supplement to the public school, conducted in the same building and by the same teacher after the [public] funds are exhausted."[30]

Whites also turned to private education to fill gaps in the public system. In 1877 and 1878 about a thousand white students attended private schools, many of which offered secondary as well as primary education. Among the most important white private schools were Wilson Collegiate

29. *Report of the Industrial Commission*, X, 425–27; Logan, *Negro in North Carolina*, 150. For a partial listing of Negro private schools, see Hugh Victor Brown, *A History of the Education of Negroes in North Carolina* (Goldsboro, N.C., 1961), 27–40.

30. *Report of the Industrial Commission*, X, 425, 427. For an illustration of this public-private combination, see J. C. Price's diary comments on his experience in Wilson in 1877. Josephine Price Sherrill, "A Negro School-Master of the 1870's," *Journal of Negro Education*, XXX (Spring, 1961), 163–72.

Institute (whose alumni included Josephus Daniels, Charles Aycock, and Fred Woodard), Newbern Academy, established in 1766, and Kinston Collegiate Institute. The number of private students in white schools increased over the years, despite the establishment of public graded schools in a number of towns, and incomplete statistics indicate at least two thousand attending such schools by 1892.[31]

Whether public or private, integrated education was out of the question. Whites sensitive to the dangers of "social equality" instinctively approved separate schools, whereas Negroes were too busy resisting attempts to exclude them from public education altogether to be concerned with integration. William H. Kitchin was not alone in his antipathy to "wasting" money on black education. "We are out of patience," he wrote, "with the educational cranks who are ever and anon calling for more money to educate the negro." Blacks were not grateful for the state-supported insane asylums, normal schools, and other institutions already provided them, Kitchin complained. And there was a widespread feeling among whites that "education spoils the colored people as laborers." In education, as Howard N. Rabinowitz has noted for race relations in general, the issue was between "a policy of exclusion" and one of "segregation."[32]

North Carolina Negroes felt particularly threatened by a movement to separate taxes according to race which flourished in the 1880s and persisted into the twentieth century. In 1880 the general assembly passed a bill allowing Goldsboro to establish two graded schools, one for each race, to be supported by the local taxes of the respective groups. As defenders of the law saw it, the measure simply allowed the whites in Goldsboro to tax themselves above the normal level in order to add to the basic system established by state funds. The general school funds, to which whites contributed far more than blacks, would continue to be distributed impartially to sustain the common school system. Blacks

31. U.S. Department of the Interior, *Report of the Commissioner of Education, 1877* (Washington, D.C., 1877), 420–21; North Carolina, *Report of the Superintendent of Public Instruction, 1891–92,* 64–75.

32. Scotland Neck *Democrat* quoted in Raleigh *Signal,* May 5, 1887; Logan, *Negro in North Carolina,* 140; H. N. Rabinowitz, "From Exclusion to Segregation: Southern Race Relations, 1865–1890," *Journal of American History,* LXIII (September, 1976), 325–50. On the issue of school integration, see William Preston Vaughn, *Schools for All: The Blacks and Public Education in the South, 1865–1877* (Lexington, Ky., 1974).

realized that they would be fatally handicapped if their hopes for graded schools rested on the narrow Negro tax base, and Negro voters helped defeat the Goldsboro scheme in a local election in May, 1880. The plan finally passed in another election a year later.

The legislature of 1883 approved a measure extending the principle of the Goldsboro law, making it possible for the citizens of any school district to vote to divide local school taxes by race. This law, sponsored by Goldsboro Democrat William T. Dortch, a former member of the Confederate senate, led to the establishment of white graded schools in a number of towns. (In Tarboro and New Bern Negroes helped defeat segregated taxation, however.) When the Dortch Act was declared unconstitutional by the state supreme court in 1886, many schools closed. "Some towns, notably Wilson, openly defied the supreme court ruling for years. . . . and some smaller towns such as Kinston converted their public schools to private schools rather than support Negro education." In Goldsboro black and white leaders, including Charles Aycock and George T. Wassom, worked together to win public support for a continuation of the town's graded school on the basis of nondiscriminatory taxation.[33]

Ironically, it was Aycock who later built an anti-Negro campaign upon promises of educational reform and used illiteracy—black but not white—as an excuse to limit the electorate. After 1901 white education expanded dramatically, but according to Harlan, "the Aycock era was one of rapid deterioration in the concept of universal education, and of retrogression in the actual facilities provided for Negro schoolchildren."[34]

The racial polarization which was so clear in the early twentieth century, as some lawmakers called for an end to any support of Negro schools by white taxes, began in the late 1880s when the understandings of the Bourbon equilibrium came unraveled. The educational policies of the eastern black counties anticipated the movement of the entire state. As black political influences waned, counties like Edgecombe, Halifax, or Craven did not hesitate to divide school funds with outrageous inequity. The school system, like the judicial system, reflected the basic change in political life.

33. Logan, *Negro in North Carolina*, 155–58, 160–63; Harlan, *Separate and Unequal*, 47; Orr, *Charles Brantley Aycock*, 70–74; Charles L. Coon, "The Beginnings of the North Carolina City Schools, 1867–1887," *South Atlantic Quarterly*, XII (July, 1913), 235–47.
34. Harlan, *Separate and Unequal*, 110.

Chapter 18

THE LEGACY OF THE SECOND DISTRICT

The machine now was not run by the old Colonels; for they were nearly all gone to their eternal rest. . . . Men of my generation—some younger than I—were come into political management. They had seemed to us hitherto to be commonplace lawyers without clients, editors of newspapers that did not make a profit, hangers-on to legitimate industry. . . . But suddenly they assured us that they were society's most zealous guardians. . . . We were about to be engulfed in a flood of African despotism, they said.

—Nicholas Worth [Walter Hines Page], 1906[1]

Two thousand years ago the proud Romans looked down upon the uncouth Teutons, even as you white men today despise the blacks. And note the result. Ere long the haughty Roman was an humble Italian, grinding an organ, as his monkey, tricked out in cap and bells, was holding out his hand for a penny. Today the despised Teuton is ruling the world.

—Samuel Phillips, 1870[2]

THERE WAS A TONE OF OPTIMISM in James O'Hara's testimony before the Senate exodus committee. Yes, there was prejudice against Negroes in the North Carolina of 1880, the black lawyer told the senators, but less than in the North, and blacks voted freely and were quietly acquiring land. ("There is one thing peculiar about this matter; when a colored man possesses land you cannot get him after he has paid for it to mortgage it; he will mortgage anything else in the world; he will cling to it under all circumstances," O'Hara had said.) Negroes did not always receive justice from the courts, but then "a poor man, or an ignorant man, in any community, is at a disadvantage." O'Hara seemed to take for granted that the rights won by Negroes in Recon-

1. Nicholas Worth [Walter Hines Page], "The Autobiography of a Southerner," *Atlantic Monthly*, 98 (July-October, 1906), 484.
2. Quoted in Winston, *It's a Far Cry*, 84.

331

struction would be permanent. It did not occur to him, apparently, that slow progress—even stagnation—might be replaced by swift deterioration. His confidence in the enduring legacy of Reconstruction led him to declare: "I am one of those who think the American negro ought to be left to work out his own destiny, and that he has been a foundling and a ward too long already."[3]

Two decades later the atmosphere had changed. Writing in 1903, the historian John Spencer Bassett saw "a notable increase in the general opposition to the negro" in the "last five years." "There is today more hatred of whites for blacks and of blacks for whites than ever before," he wrote in the *South Atlantic Quarterly*. James O'Hara's black successor offered similar testimony. Remembering his legislative service of 1881 and 1885, George White touched a note of infinite sadness. Those were years, he said, "when times were better with us than now." "Have you any suggestion for a State law for the benefit of the colored people in your State?" he was asked in 1900. "Yes," he replied, "but wholly without hope."[4] What had happened between 1880 and the turn of the new century to change mild confidence into despair? Negro progress, ironically, was at the heart of the matter, inspiring both optimism and, later, hopelessness.

James O'Hara's 1880 assessment was more than wishful thinking; second district blacks were indeed making headway against powerlessness, poverty, and illiteracy. But their advance created new problems. As Bassett recognized: "It is important for us to note that the progress of the negro has brought him opposition as well as his regression. . . . The advance of the negro in education and economic conditions brings him ever into new conflicts with the white man." George White said much the same thing in 1899 when he attributed the nation's race crisis "more than any other thing" to the Negro's steady progress in the face of oppression. The "tendency on the part of some of us to rise and assert our manhood along all lines" had brought about the change for the worse in race relations.[5]

"Progress" and "advance" are vague words, redolent of such wholly

3. *Exodus Report*, 49–71.
4. John Spencer Bassett, "Stirring Up the Fires of Race Antipathy," *South Atlantic Quarterly*, II (October, 1903), 297, 304; *Report of the Industrial Commission*, X, 430.
5. Bassett, "Race Antipathy," 300; *Congressional Record*, 55th Cong., 3rd Sess., 1124.

material measurements of change as increasing per capita income, longer school terms, and better plumbing. Essential as these things are, black "progress" in the second district had a broader meaning. Any single aspect of material or social "advance" appeared in the larger context of weakening white supremacy—or, to put it another way, increasing black ability to influence community decisions. The confusing, often painful adjustment from a slave society to a free one continued long after emancipation, with each race testing new arrangements to replace the old. The complex, all-pervading relationship of paternalism, which had dominated under slavery, gradually lost its force, leaving only disjointed fragments to influence southern life. In the minds of both black and white, Negro "advance" meant the negation of paternalism—and the rise of a new interdependence. In this sense, men like O'Hara and White were themselves the best symbols of black progress. The growth of black leadership after Reconstruction is one of the most fascinating aspects of the history of the "black second," and, more than that, the most vivid manifestation of increasing black autonomy.

In 1877, as Zebulon Vance returned to the North Carolina governor's chair, black leadership had only begun to develop. Although eight of the seventeen Republicans representing the district in the general assembly were Negroes and twelve black county commissioners held office in six different counties, white Republicans generally controlled party machinery and no blacks served in major county executive offices such as sheriff, clerk of the superior court, and register of deeds. Two of three Republican congressional nominees in the short history of the black district had been white men, and whites held most significant federal patronage positions.

Not until after Reconstruction did black officeholding reach its zenith. Black aspirants won six terms in Congress, and only in 1880 and 1900 was a white Republican the party nominee. The three Negroes elected to the House of Representatives in the post-Reconstruction period illustrated well the changing character of black leadership. They had been born free or were too young to have felt the full rigors of slavery, and unlike their ill-educated predecessor John Hyman, all were professional men, trained in the law, education, or both. The two younger men, Henry Cheatham and George White, graduated from Negro colleges established in the postwar era and entered politics only in the 1880s.

Taken as a group, the three black congressmen symbolized the sort of leadership that might have developed many places in the South had blacks been able to vote without interference in the two decades after Reconstruction.

Success at the congressional level reflected—and stimulated—increased black officeholding at other levels. Black lawyers filled the office of district solicitor for the Second Judicial District from 1878 to 1894, and even distinguished white attorneys like Charles A. Cook and Francis D. Winston could not secure the party nomination for the post. A Negro presided over the district executive committee for the first time from 1880 to 1882. Voters elected black Republican registers of deeds in Warren, Edgecombe, Halifax, Bertie, Northampton, and Vance in the 1880s, though several of the successful candidates lost their offices through legal maneuvers. Representation in the general assembly remained about the same, with eight or more black legislators from the district in every session of the legislature until 1891. Under the Harrison and McKinley administrations, Negroes began holding important patronage jobs, particularly postmasterships, in considerable numbers. Black leadership declined only when the Democrats ended popular election for an office, as in the case of magistrates and county commissioners.

Black success was still Republican success, for in the extensive area of a congressional district (especially this oddly contorted one) victory depended on an organization that could confederate county chieftains and factions, raise campaign expenses, distribute rewards, ordain nominees for lower offices (with their natural interest in getting out the vote and fair elections), and give voters a rhetorical system that inspired allegiance. Powerful white supremacy sentiment in the Democratic party made Negro participation in that organization awkward. In the 1890s, Populists were willing to appeal for Negro votes but seldom rewarded black leaders with office. For most blacks there was little question about political fealty, though they often complained, like their white brethren of all parties, about patronage and party policy. Indeed, the late nineteenth century was an age of party regularity, and in the second district an ambitious man seldom advanced by being an independent. Republican "bolters" insisted that they were "regular" and usually won only when bold assertion made their claims plausible. As popular a leader as George White failed when he challenged the regular state senate candidate in 1882, despite the fact the organization man was a white running in a black county.

The "Republican party" did not mean, of course, a centralized, Washington-run machine. It was rather a local organization, operated for largely local purposes, preoccupied with county and district affairs and only occasionally looking beyond North Carolina. It cannot be adequately studied from a national or even a regional perspective.[6] Year in and year out, this local political organization, inconsistent and opportunistic as it often was, more strongly defended black interests than any other group. As a biracial institution, the party was able to treat as political disputes situations that otherwise would have been purely racial conflicts. Ordinary pressure for a fair election was less likely to be seen as "Negro impudence" if it came from white Squire Smith as well as colored Teacher Jones, and their efforts were in behalf of a biracial ticket. But the fragile biracial character of the party was susceptible to deadly attack. In time of crisis, particularly in 1898 and 1900, white supremacists concentrated their attack on the GOP as the vehicle of Negro political aspirations—which it was—and by strident appeals to white solidarity put almost unbearable pressure on the party's white minority in the black belt. Democrats sensed that if they could politically isolate Negroes by driving all whites into one party, suppressing "Negro domination" would be much easier.

History was on the side of the white supremacists. The major tendencies of the last quarter of the century—rising black ability to produce leaders and intermittent but gradually intensifying white pressure for race solidarity—quietly prepared a disaster. Black progress toward autonomy, if that is the term to describe the changing Negro role, also served to isolate blacks, just as their worst enemies desired. As blacks assumed greater control in the Republican party, white supremacists turned progress into a trap, using black success to stir up race hatred and depicting the Democratic party as the only home for "true" white men.

Again and again in the history of the "black second," Democrats

6. George W. Reid overlooks the local structure of the Republican party in his brief article, "Congressman George Henry White: His Major Power Base," *Negro History Bulletin*, XXXIX (March, 1976), 544–54. See the same author's "A Biography of George Henry White, 1852–1918," (Ph.D. dissertation, Howard University, 1974). Reid's dissertation is extremely inaccurate and incomplete and must be used with care.

worked to exacerbate the tensions generated by Negro advance. In the 1880s and 1890s they intensified what might be called "natural" friction between white leaders in the Republican party, many of them veterans of Reconstruction, and the rising generation of new black leaders. Using techniques invented during Reconstruction, molders of white opinion pilloried white Republicans as hypocrites (if they made any concessions to southern prejudice) or traitors (if they offered any criticism of the treatment accorded blacks). Depending on the occasion, a man might be accused of being an insincere manipulator of Negro voters, or a party loyalist bound hand and foot to a black-dominated organization. Despite antiblack features of the Democratic ideology, the party covertly encouraged black power in the Republican party as a way of encouraging factionalism and weakening the enemy. Bribery, deception, and propaganda were tools used to batter away at the fault lines within the GOP.

If losers can reveal as much about history as winners, the white Republicans of the South deserve more study than they have received. To say that many of them were opportunists tainted with racism would be to belabor the obvious. When a Charles R. Thomas, a Lotte Humphrey, a Leonidas Moore abandons a party that has refused to give him high office, the element of self-interest is apparent. What is perhaps more interesting, and ultimately more tragic, is that a man might for twenty-five years attend "Negro conventions," collaborate with black leaders, address primarily Negro audiences, crusade for honest elections, support black candidates—and then renounce it all in the upheaval of 1898 to 1900. Was a man like Hiram L. Grant merely an opportunist? As a Yankee commanding Negro troops, as a dedicated supporter of Wayne County's usually unsuccessful GOP, as a leader in the fusion movement, he had not shown particular fear of unpopular stands or partisan abuse. Yet in 1900 he denounced George White and complained about the educated few among Negroes who sought offices, asserting that he had always opposed black officeholding.

Only with an effort of the imagination can the modern observer grasp the complete defeat white Republicans felt. The tides of contemporary events were unmistakable; in the struggles of the past quarter century the men who had defended Negroes had been wrong. The struggle was coming to a final end with white supremacists triumphant, northern opinion unconcerned, and the national government impotent. The Republicans suffered the kind of massive defeat that leaves the vanquished apathetic, wondering if they have been wrong all along. Their defeat was something like that endured by prohibitionists in the 1930s or by American defenders of South Vietnam in the 1970s. In such circumstances, most white Republicans failed to notice the much greater tragedy of George White and other black leaders.

It would be unrealistic to expect a majority of ordinary men to possess the detached, calm historical perspective of John Spencer Bassett. "In spite of our race feeling, of which the writer has his share," he commented, "Negroes will win equality at some time. We cannot remove them, we cannot kill them, we cannot prevent them from advancing in civilization. They are now very weak; some day they will be stronger. . . . I do not know just what form the conflict will take. It may be merely a political conflict; it may be more than that. I am persuaded that it is in many respects the old conflict between Roman plebs and Roman patricians over again." But, he added optimistically, "it ought to be shorter than that struggle and the issue ought to be more fortunate than the issue of the Roman conflict; for American life is richer and better than Roman life."[7]

Equally rare was the reaction of Thurston Titus Hicks, a lawyer and former Democratic mayor of Henderson. Hicks joined the Republican party after the election of 1900, explaining that "the Democratic party of North Carolina jumped the fences of Constitution and law and put itself at large." Unlike most white men, he refused to register to vote under the grandfather clause but insisted that he be given a literacy examination. "There are only two such cases known in Vance County," recorded a local historian.[8]

For a black and Republican stronghold, the second district produced a remarkable number of important white leaders. Former Confederate General Matt W. Ransom, party leader from eastern Carolina and United States senator from 1872 to 1895, was born in Warren County and lived most of his life in Northampton. Furnifold M. Simmons, who

7. Bassett, "Race Antipathy," 304.
8. Samuel Thomas Pearce, *"Zeb's Black Baby": Vance County North Carolina, A Short History* (Henderson, N.C., 1955), 411.

served for thirty years in the Senate, was first elected to Congress in 1886 as representative of the second district. For years North Carolina's most powerful journalist, Josephus Daniels began his career as editor of the Wilson *Advance*, early evincing the fascination with politics that was to carry him to a place in Woodrow Wilson's cabinet. The House majority leader during the Wilson administration, Claude Kitchin, was the immediate successor of George White and the son of a three-time Democratic nominee in the "black second." Charles B. Aycock, North Carolina's famous "progressive," "educational governor," was a native of Wayne County. Henry G. Connor of Wilson County served as speaker of the North Carolina house and justice of the state supreme court, and "Fighting Judge" Walter Clark, a man with long service on the North Carolina Supreme Court, including twenty-one years as chief justice, came from Halifax County. Elias Carr, leader in the Farmer's Alliance and governor from 1893 to 1897, hailed from Edgecombe.

What was there about the second district that produced this strange profusion of eminent white Democrats? What kind of "soil" grows a Daniels, a Simmons, and an Aycock? These questions must be taken into account in any conclusions about the history of the second district.

V. O. Key observed, in his classic study *Southern Politics in State and Nation*, that the whites of southern black belts have historically exercised influence far out of proportion to their numbers: "Although the whites of the black belts are few in number, their unity and political skill have enabled them to run a shoestring into decisive power at critical junctures in southern political history."[9] The surprisingly large number of important white leaders from the "black second" may simply be a specific illustration of the general principle noted by Key.

Yet if the second district's unusual production of white leaders illustrates a typical pattern, the district certainly was irregular in meeting its quota. When Elias Carr won the governorship in 1892, no second district Democrat had been nominated or elected to the position in thirty years. Then twice in three elections, in 1892 and 1900, the Democratic standard-bearer came from the second district. Indeed, the nominee in 1908 was a transplanted second district man, William W. Kitchin, the son of "Buck" Kitchin.

9. V. O. Key, Jr., *Southern Politics in State and Nation* (New York, 1949), 5–6.

It was in the decade following 1892 that the district's sons most notably rose to prominence. Furnifold Simmons oversaw the Democratic victories of 1892, 1898, and 1900 as state party chairman and in 1901 he entered the Senate. Josephus Daniels obtained control of the *News and Observer* in 1894 and two years later replaced Matt Ransom as North Carolina's Democratic national committeeman. H. G. Connor served as speaker of the 1899 house, and Charles Aycock captured the governorship in 1900, the same year Claude Kitchin was elected to represent the second district. In 1902 Walter Clark became chief justice and Connor was elected associate justice.

What at first appears to be a remarkable region can be more correctly defined as a remarkable political *generation* from that region. The question then becomes "Why did this particular group of men rise to power in the 1890s and at the turn of the century?" It is not simply a matter of a small region providing a disproportionate number of the state's leaders.

Of the leaders emerging from the second district, only Connor, Simmons, Aycock, and Daniels can be considered members of the same generation in a chronological sense, the four men having been born between 1852 and 1862. But all of them, with the possible exception of Kitchin, the youngest, came of age politically in the 1880s.[10] Josephus Daniels was not twenty-one until 1883, the year after he purchased the Wilson *Advance*. In 1885 he became editor of the Raleigh *State Chronicle* and two years later was awarded the state's printing contract, a coveted political plum. H. G. Connor won his first election in 1884 as a candidate for the state senate, beginning a ten-year tenure as superior court judge the next year. After twelve years of private law practice in Raleigh, Walter Clark was appointed to the superior court bench in 1885. In 1886 Furnifold Simmons, who was little more than a year younger than George White, won by a plurality in a three-way congressional race. In the same year, Elias Carr began his rise in agrarian organizations as state delegate to the St. Paul Farmers' Convention. Charles Aycock, an 1880 graduate of the University of North Carolina, served as Democratic presidential elector (and campaign orator) in the election of 1888. If Claude Kitchin had no important political role in the 1880s, his political philosophy was certainly molded by the atmosphere

10. For biographical material on these men, see *Dictionary of American Biography*.

of the late eighties. Always an intense partisan, the elder Kitchin traveled across the state in 1888, the year Claude graduated from Wake Forest, speaking for the Democracy in his famous fiery way. Family friend Spier Whitaker managed the party's statewide efforts as party chairman.

Most of these men, in other words, began to succeed in politics at a time when Negro political influence was at its height. Their views of politics were not shaped by personal experience in the Civil War (except for teen-aged officer Walter Clark), nor did they have any important role to play during Reconstruction. Rather they were men maturing during the Bourbon equilibrium, familiar with an aggressive, rising black leadership class and exposed to a variety of notions on the permanent role of Negroes in southern society. They knew of the compromises, bargains, and inconsistent understandings which underlay the era's *modus vivendi* between black and white. The reactions of men like Simmons, Daniels, and Kitchin, each of whom reached voting age at a time when a Negro represented the district, helped determine the ultimate direction of a period of confusing and uneven promise.

When in the 1890s white supremacy, Negro domination, and race solidarity became paramount issues, it was not surprising that men from the section where the "problem" was most acute spoke for the entire party and state. Quite simply, Simmons, Daniels, Aycock, and Kitchin (and other men to a lesser degree) rode the race issue into power. After they passed from power, the Negro problem "solved," the counties of the second district never again produced so many state and national leaders.

One final question remains: Was the second district unique in the South? If the political patterns of the "black second" are merely an aberration, a fascinating exception to the rule, the district has limited significance to the historian—beyond suggesting political and social dynamics that may have been obscured or suppressed elsewhere. Did any other southern congressional districts have histories similar to this remarkable North Carolina district?

Three other southern districts elected one or more Negro congressmen in the period after 1878: John R. Lynch's "shoestring" district in Mississippi; Virginia's fourth district, which sent John Mercer Langston to the national legislature in 1888; and the black district in South Carolina where Robert Smalls, Thomas E. Miller, and George W. Murray won

House seats. These districts differed from the second district in that their elections were usually followed by drawn-out election contests which often kept the winner from taking his seat until late in the session. In other respects, further study would probably indicate important parallels with the North Carolina district. There was significant, long-term friction, for example, between white and black Republicans in the fourth Virginia district, and Langston's battle for the nomination bears comparison with the struggles of James O'Hara from 1878 to 1882. Both the South Carolina district and Lynch's district were gerrymandered creations, designed for much the same reasons as the "black second." In South Carolina, black power persisted long enough for the rise of a post-Reconstruction generation of leadership, just as in North Carolina's gerrymandered black district.

But the record of the second district is probably significant for more than these three "Negro" districts. In fact, any district where Republicans were strong and blacks numerous was certainly similar in many respects to the baliwick of O'Hara, Cheatham, and White. Historians have seldom noticed how many such GOP districts existed in the years from Hayes to McKinley. In four of the five congressional elections in the eighties, for example, Louisiana's second district, including part of the city of New Orleans, elected a Republican representative. Eighteen Republicans or Readjusters were elected to Congress from Virginia between 1876 and 1896, including one three-term congressman. Republicans expected to carry east Tennessee's mountain district, represented for six terms (1878–1890) by Leonidas Houk, but in every election except that of 1878 they were also able to win in one or more other districts. A total of fourteen Republicans represented Tennessee in the House in the twenty years after 1876. North Carolina Republicans perennially challenged the dominant Democrats, and they were able to carry seven of the state's nine districts at least once during this period, four of the districts going Republican on three or more occasions. Florida elected a Republican congressman in 1876, 1880, and 1882. This is not to mention the occasional independent or fusionist aided by Republicans and blacks in Texas, Arkansas, Alabama, and Georgia.[11]

Thus in scores of counties across the South, Republicans were strong

11. See *Congressional Directories* for the sessions between 1877 and 1897. For good overviews of Republican strategy toward the South, see De Santis, *Republicans Face the Southern Question*, and Hirshson, *Farewell to the Bloody Shirt*.

contenders in congressional races for years after Reconstruction. The experience of the "black second"—in evolving black leadership, in the status of white Republicans, in the role of local politics, and in the shifting white response to race relations—is relevant far beyond the boundaries of North Carolina. If nothing more, the study of southern politics from a district perspective is appropriate, and long overdue, for a time and region of intense localism. And it also demonstrates, once again, the rich diversity of an area often viewed by outsiders as uniform and unchanging.

SECOND CONGRESSIONAL DISTRICT ELECTION RETURNS, 1872–1900

The tables in this appendix are based upon an unpublished compilation of North Carolina election returns from the North Carolina Department of Archives and History.

Table 8   **Election of 1872**

County	William H. Kitchin (D)	Charles R. Thomas (R)
Craven	1,132	2,699
Edgecombe	1,444	3,443
Greene	773	944
Halifax	1,620	3,632
Jones	557	638
Lenoir	945	1,258
Northampton	1,044	1,985
Warren	1,092	2,382
Wayne	1,706	1,946
Wilson	1,314	1,145
Total	11,627	20,072

Table 9   **Election of 1874**

County	George W. Blount (D)	John A. Hyman (R)
Craven	1,129	2,316
Edgecombe	1,094	3,368
Greene	828	850
Halifax	1,292	3,509
Jones	543	645
Lenoir	1,078	1,158
Northampton	978	1,838
Warren	674	1,608
Wayne	2,038	1,795
Wilson	1,490	1,089
Total	11,144	18,176

A third candidate, Garland H. White, received 1,091 votes, the majority of them from Warren County. *Tribune Almanac* (1875), 77.

Table 10   **Election of 1876**

County	Wharton J. Green (D)	Curtis H. Brogden (R)
Craven	1,235	2,861
Edgecombe	245	3,855
Greene	885	1,064
Halifax	1,616	3,232
Jones	585	800
Lenoir	1,190	1,489
Northampton	860	1,898
Warren	1,302	2,477
Wayne	2,229	2,192
Wilson	1,727	1,192
Total	11,874	21,060

Table 11   **Election of 1878**

County	W. H. Kitchin (D)	J. H. Harris (R)	J. E. O'Hara (R)
Craven	765	284	1,383
Edgecombe	805	26	1,802
Greene	842	16	930
Halifax	1,119	709	1,348
Jones	584	114	548
Lenoir	1,164	70	702
Northampton	831	227	1,333
Warren	926	837	757
Wayne	2,244	1,353	242
Wilson	1,424	312	637
Total	10,704	3,948	9,682

Warren County returned 584 votes for J. Williams Thorne. There were 28 scattered votes for the district.

Table 12   **Election of 1880**

County	William H. Kitchin (D)	Orlando Hubbs (R)
Craven	1,035	2,771
Edgecombe	1,646	3,442
Greene	859	940
Halifax	2,487	1,772
Jones	567	802
Lenoir	1,065	1,359
Northampton	1,452	2,023
Warren	1,344	2,654
Wayne	2,292	2,136
Wilson	1,558	1,360
Total	14,305	19,259

Greenback candidate Cicero Green received 104 votes.

Table 13 **Election of 1882**

County	scattering (D)	James E. O'Hara (R)
Craven	204	1,138
Edgecombe	26	2,707
Greene	1	1,026
Halifax	212	4,340
Jones	77	708
Lenoir	549	1,160
Northampton	113	2,098
Warren		2,110
Wayne	44	1,989
Wilson		1,255
Total	1,226	18,531

Table 14 **Election of 1884**

County	Frederick A. Woodard (D)	James E. O'Hara (R)
Bertie	1,513	1,868
Craven	1,280	2,487
Edgecombe	1,602	3,353
Greene	1,031	1,067
Halifax	2,007	3,857
Jones	745	749
Lenoir	1,614	1,349
Northampton	1,703	2,351
Vance	1,113	1,625
Warren	1,047	2,113
Wilson	2,044	1,490
Total	15,699	22,309

Table 15   **Election of 1886**

County	F. M. Simmons (D)	J. E. O'Hara (R)	I. B. Abbott (R)
Bertie	1,274	1,698	117
Craven	1,238	1,195	277
Edgecombe	1,636	804	2,134
Greene	1,045	1,069	2
Halifax	2,098	2,462	212
Jones	767	724	9
Lenoir	1,555	1,273	31
Northampton	1,436	1,146	398
Vance	1,126	853	222
Warren	1,033	692	1,507
Wilson	1,950	1,144	111
Total	15,158	13,060	5,020

Table 16   **Election of 1888**

County	Furnifold M. Simmons (D)	Henry P. Cheatham (R)
Bertie	1,247	1,060
Craven	1,689	2,335
Edgecombe	1,378	1,578
Greene	1,011	1,045
Halifax	2,424	2,842
Jones	747	583
Lenoir	1,965	1,339
Northampton	1,682	1,796
Vance	1,398	1,890
Warren	544	865
Wilson	2,236	1,371
Total	16,051	16,704

Table 17 **Election of 1890**

County	James M. Mewboorne (D)	Henry P. Cheatham (R)
Bertie	1,582	1,458
Craven	1,370	2,158
Edgecombe	1,651	2,383
Greene	1,020	730
Halifax	1,737	2,825
Jones	716	470
Lenoir	1,535	795
Northampton	1,607	1,756
Vance	1,347	1,677
Warren	1,125	1,887
Wilson	2,023	804
Total	15,713	16,943

There was a scattering of 143 votes.

Table 18 **Election of 1892**

County	F. A. Woodard (D)	H. P. Cheatham (R)	E. A. Thorne (P)
Bertie	1,533	1,302	346
Edgecombe	1,894	1,514	508
Greene	869	554	267
Halifax	1,621	2,326	450
Lenoir	1,378	976	485
Northampton	1,408	1,472	604
Warren	708	1,683	681
Wayne	2,267	1,565	891
Wilson	2,247	422	1,225
Total	13,925	11,814	5,457

Giles Hinson received 74 votes.

Table 19 **Election of 1894**

County	F. A. Woodard (D)	H. P. Cheatham (R)	H. F. Freeman (P)
Bertie	1,366	1,235	212
Edgecombe	1,933	1,083	709
Greene	822	462	316
Halifax	3,158	1,496	
Lenoir	1,278	1,114	520
Northampton	1,210	906	331
Warren	845	1,511	713
Wayne	2,122	1,321	996
Wilson	1,987	285	1,517
Total	14,721	9,413	5,314

There were 20 scattered votes.

Table 20 **Election of 1896**

County	F. A. Woodard (D)	G. H. White (R)	D. S. Moss (P)
Bertie	1,440	2,199	216
Edgecombe	1,766	2,750	370
Greene	1,020	995	202
Halifax	2,056	3,955	205
Lenoir	1,662	1,395	291
Northampton	1,757	2,302	144
Warren	1,120	2,155	61
Wayne	2,811	2,159	438
Wilson	1,746	1,422	811
Total	15,378	19,332	2,738

Table 21 **Election of 1898**

County	W. E. Fountain (Ind. P.)	G. H. White (R)	J. B. Lloyd (P)
Bertie	1,151	1,871	375
Edgecombe	2,462	2,449	87
Greene	1,207	1,092	134
Halifax	1,162	2,626	78
Lenoir	1,679	1,465	279
Northampton	1,767	2,137	93
Warren	927	2,236	278
Wayne	2,444	2,102	534
Wilson	2,148	1,582	589
Total	14,947	17,560	2,447

Claude Kitchin received 85 votes in Halifax, and B. F. Aycock received 324 votes in Wayne. There was a scattering of 109 votes.

Table 22 **Election of 1900**

County	Claude Kitchin (D)	Joseph J. Martin (R)
Bertie	2,443	1,055
Edgecombe	3,028	1,621
Greene	1,401	801
Halifax	4,198	1,969
Lenoir	1,950	1,245
Northampton	2,169	1,313
Warren	1,670	1,271
Wayne	3,185	2,076
Wilson	2,857	1,170
Total	22,901	12,521

BIBLIOGRAPHY

Primary Sources

MANUSCRIPT COLLECTIONS

Library of Congress, Washington, D.C.
> Chandler, William E. Papers.
> Garfield, James A. Papers. (Microfilm).
> Sherman, John. Papers.

Duke University, Durham, N.C.
> Caldwell, Tod R. Papers.
> Hunter, Charles N. Papers.
> Smith, Edward Chambers. Papers.
> Whitford, John N. Papers.

East Carolina University, Greenville, N.C.
> Carr, Elias. Papers.
> Clarke, William E. Papers.

North Carolina Department of Archives and History, Raleigh
> Ashe, Samuel A'Court. Papers.
> Brogden, Curtis Hooks. Governor's papers.
> Clark, Walter. Papers.
> Gregory, John T. Papers.
> Harris, James Henry. Papers.
> Hawkins, Marmaduke J. Papers.
> Reid, David Settle. Papers.
> Saunders, William L. Papers.

Southern Historical Collection, University of North Carolina, Chapel Hill
> Butler, Marion. Papers.
> Clarke, William J. Papers.
> Connor, Henry G. Papers.
> Kitchin, Claude. Papers.
> Ransom, Matt Whitaker. Papers.
> Russell, Daniel Lindsay. Papers.
> Settle, Thomas. Papers.
> Thompson, Cyrus. Papers.

Tourgée, Albion Winegar. Papers. (Microfilm).
Vance, Zebulon Baird. Papers.
Winston, Francis D. Papers.
University of Chicago
Harrison, Benjamin. Papers. (Microfilm).
O'Hara, James Edward. Papers.

NORTH CAROLINA NEWSPAPERS
Charlotte *Democrat*.
Charlotte *Observer*.
Clinton and Raleigh *Caucasian*.
Daily Raleigh Tribune.
Goldsboro *Daily Argus*.
Goldsboro *Headlight*.
Goldsboro *Messenger*.
Greensboro *North State*.
Henderson *Gold Leaf*.
Kinston *Free Press*.
Kinston *Journal*.
Lasker and Rich Square *Patron and Gleaner*.
Littleton *Courier*.
Littleton *News Reporter*.
Newbernian.
New Bern *People's Advocate*.
New Bern *Republic-Courier*.
New Bern *Journal*.
New Bern *Journal of Commerce*.
New Bern *Times*.
Raleigh *Blasting-Powder*.
Raleigh *Era*.
Raleigh *Gazette*.
Raleigh *Morning Post*.
Raleigh *News*.
Raleigh *News and Observer*.
Raleigh *Register*.
Raleigh *Sentinel*.
Raleigh *Signal*.
Raleigh *Southern Illustrated Age*.
Raleigh *State Chronicle*.
Rocky Mount *Argonaut*.
Salisbury *Star of Zion*.
Scotland Neck *Commonwealth*.
Scotland Neck *Democrat*.
Tarboro *Carolina Banner*.
Tarboro *Southerner*.

Warrenton *Centennial.*
Warrenton *Gazette.*
Warrenton *Warren News.*
Wilmington *Morning Star.*
Wilmington *Post.*
Wilson *Advance.*
Wilson *Mirror.*
Wilson *Plain Dealer.*
Windsor *Public Ledger.*

OUT-OF-STATE NEWSPAPERS
New York *Freeman.*
New York *Herald.*
New York *Times.*
New York *Tribune Almanac.*
Washington (D.C.) *Bee.*
Washington (D.C.) *Colored American.*

GOVERNMENT PUBLICATIONS
DuBois, W. E. B., "The Negro Landholder of Georgia," *Bulletin of the Department of Labor No. 35.* Washington, D.C., 1901.
North Carolina. Bureau of Labor Statistics. *First Annual Report of the Bureau of Labor Statistics for the State of North Carolina, for the year 1887.* Raleigh, 1887.
————. *Fourteenth Annual Report of the Bureau of Labor and Printing, 1900.* Raleigh, 1901.
————. *Journal of the Constitutional Convention of the State of North Carolina Held in 1875.* Raleigh, 1875.
————. *Journal of the House of Representatives, 1872–73.*
————. *Laws and Resolutions of the State of North Carolina, 1876–77.* Raleigh, 1877.
————. *Laws and Resolutions of the State of North Carolina Passed by the General Assembly at Its Session of 1889.* Raleigh, 1889.
————. *North Carolina Manual.* Raleigh, 1913.
————. *Public Laws and Resolutions, 1895.* Raleigh, 1895.
————. *Report of the Commissioner of Agriculture, 1900.* Raleigh, 1901.
————. *Report of the Commission to Investigate Charges of Fraud and Corruption, Under Act of Assembly, Session 1871–72.* Raleigh, 1872.
————. *Report of the Superintendent of Public Instruction, 1877.* Raleigh, 1879.
————. *Report of the Superintendent of Public Instruction, 1878.* Raleigh, 1879.
————. *Report of the Superintendent of Public Instruction, 1879.* Raleigh, 1881.
————. *Report of the Superintendent of Public Instruction, 1880.* Raleigh, 1881.

————. *Biennial Report of the Superintendent of Public Instruction, 1883–84.* Raleigh, 1885.

————. *Biennial Report of the Superintendent of Public Instruction, 1889–90.* Raleigh, 1891.

————. *Biennial Report of the Superintendent of Public Instruction, 1891–92.* Raleigh, 1893.

————. *Biennial Report of the Superintendent of Public Instruction, 1900–1901 and 1901–1902.* Raleigh, 1903.

————. *Second Annual Report of the Board of Railroad Commissioners, 1892.* Raleigh, 1893.

————. *Sixth Annual Report of the Board of Railroad Commissioners, 1896.* Raleigh, 1897.

U.S. Congress. *A Biographical Congressional Directory, 1774–1903.* Washington, D.C., 1903.

————. *Biographical Directory of the American Congress, 1774–1961.* Washington, D.C., 1961.

————. *Congressional Directory,* 49th Cong., 54th Cong.

————. *Congressional Globe,* 42nd Cong.

————. *Congressional Record,* 43rd Cong.–56th Cong.

U.S. Congress. House. *Contested Election Case of Henry P. Cheatham v. Frederick A. Woodard from the Second Congressional District of the State of North Carolina.* Washington, D.C., 1896.

————. *Henry P. Cheatham v. Frederick A. Woodard.* House Rpt. 1809 to accompany House Resolution 337, 54th Cong., 1st Sess., 1896.

————. *O'Hara v. Kitchin.* House Rpt. 263, 46th Cong., 3rd Sess.

————. *Papers in the Case of James E. O'Hara v. William H. Kitchin, Second District of North Carolina.* House Miscellaneous Doc. 7, 46th Cong., 3rd Sess., 1881.

U.S. Congress. Senate. *Report and Testimony of the Select Committee of the United States Senate to Investigate the Causes of the Removal of the Negroes from the Southern States to the Northern States,* Pt. I, Senate Rpt. 693, 46th Cong., 2nd Sess., 1880.

————. *Report of the Committee on Agriculture and Forestry on Condition of Cotton Growers in the United States, the Present Prices of Cotton, and the Remedy; and on Cotton Consumption and Production,* Vol. I, Senate Rpt. 986, 53rd Cong., 3rd Sess., 1895.

U.S. Department of Agriculture. Division of Statistics. Miscellaneous Series, Rpt. No. 4. "Wages of Farm Labor in the United States." Washington, D.C., 1892.

————. James L. Watkins. "Production and Price of Cotton for One Hundred Years." Bulletin no. 9, Miscellaneous Series. Washington, D.C., 1895.

U.S. Department of Commerce. Bureau of the Census. *Negro Population, 1790–1915.* Washington, D.C., 1918.

————. *Religious Bodies, 1916.* Washington, D.C., 1919.

U.S. Department of Commerce. Census Office. *Eighth Census* (1860).

———. *Ninth Census* (1870).

———. *Tenth Census* (1880).

———. *Eleventh Census* (1890).

———. *Twelfth Census* (1900).

———. *Thirteenth Census* (1910).

U.S. Department of the Interior, *Official Register of the United States,* 1869, 1871, 1881, 1883, 1885, 1897, 1899.

———. *Report of the Commissioner of Education, 1877.* Washington, D.C., 1877.

U.S. Industrial Commission, *Report of the Industrial Commission,* X. Washington, D.C., 1901.

U.S. *The War of the Rebellion: A Compilation of the Official Records of the Union and Confederate Armies,* Washington, D.C., 1883, Series I, Vols. IX, XVIII, XXVII, XXIX, XXXVI, XLVII.

UNPUBLISHED RECORDS AND DOCUMENTS

North Carolina Department of Archives and History, Raleigh

    Bertie County. Election Returns, 1880–1914.

    Craven County. Election Returns, 1878–90.

    ———. Record of Elections, 1874–1908.

    ———. Tax List. 1887–88. (Microfilm).

    Edgecombe County. Record of Elections, 1880–94 [*sic*].

    Greene County. Record of Elections, 1878–98.

    Halifax County. Minutes of the County Commissioners, 1873–83. (Microfilm).

    ———. Minutes of the Superior Court, 1878–79, 1880–81.

    ———. Record of Elections, 1878–1908.

    Jones County. Record of Elections, 1878–1908.

    Lenoir County. Record of Elections, 1880–1900.

    Northampton County. Miscellaneous Records.

    Northampton County. Record of Elections, 1878–1906. (Microfilm).

    North Carolina. General Assembly. Legislative Papers, 1876–77, 1881, 1883, 1885, 1887, 1889, 1893, 1895, 1899.

    North Carolina. Supreme Court. Papers in the case of *John H. Hannon v. James M. Grizzard, et al.* 96 NC 293, February, 1887.

    Vance County. Tax Scrolls, 1883, 1885–87, 1890, 1894.

    Warren County. Record of Elections, 1878–96.

    Wayne County. Record of Elections. 1878–1904.

    Wilson County. Record of Elections, 1878–1904.

    ———. Record of Elections, 1880–1904.

    Unpublished compilation of North Carolina election returns. Second Congressional District.

    U.S. Department of Commerce. Census Office. MS Ninth Census.

————. MS Tenth Census, population schedules, agriculture schedules. (Microfilm).

National Archives

Department of Justice. Year Files, 1877–95. Record Group 60.

Post Office Department. Record of Appointments of Postmasters, Vols. 49, 69. Record Group 28.

MISCELLANEOUS

"Address of Hon. C. H. Brogden, to the Voters of the Second Congressional District of North Carolina." North Carolina Collection. (Broadside.)

Assembly Sketch Book, Session 1885, North Carolina. Raleigh: Edwards, Broughton, 1885.

Branson, Levi, ed. *The North Carolina Business Directory, 1877 and 1878.* Raleigh: L. Branson, 1878.

Biographical Sketch Book, Session 1887. Raleigh: Edwards, Broughton, 1887.

King, Edward. *The Southern States of North America; A Record of Journeys in Louisiana, Texas, The Indian Territory, Missouri, Arkansas, Mississippi, Alabama, Georgia, Florida, South Carolina, North Carolina, Kentucky, Tennessee, Virginia, West Virginia and Maryland.* London: Blackie and Son, 1875.

Proceedings of the Tenth Republican National Convention; Held in the City of Minneapolis, Minn., June 7, 8, 9 and 10, 1892. Minneapolis, 1892.

Rivers, Vera Jean O'Hara. Interview with author, February 26, 1975, Statesville, N.C.

Speech of Hon. C. H. Brogden Delivered before the Wayne County Republican Convention at the Town Hall in Goldsboro, N.C. Saturday May 29, 1880. Goldsboro, N.C.: Messenger Book and Job Printing House, 1880. North Carolina Collection, University of North Carolina.

New York Tribune Almanac. New York, 1875.

Secondary Sources

Anderson, Eric D. "Race and Politics in North Carolina, 1872–1901: The Black Second Congressional District." Ph.D. dissertation, University of Chicago, 1978.

Ashe, Samuel A., ed. *Biographical History of North Carolina from Colonial Times to the Present.* Vol. II. 8 vols. Greensboro, N.C.: Charles L. Van Noppen, 1905–1907.

Balanoff, Elizabeth. "Negro Legislators in the North Carolina General Assembly, July 1868–February 1872." *North Carolina Historical Review,* XLIX (January, 1972), 21–32.

Bassett, John Spencer. "Stirring Up the Fires of Race Antipathy." *South Atlantic Quarterly,* II (October, 1903), 297–305.

Bode, Frederick A. *Protestantism and the New South: North Carolina Baptists and Methodists in Political Crisis, 1894–1903.* Charlottesville: University Press of Virginia, 1975.

Bond, Horace Mann. *The Education of the Negro in the American Social Order.* New York: Octagon Books, 1970.

Brooks, Aubrey Lee, and Hugh Talmage Lefler, eds. *The Papers of Walter Clark.* Vol. I. 2 vols. Chapel Hill: University of North Carolina Press, 1948.

Brown, Cecil Kenneth. *A State Movement in Railroad Development: The Story of North Carolina's First Effort to Establish an East and West Trunk Line Railroad.* Chapel Hill: University of North Carolina Press, 1928.

Brown, Hugh Victor. *A History of the Education of Negroes in North Carolina.* Goldsboro, N.C.: Irving-Swain Press, 1961.

Burke, Edmund. *Reflections on the Revolution in France and on the Proceedings in Certain Societies in London Relative to that Event.* Harmondsworth, Middlesex, Eng.: Penguin Books, 1968.

Christopher, Maurine. *America's Black Congressmen.* New York: Thomas Y. Crowell, 1971.

Connor, Henry G. and Joseph B. Chesire. *The Constitution of the State of North Carolina Annotated.* Raleigh: Edwards, Broughton, 1911.

Coon, Charles L. "The Beginnings of the North Carolina City Schools, 1867–1887." *South Atlantic Quarterly,* XII (July, 1913), 235–47.

Corbitt, David Leroy. *The Formation of North Carolina Counties, 1663–1943.* Raleigh: State Department of Archives and History, 1950.

Coulter, E. Merton. *The South During Reconstruction, 1865–1877.* Baton Rouge: Louisiana State University Press, 1947.

Crow, Jeffrey J., and Robert F. Durden. *Maverick Republican in the Old North State: A Political Biography of Daniel L. Russell.* Baton Rouge: Louisiana State University Press, 1977.

Cutler, James Elbert. *Lynch-Law: An Investigation into the History of Lynching in the United States.* New York: Longmans, Green, 1905.

Daniels, Jonathan. *Prince of Carpetbaggers.* Philadelphia and New York: J. B. Lippincott, 1958.

Daniels, Josephus. *Editor in Politics.* Chapel Hill: University of North Carolina Press, 1941.

————. *Tar Heel Editor.* Chapel Hill: University of North Carolina Press, 1939.

DeCanio, Stephen J. *Agriculture in the Postbellum South: The Economics of Production and Supply.* Cambridge, Mass.: MIT Press, 1974.

————. "Cotton 'Overproduction' in Late Nineteenth-Century Southern Agriculture." *Journal of Economic History,* XXXIII (September, 1973), 606–33.

Degler, Carl N. *The Other South: Southern Dissenters in the 19th Century.* New York: Harper & Row, 1974.

De Santis, Vincent P. *Republicans Face the Southern Question: The New Departure Years, 1877–1897.* Baltimore: Johns Hopkins Press, 1959.

Dillingham, Pitt. "Land Tenure Among the Negroes." *Yale Review,* V (August, 1896), 190–206.

Dunning, William A. *Reconstruction, Political and Economic, 1865–1877.* New York: Harper & Row, 1962.

Durden, Robert F. *The Climax of Populism: The Election of 1896.* Lexington: University Press of Kentucky, 1965.

Duster, Alfreda M., ed. *Crusade for Justice: The Autobiography of Ida B. Wells.* Chicago: University of Chicago Press, 1970.

Edmonds, Helen G. *The Negro and Fusion Politics in North Carolina, 1894–1901.* Chapel Hill: University of North Carolina Press, 1951.

Elmore, Joseph Eliot. "North Carolina Negro Congressmen, 1875–1901." M.A. thesis, University of North Carolina, 1964.

Emerson, Charles, and Co. *New Bern Directory, 1880–1881.* Raleigh: Edwards, Broughton, 1880.

———, compiler and publisher. *North Carolina Tobacco Belt Directory.* Raleigh, 1886.

Evans, W. McKee. *Ballots and Fence Rails: Reconstruction on the Lower Cape Fear.* Chapel Hill: University of North Carolina Press, 1966.

Foote, Shelby. *The Civil War: A Narrative, Red River to Appomattox.* New York: Random House, 1974.

Foster, Gaines M. "Bishop Chesire and Black Participation in the Episcopal Church: The Limitations of Religious Paternalism." *North Carolina Historical Review,* LIV (January, 1977), 49–65.

Franklin, John Hope. *The Free Negro in North Carolina, 1790–1860.* New York: W. W. Norton, 1971.

———. *The Militant South, 1800–1861.* Boston: Beacon Press, 1964.

Gaston, Paul M. *The New South Creed: A Study in Southern Mythmaking.* New York: Vintage Books, 1973.

Genovese, Eugene D. *Roll, Jordan, Roll.* New York: Pantheon Books, 1974.

Gilbert, Abby L. "The Comptroller of the Currency and the Freedman's Savings Bank." *Journal of Negro History,* LVII (April, 1972), 125–43.

Grossman, Lawrence. *The Democratic Party and the Negro: Northern and National Politics, 1868–92.* Urbana: University of Illinois Press, 1976.

Hamilton, J. G. de Roulhac. *History of North Carolina: North Carolina Since 1860.* Vol. III. 6 vols. Chicago: Lewis Publishing Company, 1919.

———. *Reconstruction in North Carolina.* New York: Columbia University, 1914.

Harlan, Louis R. *Separate and Unequal: Public School Campaigns and Racism in the Southern Seaboard States, 1901–1915.* New York: Atheneum, 1968.

Headley, P. C. *Public Men of To-Day.* Tecumseh, Mich.: A. W. Mills, 1882.

Higgs, Robert. *Competition and Coercion: Blacks in the American Economy, 1865–1914.* Cambridge, Eng.: Cambridge University Press, 1977.

———. "Patterns of Farm Rental in the Georgia Cotton Belt, 1880–1900." *Journal of Economic History,* XXXIV (June, 1974), 468–80.

————. "Race, Tenure, and Resource Allocation in Southern Agriculture, 1910." *Journal of Economic History*, XXXIII (March, 1973), 149–69.

————. *The Transformation of the American Economy, 1865–1914: An Essay in Interpretation*. New York: John Wiley and Sons, 1971.

Hirshson, Stanley P. *Farewell to the Bloody Shirt: Northern Republicans and the Southern Negro, 1877–1893*. Chicago: Quadrangle Books, 1962.

History of North Carolina, VI. Chicago: Lewis Publishing Company, 1919.

Hofstadter, Richard. *Social Darwinism in American Thought*. Boston: Beacon Press, 1955.

Huggins, John E. "The Resurgence and Decline of the Republican Party, 1871–1876." M.A. thesis, Wake Forest University, 1966.

Ingle, H. Larry. "A Southern Democrat at Large: William Hodge Kitchin and the Populist Party." *North Carolina Historical Review*, XLV (April, 1968), 178–94.

Johnson, Guion B. *Ante-Bellum North Carolina: A Social History*. Chapel Hill: University of North Carolina Press, 1937.

Johnson, Talmage C. and Charles R. Holloman. *The Story of Kinston and Lenoir County*. Raleigh: Edwards, Broughton, 1954.

Katz, William. "George Henry White: A Militant Negro Congressman in the Age of Booker T. Washington." *Negro History Bulletin*, XXIX (March, 1966), 125–26, 134, 138–39.

Key, V. O., Jr. *Southern Politics in State and Nation*. New York: Vintage Books, 1949.

Kousser, J. Morgan. *The Shaping of Southern Politics: Suffrage Restriction and the Establishment of the One-Party South*. New Haven, Conn.: Yale University Press, 1974.

Lefler, Hugh T. and Ray R. Newsome, *North Carolina: The History of a Southern State*. Chapel Hill: University of North Carolina Press, 1973.

Lockert, Walter S. II. "Lynching in North Carolina, 1888–1906." M.A. thesis, University of North Carolina, 1972.

Logan, Frenise. "Influences Which Determined the Race-Consciousness of George H. White, 1897–1901." *Negro History Bulletin*, XIV (December, 1950), 63–65.

————. *The Negro in North Carolina, 1876–1894*. Chapel Hill: University of North Carolina Press, 1964.

Mabry, William A. " 'White Supremacy' and the North Carolina Suffrage Amendment." *North Carolina Historical Review*, XIII (January, 1936), 1–24.

McCormick, John G. "Personnel of the Convention of 1861." *James Sprunt Historical Monographs*, No. 1. Chapel Hill: University of North Carolina Press, 1900.

McDuffie, Jerome A. "The Wilmington Riots of November 10, 1898." M.A. thesis, Wake Forest University, 1963.

McKinney, Gordon B. "Southern Mountain Republicans and the Negro, 1865–

1900." *Journal of Southern History*, XLI (November, 1975), 493–516.

Mandle, Jay R. *The Roots of Black Poverty*. Durham, N.C.: Duke University Press, 1978.

Matthews, Donald R., ed. *North Carolina Votes: General Election Returns, by County, for President of the United States, 1868–1960, Governor of North Carolina, 1868–1960, United States Senator from North Carolina, 1914–1960*. Chapel Hill: University of North Carolina Press, 1962.

Montgomery, Lizzie Wilson. *Sketches of Old Warrenton, North Carolina*. Raleigh: Edwards, Broughton, 1924.

Moore, John H. "The Negro and Prohibition in Atlanta, 1885–1887." *South Atlantic Quarterly*, LXIX (Winter, 1970), 38–57.

National Association for the Advancement of Colored People. *Thirty Years of Lynching in the United States, 1889–1918*. New York: Arno, 1969.

Olsen, Otto H. *Carpetbagger's Crusade: The Life of Albion Winegar Tourgée*. Baltimore: Johns Hopkins Press, 1965.

Orr, Oliver H. *Charles Brantley Aycock*. Chapel Hill: University of North Carolina Press, 1961.

Osterweis, Rollin G. *Romanticism and Nationalism in the Old South*. Baton Rouge: Louisiana State University Press, 1967.

Painter, Nell Irvin. *Exodusters: Black Migration to Kansas After Reconstruction*. New York: Alfred A. Knopf, 1977.

Pearce, Samuel Thomas. *"Zeb's Black Baby": Vance County North Carolina, a Short History*. Henderson, N.C.: Seeman Printery, 1955.

Pelletreau, William S. *A History of Long Island from Its Earliest Settlement to the Present Time*. Vol. III. 3 vols. New York and Chicago: Lewis Publishing, 1903.

Poole, William J., Jr. "The Congressional Career of Joseph Haynes Rainey, First Negro Congressman." Seminar paper, University of Chicago, 1971.

Procter, Ben H. *Not Without Honor: The Life of John H. Reagan*. Austin: University of Texas Press, 1962.

Rabinowitz, H. N. "From Exclusion to Segregation: Southern Race Relations, 1865–1890." *Journal of American History*, LXIII (September, 1976), 325–50.

———. *Race Relations in the Urban South, 1865–1890*. New York: Oxford University Press, 1978.

———. "Half a Loaf: The Shift from White to Black Teachers in the Negro Schools of the Urban South, 1865–1890." *Journal of Southern History*, XL (November, 1974), 565–94.

Ransom, Roger L., and Richard Sutch. *One Kind of Freedom: The Economic Consequences of Emancipation*. Cambridge, Eng.: Cambridge University Press, 1977.

Reid, George W. "A Biography of George Henry White, 1852–1918. Ph.D. dissertation, Howard University, 1974.

———. "Congressman George Henry White: His Major Power Base." *Negro History Bulletin*, XXXIX (March, 1976), 554–55.

Rippy, J. Fred, ed. *Furnifold Simmons, Statesman of the New South: Memoirs and Addresses*. Durham, N.C.: Duke University Press, 1936.

Shaffer, A. W. "A Southern Republican on the Lodge Bill." *North American Review*, CLI (November, 1890), 601–609.

Sherrill, Josephine Price. "A Negro School-Master of the 1870's." *Journal of Negro Education*, XXX (Spring, 1961), 163–72.

Sherman, Roger B. *The Republican Party and Black America: From McKinley to Hoover, 1896–1933*. Charlottesville: University Press of Virginia, 1973.

Shotwell, R. A., and Natt Atkinson. *Legislative Record, Giving the Acts Passed Session March 1877, Together with Sketches of the Lives and Public Acts of the Members of Both Houses*. Raleigh: Edwards, Broughton, 1877.

Sinkler, George. "Benjamin Harrison and the Matter of Race." *Indiana Magazine of History*, LXV (September, 1969), 197–209.

Smith, H. Shelton. *In His Image But . . . : Racism in Southern Religion, 1780–1910*. Durham, N.C.: Duke University Press, 1972.

Smith, Samuel Denny. *The Negro in Congress, 1870–1901*. Chapel Hill: University of North Carolina Press, 1940.

Steelman, Joseph F. "The Progressive Era in North Carolina, 1884–1917." Ph.D. dissertation, University of North Carolina, 1955.

———. "Republican Party Strategists and the Issue of Fusion with Populists in North Carolina, 1893–1894." *North Carolina Historical Review*, XLVII (July, 1970), 244–69.

———. "Vicissitudes of Republican Party Politics: The Campaign of 1892 in North Carolina." *North Carolina Historical Review*, XLIII (October, 1966), 430–42.

Stewart, Patricia H. "Orlando Hubbs and the Corruption Charges of 1908." Academic paper, Molloy College, 1974.

Stover, John F. *The Railroads of the South, 1865–1900*. Chapel Hill: University of North Carolina Press, 1955.

Tilley, Nannie May. *The Bright-Tobacco Industry, 1860–1929*. Chapel Hill: University of North Carolina Press, 1948.

Tindall, George Brown. *South Carolina Negroes, 1877–1900*. Columbia: University of South Carolina Press, 1952.

Tomlinson, W. F. *Biography of the State Officers and Members of the General Assembly; Other Interesting Facts*. Raleigh, 1893.

Turner, J. Kelly and John L. Bridgers, Jr. *History of Edgecombe County, North Carolina*. Raleigh: Edwards, Broughton, 1920.

Uya, Okon Edet. *From Slavery to Public Service: Robert Smalls, 1839–1915*. New York: Oxford University Press, 1971.

Vance, Rupert B. *Human Factors in Cotton Culture*. Chapel Hill: University of North Carolina Press, 1929.

Van Deusen, John G. "Did Republicans 'Colonize' Indiana in 1879?" *Indiana Magazine of History*, XXX (December, 1934).

Vaughn, William Preston. *Schools for All: The Blacks and Public Education in the South, 1865–1877*. Lexington: University Press of Kentucky, 1974.

Wharton, Vernon. *The Negro In Mississippi, 1865–1890*. New York: Harper & Row, 1965.

Wheeler, John H. *Reminiscences and Memoirs of North Carolina and Eminent North Carolinians*. Baltimore: Geneological Publishing Company, 1966.

White, Leonard D. *The Republican Era, 1869–1910: A Study in Administrative History*. New York: Macmillan, 1958.

Whitener, Daniel Jay. *Prohibition in North Carolina, 1715–1945*. Chapel Hill: University of North Carolina Press, 1945.

Who's Who in New York City and State: A Biographical Dictionary of Contemporaries. New York: W. F. Brainard, 1911.

Wiley, Bell I. *Southern Negroes, 1861–1865*. Baton Rouge: Louisiana State University Press, 1965.

Wilson, Peter Mitchel. *Southern Exposure*. Chapel Hill: University of North Carolina Press, 1927.

Winston, Robert W. *It's a Far Cry*. New York: Henry Holt, 1937.

Woodward, C. Vann. *Origins of the New South, 1877–1913*. Baton Rouge: Louisiana State University Press, 1951.

Wooley, Robert H. "Race and Politics: The Evolution of the White Supremacy Campaign of 1898 in North Carolina." Ph.D. dissertation, University of North Carolina, 1977.

Worth, Nicholas. [Walter Hines Page]. "The Autobiography of a Southerner." *Atlantic Monthly*, 98 (July-October, 1906), 1–12, 157–76, 311–25, 474–88.

Wright, Gavin and Kunrenther, Howard. "Cotton, Corn and Risk in the Nineteenth Century." *Journal of Economic History*, XXXV (September, 1975), 526–51.

INDEX

Abbott, Israel: and 1878 campaign, 65, 70, 73, 89; and 1882 campaign, 103; and 1884 campaign, 116; and 1886 campaign, 130, 134, 135, 137, 138
Adams, Spencer B., 302, 307
Agriculture: importance of, 15; and cotton, 15, 30, 31 and n, 33; diversification and self-sufficiency in, 15, 30–32; and Civil War, 16–17, 19–20; labor systems in, 17–19 and n, 20, 25, 27, 28; landlord-tenant relations in, 20–21, 22; and black landownership, 22–27; farm laborers in, 27–29, 33; and import duties, 147–48; 1889 depression of, 171–72, 175
Anthony, C. P., 244, 246, 248
Anti-option bill, 188
Anti-Prohibition Association, 98, 100
Arrington, J. H., 238n, 247n
Arthur, Chester A., 102, 179
Atlantic and North Carolina Railroad, 32, 35, 40, 64 and n
Aycock, Benjamin F., 215, 260
Aycock, Charles B.: as white leader, x, 338, 339, 340; on 1886 election, 139, 254; and 1898 campaign, 253, 254–55, 258n, 268; and 1900 campaign, 302, 305, 306–307; and education, 330; mentioned, 15, 329
Ayer, Hal W., 234

Back salary grab, 39 and n, 41
Ballot "devices," 44, 160, 227–28. See also Vote fraud
Barksdale, Ethelbert, 122, 123
Bassett, John Spencer, 332, 337
Battle, Clinton W., 54n, 245, 246

Bennett, Risden T., 112, 126
Bergen, C. A., 187–88
Bertie County: population in, 10; black landowning in, 24, 26; 1876 election in, 54; joins second district, 115, 317; 1884 election in, 118, 119; 1886 election in, 133, 138, 139; as Republican stronghold, 146; 1888 election in, 150, 156, 161; 1890 election in, 177, 182; 1892 election in, 202, 203; 1894 election in, 210, 219n, 223; 1896 election in, 230, 238; black officeholding in, 245, 246, 247 ,249, 250, 334; 1898 election in, 266, 276, 277; 1900 election in, 304, 306; lynching in, 322n
Biggs, William, 6, 7–8
Black exodus, 9, 29–30, 80, 166, 172, 173, 186, 297
Black leadership: and congressmen, 5, 248, 316, 333–34; and solicitors, 5, 334; white reactions to, 34, 180, 190, 240, 242–43, 244, 245, 251, 252, 264, 324; and magistrates, 62, 248, 250–51, 319–20; during Bourbon equilibrium, 62, 64, 94–95, 107, 108, 250; and federal patronage, 98, 170, 334; and jurors, 98n, 318–19; revival of, 145, 146, 250; training for, 159, 316; and bonding system, 162–65, 185, 249–50; and postmasters, 168, 242–43, 244–45; and Populists, 215–16, 298, 334; and Hiram Grant, 300, 336; White on, 310; and policemen, 320. See also Negro Progress
Black suffrage: restriction of, ix, xi, 5, 15, 145, 231; in gerrymandered second district, 4; and 1880 election, 93–94;

363